C000068458

The True Face of
William
Shakespeare

Hildegard Hammerschmidt-Hummel

The True Face of
William Shakespeare

Hildegard Hammerschmidt-Hummel

THE POET'S DEATH MASK AND LIKENESSES

FROM THREE PERIODS OF HIS LIFE

Translated from the German by Alan Bance

CHAUCER PRESS

Published in 2006 by Chaucer Press
20 Bloomsbury Street
London WC1B 3JH

© 2006 this edition Chaucer Press
© 2006 German edition Georg Olms Verlag
© 2006 by Hildegard Hammerschmidt-Hummel

Designed and produced for Chaucer Press
by Open Door Limited, Rutland

Editor: Victoria Huxley
Indexer: Ingrid Lock

All rights reserved. No part of this publication may be
reproduced or transmitted in any form or by any means,
electronic or mechanical, including photocopying, recording
or any information storage and retrieval system, without
prior permission in writing from the copyright owner.

Title: The True Face of Willam Shakespeare
ISBN: 1 904449 56 5
978-1-904449-56-0
Printed by BROSMAC, Madrid, Spain

He was a handsome, well-shaped man, and of ever ready and pleasant smooth wit.
John Aubrey on William Shakespeare (*Brief Lives*, after 1667)

... but the best memorial of all is still a man's own likeness.
Johann Wolfgang von Goethe (*Elective Affinities*, 1809)

CONTENTS

PART V

APPENDIX I

APPENDIX II

PREFACE TO THE GERMAN EDITION

This book is the outcome of extensive research, stretching over a decade, with lengthy interruptions where other urgent projects intervened or demanded completion. Over that time, a process of development, expansion, and refinement occurred both in relation to the nature of the project and to the investigative methods applied. As certain questions were answered, other questions arose.

During unavoidable interruptions to the work, there was room for many thoughts and insights to mature. The circle of specialists from the most varied fields whom I consulted and whose expertise I could draw on expanded, turning the research project into a truly inter-disciplinary and even trans-disciplinary one; perhaps a model for future enterprises of this kind.

In 1996, I was granted a one-year award with travel funding by the German Research Council (*Deutsche Forschungsgemeinschaft*), enabling me to carry out specific investigations in English churches, castles, galleries, museums and libraries with regard to the authenticity and history of several of Shakespeare's portraits. But I was also able to pursue more broadly conceived studies, with a view to throwing light upon the religious and cultural-historical context within which the origins and function of these images must be seen.

I thank the German Research Council for its generous support. My special thanks go to the experts of the German Federal Bureau of Criminal Investigation, especially Reinhardt Altmann, EHK, and the medical specialists who participated: Professor Michael Hertl, Professor Hans Helmut Jansen, Professor Bernd Kober, Professor Walter Lerche and Professor Jost Metz. All of them thoroughly investigated the images by means of traditional or innovative procedures, carried out comparisons between them, identified them, or presented professional medical opinions and reports about the signs of disease they had diagnosed in them. Their contribution was indispensable to solving the problems addressed. I am also deeply indebted to a number of people who provided advice, suggestions and assistance, and often undertook laborious journeys in connection with the project or carried out time-consuming investigations using special techniques. My thanks also go to the directors and staff of my publishers, Georg Olms Verlag, especially to the two copy editors, as well as those responsible for the layout, proof-reading, and index. But it is to my husband and my daughter, without whose help, support and understanding this book could hardly have come about and who raised my spirits at difficult moments that I owe my deepest debt of gratitude.

A full list of Acknowledgements can be found on page 148.

PREFACE

In 2006, 'The Year of the Bard', the National Portrait Gallery in London mounted an extensive exhibition dedicated to the great British national poet and playwright. A large number of images of the Bard were displayed, many of them claiming to depict William Shakespeare authentically, including the Gallery's very first and most important painting, the Chandos Portrait. The preparations for this major event included subjecting a number of Shakespeare portraits to laboratory investigation, and the BBC broadcast the results in a series of TV documentary programmes. All this has served to raise public awareness and bring Shakespeare's physical appearance into focus.

The build-up to this exhibition coincided with the completion of my long-term research project on authentic images of Shakespeare, and especially with my investigations into the Davenant bust, owned by the Garrick Club in London.

In the course of my wide-ranging research I have unearthed entirely new textual and visual sources, and have made existing source material newly accessible. On this basis, and in collaboration with experts from a variety of disciplines, I have put forward startling new findings with regard to Shakespeare's life and death, and placed them in the appropriate framework of their cultural history.

By discovering new sources I have also been able to resolve previously unanswered questions concerning the provenance of these images and to rule out those painters and sculptors hitherto considered as their possible creators. These new findings and new knowledge about Shakespeare's life* have enabled me to identify other artists who closely fit the historical and biographical requirements.

This has led to the solving of centuries-old mysteries. We can now be certain that we possess not only the genuine death mask of Shakespeare but also detailed and accurate images, with clearly visible signs of disease, from three periods of his life. It will be demonstrated in this book that William Shakespeare must have sat in person for these true-to-life likenesses.

Hildegard Hammerschmidt-Hummel
Wiesbaden, February 2006

---

* The English edition of my Shakespeare biography, *The Life and Times of William Shakespeare (1564-1616)*, will also be published by Chaucer Press in 2006.

Terracotta bust of William Shakespeare, called the Davenant Bust, 62 x 59 x 29 cm, Garrick Club, London.
This bust was scientifically authenticated by Professor Hildegard Hammerschmidt-Hummel as a true-to-life likeness
of Shakespeare for which the poet must have sat in person.

I. THE CONTEXT OF CULTURAL HISTORY:

The Image of Man in the Renaissance and Baroque

THE INDIVIDUAL, CREATIVE ACHIEVEMENT, AND POSTHUMOUS FAME

In one of the most famous texts of the Italian High Renaissance, *On Human Dignity*, God the Father is given the following words to say in a dialogue with Adam:

> I have placed thee at the centre of the world, that from there thou mayest more conveniently look around and see whatsoever is in the world. Neither heavenly nor earthly, neither mortal nor immortal have We made thee. Thou, like a judge appointed for being honourable, art the moulder and maker of thyself; thou mayest sculpt thyself into whatever shape thou dost prefer.[1]

The Italian humanist and philosopher, Pico della Mirandola, who was writing these lines in 1486 at the age of only twenty-three, thereby placed mankind, endowed by God with a vast multitude of choices, at the centre of the world. According to Pico, man is free to decide whether to dwell in the depths of the "animal" realm or ascend to the heights of the "divine". The alluring image of man as his own sculptor did not in fact originate in Pico's imagination, but had already been employed in classical antiquity.[2] His emotionally charged dictum expresses a sense of human self-confidence and feeling for life that marks a high point in that age of increasing individual self-awareness.

About a hundred years later a French author gained attention in the Europe of his day; one who had witnessed the misery of the religious wars in the sixteenth century, and to his dismay observed a neighbouring country, England, altering its laws three or four times during his lifetime – including those concerning religion, the sphere of greatest importance to him.[3] The writer in question is that great sceptic of the western world, Michel de Montaigne, who, retiring to his chateau near Bordeaux, had the maxim of the classical author Terence pinned to his ceiling – "I am a man; nothing human is alien to me" – and in his essays philosophised about man: his opportunities and his limits, his internal contradictions, his dependence upon contemporary conditions, and his animal nature. Above all he asked himself who man really was. Montaigne's image of mankind was marked by a pessimism which completely contrasts with Pico della Mirandola's concept of man as practically the measure of all things.

Many examples from the civics, historiography, painting, and literature of the time attest to the positive as well as negative ways in which numerous potentates, authors, and artists seemed to make use of the options projected by Pico. This antithetical view of man was also to be found in the theatre; most especially in England, where drama enjoyed an unimaginable flowering at the end of the sixteenth century with the works of Christopher Marlowe and William Shakespeare.

The ambitious, bombastic heroes of Marlowe's plays, blinded by hubris, often exceed the bounds of humanity and in doing so come down – as with the protagonist of *The Jew of Malta* – on the side of evil. Scoundrels and villains ruled by their baser instincts abound in Shakespeare too; among them Aaron, Richard III, Macbeth, Iago, and Iachimo. But in contrast to Marlowe, Shakespeare also created largely positive parallel worlds, such as the company of exiles living in the Forest of Arden in *As You Like It*. At the end of Shakespeare's plays order and justice are always restored. It is true that in *Hamlet*, the poet's first great tragedy after he turned to that genre,[4] the prince comes to grief through the external and internal circumstances imposed upon him, but nevertheless he thinks of man as a godlike masterpiece. He holds up to his erstwhile friends, now set to spy upon him, a fascinating image of man, very closely related to Pico's ideas on the ascent of mankind to divine heights:

> What piece of work is a man ! How noble in reason! how infinite in faculties ! in form and moving, how express and admirable ! in action, how like an angel ! in apprehension, how like a god ! the beauty of the world ! the paragon of animals ! (*Hamlet*, II.2)

This central preoccupation with man (beginning with the humanists, who in their turn were influenced by classical models) rapidly took hold in philosophy, the visual arts, literature, education and other areas. It brought in its train an appreciation of the deeds not only of rulers and the politically powerful but also of those great contemporary scholars, scientists, artists and writers who had produced outstanding cultural and scientific achievements. The invention of printing and the means of reproducing images were the technical preconditions for the distribution of their works in the early sixteenth century through frequent reprinting or reproduction. These books published under the names of their authors often carried veristic, i.e. realistic and accurate images of their authors' features, their authenticity confirmed in writing by inscriptions or epigrams. In this way an author-work-identification was established, and individual authorship was thus also protected (see p. 44).

The funerary monuments of this group of people too were embellished with accurate sculptural portraits, accompanied by epitaphs chiselled in stone praising the merits of the deceased.

The radically new image of man in early modern times is surely nowhere more evident than in the Renaissance art of portraiture. Fundamentally concerned with presenting an accurate likeness, and showing an appreciation of outstanding individuals in a manner that was unknown in western culture since Roman antiquity, it created an unprecedented permanent monument to members of the intellectual elite who were also of bourgeois origin.

THE REDISCOVERY OF ARTISTS' TECHNIQUES
IN ROMAN ANTIQUITY:
DEATH AND LIFE MASKS IN
SCULPTURED PORTRAITURE

Human images played a significant role in Roman art. It had its origins in the Romans' death cult, which gave expression to their characteristic respect for their ancestors. As it was important to capture the exact features of prominent contemporaries, Roman images are characterised by a strict verisimilitude. "Images of great ancestors, death masks as well as statues and busts", states the classical historian Karl Christ, "do not idealise or heroicise", but present "the individual in all his singularity".[5]

The frequently drastic realism of Roman sculptured portraiture was made possible by the artists' use of death masks. The technique of taking a death mask is described in detail by Pliny the Elder (23/24-79 AD) in his *Historia Naturalis*.[6] However, this knowledge was lost after the demise of Roman civilisation, to be rediscovered and put into practice again only through the study of the classics in the Italian Renaissance.

It is impossible to overestimate the importance of Pliny for the Renaissance sculptors who made use of this aid in creating their life-like sculptured portraits. For them, his text was – as underlined by Mary-Jane Opie – "of inestimable value".[7] The death mask became an indispensable aid to their successful creation of images identical with nature, so to speak, in accordance with the Renaissance concept of realism.

Producing a death mask required specialised knowledge and manual skill. And yet this was a relatively simple procedure compared to what was entailed in making a stone image from the death mask and proceeding to produce, with mathematical precision and by means of special measuring instruments and tools, an accurate likeness of the original. This was true expertise.[8] Even the slightest deviations or changes could result in considerable distortions of the stone image.

Death masks were generally plaster casts made from plaster moulds of the features of the deceased. As a rule they were taken immediately after death, usually by professional plaster moulders. Georg Kolbe supplies a precise and vivid description of this ancient method of preparing death masks:

"[...] where there is hair, it is painted over with thinned-down modelling clay, or perhaps with oil, so that it does not stick to the plaster. The skin itself contains enough fat to make any preparation unnecessary. The edges of the mask, at the neck and behind the ears etc are covered with a layer of damp, extremely thin paper. [...] A big bowl of plaster no thicker than soup is ladled over the face to a depth of just a few millimetres; then a thread is laid across the middle of the forehead, down to the ridge of the nose, the mouth and the chin. A second bowl of thicker plaster, like a kind of porridge, is spread over the first layer (think of it as kind of cap to hold everything in place) and before it has set the thread is pulled away, dividing the whole into two halves. When the cap has hardened off, the bipartite mould is broken in two and carefully removed from the head; this is the most difficult step, because the mould has formed an airtight bond with the body. The two halves are then immediately fitted together again and clamped; the 'negative' is cleaned and refilled with plaster. Then the outer coating, the cap, is carefully chipped away with mallet and chisel, revealing the 'positive', the finished mask".[9]

Life masks were prepared in much the same fashion from the faces of the living (see Part IV, n102). They did require a slightly different procedure, however, to enable breathing to continue through both nostrils. This was normally done by inserting straws into the nose. Johann Wolfgang von Goethe described in graphic detail how unpleasant this whole process was for the subject, and how much he disliked the feeling of "muck on his face".

The first true-to-life bust in modern art history to have been created from a cast is probably that of the Italian banker Niccolò da Uzzano (c. 1425-30 – fig. 001), ascribed to Donatello and located in the Bargello in Florence.[10] It was the German art historian Joseph Pohl who, in the 1930s, had already noticed that this bust marked the beginning of the use of "death and life masks in quattrocento and cinquecento portraiture".[11]

Fig. 001 Bust of the Italian banker Niccolò da Uzzano (c. 1425-30).

In contrast to the age of Romanticism, when a death mask was an object of reverence keeping alive the memory of the deceased, in the Renaissance and Baroque period it was discarded or forgotten once the work based on it was completed. Having no intrinsic value, it was often lost. Newton's death mask was rediscovered by accident 112 years after the physicist's death and Beethoven's about fifty years after the composer had died.[12] Against this background it does not seem so remarkable that William Shakespeare's death mask too was lost for many years, after the sculptor Gheerart Janssen had made use of it.

FUNERARY MONUMENTS AND BUSTS

The three-dimensional funerary monument of the Renaissance had its origins in Florence. The dead were depicted first in a lying position, and then sitting, usually in a wall-niche. Funerary monuments were at first usually only provided for popes, cardinals, bishops, monarchs, and aristocrats. The first example, pointing the way, was no doubt the monument by Donatello for Pope John XXIII (Baldassare Cossa) in the Baptistry in Florence, dating from between c. 1421 and 1427.[13] Other outstanding works include the monument of the Cardinal of Portugal (S. Miniato al Monte, Florence), the work of Antonio Rossellino in the period between about 1461 and 1466. Between 1520 and 1534, Michelangelo created a new type of monument with sculptures for the tombs of the Medici in S. Lorenzo in Florence. Harald Olbrich rendered the following description:

> The deceased sit in classical costume in reflective poses in niches above their sarcophagi, while naked allegorical figures representing the hours of the day are arranged in antithetical positions on the lids of the sarcophagi, symbolising time.[14]

In fifteenth century Italy there were already isolated examples of niche monuments to the memory of humanist scholars, poets, and prominent representatives of the wealthy bourgeoisie. An example is the tomb monument of the distinguished humanist, historiographer and chancellor of the Florentine Republic, Leonardo Bruni, in the church of S. Croce in Florence. Dating from about 1448-50, it is the work of Bernardo Rossellino.[15] Or we may cite the memorial to a scholar created in 1492-98 by Bartolomeo Bellano in the church of S. Francesco in Padua which honours the Venetian doctor and philosopher Pietro Roccabonella, who died in 1491.[16]

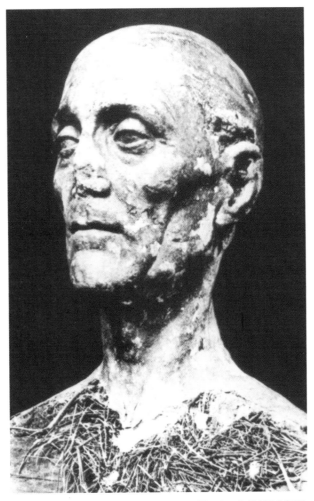

Fig. 002 Funeral effigy of Henry VII of England (1457-1509).

The chief characteristics of the type of tomb monument particularly designed for scholars and poets were the meticulous, accurate and realistic portrayal of the head and face and the carefully executed inscriptions conveying the identity, dates and achievements of the deceased. The three-dimensional image on a scale of one to one aimed at faithfully reproducing the features of the dead person. Along with the written information and explication, it was meant as a display of respect for the great individual, documenting his existence and achievements for posterity. However, as we have seen, Renaissance sculptors could only achieve a perfect likeness of their subject by using a death mask, which enabled them to transfer precisely the measurements, proportions and special morphological features of the individual's expression to the stone they were going to point and work on. In some cases they made use of a life mask, or a likeness painted in a true-to-life manner.[17]

The use of death masks for funerary monuments spread rapidly from Italy across Europe. As far as England is concerned, there is evidence that this practice came into being at the beginning of the sixteenth century. It was Henry VII (1457-1509) who, during his lifetime, commissioned the leading Florentine sculptor Pietro Torrigiano (1457-1528) to execute his tomb monument, and thus laid the foundations for true-to-life funerary sculpture in the Italian fashion in England.[18] In his will the king decreed that there should be "oon Ymage y-made of our owne figure and an other of hers [the queen's]".[19] Pohl describes the likeness of the king that resulted (*fig. 002*):[20]

> The most impressive portrait of the time is the effigy of Henry VII, who died in 1509. The death-mask characteristics are unmistakeable. The face has fallen in, the skin is slack, and lies stretched across the framework of bone.[21]

Torrigiano also created tomb monuments for the bourgeois citizens of early sixteenth-century England. The memorial sculpture (*fig. 003*) for the diplomat and cleric John Yonge (1467-1516), dating from after 1516, was quite clearly based on a death mask.[22]

The impressive funerary culture in England, with its lifelike tomb sculptures, reached its flowering in the late sixteenth and early seventeenth centuries. It mirrors not

Fig. 003 Funerary sculpture of the diplomat and cleric John Yonge (1467-1516), based on a death mask.

Fig. 004 Funerary monument of the Earls of Southampton in St Peter's Church, Titchfield.

ually and true to life, with natural colours and usually with eyes wide open, gazing at the observer. The memorial reflects the changes in building styles and art, as well as hairstyles, beards and dress fashions. The sphere of activity in which the individual achieved distinction in life is shown by a representative object.

An outstanding example of the dynastic type of tomb monument in the Elizabethan period is the splendid memorial to the Earls of Southampton (*fig. 004*), made by the Southwark sculptor, Gheerart Janssen, for St Peter's Church in Titchfield. Janssen was the father of the sculptor of the same name who later created Shakespeare's monument (see p. 41 and 128). The third Earl of Southampton, Shakespeare's patron and friend, is shown kneeling with his sister Mary at the tomb of their parents.

One of the finest artistic examples of the kneeling single figure is the funerary sculpture of Henry Howard, the first Earl of Northampton, who died in

only the social hierarchy of the country, but also the great social permeability brought about by commoners' achievements through educational and academic training, personal accomplishments, attaining of public office, entrepreneurship, and the acquisition of houses and estates. Despite the devastating effects of the English Civil War, especially the blind fury of the Puritans' iconoclasm which destroyed or severely damaged many extremely valuable cultural assets (*see fig. 103*), there still exist in English churches today numerous tomb monuments, falling broadly into three types:

> *First*: the grand, elaborate dynastic family monument often uniting several generations of a family, with fully three-dimensional, brightly painted couples lying in armour and an elegant robe respectively, surrounded by the still-living generation of (mainly) children or young adults who – like the deceased – are realistically depicted as they kneel at the tomb of their parents.
> *Second*: the lying, kneeling, or standing single figure representing an affluent and/or prominent person.
> *Third*: the monuments for scholars, writers and poets showing a half-length statue sitting in a wall niche. As with the dynastic family monument and those with a single figure, the face of the scholar is rendered individ-

Fig. 005 Funerary sculpture of the first Earl of Northampton, Henry Howard (1540-1614).

1614 (*fig. 005*).[23] This is the first known work by the English sculptor Nicholas Stone after his return to England in 1613. Stone was trained by Hendrik de Keyser in Amsterdam and was soon to become famous. As will be explained in Part IV that draws on new sources, a different work may in fact have been his first in England (see p. 99).

The monument to the Earl of Northampton was apparently based on prominent models created for the higher nobility of Spain and for the Habsburg dynasty, as a comparison with the funerary sculpture of Francisco de Sandoval y Rojas, Duke of Lerma, first minister and favourite of King Philip III of Spain, would suggest.[24] As Northampton was a committed Catholic,[25] it was probably not accidental that the type of tomb sculpture customary in Catholic countries was chosen.

The Earl of Northampton was one of the most learned men of his day. He was among the participants in a meeting of English Catholics in Rome in 1585, conducted by the leaders of the Catholic opposition, the Jesuit Father Robert Parsons and the later Roman cardinal William Allen. At this meeting the future strategy of the English Catholics in exile towards the government in London was decided, and the Armada project was born.[26] Northampton had been in prison when, in 1585, he successfully petitioned Queen Elizabeth's Lord Treasurer, William Cecil, for his release by pleading that his poor health required him to take the spa waters in Warwickshire. As soon as he was a free man, he made his way to Rome.[27]

There are countless examples of the sixteenth- and early seventeenth-century wall-niche monument reserved for scholars, scientists, poets, writers, and sometimes for meritorious individuals from other professions; it is to this type that William Shakespeare's tomb monument belongs (see pp. 38–42). For the most part they adopted typical contemporary Renaissance style architecture, employing columns. Apart from the true-to-life busts of the departed, based upon death masks, and the aforementioned signs of their profession, these monuments were often furnished with symbols signifying time and transience: attendant figures and skulls. The arms and honours of the deceased were also depicted, and marble plaques were placed under the monument-niche with inscriptions recording the age of the dead man as well as his special achievements. The monuments served not only as a memorial for posterity, but also as a mark of respect.[28] The examples displayed here date from about 1578 to 1632. They are therefore very suitable for comparison with Shakespeare's tomb

Fig. 006 Monument of Cornelius van Dun (d. 1577), St Margaret's Church, Westminster.

monument, and refute the written objection put forward in 1995 by the former Director of the University of Birmingham's Shakespeare Institute in Stratford, Professor Stanley Wells, who argued that he knew "of no death mask of any non-royal British person before that of Oliver Cromwell [1599-1658]".[29]

In St Margaret's Church in Westminster there is a wall-niche monument of Cornelius van Dun (who died in 1577), with a lively and forceful likeness of the departed (*fig. 006*). Van Dun had particularly distinguished himself – as the inscription tells us – as a soldier under Henry VIII at Tournai, and as "Yeoman of the gard and usher to K. Henry. K. Edward, Q. Mary and Q. Elizabeth". What is chiefly celebrated here is his service in the war with France. Henry VIII joined the Holy League against France in 1512. In 1513, together with the Emperor Maximilian, he defeated the French army. The peace treaty with France ceded Tournai to England. Henry's sister Mary married Louis XII.

The tomb monument of the English historian and antiquarian John Stow (1525-1603) in St Andrew

Fig. 007 Monument of the historian John Stow (1525-1603), St Andrew Undershaft, London.

Undershaft in London shows the deceased seated, holding an open book (*fig. 007*).[30] Stow was a close observer of the furious pace of change in the Elizabethan scene. He reported, for example, on the great quantity of luxury goods and status objects flooding into England, commenting among other things on the origins of the fans and wigs imported for fashion-conscious Elizabethan ladies, and pinpointing the beginnings of the trade. Originating in Italy, where they were popular among courtesans, according to Stow they reached England via France after the St Bartholomew's Day Massacre in Paris in 1572.[31] In Shakespeare's *Romeo and Juliet* Mercutio makes fun of Juliet's nurse when she asks her servant Peter to bring her fan: "Good Peter, to hide her face; for her fan's the fairer face" (II, 4). In his *Survey of London* (1598) Stow mentions that a new kind of vehicle is in use in London, and much in demand: the coach, imported from Germany. He comments: "for the world runs on wheels with many, whose parents were glad to goe on foote".[32]

As researchers have pointed out several times,[33] Stow's tomb monument bears a close resemblance to that of Shakespeare's. His hands and left forearm lie across the pages of the open book. There is a pen in his right hand, indicating (as does the book) his activity as a writer. The historian's features are faithfully reproduced, quite clearly by using a death mask.

The equally lifelike tomb bust, in a wall-niche in St Lawrence's Church in Reading, of the English mathematician John Blagrave, who died in 1611, also shows the scholar in a seated position. His eyes are wide open. In his hands he is holding instruments that typify his specialisation; a globe in his right, and a quadrant in his left hand. The allegorical figures to the left and right of Blagrave's bust symbolise the geometrical solids, the cube and the pyramid.

A funerary sculpture in the entrance to St George's Chapel in Windsor commemorates the Elizabethan/Jacobean Bishop and Dean of St George's Chapel Giles Tomson (1553-1612) (*fig. 008*).[34] He is holding a prayer book. Bishop Tomson was one of the forty-seven leading theologians and scholars at the Bible

Fig. 008 Monument of Bishop Giles Tomson (1553-1612), St George's Chapel, Windsor Castle.

conference called together by James I in 1604, which led to the famous "Authorized Version" or "King James Bible" in 1611. The size, shape, decoration and colour of the cushion placed beneath the Bible – a relatively flat, rectangular rest for writing or reading, red below, green on top, and decorated at the corners with gold tassels - corresponds to the cushion of the Shakespeare monument in Holy Trinity Church in Stratford-upon-Avon, made only about four years later as an original component of the tomb monument.

Fig. 009 Monument of the English historian and antiquary William Camden (1551-1623), Westminster Abbey.

An early plaster copy of the Shakespeare bust (*see fig.101*) can be regarded as pictorial evidence for the shape of the cushion, unchanged to this day. The pillow shape depicted in the Dugdale engraving (*see fig. 100*) is based – as will be shown – on a misunderstanding (see p. 120).

The tomb monument of the English historian and antiquary William Camden (1551-1623), who was head of Westminster School from 1593 and whose distinguished pupils included Shakespeare's fellow-dramatist Ben Jonson, is to be found in Westminster Abbey (*fig. 009*).[35] It shows clear similarities to numerous other surviving images of Camden. The scholar is shown resting his left hand upon his most important work, *Britannia*, first published in 1586 (sixth, enlarged edition 1607), while his right arm rests with bent elbow and the hand clutching his gloves.

Also in Westminster Abbey, not far from Camden's monument, is the tomb sculpture of the Elizabethan/Jacobean poet Michael Drayton (1563-1631), who belonged to the circle around Stow, Camden and

Jonson, but was also a friend of Shakespeare's, as demonstrated by his visit (together with Ben Jonson) to Stratford-upon-Avon in April 1616, which according to tradition took place only a few days before Shakespeare's death (see p. 138). In contrast to Shakespeare's, little is known about Drayton's life. As he died in relative penury, Lady Anne Clifford, Countess of Dorset, saw to it that the memory of this very prolific and popular poet (his best-known work was the sonnet sequence *Ideas Mirror*, 1594) was kept alive. At her behest, when Drayton died a costly marble monument was erected in Westminster Abbey, reproducing his features precisely (*fig. 010*).[36] Its inscription contains the lengthy eulogy:

MICHAELL DRAITON ESQR: A MEMORABLE POET OF THIS AGE.
CHANGED HIS LAVRELL FOR A CROWNE OF GLORYE A° 1631.
DOE PIOVS MARBLE LET THY READERS KNOWE
WHAT THEY AND WHAT THEIR CHILDREN OWE
TO DRAITONS NAME: WHOSE SACRED DVST
WEE RECOMMEND VNTO THY TRVST:
PROTECT HIS MEMORY, AND PRESERVE HIS STORYE:
REMAINE A LASTINGE MONVMENT OF HIS GLORYE:
AND WHEN THY RVINS SHALL DISCLAIME
TO BE THE TREAS'RER OF HIS NAME
HIS NAME THAT CANOT FADE, SHALL BE
AN EVERLASTING MONVMENT TO THEE.

Fig. 010 Monument of the Elizabethan-Jacobean poet Michael Drayton (1563-1631), Westminster Abbey.

PORTRAITS

If the individual as a subject was only marginally present in mediaeval painting, in fourteenth-century Italy – once again under the influence of the revival of classical thinking and art-forms – a new genre arose: the portrait of the individual. The new image of man in the Renaissance period is particularly evident in portrait painting. Like the portrait sculpture and drawing of the time, it reflects not only a new conception of the significance of particularly meritorious individuals, but also the desire to honour them and to record their external appearance. This was done by means of images that were created *ad vivam effigiem*, i.e. "from life", or "based on the live model". They usually reproduced the physiognomy of the subject with strict accuracy in order to create a faithful representation and a durable testimony to his actual physical existence.

In his book *Renaissance Portraits. European Portrait Painting in the 14th, 15th and 16th Centuries* (1990) Lorne Campbell states: "The basic function of portraiture was and is commemorative".[37] Next to this commemorative use of portraits Campbell also mentions a number of other functions of portraiture.[38] The standard way for contemporaries to praise a portrait, Campbell says, was to remark that "it was so like [the subject] that it lacked only speech" to make it talk.[39] Shakespeare, too, in his late play *The Winter's Tale* (V, 3) speaks about this kind of deceptive similarity between a work of art, in this case a sculpture, and a living person. The figure in question is – as Paulina initially gives King Leontes to understand – a statue of the supposedly dead Queen Hermione, who is in fact impersonating herself. This "statue" is then, as though by a miracle, brought to life before the eyes of the king, his daughter Perdita, and his royal friend Polyxenes:

PAULINA ...
The statue is but newly fix'd, the colour's
Not dry....

LEONTES: ...
What was he that did make it? See, my lord
Would you not deem it breath'd, and that those veins
Did verily bear blood?

POLYXENES:
Masterly done!
The very life seems warm upon her lips.

LEONTES:
The fixure of her eye has motion in't
As we are mocked with art. ...
Let no man mock me,
For I will kiss her.

PAULINA: ...
The ruddiness upon her lip;
You'll mar it if you kiss it; stain your own
With oily painting. ...

The fact that early modern artists generally worked from the life and true to life, as many picture inscriptions record, makes the faces of those portrayed still identifiable today. We might think of the well-known painting "The Merchant Georg Gisze" by Hans Holbein the Younger in the new Berlin Gallery of Painting, whose inscription particularly emphasises the authenticity of Gisze's features in the portrait. The face in a portrait, wrote the German art historian Rudolf Preimesberger in another context, is the "most important key to identification".[40] The ability to identify the subjects of portraits was a precondition for the work of the German Federal Bureau of Criminal Investigation (Bundeskriminalamt – BKA), and for all the other research methods and testing procedures employed as described in this book (see pp. 47ff.). Since all the symptoms of disease were also faithfully reproduced in early modern images, doctors today are able to describe and diagnose them.

THE DEPICTION AND DIAGNOSIS OF SYMPTOMS OF DISEASE

The symptoms of disease depicted in portrait painting of the sixteenth and seventeenth centuries have supplied medical research, especially dermatology, with a rich vein of visual material that has been mined intensively by numerous medical experts for many decades.[41] The exact reproduction of symptoms of illnesses has in many cases led to astonishingly precise diagnoses.

In images of Johann Sebastian Bach (1685-1750) an abnormality of the upper eyelid was established, diagnosed by Professor Ernst Engelking, Director of the Ophthalmic Clinic at the University of Heidelberg, as blepharochalasis (a slackening of the skin in the upper eyelid). This pathological symptom is more prominent on Bach's right side than his left. The new medical assessment enabled the iconography of Bach to be placed on a new footing.[42]

Fig. 011 Portrait of the patrician Ulrich Röhling (d. 1618) by Mathias Krodel the Younger, Germanic National Museum, Nuremberg.

In 1982, the dermatologist Albrecht Scholz diagnosed birthmarks (naevi) on the left cheek of the portrait of Federigo di Montefeltro, Duke of Urbino (1422-1486), painted by Piero della Francesca and hanging in the Uffizi in Florence. As Scholz points out, the Duke clearly cannot have been too concerned about these marks, since they "are unmistakeably reproduced even on a Florentine marble relief".[43]

In a portrait of an old man by Domenico Ghirlandaio in the Louvre a case of rhinophyma (bulbous nose or acne rosacea) is depicted.[44] This morbid change begins as a rule between the ages of forty and fifty and the patient would suffer from secretory problems and inflammatory affection or chronic gastro-intestinal complaints.

A drawing by Hans Holbein the Younger in the Fogg Museum at Harvard shows the distorted features of a young man suffering from syphilis or contagious impetigo.[45]

The portrait of Martin Luther by Lucas Cranach the Younger in the Germanic National Museum in Nuremberg reveals – according to the diagnosis of the dermatologist Walter Roth – a pea-sized tumour on the reformer's forehead.[46]

In the same Nuremberg museum there is an image of the patrician Ulrich Röhling (d. 1618) painted by Mathias Krodel the Younger, which shows that Röhling, too, was afflicted by rhinophyma. The picture displays realistically presented deformations, reddish-brown infiltrations, and irregular lumps and swellings (*fig. 011*).[47]

The portrait of Galileo Galilei (1564-1642) in the Pitti Place in Florence, a product of the school of Sustermans, shows on the left cheek-bone a lump the size of a grain of maize, dome shaped and clearly delineated; it was diagnosed by Walter Roth as a keratoacanthoma (a wart-like hornification).[48] This pathological phenomenon occurs on average in patients aged about sixty-four, develops a self-healing power, and remits after about six months. It is therefore a symptom that could even help to date the picture precisely.

One of the most outstanding examples of strict verisimilitude in portraiture is the image of the painter Michael Wolgemut in the Germanic National Museum in Nuremberg (*fig. 012*). It was a picture painted in 1516 by Albrecht Dürer of his eighty-two-year-old mentor, for whom he had enormous, lifelong respect. In the judgement of the German art historian Daniel Hess, Dürer succeeded here "in a unique manner in bringing waning physical strength into harmony with the visionary gifts of a seer".[49] The "truth to life" and "precise copying of nature" in this picture had already impressed the painter Johann Heinrich Tischbein in 1779 so deeply that he felt he was looking at the portrait's subject himself.[50] It was the German art historian Kurt Löcher who noticed that the painting showed the subject's face had undergone a pathological change. When Löcher called in the ophthalmologist Professor Rainer Rix, the latter concluded that this could be a case of an iridocyclitis (a combination of grey cataract and glaucoma), that is to say "a disorder of the pupil with partial synechia [adherence of the iris to cornea or lens] following inflammation of the iris".[51] This characteristic, says Löcher, was so accurately depicted that a fissure in the shape of a round hole, typical of this condition, was also visible.[52] In addition, a "localised opacity of the lens" was perceptible.[53]

I was similarly able to make out noticeable pathological changes in images of Shakespeare, also offering vivid evidence for the accuracy of Renaissance portrait art. I asked several medical experts from various disciplines to examine and report on these symptoms of disease (see pp. 67ff.).

Fig. 012 Portrait of the painter Michael Wolgemut (1434/37-1519) by Albrecht Dürer, Germanic National Museum, Nuremberg.

THE MORAL AND THEOLOGICAL REASONS
FOR LIFELIKE PORTRAITURE

The generally precise reproduction of pathological symptoms in Renaissance and Baroque painting is explicable not only in terms of the contemporary practice of faithful representation, but also in the light of the injunctions, based on moral theology, of the Catholic church to painters to paint faces true to reality, i.e. not to improve on nature, and not to omit any signs of illness.[54] The relevant regulations, agreed in a generalised form at the final session of the Council of Trent (1545-1563), written by Gabriele Paleotti, Bishop of Bologna, and published by him in 1582, represent the basis of a new order in Catholic policy towards the creation of images. In Paleotti we read:

> But as they are called portraits drawn from nature, it is necessary to ensure that the face or other parts of the body are not rendered more beautiful or more ugly, or changed in any way not in accord with what nature has bestowed upon him; but rather that, even if he should be very disfigured by congenital or accidental flaws, there should be no question of leaving them out, unless they have been disguised by artifice, just as it was written of the image of Antigonos which Apelles painted in profile, so that it could not be seen that he lacked an eye [...].[55]

The "honourable" grounds for producing portraits listed by Paleotti are especially informative in terms of cultural and social history. They are as follows:

> We would just want to recall that sometimes sufficient honourable reasons exist for someone who has been requested to do so to allow it [i.e. allow his portrait to be made], in order to please the other person; [1] as when, perhaps, the father, the mother, wife or other closely related persons with understandable benevolence towards him ask the other for a picture of himself, [in order] that the presence of the painting should relieve the hardship of absence. [2] There would be a further reason if because of disputes in distant regions it should be necessary to prove the similarity of father to son, or of children to each other. [3] Or when it is necessary to marry a woman whom he has never seen, and the husband desires to see the image of the woman he is to wed, or the bride that of the bridegroom. [4] The case is similar if one were to judge it appropriate to have a picture made to please the public or a highly-placed person or other people who are motivated by decent and Christian intentions. [5] We also believe that one may express one's willingness [to be painted] without any doubts if one wants only to be useful to the painter, who wishes in good faith to make a portrait of this or that person to further his studies and gain practice.[56]

The question of whether such regulations really were closely followed in Catholic countries must be left aside. In Elizabethan/Jacobean England at any rate they cannot have been in force officially. But the fact remains that the portrait painters of the time – whatever the motivation for their activity – by and large complied with the rules to reproduce faithfully all visible morphological and pathological facial features.

PORTRAIT ENGRAVINGS

The reproduction of portrait works dominated the early history of book illustration, from the end of the fifteenth until the beginning of the eighteenth century. As with portrait sculptures, in two-dimensional portraiture depicting princes, scholars, writers and poets the painters, too, looked back to classical examples from Roman antiquity. Pliny the Elder gives an account in Volume XXXV of his *Historia Naturalis* of the "imagines" of the Roman

Fig. 013 Albrecht Dürer, portrait of Philip Melanchthon, copper engraving, 1526.

authors M. Terentius Varro and T. Pomponius Atticus, which were accompanied by a few lines of verse. Until the end of the fifteenth century images based on type were the norm ('*Typenbilder* of princes and scholars'),[57] rarely possessing or aiming at a likeness. However, in the course of the sixteenth century – following classical Roman examples, and along with the humanists' rekindled interest in the biographies of exceptional individuals – the first subjects for "truthful" treatment were scholars, closely followed by "truthful" portraits of artists and poets. Thanks to the new but already well-developed technique of image reproduction, in combination with typeset book printing, it was possible to meet the great demand for "*imagines verae*" of important personalities that guaranteed to replicate with painstaking verisimilitude the features of those portrayed.

In 1562 G. Schnellboltz in Wittenberg published images of protestant scholars with the significant title *True Portraits of Some Learned Men* (*Wahrhaffte Bildnis etlichen gelernten Menner*). On the Calvinist side, Theodore Beza's book *Icones, id est verae imagines virorum doctrina simul et pictate illustrium*

appeared in Geneva in 1580. The portrait engravings of scholars, artists and poets, based on an authentic image ("*vera imago*") and being particularly popular engraved on copper as a frontispiece,[58] created a type of illustration that was adopted throughout Europe and frequently encountered in England. Such pictures were often accompanied by inscriptions or lines of verse, authenticating – as is the case with the portrait engraving of William Shakespeare (*see fig. 023*) – the absolute faithfulness of the engraved portraits to their subjects, and thus also the identity of the latter.

THE PORTRAIT ARTISTS' DILEMMA

When in 1526 Albrecht Dürer engraved an individual portrait of Philip Melanchthon precise in every detail (*fig. 013*), he added this text: "The skilled hand of Dürer was able to paint the living countenance of Philip, but not his mind or soul".[59] Dürer was thereby alluding to a dilemma of the portrait artist that had already been expressed in classical antiquity: it was not given to the artist to transcend the portrayal of outward appearances and capture the soul or mind of his subject as well. So, for example, in his description of a portrait of Marcus Antonius Primus, Martial commented: "*Ars utinam mores animumque effingere posset! / Pulchrior in terris nulla tabella foret.*"[60] ("If art could represent character and mind, there would be no more beautiful picture on earth.") Preimesberger brings out the point when he says: "It is clear that Dürer's real aim in this 'confession' of his inability to paint the mind of Melanchthon is not just a confession of the inadequacy of art or the artist: it invokes the theme of the 'great compliment' paid to the subject, in the face of whose greatness all art is bound to fail".[61] The engraving that Dürer made of Erasmus of Rotterdam in 1526 can be seen in this light. Its inscription reads: "The picture of Erasmus of Rotterdam, drawn from the life (as a true-to-life portrait) by Albrecht Dürer. He will be better shown by his writings."[62] And the same message is to be found in the text placed opposite the copper-plate engraving of William Shakespeare in the First Folio in 1623 (*see fig. 023*). All of these are examples of the "themes of inexpressibility" (*Unsagbarkeitstopoi*) which always represent a great tribute to their subjects (see p. 44).

II. THE IMAGES UNDER INVESTIGATION:

The Previous State of Knowledge

Among the many images of Shakespeare that have come to light over the centuries, there are just a few that, on the basis of oral or written tradition, but also for other reasons, justify the assumption that they may be authentic, true-to-life representations of the poet's person, dating from his own lifetime or immediately after his death. They are the Chandos portrait, the Flower portrait, the Davenant bust, and the Darmstadt Shakespeare death mask. In the following chapters they will be presented within the framework of the previous state of knowledge, and their identity and authenticity will then be thoroughly tested by using the latest research methods and techniques.

THE CHANDOS PORTRAIT

The so-called Chandos portrait, an oval picture executed in oil on canvas and measuring 55.2 x 43.8 cm (*fig. 014*), is the oldest known Shakespeare portrait of all. The National Portrait Gallery in London, founded in 1856 and opened three years later, acquired it as their first exhibit.[63] The picture has ever since been among the most important and best-guarded treasures of England. Its succession of previous owners came from a wide variety of social backgrounds: actors, authors, and aristocrats. From the early nineteenth century onwards it became known as the "Chandos portrait", after one of its earlier owners, the Marquis of Caernarvon, later Duke of Chandos. On 29 June 1784 the Irish Shakespeare scholar Edmond Malone (1741-1812), living in England, made a note on the back of a crayon drawing he possessed: "This Drawing of Shakspeare was made in August 1783, by that excellent artist, Mr Ozias Humphry, from the only original picture [of Shakespeare] extant, which formerly belonged to Sir William Davenant, and is now in the possession of the Duke of Chandos".[64] The basis of this drawing was the Chandos painting. When the duke's daughter married the Duke of Buckingham, her dowry included the Shakespeare picture.[65] The Duke of Buckingham's collection was auctioned off in September 1848. The Chandos portrait was acquired for 355 guineas by the

Duke of Ellesmere, who gave it to the new National Portrait Gallery.[66] The picture has suffered considerable wear and tear in the course of its history and has constantly needed repairs and restoration.[67]

In my view, the question of who painted the Chandos portrait has never been satisfactorily resolved. This has to do with, among other things, inconsistencies among the entries in the *Notebooks* (1719) of the English antiquary George Vertue, where for the first time the oral traditions of the seventeenth century were taken down in writing. According to Vertue, who relied on statements by its owner at the time, the picture had been painted by an actor called "John Taylor", a contemporary and close friend of Shakespeare's. The name "Richard Burbridge" [sic] noted in the margin of the *Notebook*-entry was later crossed out by Vertue.[68] However, no *John* Taylor is known among the actors of Shakespeare's day; but there is a *Joseph* Taylor, who lived from 1586 to 1653. He is mentioned in the First Folio of 1623 among the "principal actors in all these plays". But Joseph Taylor is not known either as a professional or an amateur artist. And it seems somewhat unlikely that, being twenty-two years younger than Shakespeare, he could have been a close friend of the dramatist. On the other hand, the actor Richard Burbage, only about five years younger, fulfils both criteria. He was, as is well-known, a close friend of the dramatist, and, as tradition has it, he is known to have been an amateur painter. In her essay "The Chandos portrait: a suggested painter" the English author Mary Edmond claims to have identified the Chandos portraitist. The artist in question, according to Edmond, was the John Taylor who belonged to the London guild of "Painter-Stainers" and died in 1651.[69] But Edmond's suggestion, too, is problematical (see p. 83).

While the Chandos portrait incontrovertibly dates from Shakespeare's period, up to the present day it could not be established that it really does depict William Shakespeare. The former director of the National Portrait Gallery, Sir Roy Strong, taking his cue from statements by his predecessors, remarked in his *Tudor & Jacobean Portraits* (1969) that the picture

Fig. 014 The Chandos portrait, oval, oil on canvas, National Portrait Gallery, London.

was "without doubt a perfectly authentic English portrait of its period".[70] On the question of identifying the subject, Strong observed that "the identity of this as a portrait of Shakespeare remains non proven and is likely to remain so",[71] but conceded that: "All that can be said is that the painting is the only one which can have any claim, on documentary and other evidence, to be rightly identified."[72] The American Shakespeare biographer Samuel Schoenbaum shared this opinion – although without undertaking any independent critical examination of his own.[73]

THE FLOWER PORTRAIT

The Flower portrait (*figs. 015 and 016*)[74] is a panel painting in oil[75] measuring 59.7 x 43.8 cm, bearing the inscription "Willm̄ Shakespeare 1609". When it was exhibited in 1892 on loan at the Memorial Picture Gallery in Stratford-upon-Avon, it caused a sensation among the public because of its striking resemblance to the Droeshout engraving (*see fig. 023*) in the First Folio of 1623. There are two ways in which its owner, Mr H. C. Clements from Sydenham or Peckham Rye near London,[76] may have come by the picture: either directly from one of the proven descendants of the Shakespeare family, in whose possession it may have been ever since the poet himself sat for it;[77] or indirectly via an unnamed dealer from whom Clements may have bought it around 1840.[78]

The meticulously conducted *Proceedings of the Society of Antiquaries of London* of 12 December 1895 also mentions a Shakespeare descendant as the former owner.[79] It is not improbable that in the early decades of the nineteenth century the portrait was still in the hands of one of the dramatist's distant relatives, forced to sell it because of financial exigencies. Shakespeare's last direct (and legitimate) descendant,[80] his grand-daughter Elizabeth Nash, née Hall, later Lady Bernard, bequeathed her grandfather's house in Henley Street in Stratford to the grandchildren of the poet's sister Joan Hart, born in 1569.[81]

During repairs to roof timbers in Shakespeare's birthplace in 1757 Thomas Hart, a fifth-generation descendant of Joan Hart, discovered the Jesuit testament of John Shakespeare, in which the dramatist's father declared his Catholic faith in writing.[82] The English Shakespeare specialists T. J. B. Spencer and Stanley Wells have followed the line of Shakespeare's descendants from his sister down to the twentieth century, as far as George Shakespeare Hart

from High Wycombe, who went to the Stratford Grammar School, had a son called Alfred Thomas Shakespeare Hart, and died in 1907.[83]

The Flower portrait was named after Mrs Charles Flower, who bought it in 1895 from Mrs Clements and presented it to the Stratford Gallery, where it remains today. The history of the Flower portrait has until now been full of gaps and flaws. Part IV of this book tries to correct this.

With regard to the painter of the Flower portrait, so far there has been nothing but speculation. The English Shakespeare scholar Sidney Lee comments:

> Influences of an early seventeenth-century Flemish school are clearly discernible in the picture, and it is just possible that it is the production of an uncle of the young engraver Martin Droeshout, who bore the same name as his nephew, and was naturalised in this country on January 25, 1608, when he was described as a "painter of Brabant".[84]

The possibility that the Flower portrait was painted by the uncle of the engraver of the same name, i.e. the painter Maerten or Martin Droeshout the Elder, cannot immediately be ruled out. For Droeshout the Elder may have arranged that the engraving commission should go to his brother Michiel's son, who was at the very beginning of his career as an engraver.[85]

Because of the similarity of this picture to the Droeshout engraving in the First Folio, Shakespeare researchers have never doubted the identity of the subject. A number of experts in the late nineteenth century confirmed the owner's claim to possess the original model for the Droeshout engraving. In a report by the Stratford curator W. S. Brassington of 27 November 1896 it is stated that Mr G. R. M. Murray of the botany department of the British Museum had declared the panel to be elmwood. Sir E. J. Poynter, as director of the National Gallery (by the time Brassington was writing Poynter had become President of the Royal Academy), was convinced that the portrait had been painted from life. Mr Lionel Cust, director of the National Portrait Gallery, and Mr S. Colvin, curator of the British Museum print-room, had expressed their conviction that the portrait was a genuine early seventeenth-century picture. They believed the date "1609" to be authentic.[86]

It was the English art historian Marion H. Spielmann who was the first to conjecture that the

Fig. 015 The Flower portrait, oil on panel, Royal Shakespeare Company Collection, Stratford-upon-Avon.
Its condition before the 1979 restoration.

Fig. 016 The Flower portrait, oil on panel, Royal Shakespeare Company Collection, Stratford-upon-Avon.
Its condition after the 1979 restoration of the painting by Nancy Stocker of the Ashmolean Museum, Oxford.

picture was actually painted after 1623, i.e. after the publication of the Droeshout engraving in the First Folio. He argued that:

> The character of the picture – which may be a seventeenth-century production, executed from the print – is quite inconsistent with a portrait from life. There are none of those little tentative experimental touches which are invariably present, even in the most dashing portrait, when an artist is exploring for the details about the eyes and corners of the mouth – the accidents of a face – which give expression, likeness, and life – colour and folds of the skin and the play and forms of the muscles.[87]

Spielmann's arguments are not convincing. The English Shakespeare specialist and antiquary Edgar Fripp even found "Spielmann's elaborate and interesting arguments for the priority of the engraving are convincing me of the contrary".[88]

Nonetheless, Spielmann's assertion gained ground. In the course of the twentieth century it was accepted almost without contradiction. The American biographer of Shakespeare, Samuel Schoenbaum, relied on Spielmann's opinion and adopted it uncritically. He did not feel the need to verify the arguments of the noted English art historian.[89] Schoenbaum even continued to defend them[90] long after the emergence of expert objections that once more placed a question mark over them.[91]

A long time before it became possible to subject the Flower portrait to investigation using modern forensic and medical methods, and long before the picture's extensive and radical restoration in 1979 by Nancy Stocker of the Ashmolean Museum in Oxford, it was suspected that there was an older picture beneath the Shakespeare painting.[92] Spielmann thought it was a portrait of a lady, perhaps even of Shakespeare's "Dark Lady".[93] But in fact, as the London Courtauld Institute established in 1966 by x-ray examination, the subject was a religious motif, Mary with the Christ child and St. John (see fig. 073).[94] The badly damaged painting, clearly Italian in origin, was thought to date from the second half of the fifteenth century. However, the American authors Paul Bertram and Frank Cossa produced plausible arguments for placing the painting's origins in central Italy no earlier than the early sixteenth century.[95] The unfortunate notion that obtained for a while, of removing the Flower portrait completely in favour of

the Madonna piece - regarded as artistically more valuable - was only rejected in the end because it was not compatible with the intentions of the donor, Mrs Charles Flower, who had made the picture over to the Stratford Gallery as a portrait of Shakespeare.[96] The one and only reason for contemplating and discussing such a proposal at all was the general conviction, based on Spielmann, that there was practically no likelihood that the portrait was authentic and that it therefore had little value.

As a result of the spectacular restoration of the Flower portrait in 1979,[97] Bertram and Cossa revived the old theory that the portrait had been painted in 1609 directly from life, and that the engraver Droeshout had worked from it[98]. In their support they were able to call upon the best English art experts of around 1900, who held that the Flower portrait must be older than the Droeshout print. The most important English Shakespeare specialist and biographer of the time, Sidney Lee, agreed with this opinion, and explained:

> Connoisseurs, including Sir Edward Poynter, Mr Sidney Colvin, and Mr Lionel Cust, have almost unreservedly pronounced the picture to be anterior in date to the engraving, and they have reached the conclusion that in all probability Martin Droeshout directly based his work upon the painting.[99]

In his description of the Flower portrait, Lee writes:

> Though coarse and stiffly drawn, the face is far more skilfully presented than in the engraving, and the expression of countenance betrays some artistic sentiment which is absent from the print.[100]

Although Bertram and Cossa's cautious re-opening of the case produced a wealth of interesting details that spoke against Spielmann and Schoenbaum and in favour of the truth to life of the Flower portrait, they were not in a position to prove the authenticity of the Shakespeare picture. They could go no further than to state that:

> If the painting does in fact date from 1609, it is of course one of the world's great treasures, perhaps the only surviving portrait of Shakespeare from life. If on the other hand it was painted after 1623, it is unique among fakes [...] and [...] constitutes one of the most intriguing and inexplicable deceptions in English art history.[101]

THE DAVENANT BUST

The Davenant bust, made of terracotta, measuring 62x59x29 cm (length of face 26 cm), and kept in the Garrick Club in London is – aside from the death mask - the most impressive, and also the most artistically valuable, image of the poet (*fig. 017*).[102] It was named after Shakespeare's godson, and perhaps natural son, the dramatist Sir William Davenant (1606-1668). The subject's expression has been called "intellectual",[103] and the artist a "skilled sculptor".[104] H. Snowden-Ward and Catharine Weed Ward used a reproduction of this bust as the frontispiece to their book *Shakespeare's Town and Times* (*c.* 1896), and commented that this was "by far the most beautiful likeness of the poet, and one that gives us a loftier idea of his personality than even the Chandos portrait [...]."[105] However, contrary to the authors' assertion, the original is not in the Memorial Library (now the Royal Shakespeare Collection), but – as stated – in the Garrick Club. Stratford possesses one of the two copies that the anatomist and palaeontologist Sir Richard Owen had made. The other copy is held by the British Museum. The earliest description of the discovery of this Shakespeare image is that of its then owner, the Duke of Devonshire, who must have acquired the work from Sir Richard Owen in 1849, or not much later. Owen was the son-in-law of the finder, William Clift, and previously his assistant. Clift, who for many decades was a curator of the Royal College of Surgeons museum, died in 1849 and left the bust to Owen or his daughter. In his letter of 8 December 1855 which was attached to the minutes of the Garrick Club for 15 December 1855, Devonshire sets out his intention of giving his "interesting" bust to the Club, and at the same time reports what he knows about its provenance:

> The Bust, which is in terra cotta, was in the possession of Professor Owen of the College of Surgeons, from whom I purchased it. It was discovered in pulling down the old Duke's Theatre in Lincoln's Inn Fields, where it was placed over one of the Stage doors, the Bust of Ben Jonson (accidentally destroyed by the workmen) occupying a corresponding place over the other door – Shakespeare having been rescued by the timely interposition of Mr Cliff [Clift] (Professor Owen's father-in-law) the Bust became his property and was given by him to Professor Owen.[106]

Fig. 017 Davenant bust, terracotta, Garrick Club, London.

Similar descriptions can be found in the literature about construction work in Lincoln's Inn Fields in the nineteenth century.[107]

The account of the circumstances under which the Davenant bust is alleged to have been discovered in the first half of the nineteenth century is described by Geoffrey Ashton in the Garrick Club's catalogue from 1997 as "extremely suspect".[108] This mistrust is not entirely unjustified – in a different sense, however, from that assumed by the writer or editors of the catalogue. It relates to the fact that William Clift, the bust's finder, omitted for certain reasons to state in detail in an official report of his find how, where, when and in what condition he had found the Shakespeare bust, who its actual owner was, and how it had ended up in his possession. By using new sources, however, it is now possible to answer these previously open questions about the real circumstances concerning the finding of the bust and its history (see pp. 91ff.).

Without going into detail about his reasons, M. H. Spielmann at the beginning of the twentieth century ascribed this unusual sculpture of Shakespeare to a French sculptor working in England, Louis François Roubiliac (1705-1762).[109] This, like other theories of

Spielmann's, was accepted uncritically and unreservedly during the twentieth century. While Samuel Schoenbaum, without doing any research of his own but relying entirely on Spielmann, thought that the artist in question was probably Roubiliac,[110] Geoffrey Ashton in *Pictures in the Garrick Club* (1997) definitively attributed the Davenant bust to the French-English sculptor, and dated the work at around 1758.[111]

Because of its grimy condition, the bust underwent a thorough expert cleaning in 1986/87. The restorer J. H. Larson provided an exhaustive report on all his observations, all the work he had undertaken, and all the materials he had used. He came to the conclusion that: "It is quite clear that this bust had undergone two major restorations, one in the 18th century under the supervision of Roubiliac and a second during the 19th century when the back was filled with plaster and the terracotta was painted to look like bronze."[112] The restorer's statement that a restoration had already taken place in the eighteenth century does not favour an attribution to the sculptor Roubiliac. For it hardly seems likely that Roubiliac, who died in 1762, was already carrying out a major restoration on the work – allegedly made by him around 1758 – some time during the first four years after its completion. What also argues against Roubiliac as originator of the bust is that it is not signed by the artist and bears no inscription. By contrast, in 1758 when he made a gilded bronze bust of the famous actor David Garrick, he added the inscription: "*David Garrick, Arm, /L. F. Roubiliac Sct ad Vivum / 1758* (verso)".[113] Moreover, it can be seen that the Davenant bust – as will be developed further in Part IV – is a particularly successful, imposing image of William Shakespeare (see p. 99), displaying none of the strained dramatic effects more or less typical of Roubiliac. "His figures", says a critical entry in the 1899 *Encyclopaedia Britannica*, "are uneasy, devoid of dignity and sculpturesque breadth, and his draperies are treated in a manner more suited to painting than sculpture. His excessive striving after dramatic effect takes away from that repose of attitude which is so necessary for a portrait in marble."[114]

THE DARMSTADT SHAKESPEARE DEATH MASK

In 1960 the city of Darmstadt, just forty kilometres south of Frankfurt, acquired for DM 52,000 what was then the controversial death mask of Shakespeare (*fig. 018*). It had been sent for public auction by Dr Magda Heidenreich, a member of the Becker/Heidenreich family who were joint heirs and descendants of the family to which the finder of the mask belonged. The auction in the Helmut Tenner auction hall in Heidelberg[115] took a dramatic turn when the director of the Hessian State and University Library, Dr Hans Rasp (acting for the city of Darmstadt), and the Swiss scholar Martin Bodmer entered into a bidding duel. The Darmstadt bid won the day. Since then, the mask has been on permanent loan in the library of Darmstadt Castle. The plaster mask, dating back to Elizabethan times, is 23.5 cm in length and at the back has the date inscribed into it "+Aᵒ D͞m 1616" (*fig. 019 and fig. 19 a*). It had been in the possession of the Becker family of Darmstadt for over a hundred years, after Ludwig Becker (*see fig. 081*), a former Darmstadt court painter, had discovered it under noteworthy circumstances in Mainz in 1849. In 1847 Becker had acquired from the Mainz antiquary S. Jourdan a small death-image bearing on its frame the inscription "Shakespeare" (*see fig. 082*). It is still among Magda Heidenreich's effects. The picture sent Becker off on a feverish hunt for the death mask of the great English poet (see p. 103).

When the art collection of the former canon at the cathedral in Mainz, Count Franz Ludwig von Kesselstatt, was auctioned off in 1842, item no. 738, "male image in plaster", which must have been the Shakespeare death mask, aroused not the slightest interest, and certainly did not provoke any bidding. It disappeared from public view after the auction. Without the commitment of Ludwig Becker, it would surely have been permanently lost.

Becker personally took the mask to England, where his half-brother Dr Ernst Becker (*see fig. 084*) held the post of private secretary to Prince Albert from 1851 onwards. Before Ludwig Becker set out on an expedition to Australia, he gave the mask for safe-keeping to Professor Richard Owen (*see fig. 077*), who in 1856 became head of the Natural Sciences department of the British Museum. It was in Owen's care for roughly a decade and a half, until 1865. After thorough comparative examination by Owen, Becker's find was exhibited as "Shakespeare's Death Mask" in the British Museum for many years, and also in 1864 – as part of the "Centenary Exhibition" – in Stratford-upon-Avon.[116] The anatomist Owen undoubtedly regarded the object as authentic.[117] Hermann Schaaffhausen comments:

Fig. 018 The Darmstadt Shakespeare death mask, plaster of Paris, Hesse Land and University Library, Darmstadt.

Owen's verdict on the mask was that in its anatomical details it corresponded to the image we could obtain of Shakespeare. He recognised the hair sticking to it as genuine human hair, and thought it significant that the date 1616 was written in the kind of numerals used at that time, and that its curved lines indicated it had been inscribed in the plaster before it set.[118]

It is recorded that Owen would have bought the death mask for the British Museum if there had been convincing evidence of how it had come into Count Kesselstatt's possession. The German Shakespeare expert Karl Elze reports:

> The Kesselstadt mask [i.e. the Darmstadt Shakespeare Death Mask] was offered for sale to the British Museum, and apparently the Museum would have taken up the offer if it could have been proved that any member of the Kesselstadt [sic] family had been in London, for instance in connection with some ambassadorial mission.[119]

When Ludwig Becker lost his life in the expedition to Australia, Owen handed the mask over to his half-brother Ernst, who – after the death of Prince Albert – returned to Darmstadt with this valuable object.[120] Schaaffhausen reports that Owen advised Dr Becker "to inquire whether any Count Kesselstadt [sic] had ever stayed in England".[121]

Ernst Becker made great efforts to do so, and eventually came across the former manager of the Kesselstatt estate, Josef Weismüller, who in 1872 certified "with pleasure" that Count Franz von Kesselstatt "had travelled in England at the end of the last century, just as he made many other journeys, collecting many valuable art treasures on his travels".[122] In a letter to the lawyer Zell in 1869 Weismüller wrote that he remembered the Count going to England in his youth, but that he knew nothing about a mask.[123] Although this information consisted of indications provided by a completely trustworthy source, a contemporary witness who, while admittedly elderly, was intimately acquainted with the affairs of the Kesselstatt family, it was considered unreliable.[124] It was more or less disregarded, something that from today's perspective, even for somebody inclined to be critical, is hard to comprehend. It was clear, for example, to Alois Brandl, writing in the *Shakespeare-Jahrbuch* of 1911 and dealing at length with the publication by Paul Wislicenus, *Shakespeares Totenmaske (Shakespeare's Death Mask)*, which had appeared in

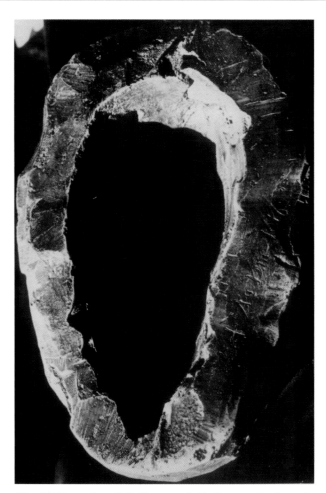

Fig. 019 Rear view of the Darmstadt Shakespeare death mask.

Fig. 019a Detail – Inscription reading "+Aº D͞m 1616".

Darmstadt in 1910, that "[…] the most serious objection so far raised to the death mask, the obscurity of its pre-history, was – as a result of this publication – still valid."[125] The long sought-after and decisive proof of a journey to England by the later Mainz canon, Count Franz Ludwig von Kesselstatt, who was the first known owner of the mask, did not come to light until June 1995. It will be presented in Part IV (see p. 117).

There is neither space enough, nor necessity, to go into the detail of the many heated debates about the mask at the end of the nineteenth and beginning of the twentieth century. Suffice it to say that those who were preoccupied at the time with the question of the authenticity of the Darmstadt Shakespeare death mask fall into two groups: on the one hand, those who sought to arrive at academically sound knowledge by using the scientific methods available at the time and on the basis of observation and investigation of the object itself; and on the other hand, those who formed a judgement without ever having seen and investigated the mask, and without reference to reliable empirical research.

The first group included (as we have seen) not only the English anatomist Richard Owen, but also the German anthropologist Hermann Schaaffhausen, the American sculptor William Page, the German historian Paul Wislicenus, and the German sculptor Robert Cauer.

At a meeting of German Nature Researchers and Doctors on 19 September 1873 in Wiesbaden ("Anthropological Section") Hermann Schaaffhausen presented a photograph of the Darmstadt death mask to the participants, and reported on his craniological and physiognomic findings, which had led to a positive outcome:

> A craniological and physiognomic verdict on this death mask, which manifests the most noble features, can find nothing to justify doubting its authenticity. As the fine lines of the skin demonstrate, it really has been taken from a dead person. The broad high forehead and the beauty of the features correspond to the image we may conceive of the great poet, and they resemble those of the well-known images of him. [...] There are grounds for believing that the mask is the original, not a copy.[126]

In 1874 the American sculptor William Page, President of the Academy of Design in New York and already advanced in years, travelled to Europe to make precise investigations and measurements in order to establish whether this image accorded with what for him were authentic likenesses of Shakespeare: the Chandos portrait, the funerary bust, and the Droeshout engraving.[127] Page reports:

> The August of 1874 arrived. [...] I had determined to go abroad to see the original. Reports in regard to it from different individuals who had seen it were conflicting. I could get no measures from other hands which I knew how to use with precision. I wished also to know more of the surface and texture of the skin, and the more delicate markings of the face as taken from nature and indicating temperament. And feeling that further effort would lack weight without personal observation of the original, I set out to see the mask itself.[128]

During his investigations of the mask in Darmstadt, lasting seven days, Page took twenty-six measurements in all, using a pair of compasses; but unfortunately he did not express these in terms of geometric units of measurement but by marking the distances between the points corresponding to the span of the compasses.[129] In comparing the mask and the funerary bust, Page found that at least ten or twelve measures "fit exactly corresponding points in the Stratford bust".[130] Where the fit was not exact, he concluded that "the failure or misfit of the other more than dozen measures is confined to those parts of the face where there is acknowledged error on the part of the sculptor of the Stratford bust".[131] Since Page, regrettably and for whatever reason,[132] failed to detail these fourteen or sixteen divergences individually or plausibly explain them - which, on closer inspection of the facts of the matter, would not have been difficult to do – he made himself an easy target for later critics.[133] He was content to point out, correctly, that it had never previously happened that about a dozen proportions had corresponded in the faces of two different (adult) persons.[134] Furthermore, he observed:

> It is, indeed, singular that such an agreement in measure with the Stratford bust should not have been noted or published by the distinguished scholars and scientists in whose care the mask was during its sojourn in England; but, so far as I know, it has not hitherto been done. There was no inquest of experts, and, hence, no verdict, except in the matter of the pedigree, which all grant is defective.[135]

In 1911 the German historian Paul Wislicenus together with the German sculptor Robert Cauer[136] turned their attention upon the mask in Darmstadt and the bust in Stratford-upon-Avon, to carry out a check on Page's measurements and his theory that mask and bust represented one and the same person: William Shakespeare. Wislicenus reports on how their preparations proceeded:

> First of all Herr Cauer checked Page's measurement one by one on the death mask, then he transferred them to a cast of the mask, 'pointing' them according to [Johann Gottfried] Schadow's description, marking on the cast as the starting point for each measurement the places where the two points of the compass touched, putting in little crosses – fifty-two in all – in those places, and writing in the number of the measurements.[137]

Wislicenus describes in minute detail the arrival of the Germans in Stratford and their work on the spot:

> With this cast and Page's notebook we travelled to Stratford, arriving at about 11 am on 4 August 1911 in the birthplace of the great poet. With a recommendation from Sir Sidney Lee to Mr Wellstood, the secretary of the 'birth house', we soon had the kind permission of Canon Melville, and by 3 o'clock in the afternoon we had already finished measuring the bust, with the help of the Canon himself. We put up a ladder next to a tomb monument, and above the latter we laid another ladder horizontally across the rungs of the first. On this second ladder we laid a plank that Herr Cauer climbed on to. Holding the compasses in his right hand, and in his left the cast with all the crosses on, he took every measurement, first from Page's book, which I handed up to him, checking it again against the cast and his crosses, and then measuring it on the head of the bust.[138]

In contrast to Page, whose results were not recorded in writing after he measured the bust, Wislicenus noted down all of Cauer's results and observations. He consulted Page's list and his cast with the crosses on it and made the same twenty-six measurements on the bust, too, and compared them with his data.[139]

According to Wislicenus, the features of the face and head showed a correspondence of about 83 per cent.[140] The only real divergences he registers are "those relating to the cheek-bones, the outer corners of the eyes, and the length of the nose";[141] i. e. in fact just two: the narrower face of the bust, and the shortness of its nose.[142] Wislicenus summarises the results as follows:

> [...] the face on the head is exactly the same size as the mask, both in height and, with a single exception, in breadth; the eyebrows are the same, the eyes are identically placed, as are the bridge of the nose, the mouth, the temples, cheeks, jawbone and chin; in short, it is the same head, whose dimensions have been – seen, nota bene, from the front – derived from this death mask.

Wislicenus presented his findings in a number of publications,[143] but failed to convince. There was one indispensable condition for the recognition of the mask's authenticity, a demand already constantly being made in England in the second half of the nineteenth century which he could not fulfil: an answer to the question by whom, when and by what ways and means the object found its way from England to Germany.

At the beginning of the twentieth century, the group of those who arrived at a verdict on the mask without ever setting eyes on it included M. H. Spielmann and the German death mask expert Ernst Benkard; and in the last third of that century the American literary scholar and Shakespeare specialist Samuel Schoenbaum. Until the problems of the authenticity of the Darmstadt death mask and the Chandos and Flower images were resolved in 1995, twentieth-century opinions were strongly influence by the doubts about the authenticity of the death mask expressed by Spielmann in his 1911 *Encyclopaedia Britannica* article. But these doubts lacked the decisive scientific basis, an inspection and investigation of the original. They were based on three main objections that never stood up to close scrutiny. In his *Britannica* article Spielmann argues "it [the Kesselstatt death mask] is not in fact a death mask at all but a cast from one and probably not even a direct cast". There, he said, was no evidence of any connection between von Kesselstatt, England and Shakespeare. Moreover, "the skull reproduced is fundamentally of a different form and type from that shown in the Droeshout print."[144]

In contrast to Richard Owen, William Page, Hermann Schaaffhausen, Paul Wislicenus and Robert Cauer, who carefully examined and assessed the mask, Spielmann never saw it. He declined an invitation to Darmstadt.[145]

Ernst Benkard, clearly basing himself on Spielmann, also vehemently denied the authenticity of the Darmstadt mask. But he did not investigate the original, either. He propagated these views in his standard work *Das ewige Antlitz. Eine Sammlung von Totenmasken (The Eternal Countenance: A Collection of Death Masks)*, first published in 1927.[146]

Just a year after Benkard's book appeared, Ernst Gundolf in his essay "Zur Beurteilung der Darmstädter Shakespeare-Maske" ("Assessing the Darmstadt Shakespeare Mask") was describing Benkard's arguments as invalid, and some of them as downright "absurd". Clearly and decisively Gundolf rejects Benkard's assertions:

> Since Benkard presents himself here as a death-mask specialist, and such assertions often take a long time to be properly scrutinized, there is a danger that this verdict will establish itself as a "scientific finding". That would be regrettable, for none of the arguments put forward are sound, and some are simply absurd.[147]

Benkard unfortunately gives no source for his reproduction of the Shakespeare mask, but according to Gundolf he obviously took them from Wislicenus's books, thus "weakening them by making a copy of a copy".[148] This would explain the author's serious errors, such as his unsustainable claim that the furrows on the brow of the mask had been drawn in later instead of being naturally produced. Gundolf, who in contrast to Benkard did examine the original, objects that:

> Any careful observation [...] will confirm it. The brow-furrows undoubtedly occurred naturally [...]. In some less-exposed placed, e.g. underneath the eyelids, even at the outer corners of the eyes (crow's feet) and under the chin the natural (organic) wrinkling of the skin is so distinct that anybody can see it [...].[149]

Gundolf rightly rejects as "strange" Benkard's main argument against the authenticity of the mask, i.e. that all the hairs had been inserted artificially.[150] Death-mask experts today, such as the pathologist Professor Hans Helmut Jansen and the expert on the physiognomy of the sick, Professor Michael Hertl, also decisively reject Benkard's objections as unsound.[151]

Like Spielmann and Benkard, Samuel Schoenbaum had never carried out or commissioned any investigation of the Darmstadt Shakespeare death mask, nor seen the original, and he based his views about its authenticity almost exclusively on Spielmann. In the second edition of his *Shakespeare's Lives* (1991) he still calls the art historian, active at the beginning of the twentieth century, "the foremost modern authority on Shakespearian iconography", and says that Spielmann "regards the relic as not properly a death mask at all but a cast from one and probably not even a direct cast" (p. 338). Schoenbaum uncritically adopts Spielmann's arguments, and even his language. Furthermore, he takes over Spielmann's mistaken account of the inscription on the mask (see p. 338). In the *Enyclopaedia Britannica* of 1911 Spielmann stated that the date of Shakespeare's death, 1616, is inscribed in three places on the back of the mask. In fact, the date appears only once. Likewise, both factually wrong and misleading is Spielmann's statement that the Kesselstatt collection was auctioned off in 1847 ("the death sale"). The correct date is 1842. Schoenbaum gave no credence to divergent opinions, for example that of Frederick J. Pohl, in the well-researched article "The Death Mask" in the *Shakespeare Quarterly* (1961), where the author comes to a positive conclusion about the authenticity of the mask.[152]

To summarise: according to the previous state of knowledge and in the absence of convincing confirmation, it could be doubted whether the images to be examined here were authentic, i.e. were made from life or – as in the case of the death mask – immediately taken after death. None of the many other images of the poet extant need be seriously considered in this respect - with the exception of the so-called Janssen portrait in the Folger Shakespeare Library in Washington (see 'Appendix I', 'Prospects', *fig. 113*).

III. TESTS OF IDENTITY AND AUTHENTICITY
ON THE BASIS OF NEW RESEARCH METHODS
AND EXPERT ASSESSMENTS

Up to the present time it has been impossible to prove beyond doubt the authenticity of the Shakespeare images introduced in Part II: the Chandos and Flower portraits, the Davenant bust, and the Darmstadt death mask. Now, however, their identity and authenticity has been subjected to fundamental tests involving numerous experts from various disciplines and employing new and innovative scientific methods.

EXAMINING THE BASIS OF INVESTIGATION

The basis for the following investigations will be the funerary bust of William Shakespeare and his portrait engraving in the First Folio, representing certain types of image widely used in the monumental funerary sculpture and graphic reproduction of the Renaissance and Baroque period. They will be presented here and subjected to critical examination.

The Funerary Bust of Shakespeare in the Church at Stratford-upon-Avon

The Shakespeare monument on the left-hand side of the chancel in Holy Trinity Church at Stratford-upon-Avon (*fig. 020*) contains a brightly-painted limestone bust (*fig. 021*).[1] As will become clear beyond doubt from the sum of my observations, this bust accurately represents the playwright's appearance, leaving aside the damage and repairs it has undergone over the course of its history (see p. 118ff.). The monument can be classed among the funerary memorials of scholars and writers of Tudor and Stuart times.[2] As we have seen, they typically feature a true-to-life bust, based on a death mask, situated in a wall-niche and forming the centre-piece of the monument. Also typical is the representation of objects signalling the activity by which the deceased distinguished himself in his lifetime.

Fig. 020 The funerary monument of William Shakespeare on the left wall of the chancel in Holy Trinity Church, Stratford-upon-Avon.

*Fig. 021 The funerary bust of William Shakespeare, coloured limestone, Holy Trinity Church,
Stratford-upon-Avon; original photograph taken before 1968.*

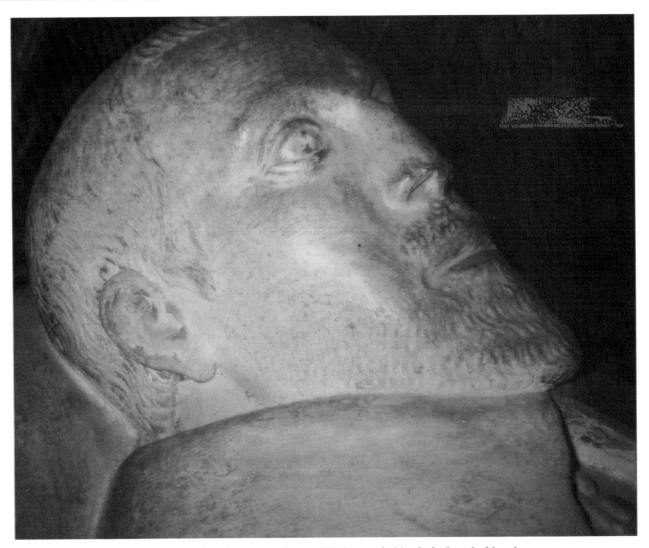

Fig. 022 Recumbent funerary sculpture of Shakespeare's friend, the Stratford burgher and moneylender John Combe, by Gheerart Janssen. Detail of head.

Shakespeare's monument significantly presents the author with the characteristic trappings of his profession: paper, pen and writing cushion. The pen – originally made of stone, but replaced by a goose-quill ever since it broke in the late eighteenth century – is held in a typical writing position in the right hand, and the paper lies on a cushion that serves as a writing support or a rest for reading. It is important in this connection that the bust and the cushion have not been assembled, but carved out of a single stone block. The paper has moulded itself to the curve in the cushion, and overhangs slightly at the front. The sheet is held in the dramatist's left hand in an equally typical position. The fact that this cushion (as already mentioned: see p. 19) corresponds to that of the monument to Bishop Giles Tomson in St George's Chapel (*see fig. 008*) in Windsor Castle proves it to be an authentic form of rest for writing or reading in use in the second decade of the seventeenth century. The two attendant figures flanking Shakespeare's coat of arms duplicate the allegorical figures of the Earl of Rutland's monument in Bottesford.[3] Contrary to the supposition of twentieth century researchers down to Samuel Schoenbaum, they do not only seem to stand for "Labour" and "Rest"; or for "Comedy" and "Tragedy", as assumed in the mid-eighteenth century by the Stratford schoolmaster and antiquary, the Reverend Joseph Greene (1712–1790),[4] but rather, in view of the items they are equipped with (a spade and a lowered torch respectively), in symbolic terms also embody life – or to be precise the *vita activa* – and life after death. In classical antiquity, which in general greatly influenced the Elizabethan period the torch pointing downward was conceived as a funeral symbol, for it illuminated "the darkness of death" and "brought light into the world to come".[5]

The creator of this monument was – according to a tradition handed on by the antiquary Sir William Dugdale – Gheerart Janssen,[6] who enjoyed great respect as a sculptor, and together with his four sons maintained a sculpture workshop in Southwark, on the south bank of the Thames near the Globe Theatre. The Janssens worked for prominent aristocratic families; they created, among others, the lavish monument to the Earls of Rutland in Bottesford (Leicestershire)[7] and that of the Earls of Southampton in Titchfield (see p. 17).[8] It was the Janssens who were responsible for the recumbent figure of Shakespeare's friend John Combe, (*fig. 022*), the Stratford burgher and moneylender, who died in 1614 and whose monument was also installed in the Stratford church – just a few metres away from Shakespeare's (*see fig. 020*).[9] Shakespeare's family must have commissioned the Janssens to make the monument to the playwright. Since the head of the family, Gheerart Janssen the Elder, died in 1616, it can be assumed that the work was undertaken by his son of the same name.[10]

As was customary at the time, to achieve the desired effect of truth to detail and verisimilitude in reproducing the head and face of the deceased, Gheerart Janssen the Younger must have worked from a death mask of the poet.[11] The death mask as an aid to the sculptor had been in use in England for over a century (see pp. 14–15). In this respect, the Janssens had decades of experience behind them. As was usual at the time and in accordance with the wishes of their clientele, the workshop attributed great importance to the faithful image of the deceased. They were renowned for their precision,[12] and promoted themselves by offering customers "exact portraitures" of the dead.[13] It was an approach that brought them great success, as is shown by the large number of commissions they received to erect funerary monuments throughout England. The English scholar Katherine Esdaile was able to identify altogether over seventy tomb monuments which originated in this workshop.[14] The actual figure may well have been much higher.

The Shakespeare monument is executed in the Jacobean Renaissance style, and in accordance with the normal practice at the time may well have been completed within a year, i.e. in 1616, or perhaps in 1617.[15] It is first mentioned in the First Folio edition of Shakespeare's works by Leonard Digges in 1623.

As was usual with memorials to scholars and writers, the Shakespeare monument has a marble tablet bearing an inscription. The latter consists of two parts: an elitist Latin text aimed at the educated reader familiar with classical mythology, philosophy and literature; and a text in English giving general information about the person, addressing a wider literate public. The Latin inscription, together with an English rendering, is as follows:

> IVDICIO PYLIUM, GENIO SOCRATEM, ARTE MARONEM
> TERRA TEGIT, POPULUS MÆRET, OLYMPUS HABET.
>
> THE JUDGMENT OF NESTOR, THE GENIUS OF SOCRATES,
> THE ART OF VIRGIL, / THE EARTH ENCLOSES,
> THE PEOPLE SORROW, OLYMPUS POSSESSES.[16]

These lines are placed immediately next to the hands of the dramatist, his pen, the page on which he writes, and his writing cushion. They are particularly significant because they focus on the prominent image of his personality, while at the same time recording for posterity that William Shakespeare, a son of Stratford already famous in his lifetime, baptised and buried in this very church, distinguished himself in life by abilities and talents that (from an Elizabethan perspective) place him on a par with the greatest personalities of classical antiquity: Nestor, Socrates, and Virgil. A book published in 1598 shows that such comparisons were already being made in his lifetime: in *Palladis Tamia*, Frances Meres likewise sees the then thirty-four-year-old Shakespeare as the equal of the great classical authors.

In contrast to the English inscription on Shakespeare's grave ledger, the Latin inscription on the marble plaque of his monument is not so widely known. Shakespeare research to date has not properly appreciated its true significance.[17]

The English text on the marble tablet, taking up a phrase from classical antiquity, makes it clear to the reader *who* it was that envious death has carried off. It too lays stress on the outstanding poetry of the deceased:

STAY PASSENGER, WHY GOEST THOV BY SO FAST,
READ IF THOV CANST, WHOM ENVIOVS DEATH HATH
PLAST / WITH IN THIS MONVMENT SHAKSPEARE: WITH
WHOME / QVICK NATVRE DIDE: WHOSE NAME DOTH
DECK Ỹ TOMBE, / FAR MORE THEN COST: SITH [SINCE]
ALL, Ỹ HE HATH WRITT, / LEAVES LIVING ART, BVT PAGE,
TO SERVE HIS WITT.

OBIIT AÑO DO^I. 1616
AETATIS 53 [sic] DIE 23 AP^R.

Inscribed in the poet's grave-slab is the invocation:

GOOD FREND FOR IESVS SAKE FORBEARE
TO DIGG THE DUST ENCLOSED HEARE.
BLEST BE THE MAN THAT SPARES THESE STONES,
AND CURST BE HE THAT MOVES MY BONES.[18]

Not only are these lines known worldwide; they have also continued to serve their purpose for over four hundred years. The threat in line four of a curse that will fall upon anyone who moves, i.e. displaces, the poet's bones was frequently misunderstood in the past. It was simply designed to preserve the earthly remains of Shakespeare from the anonymity of the charnel house. In that sense it is an inscription that could have been written by the dramatist himself. The Charnel House of Holy Trinity measured 30 x 15 feet, and was nearly as high as the chancel. It held an unusually large mass of human bones piled up there over the centuries. It was demolished in 1800 when it had become structurally unsafe.[19]

Shakespeare's monument is in keeping with the individual honouring of the dead that was widespread on the continent in the early 1500s, and then extended to England. It is a manifestation of the "awareness of personality" formed by humanism, and the "glorification of the individual" that characterised the Baroque period.[20] Not only does the poet's monument belong to the type of memorial that was proper for scholars and writers, thus enhancing the fame he had already enjoyed within his lifetime; its lavish appointments also satisfied the typical contemporary desire to demonstrate one's status that was dear to William Shakespeare's heart while he lived. As a famous author and a wealthy land and house owner, who obviously from 1601 onward had the right to bear the title of "gentleman" and his own coat of arms, the poet enjoyed great acclaim among his contemporaries,

above all his Stratford fellow-citizens. The coat of arms and the title had been awarded to his father, John Shakespeare, who died in 1601, for his services as magistrate, as mayor of Stratford and as justice of the peace as well as on account of his marriage to Mary Arden, the daughter of a gentleman, and because of his possession of "Landes & tenementes of good wealth & Substance".[21] In accordance with the custom of the time, his crest and armorial bearings too are reproduced on the poet's monument as testimony to his social standing.

The inscriptions, so far almost neglected by Shakespeare scholarship, are an integral part of Shakespeare's tomb and monument. They are based on a well-thought-out design, and as a kind of concerted documentation of essential facts they address a broad spectrum of social target groups. Those who planned it must have included Shakespeare's family, particularly his daughter Susanna and her husband Dr John Hall, as well as his close friends and advisers, perhaps those mentioned in his will; but clearly also the poet himself. These texts are of great importance. For they constitute solid historical evidence showing that William Shakespeare as a historical personality was endowed with enormous powers of judgment and wisdom, and was a writer of genius. By confirming Shakespeare's identity they also – indirectly – confirm the authenticity of the features of his portrait bust. For it was precisely this authentication that was one of the most significant and indispensable demands of those who commissioned sculptures in the early seventeenth century. As the historical sources clearly testify, the fulfilling of this demand, only achievable (as we have seen) by using a death mask, was a special concern of the Janssen workshop that made the bust of Shakespeare. We are therefore on safe ground in presuming that Gheerart Janssen the Younger – following the sculptural practice at his time – based the features of Shakespeare's bust on the poet's death mask, thus faithfully recording his appearance for posterity. We may be fairly sure, too, that those who commissioned the bust, Shakespeare's family, were satisfied with it. At any rate, no objections are known.

The first known mention of Shakespeare's monument occurs seven years after his death in the First Folio edition of 1623 with the reference "thy Stratford Moniment". In the verses published in the Folio and dedicated "TO THE MEMORIE *of the deceased Authour Maister W. Shakespeare*",[22] Leonard Digges, referring to Horace (*Carmina, 3, 30, 1 f.*), predicted that Shakespeare's literary works would outlive his monument of stone and remain fresh throughout all future ages when brass and marble fade:

SHAKE-SPEARE, AT LENGTH
THY PIOUS FELLOWES GIVE
THE WORLD THY WORKES:
THY WORKES, BY WHICH,
OUT-LIVE THY TOMBE, THY NAME MUST:
WHEN THAT STONE IS RENT, AND TIME DISSOLVES
THY STRATFORD MONIMENT,
HERE WE ALIVE SHALL VIEW THEE STILL.
THIS BOOKE, WHEN BRASSE AND MARBLE FADE,
SHALL MAKE THEE LOOKE
FRESH TO ALL AGES: [...]

Already by the 1630s strangers were coming to Stratford to seek out Shakespeare's tomb and monument, among them in 1634 a Lieutenant Hammond with his military companions, and in 1636 the antiquary Sir William Dugdale, who made a drawing of it which he published in 1656 in his book *Antiquities of Warwickshire*.[23] At this time the poet's bust still appeared in its original condition, especially as regards the moustache and the length of the nose (*see figs. 100 and 101*).

In the course of its subsequent history the bust was subjected to the most varied attacks, causing damage and changes to its appearance. As the history of these vicissitudes was never recorded in writing, the altered appearance of the bust (especially the relatively short nose, the unusually long upper lip, and the form of the moustache), noted by the mid-eighteenth century at the latest, appeared inexplicable to later authors. James Boaden, who in his monograph of 1824, *An Inquiry into the Authenticity of Various Pictures and Prints [...] of Shakespeare*,[24] was the first to engage thoroughly and systematically with the images of the poet, was already drawing attention to these matters:

The nose is thin and delicate, like that of the Chandos head; but I am afraid a little curtailed, to allow for an enormous interval between the point of it and the mouth, which is occupied by very solid mustaches, curved and turned up [...]. Yet I must acknowledge, that the distance between the mouth and nose is rather greater than is common [...].[25]

Boaden's explanation was that "there was perhaps some exaggeration here in the bust".[26] But false conclusions were later drawn from these and other discrepancies. This has made it impossible until now to reconstruct the history of the bust completely and coherently. Part IV will attempt to remedy this.

Despite occasional attempts to do so in the past, the genuineness of the bust and the authenticity of Shakespeare's features represented by it have never been doubted.[27] Researchers have always accepted it as an authentic image of Shakespeare because of its location as well as its function as a funerary bust which – as was usual in the Renaissance – must have been based on a death mask, thereby naturalistically reproducing the features of the deceased; and because of its mention in print in the first edition of Shakespeare's works in 1623.

There was clarity about this as early as the nineteenth century. Thus J. Hain Friswell pronounced in his book *Life-Portraits of William Shakespeare*, published in 1864, that "The first authentic portrait [...] of our author, is, in point of time, the Stratford bust [...]."[28] Roughly twenty years later J. Parker Norris confirmed in *The Portraits of Shakespeare*: "The Stratford Bust is the oldest, and probably the best authenticated of all the representations of Shakespeare which have come down to us."[29] In 1924 M. H. Spielmann called the monument "an harmonious and compact whole".[30] Nonetheless, especially in the course of the twentieth century, its artistic quality was not esteemed particularly highly. B. Roland Lewis comments that:

The Stratford bust may not be above the average in excellence of its kind in its day. The Stratford bust may not be a good resemblance of the bard. But this, with the Droeshout engraving, provides the only likeness of William Shakespeare to exist.[31]

And he urges that "It deserves more consideration than the present century is willing to accord it."[32] Samuel Schoenbaum does not seem to have responded to this appeal. His laconic résumé in 1975 reads: "The monument in Holy Trinity, with its uninspiring bust, is authentic enough."[33]

In sum, it can be stated that Shakespeare's funerary bust in Stratford-upon-Avon provides a solid basis for the investigations described below if one takes into account the damage it has suffered in the course of its history (see pp. 118ff.).

The Droeshout Engraving in the First Folio Edition

The copperplate engraving of William Shakespeare in the famous First Folio edition of 1623 (*fig. 023*)[34] belongs to the "verae imagines" of graphic reproductions in the Renaissance and Baroque and represents its subject in an accurate manner, in accordance with the stringent artistic demands of the age. As a frontispiece it served to determine the image of the author, and by the early seventeenth century this had long since ceased to be a rarity. For, in comparison with the sixteenth century, there was now a considerable rise in the use of frontispiece plates designed to give expression to "a work/author identity related to name, respect and image" and to manifest "an emphasised awareness of authors' copyright; thus escaping from anonymity".[35]

For Heminge and Condell, too, the portrait engraving of Shakespeare was associated with the aim of establishing a "work/author identity", recording the dramatist's appearance for posterity, and keeping alive the honoured memory of his person. And Ben Jonson, the most important living playwright of the time, a friend and colleague of Shakespeare's, took it upon himself to confirm the authenticity of the deceased's features. Jonson did so by means of a charming epigram full of wit and learning. His lines attest to the engraver's accuracy in catching Shakespeare's looks. But in adding that the image was incapable of capturing his mind, he takes up the familiar "theme of inexpressibility" of his day (see p. 24) and thus shows his own very special reverence for the poet William Shakespeare. The witty culmination of his epigram advises the reader to look at his works and not the picture:

> THIS FIGURE, THAT THOU HERE SEEST PUT,
>
> IT WAS FOR GENTLE SHAKESPEARE CUT;
>
> WHEREIN THE GRAUER HAD A STRIFE
>
> WITH NATURE, TO OUT-DOO THE LIFE:
>
> O, COULD HE BUT HAVE DRAVVNE HIS WIT
>
> AS WELL IN BRASSE, AS HE HATH HIT
>
> HIS FACE; THE PRINT WOULD THEN SURPASSE
>
> ALL, THAT VVAS EUER WRIT IN BRASSE.
>
> BUT, SINCE HE CANNOT, READER, LOOKE
>
> NOT ON HIS PICTURE, BUT HIS BOOKE.

The Droeshout engraving is far and away the best-known and most often reproduced portrait of Shakespeare. It measures 15.1 x 12.8 cm, and bears the inscription at the bottom: "Martin Droeshout sculpsit London". The engraver, Martin Droeshout the Younger, was the son of the Flemish engraver Michiel Droeshout (b. *c.* 1570 in Brussels),[36] who together with his family had emigrated to London in 1585. When the young Droeshout received the commission, he cannot have been more than twenty-two-years-old, and had therefore probably not built up much professional experience.

It took about two years for the printers Isaac Jaggard and Ed. Blunt[37] to accomplish the technical task of producing this monumental work. It appeared in London in 1623 – seven years after Shakespeare's death – in a print run of about 1000 to 1200 copies and contained thirty-six plays, half of which had previously never been printed. In the course of the seventeenth century there were three further editions of the book; the second in 1632, the third in 1663 (reprinted 1664), and the fourth in 1685. Martin Droeshout's plate was re-used each time,[38] so that the quality of the engraving left more and more to be desired.

In opting for a high-quality folio edition,[39] Heminge and Condell were pursuing the great and unselfish objective of preserving Shakespeare's dramas for posterity after having amended the text as the poet had conceived it (see p.130). In harsh language they indicate that readers have previously been very badly served by stolen, forged, mutilated and deformed copies because of the destructive deceptions and thefts perpetrated by impostors.[40] Despite continuing to work in the London theatre and touring the provinces, the editors seem to have spared themselves no trouble or effort to complete their lavish project. We know that when the work was going to press, Shakespeare's troupe was visiting Stratford, where Heminge and Condell may have met Shakespeare's daughter in New Place to acquire the model for the proposed frontispiece (see p. 130).

The folio edition that appeared in October 1623[41] was in every sense a highly imposing volume, regarded today as "one of the most precious of all books".[42] The editors themselves seem to have been aware of this: they dedicated the work to the Earls of Pembroke and Montgomery, and they gave many important contemporaries, including (once more) Ben Jonson, the opportunity to honour the poet in verse. Jonson's lines will surely not have disappointed them, containing as they do the famous and still valid dictum: "he [Shakespeare] was not for an age, but for all time".

MR. WILLIAM
SHAKESPEARES

COMEDIES,
HISTORIES, &
TRAGEDIES.

Publiſhed according to the True Originall Copies.

Martin Droeſhout ſculpſit London.

LONDON
Printed by Iſaac Iaggard, and Ed. Blount. 1623.

Fig. 023 Portrait of William Shakespeare by Martin Droeshout the Younger, copper plate engraving,
First Folio Edition of Shakespeare's plays, 1623.

The Second Folio edition (1632) contains a so-called effigies-page ("Vpon the Effigies of my worthy Friend, the Author Master William Shakespeare, and his Workes"), presenting two epitaphs in verse form. Like Jonson, these poets invite the reader to turn to the incomparable and immortal works themselves, rather than to monuments of stone. While the first text is the work of an unknown and somewhat mediocre versifier, the subsequent sixteen lines of verse bearing the title "An Epitaph on the admirable Dramaticke Poet, W. Shakespeare" were by John Milton (1608–1674). In line two he alludes to Shakespeare's monument in Holy Trinity Church in Stratford-upon-Avon, just as Leonard Digges had done in the First Folio edition. Sixteen years after the death of the playwright, with the powerful eloquence of his Shakespeare epitaph the twenty-four-year-old Milton made an impressive contribution to the new edition:

WHAT NEED MY SHAKESPEARE

FOR HIS HONOUR'D BONES,

THE LABOUR OF AN AGE, IN PILED STONES

OR THAT HIS HALLOW'D RELIQUES

SHOULD BE HID

UNDER A STARRE-YPOINTING PYRAMID?

DEARE SONNE OF MEMORY

GREAT HEIR OF FAME, WHAT NEEDST THOU

SUCH DULL WITNESS OF THY NAME?

THOU IN OUR WONDER

AND ASTONISHMENT

HAST BUILT THY SELFE

A LASTING MONUMENT:

FOR WHIL'ST TO TH'SHAKE

OF SLOW-ENDEVOURING ART

THY EASIE NUMBERS FLOW,

AND THAT EACH PART,

HATH FROM THE LEAVES

OF THY UNVALUED BOOKE,

THOSE DELPHICKE LINES

WITH DEEP IMPRESSION TOOKE

THEN THOU OUR FANCY OF

HER SELFE BEREAVING

DOST MAKE US MARBLE

WITH TOO MUCH CONCEIVING,

AND SO SEPULCHER'D

IN SUCH POMPE DOST LIE

THAT KINGS FOR SUCH A TOMBE

WOULD WISH TO DIE.

In spite of such tributes, in the course of history – as in the case of the bust of Shakespeare – there were criticisms of Droeshout's engraving, some of them quite fierce. There were negative and frequently emotional views upon it, especially during the late eighteenth century and during the nineteenth.[43] The Shakespeare editor George Steevens (1736–1800), well known to his contemporaries for his acerbity,[44] was the first to take a determinedly ironic and conde-scending attitude to Shakespeare's features in the Droeshout print and their authentication by Ben Jonson in the form of an address to the reader. Steevens thought it fortunate that Jonson was not under oath when he wrote the lines that appear opposite the engraving confirming the authenticity of Shakespeare's portrait. At the same time, Steevens assumes that Jonson understood very little about art, and that it was a matter of indifference to him whether or not the features in the portrait actually were in agreement with those of his dead friend. However, James Boaden defended Jonson and emphatically rejected Steevens' inept comments:

He [Jonson] was neither ignorant of art, nor indifferent to Shakespeare; and I make not the smallest doubt that to him, Heminge and Condell, a whole "tyring room" of admirers, it did appear "a strife of art with nature", to outdo the life; so perfectly did the print exhibit their great and lamented friend.[45]

His concluding reflections on the choice of the Droeshout engraving (or the model it is based on) are that:

It [the Droeshout engraving] has a verification certainly more direct, than any other. Ben Jonson is express upon its likeness – Shakspeare's friend and partners at the Globe, give this resemblance, in preference to some OTHERS, equally attainable. There can be no ground of preference, but greater likeness. If they knew, absolutely, of no other portrait, which I cannot think, the verisimi-litude of this is equally undisturbed.[46]

Friswell came to the same verdict; he clearly and rightly recognised that the Droeshout engraving (like the funerary bust) made a reliable basis for examining the authenticity of the many Shakespeare images that might have a valid claim to depict the poet. He writes:

Certainly this print has a verification of, and a testimony to, its worth such as no other existing portrait has or can have, […] What he [Ben Jonson] saw before him was […] an admirable likeness, and he says so. […]

We may therefore, after weighing the evidence carefully, [...] assume that the most authentic representation of the poet is that of the head attached to the first folio of 1623, and that we may take it, together with the bust at Stratford-on-Avon, as a test of the genuineness of the many other assumed portraits of the poet.[47]

Parker Norris came to an equally positive conclusion towards the end of the nineteenth century:

> It [the Droeshout engraving] is as well authenticated as the Stratford bust, for Ben Jonson's testimony is of the highest value. He knew Shakespeare well, and loved him too, in spite of what his detractors have tried to show. It is not probable, therefore, that Jonson would have given such a high testimonial to its merit as a likeness if it had not been so.[48]

Since then, the Droeshout engraving has been accepted simply as *the* authentic image of Shakespeare, even though attempts were made now and again in the twentieth century to criticise it.

In summary, it may be said that the Droeshout engraving, along with the Stratford bust, can serve as a reliable basis for the tests of genuineness presented here. These investigations will confirm that both images represent one and the same person, thus further reinforcing and substantiating the solid basis for the following investigations.

THE METHODS OF INVESTIGATION
AND THEIR RESULTS

The Conventional Comparison of Images by the German Federal Bureau of Criminal Investigation (BKA)

The conventional comparison of images using criminological investigation techniques[49] is a very old, thoroughly tested and reliable procedure employed by BKA experts to identify people by means of photographs, i.e. to check whether two different photographs represent one and the same person. It does not involve much use of technology, but does require a great deal of expertise and experience.

Such comparisons are possible because "every person's appearance is different",[50] making everyone distinctive, recognisable, and identifiable, even if the pictures were taken at different times or individual changes had occurred in their appearance.

Identification is based "on visible distinguishing features of the face or head area",[51] which do not alter over long periods in a lifetime, including "the shape of the skull, hairline, eyes, nose, lips, chin and ears", together with "scars, birthmarks and liver spots".[52]

The examination consists of a "general comparison" and a "detailed comparison". The former tests for "similarities and optical correspondences or divergences"; the latter scrutinises and evaluates "recognisable features of the facial area", "which are conclusive evidence for or against a particular identity".[53]

The outcome of comparing morphological features and evaluating the comparison leads to a statement of probability regarding the identity of those represented, using a scale that ranges "from possible, to probable, highly probable, very highly probable, and with the utmost probability".[54]

The investigations presented here were undertaken by kind permission of the then president of the BKA, Hans-Ludwig Zachert, in 1995 and 1998 in the German Federal Bureau of Criminal Investigation in Wiesbaden. They were carried out by the BKA specialist Reinhardt Altmann in conjunction with the BKA experts Jörg Ballerstaedt and Dietrich Neumann. The specialist was presented with black and white photographs of the Droeshout plate and the death mask, as well as colour photographs of the Chandos portrait, the un-restored and restored Flower portrait, and the funerary bust. Altmann inspected the death mask in Darmstadt Castle, photographing it from many angles. Present were the then Director of the Hesse *Land* and University Library Dr Yorck Alexander Haase, Senior Librarian Werner Wegmann, and myself.

For the project to achieve viability and obtain clear results, it was crucial that the images to be compared were painted or produced to give a true likeness, and that their essential details were faithfully reproduced.

Comparison of the Chandos and Flower portraits and the Droeshout engraving

Parallel investigations were carried out on precise reproductions of the Chandos portrait, the Flower portrait, and the Droeshout engraving. The results documented in the BKA report of 3 May 1995 are astonishing. Seventeen morphological features were found to be in agreement in all three images (*figs. 024, 025, 026*). On the basis of this finding and of a general comparison of the images the expert concluded "that with a degree of utmost probability they [the images] represent one and the same person". That person is Shakespeare, since the identity of the subject of the Droeshout engraving cannot be doubted (see pp. 44ff).[55]

1. Gesichtsumrißform	1. Outline of face
2. Stirn	2. Forehead
3. Augenbrauen	3. Eyebrows
4. Lidplattenanteile	4. Eyelid plate area
5. Besonderheit	5. Special feature
6. Oberlidraumhöhe	6. Height of upper eyelid area
7. Nasenwurzel	7. Roof of nose
8. Nasenrücken	8. Bridge of nose
9. Nasenspitze	9. Tip of nose
10. Nasenloch	10. Nostril
11. Nasenflügel	11. Wing of nose
12. Hautoberlippe	12. Upper lip
13. Schleimhautoberlippe	13. Mucous membrane of upper lip
14. Mundspalte	14. Oral fissure
15. Schleimhautunterlippe	15. Mucous membrane of lower lip
16. Hautunterlippe	16. Lower lip
17. Kinn	17. Chin

Fig. 024 Conventional comparison of images by Reinhardt Altmann, German Federal Bureau of Criminal Investigation (BKA): arrows indicate seventeen facial features of the Chandos portrait matching those of the Flower portrait and the Droeshout engraving, BKA image report (1995).

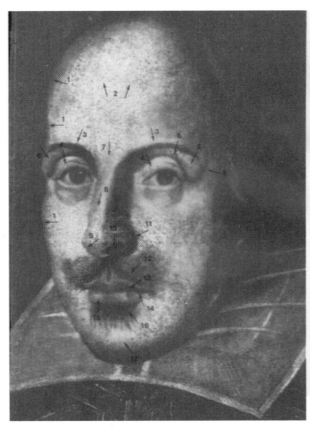

1. Gesichtsumrißform	1. Outline of face
2. Stirn	2. Forehead
3. Augenbrauen	3. Eyebrows
4. Lidplattenanteile	4. Eyelid plate area
5. Besonderheit	5. Special feature
6. Oberlidraumhöhe	6. Height of upper eyelid area
7. Nasenwurzel	7. Roof of nose
8. Nasenrücken	8. Bridge of nose
9. Nasenspitze	9. Tip of nose
10. Nasenloch	10. Nostril
11. Nasenflügel	11. Wing of nose
12. Hautoberlippe	12. Upper lip
13. Schleimhautoberlippe	13. Mucous membrane of upper lip
14. Mundspalte	14. Oral fissure
15. Schleimhautunterlippe	15. Mucous membrane of lower lip
16. Hautunterlippe	16. Lower lip
17. Kinn	17. Chin

Fig. 025 Conventional comparison of images by Reinhardt Altmann, German Federal Bureau of Criminal Investigation (BKA): arrows indicate seventeen facial features of the Flower portrait matching those of the Chandos portrait and the Droeshout engraving, BKA image report (1995).

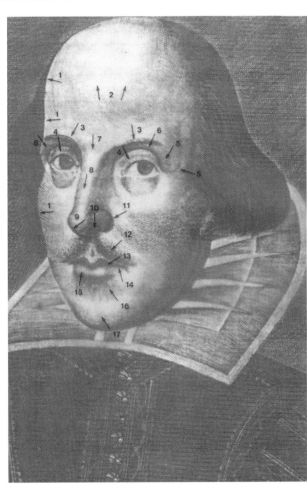

1. Gesichtsumrißform	1. Outline of face
2. Stirn	2. Forehead
3. Augenbrauen	3. Eyebrows
4. Lidplattenanteile	4. Eyelid plate area
5. Besonderheit	5. Special feature
6. Oberlidraumhöhe	6. Height of upper eyelid area
7. Nasenwurzel	7. Roof of nose
8. Nasenrücken	8. Bridge of nose
9. Nasenspitze	9. Tip of nose
10. Nasenloch	10. Nostril
11. Nasenflügel	11. Wing of nose
12. Hautoberlippe	12. Upper lip
13. Schleimhautoberlippe	13. Mucous membrane of upper lip
14. Mundspalte	14. Oral fissure
15. Schleimhautunterlippe	15. Mucous membrane of lower lip
16. Hautunterlippe	16. Lower lip
17. Kinn	17. Chin

Fig. 026 Conventional comparison of images by Reinhardt Altmann, German Federal Bureau of Criminal Investigation (BKA): arrows indicate seventeen facial features of the Droeshout engraving matching those of the Chandos and Flower portraits, BKA image report (1995).

Comparison of Funerary Bust and Death Mask

As was to be expected, comparing the tomb bust and death mask was more difficult. Five similarities and two divergences (upper lip and length of nose) were established (*figs. 027 and 028*). These divergences can be satisfactorily explained by reference to the Dugdale engraving (*see fig. 100*) and to damage inflicted by Puritan zeal during the seventeenth century (see pp. 23–27). Together with the experts' findings, this leads to a statement of probability that the two images represent the same person, and therefore also to the conclusion that the Darmstadt death mask is indeed that of Shakespeare.[56] This statement will be reinforced by further factual evidence and the results of other investigations.

The Trick Image Differentiation Technique employed by the German Federal Bureau of Criminal Investigation (BKA)

The Trick Image Differentiation Technique developed by the German Federal Bureau of Criminal Investigation is another method used for comparing photographs of persons. According to the BKA experts this procedure has proved its value over decades, and has never yet failed. In the present case, too, the experts found this method extremely well suited to dealing with the problems involved.

The procedure,[57] based on electronically blending images, uses photomontages to compare images as follows: a suitable photo shot is made of a person by TV camera I, while TV camera II simultaneously supplies a suitable photo of another person of whom there is reason to think that he or she is identical with the first.

1. Gesichtsumrißform	1. Outline of face
2. Stirn	2. Forehead
3. Nase	3. Nose
4. Kinnbart	4. Beard
5. Kinn	5. Chin

Fig. 027 Conventional comparison of images by Reinhardt Altmann, German Federal Bureau of Criminal Investigation (BKA): arrows indicate seven facial features of the funerary bust which were compared with the corresponding features on the death mask, BKA image report (1995)

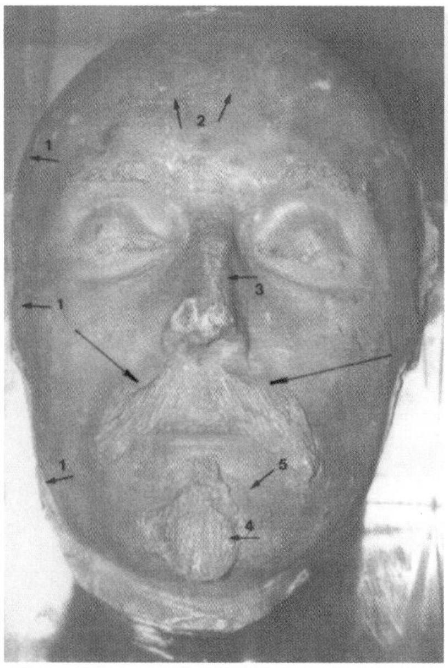

1. Gesichtsumrißform	1. Outline of face
2. Stirn	2. Forehead
3. Nase	3. Nose
4. Kinnbart	4. Beard
5. Kinn	5. Chin

Fig. 028 Conventional comparison of images by Reinhardt Altmann, German Federal Bureau of Criminal Investigation (BKA): arrows indicate seven facial features on the death mask which were compared with the corresponding features on the funerary bust, BKA image report (1995).

With the help of an effect generator, and after the pictures have been blended together by passing them through a video trick mixer, projection takes place automatically onto a TV monitor. The image produced in this way consists of two parts joined together; usually two halves of the images to be compared. The line of the join can be determined at will. The new picture is photographed and evaluated. This involves examining whether the details along the line of the join are a perfect fit, and whether symmetry, correspondences, and harmony are to be found in the individual parts of the face. As with all procedures of this kind, with the Trick Image Differentiation Technique it must also be borne in mind that the two halves of a human face are never absolutely symmetrical.

As the BKA expert Altmann explains in his report of 3 May 1995, this procedure allows the investigator "a much greater opportunity to recognise how the shapes and proportions of the soft parts of the face relate to each other with regard to solidly differentiated marks of identity".[58] In another report, of 6 July 1998, Altmann explicitly points out "that the harmony of sections and outlines of the face represents consonance, not just the sum of individual correspondences".[59]

While employing the Trick Image Differentiation Technique certainly demands considerable use of computer hard and software, interpreting images to identify people by this method also requires a great deal of expertise and experience.

The Trick Image Differentiation investigations were also carried out by kind permission of the then BKA president Hans-Ludwig Zachert in 1995 and 1998 in the Federal Bureau of Criminal Investigation in Wiesbaden. With the collaboration of the BKA experts

Jörg Ballerstaedt and Dietrich Neumann, they were undertaken by the BKA specialist Reinhardt Altmann. For this procedure, too, the specialist had available to him a black and white photograph of the Droeshout engraving, plus colour photographs of the Chandos portrait, the un-restored Flower portrait, and the Stratford bust, as well as the photographs he took of the death mask from various angles.

Comparison of the Chandos and Flower portraits and the Droeshout engraving

As documented in the report of 3 May 1995, ten different photo-montages were put together from the Chandos and Flower portraits and the Droeshout engraving, using vertically or horizontally divided halves of the face. All the combinations selected showed correspondences that were a perfect fit, seamless joins, and convincing harmonies. Three of the photo-montages are illustrated here (*figs. 029, 030, and 031*). By means of these investigations, too, it was possible to prove that all three pictures represent one and the same person: William Shakespeare.[60]

Fig. 030 Trick Image Differentiation Technique employed by Reinhardt Altmann, German Federal Bureau of Criminal Investigation (BKA): montage of the Chandos portrait (left half) and the Droeshout engraving (right half), BKA image report (1995).

Fig. 029 Trick Image Differentiation Technique employed by Reinhardt Altmann, German Federal Bureau of Criminal Investigation (BKA): montage of the Chandos portrait (upper half) and the Flower portrait (lower half), BKA image report (1995).

Fig. 031 Trick Image Differentiation Technique employed by Reinhardt Altmann, German Federal Bureau of Criminal Investigation (BKA): montage of the Droeshout engraving (left half) and the Flower portrait (right half), BKA image report (1995).

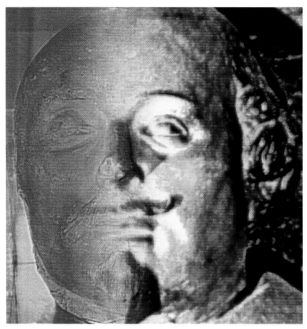

Fig. 032 Trick Image Differentiation Technique employed by Reinhardt Altmann, German Federal Bureau of Criminal Investigation (BKA): montage of the death mask (left half) and the funerary bust (right half), BKA image report (1995).

Fig. 033 Trick Image Differentiation Technique employed by Reinhardt Altmann, German Federal Bureau of Criminal Investigation (BKA): montage of the Chandos portrait (left) and the death mask (right), BKA 1995.

Comparison of funerary bust and death mask

As was also described in the BKA report of 3 May, the identity of the funerary bust and the death mask was examined using three different montages. They showed astoundingly good fits, agreements and harmonies, as demonstrated particularly vividly by the montage consisting of the left half of the death mask and the right half of the Stratford bust (*fig. 032*). This picture offered very special and convincing proof that the persons represented by bust and mask are identical. The subject in both cases is William Shakespeare, since there is no doubt that the funerary bust in Stratford is an authentic image of the poet.[61]

Comparison of the Chandos portrait and the death mask

The montage of the Chandos portrait and the mask produced by the BKA experts by means of the Trick Image Differentiation Technique (*fig. 033*) shows clear harmonies and agreements – despite the very different ages of the persons portrayed and the not quite identical angles from which the images were taken.[62] These harmonies and agreements indicate that we are dealing here with one and the same person, a result that will be reinforced by the outcome of further investigations.

Comparison of the Davenant bust with the Chandos Portrait, the Un-restored and Restored Flower Portrait, the Death Mask, the Funerary Bust, and the Droeshout Engraving

Documented in the BKA report of 6 July 1998 are the results of comparing the Davenant bust with the Chandos portrait, the Flower portrait before and after its 1979 restoration, the death mask, the funerary bust, and the Droeshout engraving. The BKA specialist, Reinhardt Altmann, put together nine photo-montages using this pictorial material (*figs. 034 to 042*)[63] which self-evidently prove that their subjects are identical. Nonetheless, further information and explanations follow, drawing upon the text of the report.

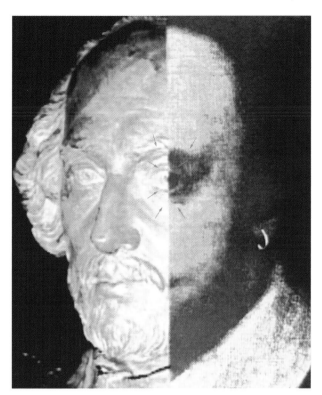

Fig. 034 Trick Image Differentiation Technique employed by Reinhardt Altmann, German Federal Bureau of Criminal Investigation (BKA): montage of the Davenant bust (left) and the Chandos portrait (right). The section runs through the left eye, with red arrows indicating the agreements, BKA image report (1998).

Fig. 035 Trick Image Differentiation Technique employed by Reinhardt Altmann, German Federal Bureau of Criminal Investigation (BKA): montage of the Davenant bust (left half) and the Flower portrait (right half), BKA image report (1998).

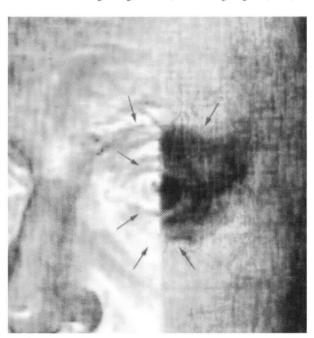

Fig. 034a BKA Trick Image Differentiation Technique: detail of montage of the Davenant bust (left) and the Chandos portrait (right). The section runs vertically through the left eye. The BKA expert stresses the "significant agreements in the line of the eyebrow, left, the margin of the upper and lower eyelids, and the fold of the lower eyelid" by using red arrows to mark the perfect transitions. BKA image report (1998).

Fig. 036 Trick Image Differentiation Technique employed by Reinhardt Altmann, German Federal Bureau of Criminal Investigation (BKA): montage of the Davenant bust (left) and Flower portrait (right). The section runs through the left eye, with red arrows indicating the agreements, BKA image report (1998).

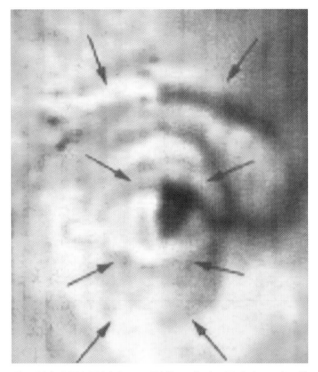

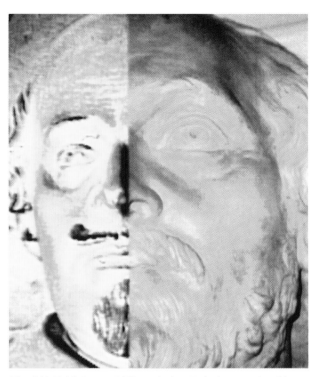

Fig. 036a BKA Trick Image Differentiation Technique: detail of montage of the Davenant bust (left) and the Flower portrait (right). The section runs vertically through the left eye. In this case too the BKA expert stresses the same significant agreements as were identified in fig. 034 a, again using red arrows to mark the perfect transitions. BKA image report (1998).

Fig. 038 Trick Image Differentiation Technique employed by Reinhardt Altmann, German Federal Bureau of Criminal Investigation (BKA): montage of the funerary bust (left half) and the Davenant bust (right half), BKA image report (1998).

Fig. 037 Trick Image Differentiation Technique employed by Reinhardt Altmann, German Federal Bureau of Criminal Investigation (BKA): montage of the restored Flower portrait (left half) and the Davenant bust (right half), BKA image report (1998).

Fig. 039 Trick Image Differentiation Technique employed by Reinhardt Altmann, German Federal Bureau of Criminal Investigation (BKA): montage of the Droeshout engraving (left half) and the Davenant bust (right half). The expert comments that the "consonance" of this montage and the one in figure 040 was "particularly impressive". BKA image report (1998).

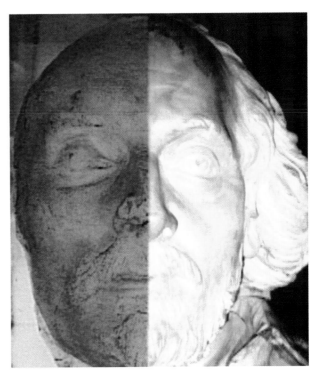

Fig. 040 Trick Image Differentiation Technique employed by Reinhardt Altmann, German Federal Bureau of Criminal Investigation (BKA): montage of the Droeshout engraving (left) and the Davenant bust (right). The section runs through the left eye. What is striking and convincing here is not just the way that the eyebrow of the Droeshout engraving flows perfectly into that of the Davenant bust, but the absolutely consistent continuity of the upper and lower eyelids. Such refined details of agreement are identifying marks of the very highest order. BKA image report (1998).

Fig. 041 Trick Image Differentiation Technique employed by Reinhardt Altmann, German Federal Bureau of Criminal Investigation (BKA): montage of the death mask (left half) and Davenant bust (right half). The expert comments that the "clearly recognisable agreements in the areas of the root of the nose, the size of the nose and the mucous membrane section" in figures 038, 041, and 042 led him to conclude "that what we are seeing here is one and the same person". BKA image report (1998).

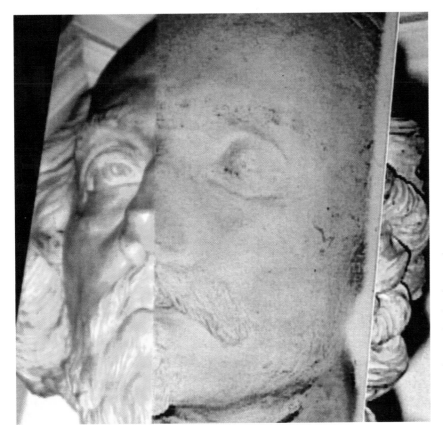

Fig. 042 Trick Image Differentiation Technique employed by the German Federal Bureau of Criminal Investigation (BKA): montage of the Davenant bust (left and right) and the death mask (centre). The specialist stresses that figures 041 and 042 also demonstrate the perfect match of the shape of the moustache. BKA image report (1998).

In a general comparison, the expert noted correspondences in the "shape of the face outline", the "areas of the forehead, eyes, nose and lips", as well as the "lower jaw and chin section".[64] On his evidence, in a standard comparison of images this would remove "all room for doubt about identity".[65]

When it came to detailed comparison of the separate parts of the face and morphological characteristics, the expert again confirmed striking agreements. Thus, figures 034 and 036 demonstrate that the subjects of the Davenant bust and the Chandos portrait, as well as that of the Davenant bust and the un-restored Flower portrait, are identical. In both cases the images were lined up through the left eye. It became apparent that the morphological characteristics of this markedly individual area were in clear agreement in the two montages (*figs. 034a and 036a*). The specialist goes so far as to speak of "significant agreements in the line of the left eyebrow, the margins of the upper and lower eyelids, and the furrow beneath the lower lid"[66]; he uses red arrows to indicate these areas.

The same positive result is found with figures 035 and 037, which show respectively the juxtaposed halves of the Davenant bust and the non-restored Flower portrait, and the restored Flower portrait and the Davenant bust. In both cases the section runs through the middle of the face. The BKA expert found that these montages, especially figure 035, show "harmony with respect to the root of the nose, the left-hand side of the nose (particularly the lower edge of the nostril), the length of the upper lip, the edge of the mucous membrane, and the length of the chin".[67]

Figures 039 and 040 display montages of the Davenant bust and the Droeshout engraving produced by making sections across the images at varying points. Even with a conventional comparison, said the BKA expert, there would be "no doubt about their identity". The specialist said that the "consonance" of these montages was "particularly impressive".[68] In figure 039, the astonishing agreements in the shape of the face outline and other parts of the face are convincing. In figure 040, where the section runs through the left eye, the joins are all seamless. What is striking and convincing here is not just the way that the eyebrow of the Droeshout engraving flows perfectly into that of the Davenant bust, but the absolutely consistent continuity of the upper and lower eyelids. Particularly amazing and convincing is the harmonious, indeed imperceptible, transition of the

eyelid cleft (palpebral fissure) from the engraving to the bust. Such refined details of agreement are identifying marks of the very highest order.

The "clearly recognisable agreements in the areas of the root of the nose, the size of the nose and the mucous membrane section" in figures 038, 041, and 042 (the comparisons are between the Droeshout engraving and the Davenant bust, the death mask and the Davenant bust, and a section of the death mask that was merged into the Davenant bust) led the BKA specialist to conclude "that what we are seeing here is one and the same person".[69] Figures 041 and 042 demonstrate that the shape of the moustache also forms a perfect match. The Davenant bust, too, is completely in accord with the death mask in this respect – in contrast to the results of comparing the Davenant bust with the funerary bust (*fig. 038*) and the death mask with the funerary bust (*see figs. 027, 028, and 032*). In these latter cases there is a discrepancy which, however, can be attributed to the damage caused by the Puritans. (see pp. 125–27).

Figure 042 is remarkable for the way in which the BKA expert has succeeded in finding shots with matching perspectives in the images at his disposal, and merging them by means of Trick Image Differentiation Technique. In this case one part of the death mask was, as it were, projected on to the bust. Even viewing the image from underneath in this arbitrary perspective, with its effect of distorting proportions, it is impossible to overlook the astounding agreements at all important points. It is particularly stunning that the lock of hair whose beginnings are visible on the left-hand edge of the mask continues as a lock of hair on the Davenant bust. The complete harmony of the moustache in this montage has already been pointed out.

To sum up the results of these comparisons carried out on the Davenant bust by the BKA expert using Trick Image Differentiation Technique, we can say that the Davenant bust depicts a person who is identical with the persons represented in the Chandos portrait, the restored and un-restored Flower portrait, and the Droeshout engraving; moreover, the same person is also the subject of the death mask and the Stratford bust. The BKA specialist summarises his findings in the report of 6 July 1998 as follows: "The striking harmony between the facial areas presented and between the morphological characteristics leads to the inescapable conclusion that one person is represented here."[70] This proves that the Davenant bust too is an authentic image of William Shakespeare. Further, the authenticity of those images which have been compared with the Davenant bust is confirmed once more; i.e. the Chandos portrait, the Flower portrait in its un-restored and restored condition, the funerary bust, and the Droeshout engraving.

Moreover the agreement, even in the most minute lifelike details, of the Davenant bust with the lifelike details of the other images examined proves conclusively that the eminent eighteenth century sculptor Louis François Roubiliac (1705–1762), who until now has been credited with creating the Davenant bust, cannot possibly have done so. For he could not have had at his disposal a lifelike or live model with all these precisely reproduced features of William Shakespeare (see also p. 97f.).

Computer Montage

To produce a computer montage, the images to be investigated are all equalized in size using an image-processing programme. They are then cut and combined in a montage. By evaluating this montage the investigator examines whether and to what extent the halves fit harmoniously together along the lines of the cuts and in their symmetrical features. He immediately recognizes the degree to which the sections he has introduced fit into the picture he is comparing them with. However, in the case of computer montage, as in other similar procedures, it must always be remembered that perfect symmetry is never found between the two halves of a human face. As with the Trick Image Differentiation Technique, the section to be made can be selected at will. The difference between this procedure and, for example, the Trick Image Differentiation Technique essentially depends on what hard- and software are used. It must be added that the evaluation of the montages in the present case was not carried out by BKA experts.

Comparison of the Davenant Bust and the Death Mask

Using the image processing programme "Photoshop", in 1998 Andreas Kahnert, photographer at the Hesse *Land* and University Library in Darmstadt, set up two computer montages, a frontal view (*fig. 043*) and a view of the right profile (*fig. 044*), in order to compare the Davenant bust and the death mask. Figure 043 shows the right–hand side of the Davenant bust, which has been fused with the left-hand side of the mask along the line of the section. Figure 044 shows the right-hand profile of the death mask, with which a piece of the Davenant bust has been merged.

Both montages display an internal consistency within the image as a whole. In figure 043 there are striking correspondences in the areas of the outline of head shape, chin, beard, moustache, the eyes, eyebrows, and forehead. Only the lower lip of the Davenant bust section is by its nature fuller than that of the death mask (see pp. 65 and 97f.). But all the joins, particularly those around the mouth, nose, eyes and eyebrow regions, show such a precise fit and harmony that we must assume the subjects are identical. Figure 044 likewise demonstrates that the merged-in section of the Davenant bust blends convincingly into the profile of the death mask.

Photogrammetry

In the process of photogrammetry the three-dimensional form of an object is reconstructed from photographic images. By expressing the measurements in digital form and with the aid of suitable software, a virtual three-dimensional picture can be produced that can be viewed and measured from all sides and compared or combined with similar pictures.

Photogrammetry was originally developed for geodetic land surveying (for example, using aerial photography). It is now employed in many different fields.

The photogrammetric images of the Darmstadt Shakespeare death mask were prepared for the current project in 1997 by the German physicist Dr Rolf-Dieter Düppe of the Institute for Photogrammetry and Cartography at the Technical University of Darmstadt, in the Hesse *Land* and University Library in Darmstadt Castle. The then Director of the Library Dr Yorck Alexander Haase was present, as was myself. In 1998 the English mathematician and physicist Dr J.M.N.T. Gray (at that time of the Technical University Darmstadt and now at Manchester University), together with Rima Astrauskeite, conducted photogrammetric measurements on the Davenant bust in the Garrick Club in London. Kind permission had been granted by Mr Anthony Butcher, then chairman of the club's Works of Art Committee, and once again I was in attendance. The same procedure was used for a copy of the

Davenant bust in the depository of the Royal Shakespeare Collection in Stratford-upon-Avon, in the presence and with the kind permission of Mr Brian Glover, at that time director of the collection (*fig. 045*). Dr Gray also measured an old marble copy of Shakespeare's Stratford funerary bust in Charlecote Park (Warwickshire), by kind agreement with Sir Edmund Fairfax-Lucy Bt. of Charlecote Park and Geoffrey Howarth, National Trust Severn, Tewkesbury.

It later became clear that suitable software for producing three-dimensional images of both objects was not available without considerable extra expense. Hence in 2004 and 2005 the technique of laser scanning which had been developed in the meantime, was employed (see p. 59).

After the processing and evaluation of part of the material, many of the high-grade photogrammetric images taken with a special camera by Dr Gray have been included as impressive and informative pictorial documentation in the present book (*figs. 046, 047, 048, 049, 050*). Because of their precise detail they yielded new discoveries about the images under investigation (*see fig. 064*) and played a significant role especially in medical analysis (see p. 67ff.).

Computertomography

Computertomography is a well-known medical x-ray procedure using a thin bundle of x-rays passing over the part of the body to be examined, and scanning it slice by slice. The computer's digital analysis of the data so collected generates a precise 3D virtual image of that region of the body, showing up even the finer details.

The potential of this procedure led to the idea of applying computertomography to compare the three-dimensional images of Shakespeare; for example the Darmstadt Shakespeare death mask and the Davenant bust. The technique is of course normally used to

Fig. 043 Computer montage of the Davenant bust (left half) and the death mask (right half), generated by Andreas Kahnert, Hesse Land and University Library, Darmstadt (1998).

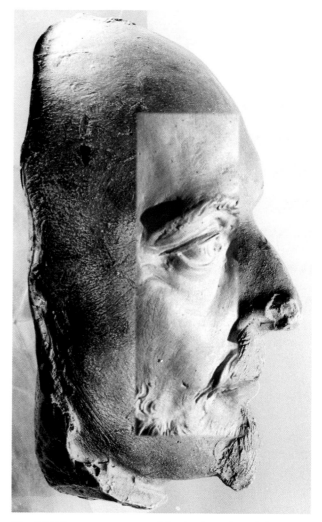

Fig. 044 Computer montage of the death mask and the Davenant bust, right profile, generated by Andreas Kahnert, Hesse Land and University Library, Darmstadt (1998).

Fig. 045 One of the two copies of the Davenant bust commissioned by Sir Richard Owen before he sold the original bust to the Duke of Devonshire. This one is kept in the repository of the Royal Shakespeare Company, Stratford-upon-Avon, the other one in the British Museum (see Part II, 'Davenant bust'). On the left, Rima Astrauskeite and the English mathematician and physicist, Dr Nico Gray, Manchester University; on the right, the author and the former Director of the Royal Shakespeare Company Collection, Brian Glover.

locate pathological characteristics inside the body; in principle, however, it can also be used simply to scan the outlines of an object and so obtain a three-dimensional virtual image that can be viewed and measured from all sides, but can also be compared with other virtual images or examined for its authenticity.

Technically there was no great difficulty about transporting the death mask to the Darmstadt Hospital. This took place in August 2004 by kind permission of the mayor of Darmstadt Peter Benz and under the supervision of the head of conservation at the library, Bernd Becker, and his deputy Rui Linnartz. It must be said, however, that the vulnerability and great value of the mask imposed elaborate security precautions[71] and a high insurance premium.[72]

Professor Bernd Kober (*fig. 051*) and his team at the Darmstadt Hospital supplied remarkable 3D images of the death mask (*fig. 052*). They were produced by the computertomograph of the Institute for X-Ray Diagnosis and Nuclear Medicine (Professor Peter Huppert).

To investigate the Davenant bust, a computertomograph of the same make was located in London, and arrangements were made for measurements to be carried out under the direction of the radiologist Professor Rodney Reznek (St Bartholomew's Hospital) in the Princess Grace Hospital in collaboration with superintendent radiographer Mrs Margaret Rintoul. But in the end it was the great security risks involved that

persuaded the Works of Art Committee of the London Garrick Club and its chairman Mr John Baskett to withhold permission for the bust to be transported to a London hospital. As a terracotta bust is indeed vulnerable to mechanical procedures, the decision was understandable. A method was sought whereby the measurements could be taken on the spot. In this situation the technique of laser scanning came to mind.

Laser Scanning

Laser scanning is an optical method of measuring in which the surface of an object is scanned (without risk of damaging it) by means of a laser beam. In this way objects, freeform surfaces, models etc. can be surveyed in three dimensions without physical contact. Digitalising the data thus obtained generates extremely precise three-dimensional colour images on the computer; these can be turned and angled at will in virtual space, and so viewed from all sides, measured, enlarged and – after the construction of models and equalizing the size – combined and compared with other images of this type. The procedure has become extremely important in various fields, being used very successfully in plastic surgery, dentistry, machine manufacture (especially car and tool production), as well as contoured textile design. Furthermore, it has been applied most successfully to the measurement, documenting, restoration, and conservation of cultural heritage objects, and to producing replicas of them.

With a 3D Laserscanner VI-910 made available by the firm of Konica Minolta Photo Imaging Europe, the investigations took place in November 2004 in the Hesse Land and University Library in Darmstadt (*fig. 053*) and in February 2005 in the London Garrick Club by kind permission of, respectively, director Dr Nolte-Fischer, chairman John Baskett, and Marco Zajac, head of Konica Minolta Europe. The equipment is very manageable and, in contrast to the computertomograph, there is no difficulty about taking it to the object to be measured. The geodetic specialist Dipl.-Ing. Thorsten Terboven, Sales and application engineer 3D (Germany) from the firm of Konica Minolta, carried out the measurements in Darmstadt: in attendance were Professor Kober, head of the Radiology Institute at the Darmstadt Hospital; head of Conservation Bernd Becker and deputy head Rui Linnartz; and myself. In London Herr Terboven's colleague David Lowry,

Fig. 046 Front view of the Davenant bust, Garrick Club, London. Photographed by Dr Nico Gray (1998).

Fig. 047 The Davenant bust seen in semi-profile (right), Garrick Club, London. Photographed by Dr Nico Gray (1998).

Fig. 048 The Davenant bust in semi-profile (left), Garrick Club, London. Photographed by Dr Nico Gray (1998).

Fig. 049 Right profile of the Davenant bust, Garrick Club, London. Photographed by Dr Nico Gray (1998).

Fig. 050 Left profile of the Davenant bust, Garrick Club, London. Photographed by Dr Nico Gray (1998).

sales and application engineer 3D for Konica Minolta (UK) undertook the task of measuring, in the presence of the Garrick Club archivist and librarian Marcus Risdell, Herr Terboven and myself (*fig. 054*). Using "Rapid Form" software, Thorsten Terboven initially, and subsequently his Korean colleague Maverick Kim, application engineer, INUS Technology (Europe), produced the virtual image comparisons. Since the death mask represents the head on a one-to-one scale, while the Davenant bust is larger than life size, the two objects had to be equalized in size before the work of comparison work could start.

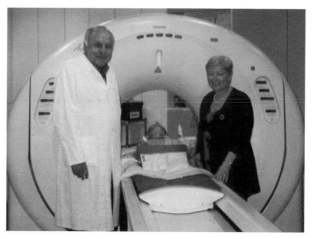

Fig. 051 *The death mask under the computertomograph (centre); left, Professor of Medicine Dr Bernd Kober; right, the author (2004).*

Comparison of the Davenant Bust with the Death Mask

Comparing the Davenant bust and the death mask with the naked eye, one is struck immediately by certain discrepancies. Primarily they result from the fact that in the former case – as will be shown – we are dealing with the image of a living person, and in the latter with that of a dead man. It is well known that the tissue collapses when the blood pressure ceases after death. Most affected are the lips, cheeks and eyes, but also (pathological) protuberances. These natural changes which occur at death are clearly recognisable in the death mask, particularly in the regions of the left eye and the lips, while the Davenant bust shows no such characteristics (see the detailed medical report, p. 76).

However, part of the explanation for the differences between the two objects also lies in the damage they have suffered in the course of their respective histories (see pp. 76–8). For example, the mask has incurred damage to the tip of the nose. The almond-shaped slit in the nasal corner of the left eye and the displaced lids indicate that there was originally a protuberance in this particular location which later either crumbled away or was removed. The Davenant bust also carries defects that must stem from damage and not from the hand of the sculptor. They can be attributed to deliberate changes, as can be seen on the left upper eyelid and on the forehead (see pp. 72ff. and 75f.).

Despite the discrepancies mentioned above, comparisons achieved by laser scanning and the use of the software "Rapid Form" to superimpose virtual images of the Davenant bust and the death mask or to create montages of them, reveal clear harmonies, correspondences and agreements. By layering individual morphological features of the mask on the Davenant bust, always within the parameters of the whole or

profile outline of the bust, it can be shown how the individual parts of the face fit together. Thus figure 055 demonstrates how perfectly the left upper eyelid (below the eyebrow and above the eyelid cleft), the left eye, the left-hand profile of the nose, the left nostril, the flesh of the upper lip, the space between the lips and the beard of the Darmstadt death mask all fit into the Davenant bust. In figure 056, where the mask is laid upon the bust, there are convincing congruencies and agreements apparent in the forehead area (from the hairline of the right temple to that of the left), the outline of the head on the left side of the forehead, the eye region, the moustache, both nostrils and the beginning of the neck. Figure 057, too, displays clear harmonies in the area of the head outline (from the right side of the forehead to the highest curve of the forehead, and on the left temple), the right cheek, the nose, the moustache and the beard.

The image created by a montage of bust and mask (*fig. 058*) created by fusing the two along the line of a section running down the middle of the face, and then turning the head to gain a view of the left profile, impressively illustrates that these images belong together. Thus the forehead of the Davenant bust flows smoothly into that of the death mask. Eyes, eyebrows and moustache correspond. Only in the area of the lips is it possible to discern a slight divergence, basically explicable because of the clear difference between the full lips of the Davenant bust (*see fig. 055* and p. 76) and the flatter ones of the death mask. Moreover, a minute difference in size between the two objects may have played its part, aside from a slight variation in the perspective. The author's comparison of the 3D images generated by laser scanning leads to

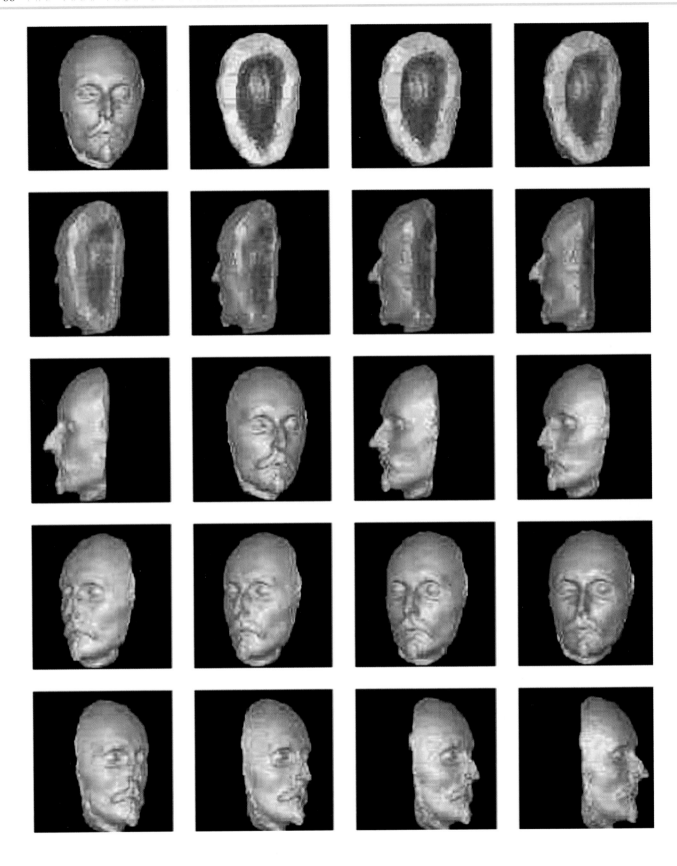

Fig. 052 Computertomography images of the death mask – Institute of X-Ray Diagnosis and Nuclear Medicine, Darmstadt City Hospital (Professor Peter Huppert) (2004).

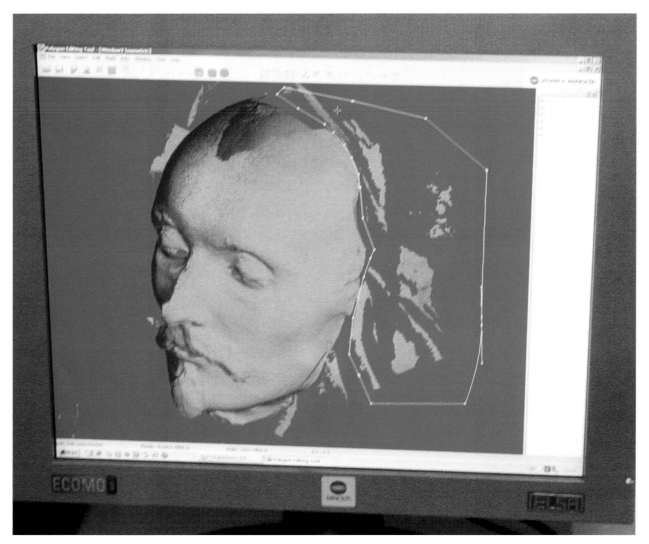

Fig. 053 Laser-scan generated image of the death mask in the Hesse Land and University Library, Darmstadt
(Dipl.-Ing. Thorsten Terboven) (2004).

the conclusion that the Davenant bust and the death mask represent one and the same person.

The images produced by this procedure were also evaluated by Professor Kober. In the expert opinion expressed in his report of 30 June 2005 the radiologist stresses that while "the soft parts of the facial structure" are markedly different in a living as against a dead person, "bone structures" normally remain unchanged. The agreement between faces can be determined by the "distance between the edges of certain bones", for example "the upper edge of the orbit (eye socket)" and the "point of the chin". In the case of the death mask and the Davenant bust there was complete accord. Kober emphasises that a key observation with respect to figure 057 is "the distance between the point of the chin and the lateral end of the eyelids corresponding to the lateral edge of the eye socket". Here too the two objects displayed "very good agreement", even though the eyelids of the

death mask were closed. In addition, referring to figure 055 and figure 056, it was established that the "curve of the forehead, and significantly also the shape of the nose and its length" were "identical". This was also true of "the total width of the skull". In his summary, the radiologist confirms the findings of the author and concludes that both objects represent "the same person".

Medical Expert Assessments of Signs of Illness

In the images investigated visible signs of sickness have been painstakingly reproduced – as is generally the case in the age of the Renaissance and Baroque. If these details have not been removed or painted over as a result of damage or restoration, to the experienced eye of the expert they lend themselves to diagnosis even today, often providing significant indications of the subject's particular stage of illness. For it is out of the question that any painter or sculptor could have arbitrarily invented signs of disease. Renaissance and Baroque artists were, however, in a position to depict these signs – from a medical point of view – in an impeccably true to life manner.

Medical assessment of illnesses delineated in painted and sculptured portraits is another way of establishing identity when comparing various images. It is possible, moreover, to determine from the various stages of illness depicted and medically diagnosed how true to life these images really are. It is also often possible to work out their date of origin and arrange them chronologically.

The medical reports were drawn up (1996) by Professor Walter Lerche, at that time medical director of the Ophthalmic Clinic at the Land-Capital Hospital, Wiesbaden, and the Teaching Hospital of the Johannes Gutenberg University, Mainz; by Professor Jost Metz, medical director of the Dermatologic Clinic at the same Wiesbaden hospital (1996); by Professor Hans Helmut Jansen, then director of the Pathological Institute of the Darmstadt City Hospital, an expert on death masks; and Professor Michael Hertl, supernumerary professor of Paediatrics at the University of Heidelberg and former medical director of the Children's Clinic at the Neuwerk Hospital in Mönchengladbach, an expert on death masks and the physiognomy of the sick (1997 and 1998).

Fig. 054 From l – r: archivist Marcus Risdell, Garrick Club, London, David Lowry of Konica Minolta (UK), Thorsten Terboven of Konica Minolta (Germany) and the author after the 3D measurement of the Davenant bust (2005).

Since a portrait painter cannot invent such conspicuous symptoms, which are still capable of diagnosis today, the case is conclusively made that Shakespeare must have sat for the Chandos and Flower portraits and that they are true-to-life. As the protuberances are very different in size, about half as big in Chandos as in Flower, it was also clear that these must be representations of the poet at different periods of his life. Accordingly, the Chandos portrait depicts the younger Shakespeare, and the Flower portrait the older man. The swelling of the upper eyelid in both paintings and in the engraving is, moreover, a significant criterion of identity.

The Swelling on the Left Upper Eyelid in the Droeshout Engraving, the Chandos Portrait, and the Flower Portrait

In the Droeshout engraving (*fig. 023*), the Chandos portrait (*fig. 014*) and the Flower portrait (*fig. 015*) I noticed in January 1995 a conspicuous, clearly pathological protuberance on the left upper eyelid which had never been remarked upon before, in spite of the intensive examination of the pictures by many (art) experts in the past. In his expert medical appraisal of 11 April 1995, Professor Lerche confirmed that the swelling was indeed a pathological symptom, probably the Mikulicz Syndrome, which is a disorder in the area of the tear glands.[73] It is bilateral, and can occur – as the clinician pointed out – "together with general disease conditions such as lymphomas and sarcoidosis".[74] This symptom is particularly marked on the *left* in all three portraits. With differential diagnosis, a fatty prolapse was also considered a possibility.[75]

The Swelling on the Left Caruncle in the Flower Portrait and the Droeshout Engraving

Both the Chandos portrait (*fig. 014*) and the Flower portrait (*fig. 015*) exhibit a protuberance on the left caruncle which Professor Lerche says might be interpreted as a "fine caruncular tumour".[76] This pathological change is missing from the Droeshout engraving (*fig. 023*), as the ophthalmologist expressly noted in his expert medical appraisal. In his words: "The swelling of the caruncle in the nasal corner of the left eye visible in both paintings (but not in the engraving) could perhaps be interpreted as a fine caruncular tumour, which however need not have any general clinical causation."[77]

As the engraver has left out this symptom, or merely indicated it vaguely, we can conclude that the engraving was produced from the painting and not vice versa. For the point has already been made that it is inconceivable that a painter of the early seventeenth century would have invented a clearly

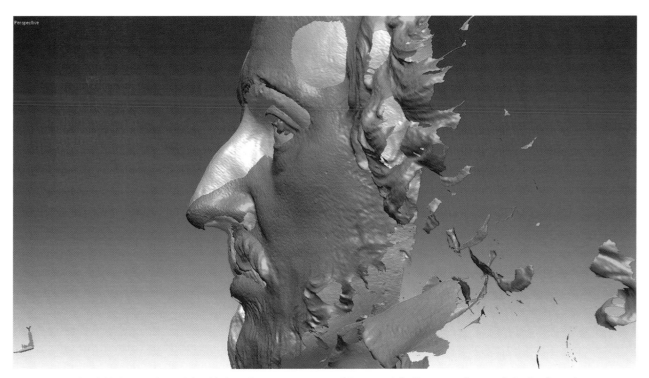

*Fig. 055 Comparison of details from laser-scan generated images of the Davenant bust and the death mask
(Dipl.-Ing. Thorsten Terboven / David Lowry) (2005).*

*Fig. 056 Comparison of details from laser-scan generated images of the Davenant bust and the death mask
(Dipl.-Ing. Thorsten Terboven / David Lowry) (2005).*

recognisable, still diagnosable and even disfiguring sign of illness if his model (the engraving) had not shown it. This settles the chronological order of the two works (see also p. 90). Furthermore, it tells us that the painter must have seen the protuberance on the left caruncle of his sitter.

The Swelling on the Forehead of the Restored Flower Portrait and the Death Mask

An additional proof of the authenticity of the Flower portrait and the death mask was adduced in 1996. In contrast to the un-restored Flower portrait which was used for the authenticity tests in 1995 (see fig. 015), the restored Flower portrait (see fig. 016) shows a sign of disease on the forehead, which – as I noticed when I compared portrait and mask – is also extant on the death mask (fig. 059). Independently of each other Professors Metz and Jansen inspected the mask, examined and palpated it in situ. In their expert opinions they confirmed that the two images correspond in portraying the same pathological phenomenon, with the same proportions in the same clearly defined location.[78] While Professor Metz interprets the symptom in the restored Flower portrait as "a chronically inflammable, granulomatous infiltration (inflammation)", instantly recognisable on the mask as well[79], Professor Jansen thinks that it might be a (benign) "bone tumour", i.e. an "osteoma" or "exostosis".[80] Taking into account the ophthalmologist's diagnosis of the Mikulicz Syndrome, the dermatologist proposes that "a chronic, annular skin sarcoidosis is most likely", which as a "systemic disease" leads to death normally after many years. Sarcodosis is an immune system disorder characterised by small inflammatory nodules and can affect any organ. In Professor Metz's view, it must remain a mere assumption that a "systemic sarcoidosis" might have been the cause of Shakespeare's death.[81]

In conjunction with the previous research results, this evidence – irrespective of the difference in diagnosis – shows once more that the Flower portrait and the death mask depict one and the same person, i.e. Shakespeare, and that both are authentic.

The Distorted Left Eye of the Death Mask

The swelling of the upper left eyelid so clearly delineated in the Chandos and Flower portraits (see p. 68) also appears on the death mask, although in a different form. Professor Hertl, the medical expert on death masks and the physiognomy of the sick, took this up at length in his expert report of 15 August 1997, where he accepted my explanations[82] and indeed expanded on them.[83] The medical specialist, who had also inspected and palpated the death mask in situ, mentions for example a "considerable reduction" post mortem of "what are known as the dependent parts of the body (in backwards dorsal position)" and refers to the long, consuming "disease process" which had led to a "shrinkage of the fatty tissue in the eye area, so that the eyes and the other contents of the eye sockets were already very sunken before dying and death." "The death mask", says Professor Hertl, "very shockingly reveals this deep setting of the eyes and the deep furrows in the orbital margin at the base of the eyelid."[84] The deformation of the whole of the left eye of the mask, and the way it protrudes in comparison with the right eye, is shown in a special photographic image (fig. 060).[85]

This pathological phenomenon is one of the main components in the network of evidence for the identity and authenticity of the persons represented by the mask and the portraits.

The Organic Substance and Skin Structures on the Death Mask

The fact that there is still an organic substance attached to the mask, in the form of the hairs found in the areas of the brows, eyelashes and beard, is a further proof of its genuineness, and is singled out for particular attention by the medical expert Professor Hertl:

> The Darmstadt mask is indisputably the original mask. From a biological standpoint this is emphasised by the fact that as the hardened plaster was pulled away countless tiny hairs came away from the skin of the face, as well as some hairs from the eyebrows, eyelashes, and beard. They were not artificially introduced with fraudulent intent, as Benkard asserts in his unfounded (mis)judgement on the mask. (p. 71).[86]

The enlarged photographic detail, by making visible the skin structures and individual hairs (see fig. 074), also offers proof that we are dealing with the original mask.

Fig. 057 Comparison of details from laser-scan generated images of the Davenant bust and the death mask (Dipl.-Ing. Thorsten Terboven / David Lowry / Maverick Kim) (2005).

Fig. 058 Comparison of details from laser-scan generated images of the Davenant bust and the death mask (Dipl.-Ing. Thorsten Terboven / David Lowry / Maverick Kim) (2005).

The Swelling on the Forehead of the Davenant Bust

The photogrammetric measurement of the death mask and the Davenant bust in 1997 and 1998 generated photographic images of the two objects that revealed in detail peculiarities and signs of disease. The special lighting needed for the measuring process had the effect of bringing out for the first time the finer features of the surface of bust and mask.

When I inspected the Davenant bust in situ in January 1998 (*fig. 061*), I noticed a considerable swelling on the forehead (*fig. 062*). Dr Gray and I explored and palpated this feature. It seemed to correspond to the pathological symptom on the death mask (*see fig. 059*) and in the restored Flower portrait (*see fig. 016*). On the upper and lateral edges of the protuberance, which in general conveyed a very uneven impression, I noted a number of smaller or larger scratches disfiguring that part of the forehead, and indicating that in the course of the sculpture's history attempts must have been made to remove or smooth out this pathological alteration on the forehead.

Commenting on the forehead region of the Davenant bust, Professor Hertl points out first of all that the latter displays a strikingly large bald area, similar to that shown in the Chandos and Flower portraits. He registers on the forehead of the photograph supplied to him (*see fig. 017*), despite attempts at "cosmetic" improvements in this area, a "polygonal, slight and poorly defined protuberance [...], of the kind and dimensions of that [on the death mask and in the restored Flower portrait] previously described and assessed by Professor Metz and Professor Jansen".[87] Hertl concludes that: "This means that an identical formation is also present on the forehead of the Davenant bust".[88] He refers, furthermore, to the "conclusions from the inspection and palpation"[89] the author, Dr Gray, and Rima Astrauskaite had drawn immediately after examining the bust *in situ*.

The pathological alteration on the forehead of the bust demonstrates that the artist must have worked from life or from a life mask; he would not have known about such a symptom otherwise. The theory that the Davenant bust is taken from life is strongly supported by the fact that the Shakespeare sculptures created in the eighteenth century – for example, the larger than life statue officially made by Roubiliac that has now been installed in the foyer of the new British Library in London (*see fig. 080*) – do not display this characteristic.

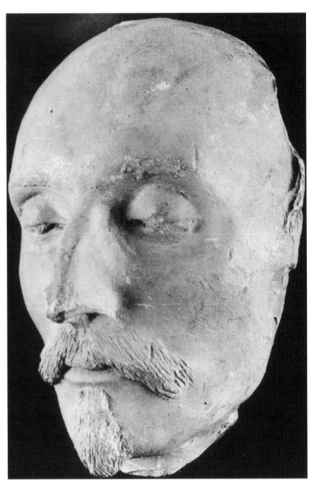

Fig. 059 The death mask with clearly visible protuberance on the forehead, Hesse Land and University Library, Darmstadt.

Since the thorough and professional restoration of the bust by the English restorer J. H. Larson in 1986/87, the marks caused by unprofessional interference with the forehead (*see fig. 062*) have become particularly conspicuous. It seems that they were inflicted not by the artist but by one of the later owners of the work in an obvious attempt to remove or at least level out the offending bump. The scratches, some of them deep enough to disfigure the bust, can now be attributed to the actions of the finder of the Davenant bust, who was personally responsible for changes in the bust's appearance that took place under unusual circumstances (see p. 95).

The Left Upper Eyelid of the Davenant Bust

The left upper eyelid of the Davenant bust is markedly flattened in the area of the tear glands (*see fig. 064*), as I noticed on first inspecting the bust in 1996 (*see fig. 061*). In the same place in the Chandos portrait (*see fig. 014*) and in the Flower portrait (*see fig. 016*) there is a considerable, clearly visible swelling (see p. 68).

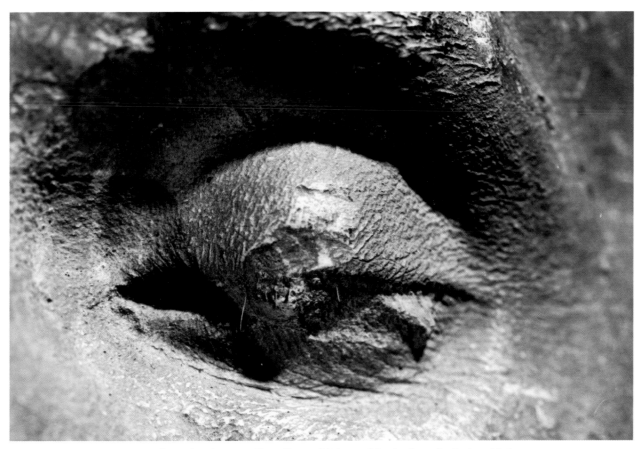

Fig. 060 The strikingly protruding, distorted left eye of the death mask. Andreas Kahnert,
Hesse Land and University Library, Darmstadt (1997).

Once computer enlargements of both eye areas had been made by myself from a special image produced by Dr Gray (*see fig. 046*), it was possible to examine this feature more closely. It then became obvious that in the course of its history the area of the left eye on the Davenant bust, like the protuberance on the forehead, had been tampered with (*figs. 063 and 064*).

Between the left eyebrow and the fissure of the upper eyelid there is an unstructured, smooth surface where all the lines that had been following the natural contours of the original model simply come to an end (*see fig. 064*). There are fundamental differences between the right and left eyelids. While the former is full, not to say swollen, and the brow above it takes a normal course (*see fig. 063*), the latter is conspicuous for its pronounced flattening off, and the raising of the brow above it, which has obviously been pushed upwards (*fig. 064*). At the same time the whole area of the left eye seems to have suffered from a pathological change, and that includes the uneven lower eyelid and nasal corner of the eye.

In his expert report of 11 September 1998 Professor Hertl refers to the "systemic swelling" observed in the Chandos and Flower portraits, which was interpreted

as "part of a Mikulicz Syndrome"; he states that in this object too [the Davenant bust] the "lateral upper eyelid area [of the right eye]", where the tear gland is situated, appears "distinctly swollen".[90] But he notes that one difference from the two painted portraits is that "the epidermis and subcutaneous tissues lie in a looser formation over the lump of the tumour".[91] With regard to the "comparable area around the left eye", the clinician notes that "there is no sign of bulging". [92] In his description he explains that:

> This area appears flatter, without any bulging of the surface structure, and noticeably depleted and smooth. It is striking that the curve at the side of the eyebrow on the left forms a steeper arc than on the right, leading to the supposition that this eyebrow has been pushed upwards by some excess tissue. The edge of the left upper eyelid falls rather lower over the eye, and the left eye gives the effect of being somewhat "hooded".[93]

The medical expert presumes that initially the region of the left upper eyelid had "in principle the same tumour swelling, in keeping with the Mikulicz Syndrome", but that "some material was scraped off

Fig. 061 The author inspecting the (larger than life-sized) Davenant bust in the London Garrick Club. She discovers the pathological changes in the area of the left eye, the slight squint (see fig. 017), which is already emerging in the Chandos portrait, and a hidden ring fixed to the left ear, reminding us of the earring in the Chandos portrait (see fig. 014). Dr Nico Gray (1998).

during one of the restorations of the bust",[94] so that today the symptoms of the Mikulicz Syndrome no longer appear bilaterally on the Davenant bust.

By drawing on new sources which I uncovered while researching the finding and early history of the Davenant bust, it is now possible to explain convincingly when, by whom, and under what circumstances the removal of the tumour swelling was carried out (see p. 92f.).

From what has been said we can conclude that there must have been a protuberance of considerable size and extent on the left upper eyelid of the Davenant bust in the region of the tear gland, corresponding to the

symptoms found in the same position in the Chandos and Flower portraits. Moreover, we can also draw the conclusion that the artist of the Davenant bust must have worked from a life mask or from the living model. Based on his many individual findings regarding the bust, Professor Hertl's conclusion is that "identity with the person of William Shakespeare can be taken for granted with utmost probability".[95] His further conclusion is that Shakespeare must have "sat for" the sculptor of the Davenant bust, and done so at a time when "the changes in the area of the eyes associated with the Mikulicz Syndrome"[96] had already taken place.

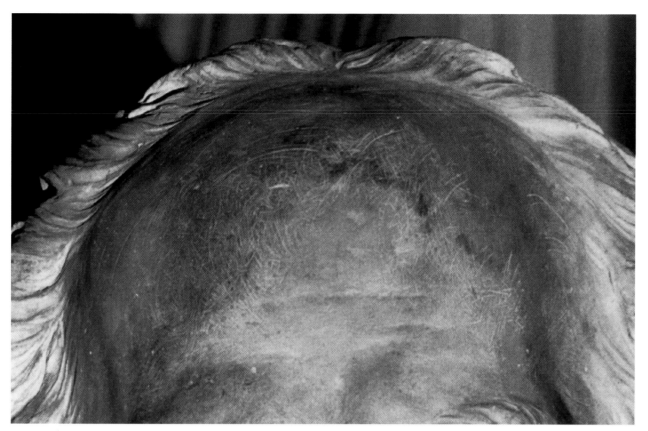

Fig. 062 Swelling on the forehead of the Davenant bust, with many scratch marks. Dr Nico Gray (1998).

The Nasal Corner of the Left Eye of the Davenant Bust

In the process of his medical appraisal of the corners of both eyes on the Davenant bust, Professor Hertl established that the corner of the right eye was "not abnormal" and that the small tear gland in this location (caruncle) appeared "normal" (*see fig. 063*). This was also true of the nasal corner of the left eye, except that "in the area of the conjunctiva towards the iris" there was "an uneven, polygonal nodulated zone" (*see fig. 064*) which "undoubtedly shows great resemblance to, if not actual identity with, the structures most distinctly visible on the Berlin copy of the mask"[97] (this is a copy, produced around 1910, of the Darmstadt Shakespeare death mask: *figs. 065 and 066*). In the expert's view an "almond-shaped displacement of the eyelid margin", the existence of which he was able to demonstrate in the same place on the death mask (*fig. 067*)[98], was however not to be expected on the Davenant bust. But in his expert assessment he did record that the left and right eyelid margins of this bust, where the eyes are open, "take different courses".[99] From the fact that there is a more "rounded curve" (*see fig. 064*) in the nasal corner of the left eye "between the iris and the caruncle",[100] as against the more "acutely

shaped corner" of the right eye[101] (*see fig. 063*), the expert draws the conclusion that:

> In the nasal corner of the left eye there is a space-occupying lesion, a lumpy thickening of tissue in the manner of a pinguecula [Lidspaltenfleck], as well as an indication of an eyelid margin deviation such as a space-occupying process induces – a picture identical in principle to earlier findings.[102]

In his assessment of 15 August 1997 Professor Hertl, who had called in the ophthalmologist Emeritus Professor Hans Pau of the University of Düsseldorf to make the diagnostic classification, had already interpreted the "nodule-like protuberances in the nasal corner of the eye" (on the Berlin copy, and therefore also on the original) as a "macule on the eyelid cleft (Lidspaltenfleck)".[103] With reference to the two painted images of Shakespeare, the Chandos and Flower portraits, Professor Lerche had interpreted this sign of illness as a small caruncle tumour (see pp. 68 and 71 – *figs. 014, 015, and 016*). Professor Hertl holds that the sculptor of the Davenant bust had "seen and faithfully reproduced" the changes in the nasal corner of the left eye – just as he had seen the "extensive protuberance on the forehead".[104]

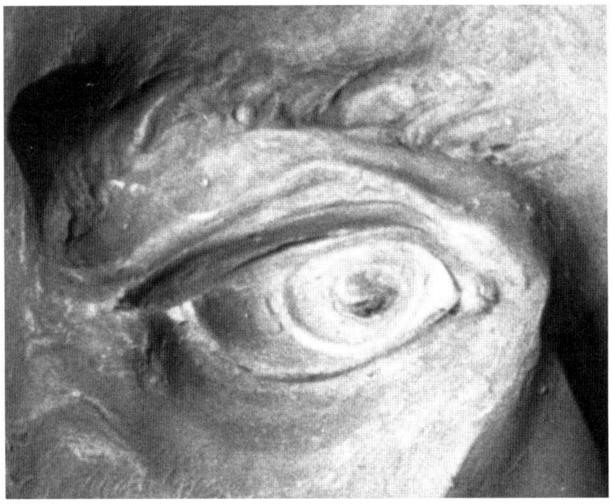

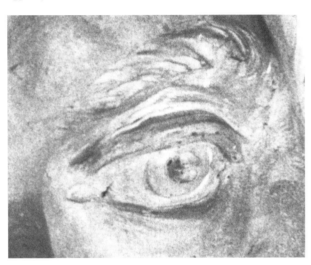

Fig. 063 Enlargement of the right eye of the Davenant bust.
A swelling (Mikulicz Syndrome) can clearly be seen in the
upper eyelid area. Dr Nico Gray (1998) - Detail of fig. 046.

Fig. 064 Enlargement of the left eye of the Davenant bust.
A pronounced swelling (Mikulicz Syndrome) must originally
have been visible in the upper eyelid area. It was reproduced at
different stages of its development in the Chandos and Flower
paintings. The enlargement shows that in the course of the
bust's history this spot underwent considerable flattening.
Dr Nico Gray (1998) - Detail of fig. 046.

Surveying the "surprising agreement" of a "series of very individual details of identical size, medically significant but unintelligible to a portrait painter", Hertl concludes "that Shakespeare not only personally sat [for the Davenant bust], but that given the accuracy of its facial anatomy a life mask must have been used as well".[105] For in no other way would it have been possible to convey "so meticulously all the constitutional features of the face, including so many pathological particularities".[106]

To sum up, it can be said that a distinctive symptom of disease must have been present in the nasal corner

of the left eye of the Davenant bust in the same place as the corresponding pathological symptom on the Darmstadt Shakespeare death mask (see pp. 77f.), but that in the course of the history of this object – for whatever reason – it must have been removed.

The Lips of the Davenant Bust and the Flower Portrait

Professor Hertl thinks the "well-filled" or "plump" lips of the Davenant bust are worthy of comment; for him they are reminiscent "of the Chandos and Flower portraits".[107] Their surface structure is however "not abnormal" and shows no signs of disease.[108] On the lips of the restored Flower portrait, however, Hertl does find a pathological change. The lower lip looks "distinctly swollen" and seems "somewhat pendulous".[109] The three sizeable yellowish spots that are visible suggest to the medical expert "an inflammation of the oral mucous membrane (stomatitis)", which was probably not just an ephemeral occurrence but possibly indicative of "a weakened condition of the body's defences (immune paresis)".[110] "The idea of sarcoidosis or chronic-lymphatic leukaemia is not far to seek"[111], says the expert. An exogenous cause – such as e.g. pipe-smoking – was possible, but could probably be ruled out in the case of Shakespeare.

Comparison of the Nasal Corner of the Left Eye on an Early Marble Copy of the Stratford Bust with the Nasal Corner of the Left Eye of the Death Mask

In August 1996 I came across an older marble copy of the Stratford bust (*fig. 068*) in Charlecote Park in Warwickshire. It was my companion, Dr Christoph Hummel, who first noticed three swellings (*fig. 069*) in the nasal corner of the left eye on this copy, obviously faithfully replicated by the sculptor from his model, the bust in Stratford.[112] There was an evident parallel to the pathologically altered left caruncle in the Chandos and Flower portraits. However, the protuberance must have grown considerably after the portraits were painted.

This marble copy was measured by Dr Gray in January 1998 (*fig. 070*). The author had already noticed when inspecting the original bust in Stratford in August 1996 (*see fig. 104*) that the sculpture there does not display this sign of illness – or more accurately, no longer displays it. Since it was overpainted in white[113] (in accordance with the prevailing neoclassical ideal at the time) in 1793, with a coat of paint that covered the bust for the next seventy years or so until removed in 1860 by the restorer Simon Collins,[114] the latter may well have thought the swellings in the corner of the eye were an accumulation of dirt, and removed them.

An additional proof that there had originally been prominent caruncular swellings on the Stratford bust is supplied by the Hunt portrait (*fig. 071*),[115] discovered in 1860, which is based on the bust.[116]

The Chandos portrait shows three protuberances juxtaposed (*fig. 072 a*) in the same place, clearly visible in an older infrared [sic] photograph (*fig. 072*)[117]. Closer inspection of the Flower portrait, and especially of the x-ray picture of the painting taken by the Courtauld Institute in London in 1966 (*fig. 073*), reveals a larger and more diffuse pathological change in this area than is immediately apparent in the painting today (*see fig. 016*).

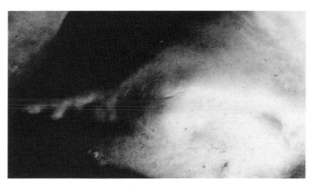

Fig. 066 Nasal corner of the left eye on the Berlin copy of the death mask, with noticeable protuberances: photogrammetric image by Dr Rolf-Dieter Düppe, Institute for Photogrammetry and Cartography, Technical University Darmstadt (1997).

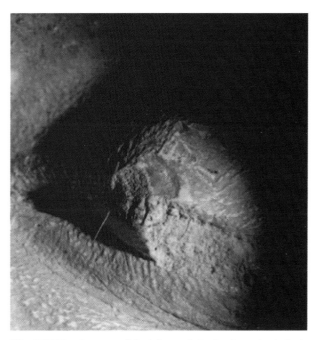

Fig. 067 Nasal corner of the left eye of the death mask. A dark almond-shaped slit can be seen. Photographed by Andreas Kahnert, Hesse Land and University Library (1997).

As the death mask had served as the basis for the Stratford bust, and must once have exhibited this pathological symptom, the nasal corner of the left eye of the mask was thoroughly inspected once again. At first sight there was nothing to be seen apart from the almond-shaped opening already mentioned (*see fig. 067*). The eyelids (especially the upper lid) had obviously been pushed aside. On the Berlin copy of the death mask (*see fig. 065*) clear protuberances are still visible in the place in question, as Dr Düppe's spatial-digital measurements of 1997 demonstrate (*see fig. 066*). This clearly established that the original mask must once have possessed the same distinctive sign of illness. However, it must have been broken off or removed by mistake in the course of the centuries.

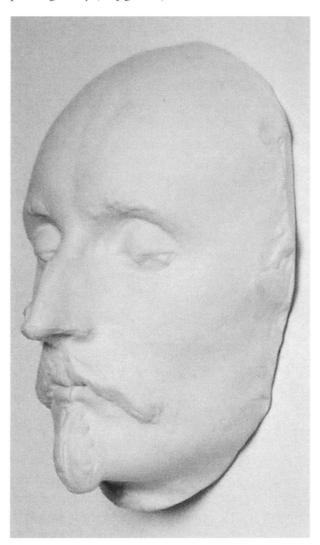

Fig. 065 Berlin copy of the death mask, Staatliche Gipsformerei (State Plaster-moulding Works), Berlin (c. 1910).

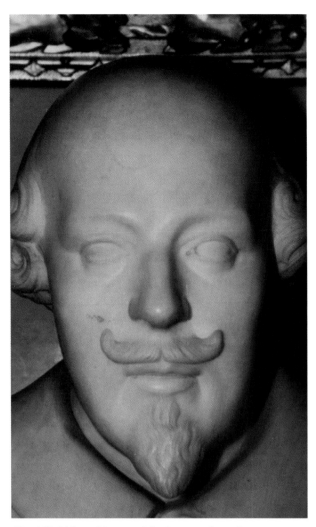

Fig. 068 Old marble copy of the funerary bust of
Shakespeare in Charlecote Park near Stratford-upon-Avon.
George E. Shiers (1997).

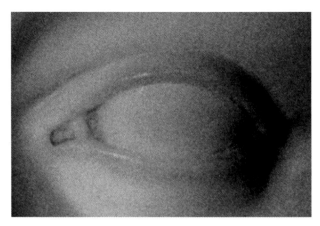

Fig. 069 Nasal corner of the left eye of the marble copy
in Charlecote Park with striking trilobate protuberance.
George E. Shiers (1997) - Detail of fig. 068.

Fig. 070 Marble copy of the funerary bust in Charlecote Park
– left to right, George Shiers, formerly Headmaster and
Teacher of Mathematics of the Grammar School in Stratford-
upon-Avon, the author, Rima Astrauskaite, and the English
physicist Dr Nico Gray (1998).

In his medical assessment of these new findings
Professor Hertl comments: "There is no doubt that
during his lifetime and at the time of his death the
person's [left] eyelids [on the death mask] encom-
passed a body, or rather were pushed aside to make
room for an extensive body."[118] The expert goes on to
say that this "body" in the inner corner of the eye is
now missing on the Darmstadt mask. However, it had
"evidently not been missing when the sculptor
Gheerart Janssen formed the Stratford bust using the
death mask as his model."[119]

By means of spatial-digital measurement in 1997,
also carried out by Dr Düppe, beneath the almond-
shaped slit in the nasal corner of the eye on the original
death mask a hollow space was detected (fig. 074), on
the bottom of which the craters of three swellings can
be recognised. In Düppe's report, which has been
incorporated into Professor Hertl's expert assessment
of 15 August 1997, we read:

With the most powerful enlargement and spatial evaluation (stereoscope) I saw a hollow space surrounded by
a wall of highly porous and granular appearance, on the
uneven floor of which two smaller and one larger crater-
like formations were to be recognised. One has the
impression here that something has crumbled out by
itself or was removed by "cleaning work". The – in terms
of extent – larger ruin of a protuberance is the one lying
closest to the iris.[120]

The medical evidence presented here speaks for itself. It
provides convincing proof that the swellings visible on the
marble copy of the Stratford bust were originally also
present on the death mask. These findings prove,
furthermore, that the death mask, the Stratford bust, the
marble copy, the Berlin copy of the death mask, and the
Chandos and Flower portraits belong together and
represent one and the same person: William Shakespeare.[121]

Fig. 071 Hunt portrait (from Shakespeare's funerary bust),
Shakespeare Birthplace Trust, Stratford-upon-Avon.

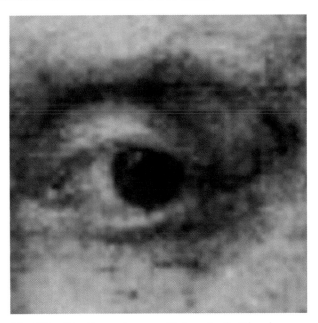

Fig. 072 a Detail: nasal corner of left eye in the Chandos
portrait with an incipient trilobate swelling.

Fig. 072 Infrared image [sic] of the Chandos portrait.

Fig. 073 The Madonna beneath the Flower portrait;
X-ray image, Courtauld Institute, London (1966).

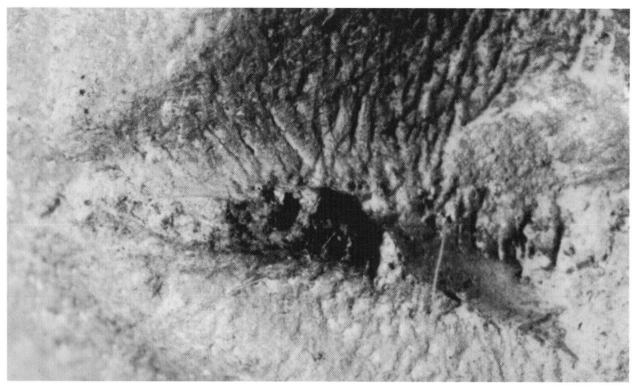

Fig. 074 Nasal corner of the left eye of the death mask with the clearly visible remains of a trilobate swelling. The skin structure of the death mask is also visible. This proves that we are dealing with the original. Photogrammetric measurement by Dr Rolf-Dieter Düppe, Institute for Photogrammetry and Cartography, Technical University Darmstadt (1997).

SUMMARY

The tests of identity and authenticity described here were carried out along new lines through interdisciplinary collaboration with criminologists, medical experts, physicists and engineers. The results of these investigations can be summarised as follows:

All of the images investigated reproduce Shakespeare's appearance authentically. The two paintings, Chandos and Flower, were painted from life and are faithful portraits of the poet. The Davenant bust too is an authentic image created during Shakespeare's lifetime, which must have been based on a life mask, and meticulously depicts all the characteristics of Shakespeare's face, including even the finest detail. The death mask is also authentic and an exact likeness of Shakespeare. It was taken soon after the poet's death and served as the model for the sculptor of the funerary bust, which accurately copies the death mask on a scale of one to one; the bust too is authentic. The Droeshout engraving was based on the Flower portrait, which the engraver used as a model. The separate steps in the presentation of evidence are conclusive not only when taken altogether, but for the most part also when they are considered individually.

In addition, the signs of disease shown in the images offer unambiguous proof of the identity of the persons represented. They show how the painters, plaster moulders and sculptors of the sixteenth and seventeenth centuries must have strived to make their work accurate and true-to-life. The truth to life of the Chandos and Flower portraits and of the Davenant bust, and the truth to nature of the death mask, is further underpinned by the fact that the same pathological manifestations are still extant in all of them, at different stages of development and in different states of preservation.

Moreover, when suitably enlarged the skin structure of the deceased Shakespeare becomes visible on the death mask (*see fig. 074*), and this, in conjunction with the proof of identity, shows that the plaster cast really does derive from the mould taken from the poet's face after death.

The organic substance still extant on the mask in the form of individual hairs is a further very decisive and unmistakable sign of its genuineness – as are the "ruins" or craters of a once trilobate protuberance in the nasal corner of the left eye, revealed by spatial-digital measurement. The funerary bust of Shakespeare must also once have possessed this sign of illness, because it appears on a marble copy derived from the bust.

IV. THE NEW RESULTS

THE CHANDOS PORTRAIT

History and Ownership

On the basis of the proofs of identity and authenticity established for the Shakespeare images examined in Part III, the Chandos portrait (*see fig. 014*) must now be regarded as a genuine portrait of William Shakespeare painted from life. It had a succession of early owners. According to James Boaden's account,[1] they range from Joseph Taylor (1586-1653), a leading actor in Shakespeare's group of players, The King's Men, to the poet laureate and eminent playwright Sir William Davenant (1606-1668); the famous actor Thomas Betterton (1635-1710); and his noted actress colleague, Mrs Elizabeth Barry (1658-1713). Boaden's version of this series of owners is – as will be seen (p. 87f.) – basically in agreement with that passed on by the antiquary and engraver George Vertue (1683-1713), and that of the antiquary and scholar William Oldys (1696-1761). As far as is known, the English poet and dramatist John Dryden (1631-1700) owned the first copy of the Chandos portrait (*see fig. 075 a*), painted by Sir Godfrey Kneller (1646/49-1723).

Up to the beginning of the eighteenth century, the original and the copy were therefore exclusively in the hands of actors and playwrights who had a high regard for Shakespeare and, by revising and performing his works, ensured that his intellectual heritage was not forgotten, but was handed on. Through their possession of the Shakespeare image they maintained, as it were, their link with the person of the poet, a link which they hoped would serve as their guide and inspiration. After Kneller, whose copy is significant in relation to the early history of the picture and to identifying its originator (see p. 85f.), this Shakespeare image was copied very frequently. Boaden mentioned in 1824 that no picture had been copied more often than the Chandos portrait.[2] In the process, however, numerous reproductions came about that distorted the poet's appearance.

Joseph Taylor, the first known proprietor of the original, like Richard Burbage (*c.* 1567-1619), who was famous for creating Shakespeare roles, was a gifted inter-preter of Hamlet. And like John Lowin (1576-1653) he is said to have been taught acting by Shakespeare himself.[3] From the death of Burbage until the outbreak of the Civil War, Taylor was held to be the greatest stage actor in England. Significantly, in Gayton's *Wit Revived* (1655), in reply to the question "Which of our Tailors were the most famous?", his is the first name to be mentioned.[4] When the theatres reopened after the restoration of King Charles II (1660), Thomas Betterton took Taylor's place. He was to become equally prominent as a member of Davenant's theatre company The Duke's Men. According to a contemporary witness and connoisseur of the theatre scene, the former prompter and later theatre historian John Downes (c. 1640-c. 1710), Betterton was tutored by Davenant, who had known the great Shakespearian actors Taylor and Lowin personally, and seen them on the stage. Downes recorded that:

> *Hamlet* [sic] being Perform'd by Mr. *Betterton*, Sir William [Davenant] (having seen Mr. *Taylor* of the Black-Fryars Company Act it, who being Instructed by the Author Mr. Shaksepeur [sic]) taught Mr. *Betterton* in every Particle of it; which by his exact Performance of it, gain'd him Esteem and Reputation, Superlative to all other Plays [...]. No succeeding Tragedy for several Years got more Reputation, or Money to the Company than this.[5]

And he continued that:

> The part of the King [Shakespeare's *King Henry VIII*] was so right and justly done by Mr. Betterton, he being Instructed in it by Sir William [Davenant], who had it from Old Mr. Lowen, that had his Instructions from Mr. Shakespear himself [...].[6]

It was at the beginning of the eighteenth century that the original portrait first left the circle of actors and dramatists, for whom it always had a very special senti-mental value. When Betterton's collection – he had been quite impoverished towards the end of his life – was auctioned after his death, the picture was acquired first by his partner and close confidante, the actress Mrs

Walker & Boutall ph. Sc.

Richard Burbage the Actor
from the original painting ascribed to himself
in the Gallery at Dulwich.

Fig. 075 Portrait engraving of Richard Burbage (c. 1567-1619) from his self-portrait in the Dulwich Picture Gallery.

Barry, but she sold it soon afterwards to the London lawyer Robert Keck for forty guineas.[7] Through marriage, the picture then passed into the possession of a Mr Nicoll (or Nicholl or Nicholls), who lived in Michendon House in Southgate (Middlesex). Nicoll's only daughter married the Marquis of Caernarvon, the later Duke of Chandos, and took the portrait with her into the marriage (see p. 26). The Chandos portrait changed hands once again when Anna Eliza, daughter of the Duke of Chandos, married the Duke of Buckingham. Until 1848 it was kept in the ducal collection in Stowe, and in September of that year it was put up for sale along with Buckingham's other paintings. It passed into the possession of the Duke of Ellesmere for 350 guineas (see p. 26). Eight years later, in 1856, Ellesmere donated the Shakespeare portrait to the newly-founded National Portrait Gallery, London,[8] where it has stayed as portrait no. 1 (literally and metaphorically) ever since, and has long been a national icon.

The Painter

The findings of the authenticity and identity tests which the Shakespeare images we are investigating have been subjected to provide decisive clues as to the identity of the painter. As the Chandos portrait must have been painted many years before the Flower portrait (see pp. 67ff.), we can exclude all the people – bar one - who have been considered as the possible artist.

Ruling out the Painter John Taylor (d. 1651)

The professional painter proposed in recent years by Mary Edmond as the artist of the Chandos portrait, John Taylor (d. 1651)[9] belonged – as mentioned in Part II (see p. 26) – to the London Guild of "Painter-Stainers" and appears in a painting of 1631/32, reproduced in Edmond's article "The Chandos portrait: a suggested painter". He is shown on the right-hand side of the picture as an office bearer of the Guild, a Lower Warden, with the Master of the Guild in the centre, and the Upper Warden on the left.[10]

According to Edmond, John Taylor is clearly aged over fifty in the picture.[11] But there are grounds for questioning this assumption. They arise from considering Taylor's career in his Guild, starting as Lower Warden (1631-32), continuing four years later as Upper Warden (1635-1636), and culminating at the high point of Master (1643-1644).[12] It is unrealistic to reckon that this career was only begun when Taylor was

already in his sixth decade. And it is rather improbable that he only achieved the highest and most influential office of Master at the relatively advanced age of about sixty-five. My opinion is that the artist probably served as Lower Warden in his forties or perhaps even his thirties. The clearly discernible face of the painter as it appears in the picture reinforces this assumption.

Edmond's starting point, however, is that "John Taylor appears to be in his fifties in 1631-32",[13] and she concludes from this that the painter was in his thirties during the last years of Shakespeare's literary career in London. This would make him old enough to have painted the portrait of the poet. In her discussion Edmond makes the tacit assumption that the Chandos portrait was only painted between about 1608 and 1613, in the last phase of Shakespeare's creative life in London. But in the light of medical expert opinion on the Shakespeare images that have been investigated, this is untenable. The new findings about the markedly differing life-stages of the subject in the Chandos and Flower portraits respectively reveal that the Chandos picture shows the poet at a much younger age than the Flower portrait, painted in 1609; so that John Taylor would have been too young to have painted this image of Shakespeare (see p. 88).

Another argument against Taylor is the well-founded assumption that the Chandos portrait was not painted by a professional artist. James Boaden remarked as long ago as 1824 that: "the reader will have found the Chandos picture to have been painted by an ordinary hand, but to possess unquestioned resemblance to the poet".[14] The painter and graphic artist George Scharf, the first secretary of the National Portrait Gallery and later its director, in his essay "The Principal Portraits of Shakespeare" (1864) lays particular emphasis not only on the coarse, crude canvas used for the Chandos portrait, but on the fact that it is remarkably well painted for an amateur.[15]

Finally, against John Taylor it must also be said that he does not fulfil the essential condition mentioned by Vertue in his *Notebook* entry: the painter of this Shakespeare image would have had to be an actor and also a close friend of Shakespeare (see p. 26).

The Early Sources and Secondary Literature Revisited

A second glance at Vertue's first entry, which tells us (without mentioning any given name) that the picture was "painted by one *Taylor*",[16] initially prompts the supposition that the names John and Joseph later became confused. If this is so, then the man in question would be the famous actor and player of Shakespearean roles Joseph Taylor, mentioned earlier. He was among the "principall actors" of Shakespeare who are named in full in the First Folio Edition. From 1611 to 1616 Joseph Taylor was officially a member of Lady Elizabeth's Men, a company that was practically "orphaned" after 1613, the year when the daughter of King James I and his queen, Anne of Denmark, Princess Elizabeth, married the German Count Palatine Friedrich V and took up residence with him in Heidelberg. It was not until early 1616, the year of Shakespeare's death, that this theatre troupe was granted the protection of Prince Charles, the heir to the throne. Taylor may therefore have performed with the King's Men during Shakespeare's lifetime. When Burbage died in 1619, Taylor succeeded him.[17]

However, for a number of reasons the actor must be ruled out as the possible painter of the Chandos portrait. As already mentioned, he could hardly have fulfilled the requirement of being Shakespeare's close friend, since he was twenty-two years younger than the poet. And in contrast to Burbage, there is no indication in Taylor's case that he engaged in amateur painting. Purely in terms of age Taylor cannot have been the originator of the Chandos portrait, since he must have been too young when the picture was painted (see p. 88).

What points to Richard Burbage as the painter of this Shakespeare picture is not only Vertue's (later crossed out) note in the margin naming the great actor and amateur painter, but also an entry by the antiquary Oldys: "Mr Nicholas [Nicholl] of Southgate has a picture of Shakespeare which they say was painted by old Cornelius Jansen, others by Richard Burbage the player".[18] Since it can be shown that Jansen did not come to England until after Shakespeare's death, he can be excluded, leaving Burbage once more as the only candidate.

There is no apparent reason to doubt this early evidence of the antiquary and scholar Oldys based on oral tradition, especially since he had collected a substantial amount of material for a Shakespeare biography,[19] and was prevented from publication only by his untimely death.[20] Furthermore, his information coincides with Vertue's already frequently cited statement that the Chandos painter must have been an actor and a close friend of Shakespeare. This applies (as already mentioned – see p. 26, n. 68) only to Richard Burbage (*fig. 075*). It is also true that Burbage was a painter. His talent as a portraitist is demonstrated by his famous self-portrait in the Dulwich Gallery.

The simple style of dress seen in the Burbage self-portrait corresponds to that in the Chandos portrait. Both pictures are quite obviously not official portrait studies, but informal images showing the subjects in their everyday dress.[21] The form of the collar is similar in each picture, being worn open by both Burbage and Shakespeare, which likewise points to an everyday setting.

It would certainly be interesting to establish through technical comparisons, for example by investigating the painting technique and analysing the paints, canvas, brushes etc, whether the Chandos picture and the Burbage portrait are by one and the same painter.

In addition, on consulting the early secondary literature about the Chandos portrait, it emerges that apart from George Vertue's *Notebooks* and the information supplied by William Oldys there exists another tradition, clearly independent of these sources, which likewise names Richard Burbage the actor and friend of Shakespeare as the painter of the Chandos portrait, and the actor Joseph Taylor as its first owner.

This tradition was first documented by James Boaden, who initially had to put up the most determined defence against the unfounded and untenable scepticism about the authenticity of the Chandos portrait expressed by George Steevens (1736-1800), the eloquent Shakespeare editor. Boaden says that: "He [Steevens] undertook to depreciate the present portrait. The means he used were these: If there had been any scandal about the possessors of this picture, such demerit in the owner was made to bear against the picture. Gossip and rumour had given out that Davenant was more than Shakspeare's godson." Furthermore, the Shakespeare editor had described it as "folly [...] to suppose that HE [Davenant] should possess a genuine portrait of the poet, when his lawful daughters had not one!"[22]

These objections are not only extremely strange, but also lack logic. They throw a significant light on Steeven's prejudices and his narrow-minded concept of morality. Well known for his habit of publishing anonymous attacks in the press on his friends, and therefore constantly embroiled in disputes,[23] in announcing his Shakespeare edition of 1793 Steevens set out to attack and disparage the publishers of the First Folio Edition, John Heminge and Henry Condell, Shakespeare's friends and colleagues. He remarked with a sneer that: "We have sometimes followed the suggestions of a Warburton, a Johnson, a Farmer, or a Tyrwhitt [later editors of Shakespeare], in preference to the decisions of a Heminge or a Condell, notwithstanding their choice of readings might have been influenced by associates whose high-sounding names cannot fail to enforce respect, viz, William Ostler, John Shanke, William Sly, and Thomas Poope."[24] Those named were actors and belonged to Shakespeare's company The King's Men, which enjoyed great esteem in their day.

The baseless doubts and reservations of this commentator concerning the Chandos portrait - Boaden accurately calls him the "PUCK of Commentators" [25] - would surely have had a real formative effect on later opinion, had Boaden not been able – as he tells us himself - to come up with a discovery which helped him to confirm the credibility of the tradition and remove practically all doubt about the genuineness of the picture.

The Significance of the Early Copy of the Chandos Portrait by Sir Godfrey Kneller

Boaden reports that during his work on a biography of the dramatist John Dryden the Shakespeare scholar Edmund Malone (1741-1812), known to Boaden personally, had by chance come upon the fact that the much-praised copy of a Shakespeare portrait, owned by Dryden, was actually a copy of what was later to be called the Chandos portrait. It was not known until that point that Dryden possessed a replica of the painting. All that was known was that the dramatist's friend, the eminent portrait painter Kneller (see p. 81), had made a copy of a Shakespeare portrait, not known by name, and given it to Dryden, who expressed his extravagant gratitude in the well-known lines:

SHAKSPEARE, THY GIFT,

I PLACE BEFORE MY SIGHT,

WITH AWE I ASK HIS BLESSING AS I WRITE;

WITH REVERENCE LOOK

ON HIS MAJESTICK FACE

PROUD TO BE LESS,

BUT OF HIS GODLIKE RACE.

HIS SOUL INSPIRES ME,

WHILE THY PRAISE I WRITE,

AND I LIKE TEUCER UNDER AJAX FIGHT;

BIDS THEE, THROUGH ME,

BE BOLD; WITH DAUNTLESS BREATH

CONTEMN THE BAD,

AND EMULATE THE BEST:

LIKE HIS, THY CRITICKS

IN THE ATTEMPT ARE LOST,

WHEN MOST THEY RAIL,

KNOW THEN THEY ENVY MOST.[26]

Fig. 075 a Sir Godfrey Kneller (1646 or 1649-1723), first copy of the Chandos portrait. Before 1683.

Kneller's impressive copy of the Chandos portrait (*fig. 075 a*) was clearly painted shortly before 1683, since Dryden's lines were written between 1683 and 1692,[27] and the painter was intensely productive precisely from this time onwards – after a period of some years (1678-1682) about which we know nothing – creating hundreds of documented paintings.[28] By the time Malone realised what the original of Dryden's copy was, the latter was already in the possession of Earl Fitzwilliam in Wentworth Castle, where it remains today.[29] The close correspondence of this early copy to that hanging in the National Portrait Gallery in London, which is known to have been restored several times in the course of its history, also serves to confirm that the Chandos portrait can be traced directly back to the seventeenth century.

Boaden, who quotes the first four lines of Dryden's poem of thanks to Kneller,[30] rightly makes the point that the Chandos portrait had already attracted attention before the early eighteenth century: "Here then we at once step back to the seventeenth century, instead of being obliged to consider the picture as one that excited no notice until the early part of the eighteenth."[31] Even though Boaden can offer no documentary proof of his statement that Dryden had seen the original for years in Davenant's or Betterton's house,[32] it is none the less credible and persuasive. In support of Boaden's remark it can be noted that Dryden, who lived in London from the middle of 1657 onwards, became a member of the Royal Society as early as 1662, and rapidly made his mark as a dramatist, could have seen the Chandos portrait during the 1660s after the opening of the theatre under the direction of Davenant in Lincoln's Inn Fields (1661).

The Chandos Portrait in
Sir William Davenant's Collection

Specific opportunities to see the Chandos portrait were provided when Davenant and Dryden met to work on an adaptation of Shakespeare's *The Tempest*. It was staged in 1667, a year before Davenant's death, by Davenant's theatre company The Duke's Men in the Lincoln's Inn Fields Theatre. Dryden always spoke of Davenant with great respect. According to Davenant's biographer Arthur H. Nethercot, he acknowledged that he learned more from the Shakespeare expert and experienced playwright than from any other mentor. And he regarded it as a particular honour for his name to be associated with those of Shakespeare and Davenant through their adaptation of the *Tempest*.[33] At the latest, it was during the time when he was becoming more closely acquainted with the grand old man of the theatre (Davenant)[34] that the latter might have shown him the Chandos portrait, which must have been in the Lincoln's Inn Fields Theatre, or in its annexe where Davenant lived (*see fig. 78*). The latter information (about Davenant's private residence) is supplied by the antiquary John Aubrey, frequently mentioned here, whose evidence is generally regarded as very reliable.[35] That this was indeed the home of the dramatist and theatre director is also apparent from Aubrey's report of Davenant's solemn funeral procession to Westminster Abbey, which set out from the theatre in Lincoln's Inn Fields. In Aubrey's eyewitness account:

> I was at his funeral. […] His body was carried in a Hearse from the Play-house to Westminster abbey […] to his Grave, […] on which, on a paving stone of marble, is writt, in imitation of that on Ben Johnson [sic]: O rare Sir Will. Davenant.[36]

When The Duke's Men presented their adaptation of the *Tempest* in 1667, Shakespeare had already been dead for fifty years, but his godson Davenant, by then almost equally famous, definitely knew him when he was a child, admired him enormously all his life, and had himself all too willingly nourished the rumour that he was Shakespeare's natural son. This too is recorded by Aubrey.[37]

Davenant, who was one of the few contemporaries and closer acquaintances of Shakespeare still alive in the 1660s, was therefore in a position to know what the playwright William Shakespeare from Stratford-upon-Avon really looked like. He was able to confirm that the Chandos portrait, which he himself owned, was a true to life depiction of the poet. He was ten when Shakespeare died, and therefore quite able to recall his features, especially as on his annual visits to Stratford the poet lodged at the Crown Tavern in Oxford, where Davenant's parents were the innkeepers. Naturally, Davenant also knew who had owned the portrait immediately before him, and how he had acquired it. It is fairly certain that he knew who painted it. Seen in this light, Sir William Davenant can be regarded as a direct, and perhaps the most authoritative and reliable, source for confirming the authenticity of the Chandos portrait and for evidence of the artist's identity.

Evidence from Seventeenth Century Witnesses

At this point, we can also call upon the actor and theatre manager William Beeston (*c.* 1606-1682), the son of the Shakespearean actor Christopher Beeston, who was a member of the Chamberlain's Men until 1602 and is known to have appeared in 1598 – together with William Shakespeare and Richard Burbage – in Ben Jonson's *Every Man in His Humour*. As a child, Beeston too must have known and seen Shakespeare, at least as long as the poet was in London. Having been old enough to consciously experience the stage in the late Shakespeare period, Beeston is regarded as a particularly important transitional figure, a living bridge between the great epochs of the English theatre in late Elizabethan and early Stuart times, and the age of Restoration theatre.[38] It is well known that for John Aubrey he was an incomparable source of biographical information and knowledge of theatre history, which but for him would doubtless have been consigned to oblivion. After their first meeting, Aubrey was full of enthusiasm, reporting that: "I have met with old Mr Beeston who knew all the old English Poets, whose lives I am taking from him: his father was Master of the Playhouse."[39]

John Dryden had a similarly high regard for the old actor and theatre director as a contemporary witness of the Elizabethan stage and its playwrights. "Mr Dryden", Aubrey records, "calles him [William Beeston] the Chronicle of the Stage".[40]

Another particularly useful contemporary witness is Sir Henry Herbert (1595-1673), the younger brother of the philosopher Lord Herbert of Cherbury (1583-1648) and of the poet George Herbert (1593-1633). In 1622, through the mediation of his influential relative William Herbert, Earl of Pembroke (1580-1630), he gained a place at court, was knighted in 1623 by James I, and a year later purchased the office of Master of the Revels, giving him control over all public theatre performances. Herbert vetted and censored all plays submitted to him, granted rights and privileges, threatened punishment for infringing the rules, and kept scrupulous records. It goes without saying that he also knew all the actors. Herbert held office until 1642. Although he resumed these functions after the Restoration, he soon resigned because he was not able to hold his own against the theatre companies of Davenant and Killigrew, who operated under royal licence.[41] The future censor not only experienced the theatre of the Shakespeare period at first hand, but also clearly followed it with great interest. At the age of twenty-eight, when Heminge and Condell were dedicating their Folio edition of Shakespeare's plays to his (distant) cousin, the Earl of Pembroke and Montgomery, Herbert already had ultimate control over all public performances. His "office-book", of which only extracts now survive, was a kind of chronicle of the theatre.[42] During the Restoration period he (besides William Beeston) was the best informed surviving witness of the early Jacobean theatre and its actors.

If Dryden was sure, therefore, that in his high-quality reproduction of the Chandos portrait he possessed an accurate representation of Shakespeare's features, he could count on the support of at least three reliable contemporaries of Shakespeare, who not only knew Shakespeare as by far the most popular playwright of his age and an outstanding personality, but who must have met him personally on many occasions.

The admiration that Davenant had for Shakespeare was reflected in, among other things, his possession of certain mementos of the dramatist. These included not only the subsequently famed Chandos portrait, but also the Davenant bust (*see fig. 017*). Dryden, who in any case had a particular fondness for all things Elizabethan,[43] shared this love of Shakespeare. The lines of praise in verse quoted above (see p. 85), addressed to the painter Kneller, bear vivid testimony to this.

Against this backdrop, it is simply inconceivable that the two most important playwrights of the early Restoration period, who preserved and transmitted Shakespeare's heritage, should not have made the Chandos portrait, kept in Davenant's home in the annexe to Lincoln's Inn Fields Theatre, the subject of intense contemplation and discussion. Boaden remarked that "Dryden had seen the original for years together, at the residences of either Davenant or Betterton, or both."[44] He too thought that "He [Dryden] had no doubt often conversed with them [Davenant and Betterton] as to its authenticity".[45]

There can be no doubt that Dryden saw and admired this Shakespeare image. That alone explains his fervent wish to own a copy of the picture, a desire fulfilled by his friend Sir Godfrey Kneller.

The Chandos portrait was acquired after Davenant's death (1668) by the stage luminary Thomas Betterton, who now ran the Duke's Theatre in Lincoln's Inn Fields. Peter Thomson's interesting comment in his essay "English Renaissance and Restoration Theatre" (1995) resonates here: "Davenant died in 1668 but his spirit lived on in Betterton".[46] It is well known that Davenant's successor as Poet Laureate was John Dryden.

Boaden's Account in the Early Eighteenth Century

The facts and circumstance set out here further serve to reinforce what is in itself a credible account by Boaden of the history of the Chandos portrait. It is especially significant that Boaden does not call upon Vertue's *Notebooks*; in fact he does not seem to have known them at all, given that they were not yet published. At any rate, he does not mention them anywhere. With Kneller's copy of the Chandos portrait, he can reach directly back to the seventeenth century and to the man who is not only mentioned in all the sources as the owner of the picture, but also had – as we have seen – a close private connection and, it seems, blood ties with Shakespeare himself: William Davenant. Davenant commanded much more comprehensive and first-hand knowledge than the lawyer Keck, who, according to Mrs Barry, was the fifth owner of the Shakespeare picture, some fifty years after

Davenant's death, and could not pass on to the antiquary Vertue any more than he knew only through what was by this time a very sketchy oral tradition. However, leaving aside these errors in Vertue (and especially in his informant Keck), which are the kind that always tend to occur when names and facts are transmitted purely orally over a longer span of time, Boaden's account very much accords with that of Vertue, and chimes with Oldys's version. The historical and biographical facts and connections presented here confirm Boaden's scenario regarding the early history of the Chandos portrait. Apart from the incorrect dating of Davenant's death, it can therefore be accepted as accurate. Boaden summarizes:

> It [the Chandos portrait] is said to have been the property of Joseph Taylor, our poet's Hamlet, who dying about the year 1653, at the advanced age of 70, left this picture by will to Davenant. At the death of Davenant, in 1663 [sic], it was bought by Betterton the actor; and when he died, Mr Robert Keck, of the Inner Temple, gave Mrs Barry the actress 40 guineas for it. From Mr Keck it passed to Mr Nicoll of Southgate, whose only daughter married the Marquis of Caernarvon [who later became Duke of Chandos].[47]

Whereas initially Boaden expressed himself tentatively on the question of the painter's identity ("It was very probably painted by Burbage, the great tragedian, who is known to have handled the pencil")[48], later he firmly concludes that:

> The Chandos picture is traced up to [Joseph] Taylor, [...] and was no doubt painted by Burbage.[49]

The Painter of the Chandos Portrait: Richard Burbage

As we have seen, the painter John Taylor (d. 1651) and the King's Men actor Joseph Taylor can both be ruled out as possible originators of the picture. On the basis of written and oral sources, only Burbage meets the conditions that the painter of this Shakespeare image is required to fulfil. And the expert medical assessment has revealed that the Chandos portrait must have been painted no later than the 1590s (see pp. 67ff. and 131f.). Therefore we can now be certain that the Elizabethan actor and amateur painter Richard Burbage (*see fig. 075*)

was indeed the creator of the Chandos picture, and that he was portraying his friend William Shakespeare.

The Client and the Fee

Since the Chandos picture was obviously painted by Richard Burbage as a kind of 'friendship portrait', strictly speaking there can be no question of a commission nor would the amateur artist Burbage have received a fee. In addition, the history of the portrait forcefully suggests that the Chandos portrait was never owned by Shakespeare or his family, but that Richard Burbage, the great Shakespearean actor of the first generation, passed it straight to Joseph Taylor, the outstanding Shakespeare actor of the second generation, and that in the later course of the seventeenth century it remained in the hands of the most important representatives of Shakespearean theatre (see p. 81).

Dating

The time separating the Chandos and Flower portraits must have been considerable. Evidence of this is the substantial progress made by the pathological signs, attested by expert medical opinion in Part III (see pp. 67ff.), in the Flower portrait as against the Chandos. The expert medical reports talk unanimously – because of the suspected systemic illness of the poet – of the disease having taken a very protracted course (see p. 71 and 131f.). A time span of about ten to fifteen years therefore seems realistic. As Richard Burbage and William Shakespeare began working together from 1594 onwards, taking the lead in the theatre company The Chamberlain's Men, founded in that year, Burbage's Chandos portrait could not have been painted before 1594. Given that the Flower portrait can now be definitively dated at 1609, we can assume that the Chandos portrait originated at some point between 1594 and 1599. This is also consistent with the historical and biographical context. For it was in this period that Shakespeare rose to the height of his fame as the most eminent poet in England, and in 1598 he was acclaimed as the equal of the great authorities of antiquity (see p. 41f.). But only a year later a crisis was beginning to develop, centring on the bearer of Shakespeare's political and religious hopes, the Earl of Essex, whose execution (1601) caused a trauma that was to have a decisive impact on the future of Shakespeare's creative work.[50]

THE FLOWER PORTRAIT (1609)

History and Ownership

The first known owner of the Flower portrait was an art-lover called H. C. Clements from Peckham Rye near London, who bought the picture around 1840 (see p. 27). In his Shakespeare biography *A Life of William Shakespeare* (first edition 1898) Sidney Lee gives the text of a note that Clements evidently attached, after he bought the portrait, to the box in which he kept it:

> The original portrait of Shakespeare, from which the now famous Droeshout engraving was taken and inserted in the first collected edition of his works, published in 1623, being seven years after his death. The picture was painted nine years before his death, and consequently sixteen years before it was published [...] The picture was publicly exhibited in London seventy years ago, and many thousands went to see it.[51]

Lee, who appears to have had access to the original text of this note, corrected the two mistakes made by Clements, and stated that the picture had been painted seven and not nine years before the death of the poet, and *fourteen*, not *sixteen* years before its publication (as an engraving). Whether the painting really was publicly exhibited as early as the eighteenth century, as this statement asserts, cannot be confirmed from any other source.

Before the Shakespeare image was delivered on permanent loan to the Stratford Memorial Gallery,[52] and before Mrs Flower acquired it in 1895 in order to present it to the Stratford gallery, it had - while in Clements's possession - been exhibited twice in public: at the Great Exhibition at the Crystal Palace in 1851,[53] and from May to June 1873 at the Alexandra Palace in London. In a fire that completely destroyed the palace on 9 June 1873, the picture was badly damaged.[54] As the Stratford curator William Salt Brassington emphasised, "it had been exhibited at the Alexandra palace, but, owing to its dingy appearance, it excited little attention".[55]

When the Flower portrait was acquired by the Stratford Memorial Gallery in 1895, it was professionally cleaned,[56] restored, and examined by experts (see pp. 27ff.). The Shakespeare scholar Sidney Lee summarised the results of the investigation in his Shakespeare biography, published in 1898. He established that: "In all its details and comparable dimensions, especially in the disproportion between the size of the head and that of the body, this picture is identical with the Droeshout engraving." And, he went on, that the experts had estimated almost without reservation that the painting pre-dated the engraving. They concluded that Martin Droeshout had in all probability used the picture directly as his model.[57] From as early as 1892, when the painting was made accessible to a wider public, the prevailing opinion began to form that the portrait engraving in the First Folio edition of Shakespeare's plays must have been based on the Flower portrait. And by the turn of the century it had already become quite usual for encyclopaedias (e.g. Brockhaus) to refer to the painting as "the original used by Droeshout". To a significant extent this was due to Sidney Lee, who judged that only the Flower portrait had a claim to have been painted during the lifetime of the poet.[58]

As mentioned in Part II, the art historian Spielmann did everything he could to reverse the priority of painting and engraving and prove that the painter had worked from the engraving (see p. 27ff.).[59] As he published his opinion in the *Encyclopaedia Britannica* of 1911, it became the prevailing doctrine for many decades – irrespective of the preceding expert reports, and despite the fact that authorities, as for instance the famous Shakespeare scholar Edgar Fripp, had been convinced of the contrary by Spielmann's arguments (see p. 30).

The American Shakespeare specialist Samuel Schoenbaum was still maintaining Spielmann's sequence towards the end of the twentieth century,[60] even though a completely new state of research had come about which could have led him to different insights. It may be recalled that when the painting was being x-rayed in 1966 at the Courtauld Institute in London a valuable old painting of the Madonna, from the late fifteenth or early sixteenth century, was discovered beneath the Shakespeare portrait (see p. 30). This fact later led me to a revision of the question of the poet's religion,[61] which in turn yielded additional significant clues to the dating of the Flower portrait (see pp. 134–36ff.). It may be further recalled that a fundamental restoration of the picture by Nancy Stocker[62] in 1979 revealed sharply delineated pathological signs, faithfully reproduced, which after intensive medical analysis allowed definitive conclusions to be reached about the truth to life of the Flower portrait and the chronology of painting and engraving.

Schoenbaum was evasive and unconvincing on the question of what model the engraver Martin Droeshout might have used if not the Flower portrait, which agreed with the engraving. Schoenbaum thought that the engraver "probably worked from a line drawing supplied to him".[63]

When the American authors Paul Bertram and Frank Cossa took up and discussed once more the old theory that the Flower portrait was an authentic image of Shakespeare, they found they had no scientific evidence to support it.[64]

Only on the basis of the results obtained by the criminological and medical investigations presented in Part III was it possible to re-open the question of the sequence of painting and engraving, and to resolve it convincingly.

In the spring of 2005 the genuineness of the Flower portrait was back in the public eye and was denied by the English art historian Dr Tarnya Cooper of the National Portrait Gallery in London. Nonetheless, I hold to the positive evidence presented here. The contradiction will be discussed and clarified in a separate chapter of this book: "The Flower portrait in the Royal Shakespeare Company Collection, Stratford-upon-Avon: original or copy?" (see "Appendix I").

The Sequence of the Flower Portrait and the Droeshout Engraving

Let us recapitulate briefly the chief argument against the authenticity of the Flower portrait; "the most telling evidence of Droeshout's priority",[65] argues Schoenbaum, relying on Spielmann, is the shadow on the collar of the Flower portrait.[66] Since this shadow was not present on the original plate, but was only added at a second stage, the anonymous painter of the Flower portrait, according to Schoenbaum, "presumably" used a copy of the First Folio as his model, in which a later state of the engraving was reproduced.[67]

However, this argument – as becomes apparent on closer examination – is intrinsically inconclusive. For the mere conjecture that an anonymous painter worked from the engraving in a copy of the First Edition cannot be regarded as proof of the priority of the engraving. Even if an unknown artist had painted a picture from the engraving in the First Folio in which the shadow on the collar is visible, a chronology of the two objects could not be possibly be inferred from this, but only that both reproduce the same phenomenon.

It was possible to establish the sequence of painting and engraving only within the framework of tests of identity and authenticity, especially – as previously mentioned – on the basis of the findings of medical reports. Medical specialists diagnosed and precisely defined pathological signs that appear in almost spectacular fashion in the Flower portrait, especially since its fundamental restoration in 1979 (*see figs. 015 and 016*). These signs agree with the symptoms of illness displayed in the same location by other authentic images of Shakespeare, differing only because of the varying ages of the sitter, and the progress of the symptoms in size and extent – provided that no inadmissible changes were made. With this background in mind, it is completely out of the question for a painter to have used the Droeshout engraving in the First Folio Edition as the basis of the Flower portrait. For it is inconceivable that he would have been in a position to invent, let alone present in a diagnosable form, the particularly distinctive and highly accurately reproduced signs of disease in Shakespeare's face, if the original from which he was working had not possessed them, or had only vaguely indicated them (see pp. 68 ff.). So we can be absolutely certain that no painter could have represented the striking symptoms of disease in the Flower portrait with such truth to life and in such precise detail if he had not actually seen them; and seen them, moreover, on the living person. Just as the other artists of authentic Shakespeare images could only have achieved their knowledge of the sitter by observing him in person, and the plaster moulder must have had the corpse of Shakespeare in front of him when he made the death mask, so must the painter of the Flower portrait have worked in the presence of the poet himself. Only thus could he have seen the clearly defined protuberance on the forehead, which was diagnosed as a sarcoidosis or an osteoma (see p. 71); the very prominent, pathological swelling on the upper eyelid, due to the Mikulicz Syndrome (see p. 68); the obvious outgrowth(s) in the nasal corner of the left eye, interpreted as a caruncular tumour or a macule on the eyelid cleft (see pp. 68ff. and 76ff.); or the whitish-yellow mark on the lower lip, which suggests a stomatitis (see p. 76).

From what has been said, there are compelling reasons to conclude that it was not the painter who used the *Droeshout* engraving, but the engraver *Droeshout* who used the *Flower* painting as the basis for his portrait.

The Painter

The painter of the Flower portrait could have been the uncle of the engraver, already mentioned in Part II (see p. 27), but also the famous Elizabethan portrait painter Marcus Gheeraerts the Younger (1553-1635). Gheeraerts and Shakespeare must have known each other well, and worked closely together.[68] It does not seem too fanciful, therefore, to speculate that Shakespeare might have placed his trust in him for this purpose. For it was not a blank piece of board that was used for this Shakespeare image, but an old panel from the fifteenth or early sixteenth century, and on it there was an artistically very valuable painting of the Madonna (see pp. 30, 89 and 134ff.).[69] If this picture had been discovered, both the painter and his subject would have been suspected of being adherents of the old religion. In early seventeenth century Protestant England this represented a danger to life and limb.[70]

However, at the moment there is no definitive answer to the question of who painted the Flower portrait.

The Client and the Fee

The only person who might have commissioned the Flower portrait is William Shakespeare himself. There remains the question, however, of whether the Madonna painting belonged to the painter or the poet. But since the artist would hardly have kept a painting with such a treacherous subject simply in order to re-use the panel, the picture may well have belonged to Shakespeare. This theory is all the more plausible since Mary Shakespeare, née Arden, the poet's mother, died in 1608, the year before the Flower portrait was painted. She came from a lateral branch of the arch-Catholic Ardens of Parkhall; she was a strict Catholic herself – like her husband John Shakespeare - and might have brought the Madonna with her when she married.[71] Shakespeare could therefore have inherited it in 1608/09, and then decided for safety's sake to have it overpainted with a portrait of himself, carried out by a painter he trusted. If this was the case, then he probably paid the kind of fee that was usual at the time.

Dating and Inscription

Since the Flower portrait has now been shown to be a genuine and faithful portrait of William Shakespeare, painted from life, there is no reason to doubt the date

on the picture, "*Willm Shakespeare 1609*". The medical reports in particular have made clear that a long time must have elapsed between the painting of the Chandos and Flower portraits. The year in which the Flower portrait was created, 1609, is given added credence by the historical and biographical circumstances. It has been claimed that the date is too early for an inscription in cursive script, and this has been seen as tending to cast doubt on the genuineness of the picture.[72] In point of fact, though, the cursive inscription on the Flower portrait may be taken to indicate that we are dealing here with a private rather than an official image, something that the special circumstances of its origins would also suggest. The inscription on the Flower portrait is far from unique in the early modern period: see, for example, the 1516 portrait of Albrecht Dürer painted by Michael Wolgemut (*see fig. 012*). The art historian Kurt Löcher writes of "the inscription in cursive writing and in the German language" on this picture that it signifies "the private nature of the portrait".[73] If the engraver omitted the inscription of the Flower painting (perhaps at the behest of the editors of the First Folio Edition, or the poet's family), the private nature of the picture may have had something to do with it.

THE DAVENANT BUST (C. 1613)

Discovery, Ownership, and History

While researching in the library and museum of the Royal College of Surgeons in Lincoln's Inn Fields in London on 12 January 1998, I came across source material that neither art historians nor Shakespeare scholars had examined or evaluated before. These new finds make it possible to reveal and reconstruct the true context of the discovery and history of the Davenant bust early in the nineteenth century.[74] Furthermore, they show that the finder, William Clift (1775-1849) (*fig. 076*) did not disclose the precise circumstances of his discovery to the public, nor even to his family - including his famous son-in-law, Professor Richard Owen (1804-1892) (*fig. 077*). But he did confide them to his diary. This diary was utilized by Jessie Dobson for a biography of Clift[75] in which he recounts the timing and circumstances of Clift's discovery and appropriation of the Davenant bust so precisely that the actual course of events can be clearly traced. The following account is based upon Dobson's Clift biography, on other relevant writings

Fig. 076 Portrait of William Clift (1775-1849), first Curator of the Hunterian Museum of the Royal College of Surgeons of England, London.

Fig. 077 Portrait of Sir Richard Owen (1804-1892), Professor of Anatomy, British Museum, London.

about Clift, and on publications concerning the old Duke's Theatre in Lincoln's Inn Fields originally run by Sir William Davenant; in particular concerning the building history of a place that is so significant for the theatre history of London.

The Extension of the Museum of the Royal College of Surgeons of England

In the spring of 1834, Clift who was the first curator of the Hunterian Museum in the Royal College of Surgeons, suggested to the trustees of the museum that the space for his collection should be expanded because of overcrowding. This proposal was accepted, and in the same year neighbouring buildings were purchased and extensive rebuilding and renovation work begun, so that the museum did not re-open until 1837.[76] Houses nos. 40 and 39 were bought up, as well as parts of the land belonging to No. 39, owned by a Mr Dennett. Before the beginning of demolition work, which was to last a fortnight, Clift must have inspected among other areas the inner yard of Dennett's house, and found there two busts placed in niches in a wall of the house. These niches probably looked more or less like those in the façade of the smaller neighbouring building, built against the right-hand side wall of the massive Lincoln's Inn Fields Theatre, also known as Duke's Theatre (*fig. 078*). The house was clearly intended as a residence for the theatre director (see p. 93f.).

The Date and Circumstances of William Clift's Discovery of the Davenant Bust

Clift recorded in his diary his inspection of the building adjacent to the theatre and the yard of a neighbouring house. Dobson comments that: "Apparently, part of the land belonging to No. 39 was also bought, for Clift mentions in his diary that he rescued two busts from 'the yard of the house of late Mr Dennett's'".[77] Dobson goes on to say that "the busts had been placed high up on the wall 'under an alcove but exposed to the weather and over a pump and covered with a dozen coats of paint'".[78] Clift cannot have noticed them later than 11 March or, at the very latest, 12 March 1834. For by 12 March he was writing a letter to the owner "requesting permission to remove the busts".[79] The reason he gave was that "one of them was 'so decomposed from the weather, as to be little more than a ball of dust, and the other has suffered considerably from the same cause'".[80] "Being fond of antiquities",[81] he

(Clift) hoped to be able to preserve some parts of their original form. However, the finder omitted to tell the owner the names of the sculptures' subjects: Ben Jonson and William Shakespeare. It is also clear that he greatly exaggerated the poor condition of the two objects. This applies at least to the Shakespeare bust, which like that of Ben Jonson had indeed been exposed to the weather in an outdoor niche, but – in contrast to that of Ben Jonson - had been excellently preserved by numerous layers of paint and was therefore undamaged.[82] It is obvious that Clift, who himself possessed considerable talent as a painter, was extremely eager to acquire these representations of Shakespeare and Ben Jonson. Because of the location of his find, he rightly assumed that they dated from Shakespeare's own time; and naturally, this was something else he failed to mention to the owner. The busts were found at a site which was in fact in many ways very closely connected with the theatre in Lincoln's Inn Fields. This aspect will be discussed more fully in what follows.

The residence of the directors of the Lincoln's Inn or Duke's Theatre

The smaller house built against the right flank of Lincoln's Inn Theatre was – according to Dobson, drawing upon Clift – the residence of the theatre director, Mr Fleetwood, one of Davenant's successors, who thus had direct access to his workplace (*see fig. 078*). In 1721 Fleetwood's troupe moved to the Covent Garden Theatre. On this basis Clift, according to Dobson, believed he could trace the history of the busts practically back to Shakespearian times:

The house, on the wall of which the busts were found, had originally been the residence of the manager of the Duke's Theatre, Mr Fleetwood, and at one time there existed a passage connecting it with the theatre. Fleetwood's company moved from Lincoln's Inn Fields to Covent Garden Theatre in 1721 and this fact, as Clift remarks, 'consequently removed this bust a long way towards the time in which Shakespeare lived'.[83]

Fig. 078 View of the Lincoln's Inn Fields Theatre or Duke's Theatre, about 1700. The residence of the dramatist and first theatre director, Sir William Davenant (fig. 079), was built adjoining the right side of the theatre. Davenant's successor, the actor Thomas Betterton (1635-1710), also lived there.

Fig. 079 Portrait of the dramatist Sir William Davenant (1606-1668). Following the Restoration of Charles II in 1660, he founded the Lincoln's Inn Theatre or Duke's Theatre (see fig. 078). Davenant revised many plays of Shakespeare, whom he admired intensely, and produced them to great public acclaim.

But Clift and Dobson had overlooked the fact that No. 39, the small house connected to the theatre by an inner yard and a passageway, must already have been occupied by the first director of the theatre, the playwright and poet laureate Sir William Davenant (1606-1668) (*see fig. 079*). Thus it is Davenant and not Fleetwood who is the decisive link in the chain practically leading back all the way to Shakespeare.

The Duke's Theatre in Lincoln's Inn Fields: History of the Building and its Uses

It was previously assumed that Lincoln's Inn Fields Theatre (*see fig. 078*) was built decades after Davenant's death (1668). While Oscar James Campbell and Edward G. Quinn assert in their *Shakespeare Encyclopaedia* (1966, repr. 1974) that the building was erected in 1695,[84] the art historian Geoffrey Ashton dates it at 1714.[85] Both dates were incorrect, but led to the rejection of any theory that

the terracotta bust of Shakespeare found in the nineteenth century could have belonged to Davenant or could have originated in the early seventeenth century, and may have been an authentic representation of Shakespeare.

But the fact is that the Duke's Theatre in Lincoln's Inn Fields was established by royal licence in 1661 by Sir William Davenant in a large, apparently solidly built tennis court. This theatre building had certainly been much altered by the 1840s and undergone a number of changes and of use, but it was not demolished until 1848 when the Royal College of Surgeons museum was greatly extended. The history of the building is described in precise and complete detail in the *London Encyclopaedia* (1983) by the London architectural bookseller, Ben Weinreb, and the English historian, Christopher Hibbert:

> LINCOLN'S INN FIELDS THEATRE *Portugal Street.* Opened in 1661 by Sir William D'Avenant for the Duke's Company in a converted tennis court […]. In 1671 the company moved to DORSET GARDEN THEATRE. In 1672-4 the theatre was used by Thomas Killigrew and his company while the Theatre Royal, Bridges Street was being rebuilt. Thereafter it became a tennis court once more. In 1695 it was refitted as a theatre by Congreve, Betterton, Mrs Bracegirdle and Mrs Barry […]. In 1704 the company moved to the Queen's Theatre in the HAYMARKET. In December 1714 the theatre was refitted by John Rich […]. In 1732 Rich moved to COVENT GARDEN. The theatre was afterwards used as a barracks, an auction room and a china warehouse. It was demolished in 1848 to make way for an extension to the museum of the ROYAL COLLEGE OF SURGEONS.[86]

Both the old theatre and the adjacent house of the director, connected by an inner courtyard, still existed in 1834, as William Clift's diary entries clearly prove. The wall with niches containing the busts of Shakespeare and Jonson was most probably the side wall on the right of the former Duke's Theatre (*see fig. 078*).

Restoration Work on the Davenant Bust

In his report on the work he carried out on the Davenant bust in 1986/87, the restorer J. H. Larson particularly stresses that *two* extensive restorations had already taken place: one by Roubiliac in the eighteenth century, and another in the nineteenth century. They had involved filling and strengthening the open back of the thin-walled terracotta bust with an iron rod and plaster (see p. 32 and n.112, Parts I & II). But, contrary to what Larson believes, the first of these procedures cannot have taken place as early as the eighteenth century. It is likely that it was undertaken in 1834, the year in which Clift discovered the bust. The second stabilizing measure must have been carried out after 1848, once the busts had been as it were "officially" discovered. While the first, crude restoration can probably be attributed to Clift, who is known to have transported the fragile Davenant bust to Kensington Palace to present it to a select public (see below), the second appears to have been carried out at the behest of Professor Richard Owen, before he sold the bust to the Duke of Devonshire (see pp. 31).

Changes to the Appearance of the Davenant Bust Carried out by its Finder

Clift's efforts to acquire both the sculptures were quickly crowned with success. The owner must have expressed his agreement within three days. For as early as 16 March 1834 the new owner (Clift) was noting in his diary that he spent "all last night and this day decorticating the bust of Shakespeare from 4 [sic] coates of coarse paint – red, white and black".[87] The scratch marks still visible on the bust today, especially in the area of the protuberance on the forehead (*see fig. 062* and p. 72) were probably caused by Clift's - obviously unprofessional – actions, and certainly did not come about when J. H. Larson was cleaning up the very dirty terracotta bust with acetone and steam in 1986/87.[88] It is also likely that the attempts to "smooth" or "even out" the swelling on the upper left eyelid (see p. 72ff.), which are very noticeable when enlarged (*see fig. 064*), were made by Clift. They cannot have been the work of the artist, and are definitely not attributable to Larson. Clift seems to have been very concerned to remove or reduce the pathological symptoms on Shakespeare's face, which to him must have been inexplicable.

The Presentation of the Davenant Bust in Kensington Palace, London

On 10 May 1834 Clift presented his bust at a soirée held by the Duke of Sussex in Kensington Palace. There it was, as Dobson phrased it, "set off by a splendid new invented light to dazzling advantage, and gave universal satisfaction to a very large meeting".[89]

The Relationship of the Finder to his Property

The new proprietor,[90] who was at no time reticent about his find, received many offers for it in the following years and thereafter, but turned them all down because – it appears – he could not bear under any circumstances to be parted from his Shakespeare bust. Years later he wrote to a gentleman called George Jones, who was trying to have a statue of Shakespeare erected, that "he would not part with it for a thousand pounds". He also rejected an offer from an unnamed American, said to be "equally Shakespeare bitten", who bought up anything resembling Shakespeare that he came across. The American confessed to Clift that his bust had given him "a much higher opinion of Shakespeare's intellectuality than he had previously conceived".[91]

Clift became so deeply attached to this Shakespeare image that he worried about its future without him: "it has been an object of anxiety to me to know what would become of this beautiful work of art after my death".[92]

The Fictitious Account of the Discovery of the Davenant Bust

We know that Clift bequeathed the terracotta Shakespeare bust to his son-in-law, from whom, however, he must have withheld the true facts of its discovery. Why he did so is obvious: as an artist and museum curator, Clift must have recognised at first sight both the material and the non-material value of this work of art. As mentioned above (see p. 92f.), he not only concealed this from the owner, but in order to acquire the well-preserved Shakespeare bust at no cost he even persuaded him that these objects were weathered and decayed, and therefore practically worthless. Since his conduct had been improper, Clift could not and would not report truthfully when, where and how the terracotta bust came to be in his possession.[93] At first, moreover, he must have feared being sued by the real owner for compensation or the return of the bust. But since the latter died soon after the bust changed hands, Clift was able to concoct his own account of the discovery of the object. This version must have been the one passed on by his son-in-law Richard Owen to the Duke of Devonshire, which the Duke then transmitted to the Garrick Club. As I discovered during my visit of inspection to Stratford-upon-Avon in January 1988, a corresponding caption is still to be found on the copy of the Davenant bust in the Royal Shakespeare Theatre Collection there. It reads: "Workmen pulling down the old Dukes Theatre in Lincoln Inn Fields London found this bust of Shakespeare which had been covered over above a doorway." [94]

The Origins of the Davenant Bust in
Sir William Davenant's Collection

Looking for a link between the site of the Davenant bust's discovery and the person of William Shakespeare, we come back again and again to the Restoration playwright Sir William Davenant. Biographical research has rightly bestowed upon him the title of "acknowledged custodian of the Shakespeare tradition".[95] Davenant, who had already been a theatre director before 1642 and as a royalist during the Civil War had rendered outstanding services to Charles I as well as Queen Henrietta Maria, was knighted in 1643. He probably knew more about Shakespeare, who was also highly esteemed by the royal family, than any other contemporary with the exception of William Beeston.

It was not by chance that in the summer of 1643, en route from Milford Haven to join the king and his court in Oxford where they had taken up quarters, the queen broke her journey to stay at Shakespeare's imposing property, New Place, as the guest of his eldest daughter and chief heir, Susanna Hall.

According to tradition, Davenant owned an autograph letter from King James I to Shakespeare.[96] After the opening of the Duke's Theatre (1661), he revised and produced Shakespeare's plays. He staged an adaptation of Shakespeare's *Hamlet* to great public acclaim in August 1661.

Davenant, the godson and perhaps natural son of Shakespeare, had not only followed in the footsteps of his illustrious predecessor, adapting his works for the Restoration stage, but was also a passionate collector of Shakespeare memorabilia. It is thanks to Davenant that the famous Chandos portrait was not only preserved and safeguarded, but also handed on to his successor, the actor and theatre director Thomas Betterton, who had a similarly high regard for Shakespeare. Nobody but Davenant could have been the owner of the Shakespeare and Ben Jonson busts. It seems that, having kept them out of the clutches of the Puritan zealots, he later placed them as icons at the entrance of his theatre. The now corrected story of their discovery supports this, and (in conjunction with

the likewise amended history of the theatre building) it is further attested by William Clift's diary entries, which provide documentary evidence that in March 1834, some 170 years after the opening of the Duke's Theatre, both works of art were rediscovered in an outside wall of the building (see p. 92f.). On the short walk from his home in what would later be No. 39, across the inner yard to the side entrance to the Duke's Theatre that was concealed from outside, practically day in day out Davenant's eyes must have fallen upon these impressive and over life-size images of the two towering dramatists of the Elizabethan-Jacobean era. And it seems as though with these visual reminders of the two authors he wanted to create an externally visible connection to them – especially as we know that as a royalist and fervent admirer of Shakespeare he quite consciously aspired, after the end of the English Civil War and the anti-theatre reign of Oliver Cromwell, to reconnect with the great theatre tradition of the Shakespearean age.

When Clift rediscovered the busts, that of Shakespeare's was covered by at least four coats of paint, which by his own account he personally removed (see p. 95). It is therefore impossible for the bust to have been created only in 1758 by the French sculptor living in England, Louis François Roubiliac (1702/5-1762). It is also quite unlikely that a portrait bust of Shakespeare of such high artistic quality, created by the most prominent sculptor then working in England, would have been placed in such a culturally insignificant location in the second half of the eighteenth century, when the cult of Shakespeare was beginning to develop in England and Germany. For after 1732 the building was no longer used as a theatre, but for a variety of other purposes, including a barracks, an auction room, and a china warehouse (see p. 94). It is hard to imagine, and therefore extremely improbable, that a sculpture of Shakespeare by Roubiliac (together with a bust of Ben Jonson) should have been hidden away between 1758 and 1834 in a back yard, as it were, exposed to wind and weather and repeatedly given a thick coat of paint. But if we assume that Davenant himself placed it there when he set up his theatre in 1661, a complete picture emerges into which all the details convincingly fit.

However, there is no way of knowing why the two busts remained unnoticed in their wall niches, and why only the Shakespeare bust was preserved under layers of paint, and not that of Ben Jonson. Presumably the sculptures were forgotten and therefore left behind when the theatre director and actor Betterton moved out of the theatre in 1671 with his troupe and transferred to the Dorset Garden Theatre on the Thames near Blackfriars. A rival troupe to Betterton's performed in the Lincoln's Inn Fields Theatre as a temporary arrangement between 1672 and 1674, but they would hardly have been authorised to remove these objects or take them with them. We can conclude from the information and facts we have that the busts were put in place by Davenant; that they were not moved from the site until 1834; and that – perhaps in the course of renovating the façade - the Shakespeare bust received a new coat of paint, unless the paint had been applied during the Civil War to protect it.

The results of the extensive scientific investigations of Shakespeare's images in Part III have shown that the Davenant bust is an authentic representation of the poet, created by the sculptor from life and with the aid of a life mask (see pp. 72–4 and 98). Now those results are confirmed by the new findings about the discovery of the bust and its undoubted origins in Davenant's collection. The theory, first put forward by Spielmann, that the Davenant bust was the work of Roubiliac is thus no longer sustainable.

The Sculptor

Now that Roubiliac has been ruled out as the originator of the Davenant bust (see p. 96f.), we must look elsewhere, to seek a sculptor who was a contemporary of Shakespeare as well as an outstanding artist. In early seventeenth-century England there were certainly talented English stonemasons and sculptors, such as the Janssens and others (see pp. 17 and 41), but none we can point to as an outstanding established sculptor capable of creating a work of art of the quality of the Davenant bust. However, around 1613 a young Englishman returned to London from Amsterdam, where he had been apprenticed for six years to the most important Dutch sculptor and master builder, Hendrik de Keyser (1565-1621). The young man in question is Nicholas Stone (1586-1647). In the course of the seventeenth century Stone was to become the most celebrated sculptor in England.[97] He created about 210 monuments, tomb sculptures, fonts, sundials, chimneypieces, stairwells etc. in nineteen English counties as well as in Scotland and Ireland.[98] He acquired an excellent training at the hands of the Mannerist de Keyser, who took his inspiration from Italian and French models, became the founder of Dutch classicism, and achieved some remarkable sculptures. Like Quellinus the Elder, he often produced the models for his figures in terracotta.[99] It was from him, therefore, that the young Englishman was able to learn his mastery of the material which was employed for the Davenant bust. Thus there is much to suggest that Nicholas Stone could have been the creator of the Davenant bust: his great artistic talent as a sculptor; his excellent training; his knowledge and experience of working in terracotta; the coincidence of dates that saw him returning to London just as Shakespeare was preparing to withdraw from London to Stratford; and the fact that Stone at this early juncture was not yet inundated with large commissions from the English crown, the aristocracy, and the upper middle class, which would have prevented him from carrying out smaller projects.

Shakespeare may have come into contact with Nicholas Stone via the Janssens' workshop in Southwark, which must have been known to him and his family. Stone collaborated with Bernard Janssen, one of the sons of Gheerart Janssen the Elder, and later worked with him to erect many English tomb monuments, taking on the task of creating the true to life images ("the figures" or "pictures") of the deceased.[100] But Shakespeare's connection with Stone may also have come about through his (Shakespeare's) son-in-law Dr John Hall. For Hall counted among his patients the Earl of Northampton (Henry Howard), whose funerary sculpture Stone created in 1614 (see p. 17f.). In 1613, the year when Shakespeare ended his brilliant literary career in London, sold his shares as a theatre owner, contributed to the survival of the old religion with his purchase of the eastern gatehouse at Blackfriars, and retired completely to Stratford, there was a series of reasons why the poet should have had himself portrayed in sculpture.[101] The sculptor may have been Nicholas Stone.

The Sculptor's Model

As was established in Part III, the Davenant bust is an authentic image of Shakespeare created from life, and very probably with the aid of a life mask.[102] It is the lips that usually reveal whether a life or a death mask has been used. If they are thin and flat, it can be assumed that a death mask has been employed, whereas full, sometimes even rather thick lips[103] are a compelling indication that the artist has used a life mask.

Since the lips on the Davenant bust (*see figs. 017 and 046–050*) are "plump and full", it can be assumed that the artist had in front of him a mask taken from the face of the living Shakespeare (see p. 76). The lips of the Shakespeare death mask, on the other hand, are flat, thin, and rigid (*see figs. 018, 028 and 059*), registering the *post mortem* condition of the poet.

In the case of the Davenant mask, there are also clear indications that Shakespeare sat personally for the sculptor (see p. 76). As the prominent pathological changes to the poet's face were originally also visible on the Davenant bust – they were removed only in the later course of its history by crude and inappropriate changes (see p. 73f. and 95) – the artist must have seen and incorporated them. He must have observed for himself the misshapen left eye with its uneven contours (see p. 75f.), the protuberances in the inner corner of the left eye, causing a distinct bulge (see p. 75), the considerable swelling on the forehead (see p. 72), and the massive swelling of the left upper eyelid, which must originally have taken up so much space that it pushed the left eyebrow upwards (see p. 73). Even a life mask could not have reproduced these symptoms so clearly, especially as – like a death mask – it would have been taken in a recumbent position and the weight of the layer of plaster would to some extent have dispersed the swellings.[104]

As the signs of illness change from one stage to another, the sculptor must have reproduced their appearance when the poet had reached a specific, very advanced point in his life. This would only have been possible if the sculptor had been able to look Shakespeare in the face (see p. 75f.). That he did so is proved by the pathological changes in the inner corner of the left eye (*see fig. 064*), which are already clearly in evidence in the painted images of Shakespeare (*see figs. 014, 072 a, 016, and 073*), but which later greatly increased in size, as can be seen on the marble copy of Shakespeare's funerary bust at Charlecote (*fig. 069*) and the Berlin copy of the death mask (*fig. 066*). On the death mask itself a residue of this most significant sign of illness is still visible(*fig. 074*).

Apart from this evidence, there are further indications that Shakespeare personally sat for the artist. As the BKA expert's montages have shown, the fine lines of the skin, especially in the area of the upper eyelid, are reproduced in a true to life manner on the Davenant bust, and demonstrate an astonishing agreement with those on the Chandos portrait (*see fig. 034 a*) and the Flower portrait (*see fig. 036 a*). The sculptor could not have known about this small morphological characteristic except by seeing it on the living subject.

Fig. 080 Louis François Roubiliac (1702/05-1762), statue of William Shakespeare of 1758, British Museum, now British Library, London. Comparisons with the authentic images of Shakespeare (see figs. 014-118, 021 and 023) reveal that the forehead on the Shakespeare statue is too low, the chin is too long, and the nose does not conform either. It is therefore apparent that the sculptor cannot have been familiar with Shakespeare's true facial features.

To summarise what has been said so far: given that a later sculptor could not possibly have known about all the morphological features of Shakespeare's face, not to speak of the various highly specific and well advanced pathological signs, it has been established that the artist who made the Davenant bust worked from a life mask as well as from the living model. These conclusions also render untenable the assumed connection between the Davenant bust and the Roubiliac Shakespeare statue (*fig. 080*)[105] which originally stood in Garrick's Shakespeare shrine in Hampton, and is now in the British Library in London.[106]

The Client

Since the Davenant bust is an artistically highly valuable and obviously imposing image of William Shakespeare, it is natural to assume that it owed its creation to a particular occasion.

A glance at Shakespeare's biography reveals that in 1613 the poet was preparing for his permanent retreat to Stratford, a move that may have been precipitated by a debilitating illness (see pp. 131ff.) and the consequent waning of his creative powers. A further motive may have been the increasing discrimination against the country's Catholic population.[107]

In 1613 Shakespeare put in order not only his professional and business affairs – by selling his shares in the Globe Theatre,[108] for example - but also matters that were to do with his hidden life; that is, his activities in connection with the Catholicism that was banned in England. For in 1613 he made a significant contribution to the survival of the old faith in his homeland (see Part V p. 134ff.) by his purchase, safeguarded by a trust, of a gatehouse at Blackfriars where fugitive Catholic priests and members of religious orders were harboured and received help to escape. This was also the year in which the poet made a last journey to Rome (see p. 135).

The many activities and dispositions Shakespeare had made in 1613 all give rise to the thought that he may have decided in this year to have himself portrayed by a London sculptor, in a manner befitting his class and in order to record his appearance for posterity. This would have met the deeply-felt need among the upper and middle classes of his time to be immortalized by an artist, be it in bronze, marble or stone, on canvas, wood or board, or engraved in copper. As Joseph Pohl puts it, "The individual wanted to be perpetuated not only in the memory of posterity, but also physically. He especially wanted his face, the most essential vehicle of expression, to be preserved as a mirror of the soul."[109]

As Shakespeare's contemporary Robert Burton noted in his *Anatomy of Melancholy* (1621), the Elizabethans had an almost pathologically obsessive longing for immortality. This could be met either by pompous tomb monuments with true to life depictions of the deceased, or by painted or engraved portraits or portrait busts that were carried out during their lifetime. The desire for immortality could also be satisfied by the verses of poets, or by begetting children.[110]

In this context, the person most likely to have commissioned the Davenant bust is Shakespeare himself.

Dating

On the basis of medical findings, the Davenant bust must have been created long after the Chandos portrait (*c.* 1594-1599), and also some time after the Flower portrait (1609). Having closely examined a number of photographs of the Davenant bust, Professor Hertl, the expert in the physiognomy of the sick, in his expert report of 11 September 1998 estimated that it represents Shakespeare around the age of fifty. Since the poet was fifty on 23 April 1614, we arrive at a rough date for the Davenant bust of 1614. But as Shakespeare retired from London in 1613 (see 'Client') and the sculptor Nicholas Stone returned to London that same year (see p. 97), the Davenant bust was in all probability created in 1613.

Whereas it has previously been assumed that Stone made his debut with the tomb sculpture of the first Earl of Northampton (*see fig. 005*), fascinating because of its artistic quality and its accurate but also extremely vivid depiction of the subject and reflection of his personality,[111] we now have to consider that the Davenant bust may have been the first work of the sculptor on his return to England in 1613.

THE DARMSTADT
SHAKESPEARE DEATH MASK (1616)

Discovery, Ownership, and History

In the past quite a lot was known about the discovery, the history and the owners of the Darmstadt Shakespeare death mask (see Part II). But much of this information did not correspond to the facts, or the versions handed down contained gaps or serious factual errors. Now that the evidence of the authenticity of the mask has been presented and new source material discovered, the next step is to set out a unified account of its factual history and the emended biographies of its owners, describing the precise circumstances of its discovery in the nineteenth century, and explaining when and by whom this unique cultural artefact was brought from England to Germany. In the process it is inevitable that some things will be repeated or presented in a reorganized form.

The Painter Ludwig Becker, the Miniature Death-Portrait of Ben Jonson, and the Shakespeare Death Mask

It was by chance that early in 1847, at the Mainz antique shop of S. Jourdan, Ludwig Becker, (1808-1861 – *fig. 081*),[112] a Darmstadt painter, illustrator, explorer and naturalist, came across a miniature oil painting that was to play a decisive part in the discovery of the Darmstadt Shakespeare death mask. The miniature is dated 1637, and shows a laurel-wreathed poet on his deathbed (*fig. 082*). The detail that fascinated Becker was the inscription on the frame: "Shakespeare". The origins and purchase of the picture are extremely well documented by the vendor's dated certificate. For Jourdan supplied Becker with the written declaration that: "I *hereby* certify, by request of

Fig. 081 Portrait of the Darmstadt Court Painter Ludwig Becker (1808-1861), who acquired a miniature death portrait of Ben Jonson in Mainz in 1847 (see fig. 082). In 1849, after a hectic two-year search, he discovered the Shakespeare death mask in Mainz (see fig. 018) that had been lost after the auction sale of Count Franz Ludwig von Kesselstatt's art collection in 1842. Both objects had belonged to Count Kesselstatt.

Herr L. Becker, that the small picture with the date 1637, *showing Shakespeare on his deathbed*, was purchased by me at an auction of the effects of Graf Kesselstadt [sic] and afterwards sold to the aforementioned Herr L. Becker. (Signed), *S. Jourdan, Mainz*." He even had his signature witnessed by the Mainz burgomaster of the day, Herr Nack: "The authenticity of S. Jourdan's signature is certified by (signed) *Nack*, Mayor of *Mainz*, 17 March 1847."[113]

There is not the slightest doubt about the provenance of the picture, thanks to this document and to the auction catalogue of 1842, produced on the occasion of the sale of the collection of art and curios that had belonged to the late Canon, Count Ludwig von Kesselstatt. The catalogue lists this miniature as item no. 291 and describes it as "A deceased man crowned with a laurel wreath 1637".[114]

Ludwig Becker was highly gifted, showing promising talent as an artist at an early age. He attended the Georg-Ludwig Grammar School in Darmstadt, and received his first training as a painter at the Darmstadt Gallery. In 1829 he moved to Frankfurt am Main, where he was employed as a painter by the publisher, printer and bookbinder Heinrich Ludwig Brönner. Simultaneously, Becker studied lithography at the Städel Institute of Art.[115] The uncommonly versatile and open-minded artist earned his living primarily as a portrait painter, but also as an illustrator and engraver.[116]

In addition, Becker was an ardent naturalist. On his extensive walking tours he pursued intensive geological, mineralogical, zoological, and botanical studies. Together with Christian Schüler he created the illustrations for the three-volume standard work by the eminent zoologist Johann Jakob Kaup: *Das Thierreich in seinen Hauptformen systematisch beschrieben* (*The animal kingdom in its chief forms systematically described*), which appeared between 1835 and 1837.[117] In the production of this work Becker's invention of copper relief printing (*Kupferhochdruck*) was put to use, allowing the simultaneous printing of text and illustration.[118] It was at this time that he created a number of portraits of the heir to the Russian throne, later Tsar Alexander, who offered Becker the post of court painter. Reluctant to relinquish his independence as an artist, he turned it down.[119]

Becker collected works of art, old coins, mineral specimens etc. It is astounding, given his slender means,[120] that he possessed more than a hundred

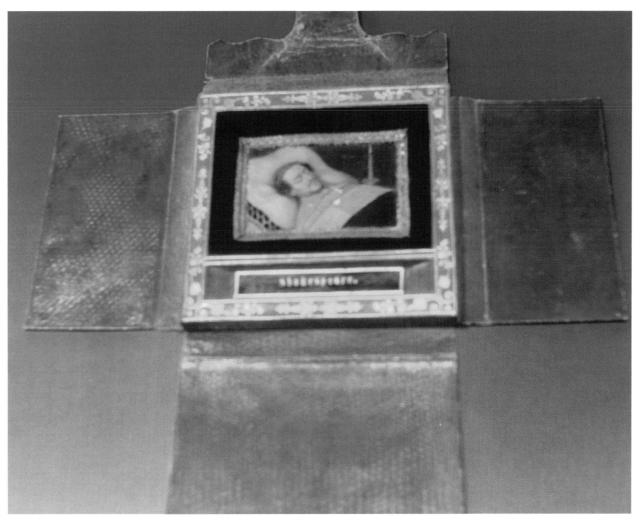

Fig. 082 Miniature death portrait of Ben Jonson (1573-1637), Shakespeare's friend and fellow dramatist.
This picture bears the false inscription "Shakespeare" on the frame. Therefore it was erroneously held
to be a genuine depiction of Shakespeare in the nineteenth century.

original drawings, including works by Raphael and Rembrandt, and oil paintings by Cranach ("Frederick II of Saxony"), Rembrandt ("St Catherine"), and the school of Van Dyck ("Bacchus and Ceres").[121]

In 1840 he became court painter at the court of Grand Duke Ludwig III of Hesse-Darmstadt. But he gave up this secure position only four years later and moved to Mainz to take care of his half-brother Karl Becker, who was ill with typhoid fever, and died of the disease in 1849. In a mentally debilitated state, and suffering from severe depression, Becker offered the whole of his collection to Grand Duke Ludwig III, if in return the ruler would assist him to recover as a human being and an artist. His offer was sternly rejected, however.[122] In this situation he came across the previously mentioned miniature oil painting with the inscription "Shakespeare", not suspecting that this find was to lead him to a sensational discovery that would fundamentally change his life.

From the certificate of the purchase of the miniature, mentioned above, it is apparent that the antiquary Jourdan procured the small oil painting at the Kesselstatt auction in 1842[123] and sold it to Ludwig Becker on or before 17 March 1847. It emerges from a correspondence between Becker and Professor Nikolaus Müller, the Mainz Gallery Supervisor, painter and restorer, that Becker had already submitted his exciting find to the latter for his expert assessment, and received an oral opinion from him. Since Becker received no written reply, however, it appears that he made another approach to Müller. This is apparent from a letter of 28 February 1847 from Müller, where he confirmed that the painter had sought his expert opinion and had later (at the end of February 1847) contacted him again asking to be sent in written form the reasons Müller had already given him orally for his (Müller's) view that the person depicted in the miniature oil painting was indeed William Shakespeare. Müller's letter runs:

Mainz, 28 Feb. 1847

Dear friend Becker Some time ago you asked me for my opinion about a small oil painting, a kind of miniature, by the English school, painted in the 17th century. The picture depicts a very famous Englishman, lying in state on his deathbed. I immediately recognised the features of the deceased as those of the great dramatist William Shakespeare, born in Stratford in 1564, and on his deathbed, sadly! in 1616. You now ask me in writing to give my reasons for the stated view, since it is at present important to you to know them.[124]

This letter, too, was certified by the mayor of Mainz, Herr Nack. However, the Gallery Supervisor had made a serious error concerning the identity of the subject. Quite clearly – like the antiquary Jourdan - he allowed himself to be guided by the inscription. It is, however, not Shakespeare who is shown in the picture, but Ben Jonson, as demonstrated by comparisons with authentic pictures of Ben Jonson, and indicated also by the date of the death portrait; 1637 is the year that Jonson died. This incorrect identification had a negative effect on the later debate about the genuineness of the Darmstadt Shakespeare death mask.[125]

But Müller's letter contains other interesting information. The miniature, he states, had always had "a prominent place" in the Kesselstatt collection because it bore the inscription "*Traditionen nach*, Shakespeare / "Shakespeare, *nach der Tradition*"[126] (Shakespeare, according to traditions / tradition has it, Shakespeare); was believed by scholars and artists to be an authentic image of Shakespeare; and was regarded as a "world-famous rarity". In Müller's words:

I will not omit to state here that among the numerous scholars, antiquaries and outstanding artists who have visited Graf Kesselstatt's gallery, not the slightest doubt obtained about the authenticity of the picture of Shakespeare […].

He added that many of the distinguished visitors had asserted that "the sketches they had seen in England showed a great resemblance to him [Shakespeare]". The Count had to his knowledge "turned down many very large offers from those who wanted to buy it."[127]

Ludwig Becker placed his trust in the "expertise" of the Mainz Gallery supervisor and the apparently well-informed additional detail he had supplied. He therefore felt confirmed in his assumption that the small deathbed painting from the Kesselstatt gallery was a genuine Shakespeare portrait.

Becker could not know that the Gallery Supervisor was only well informed up to a point.[128] Müller's claim to have been "on familiar terms" with Count Kesselstatt from 1790 onwards can be seen from today's perspective as self-aggrandizement. For if there really had been friendly contacts for over fifty years between the later Mainz Canon and the later Gallery Supervisor, Müller could hardly have put into circulation those factually mistaken assertions, which have been repeated in print ever since, that the Count's family, the von Kesselstatts, had their seat in Cologne, and that the line had died out with Count Franz Ludwig von Kesselstatt. Müller's actual words are:

The picture in question was in the hands of the aristocratic Kesselstadt [sic] family in Köln, which city, as is well known, maintained a brisk trade in works of art with London for almost three hundred years. The late Canon Count Franz von Kesselstatt (with whom I had been on familiar terms since 1790), the sole surviving heir, inherited the family fortune and acquired all the pictures and masterpieces.[129]

However, the fact is that the von Kesselstatts never had their seat in Cologne at any time. This was confirmed in a communication to the author of 16 December 1996 by Imperial Count Franz Eugen von Kesselstatt (*fig. 083*), who lives with his family at Föhren Castle near Trier, also known as Kesselstatt Castle. In his comments on the manuscript of this book referring to Müller's account he says: "Müller cannot […] have known Franz 'very well'; too many of his statements are pure invention and completely wrong."

For all its serious errors and misinterpretations, Müller's letter of 28 February 1847 nonetheless contains informative details, which seem particularly convincing because they are quite obviously based on direct experience and observation. It sounds plausible that, because it was thought to depict the great English poet, the miniature was highly regarded by everybody, and that Count Kesselstatt received various offers for it which he rejected. It is true that the former Canon – as Müller relates – had a large collection, and that he particularly valued historical scenes, among which in those days the numerous biblical motifs were also numbered.

Fig. 083 Count Franz Eugen von Kesselstatt and Countess Louisette von Kesselstatt, at Kesselstatt Castle in Föhren near Trier.

To see that von Kesselstatt really did possess a truly impressive picture gallery, we need only look at the auction catalogue of 1842, which lists over a thousand art objects; or, alternatively, Victor Chailly's 1830 painting of the interior of the grand Kesselstatt house on the Höfchen in Mainz (*see figs. 096 and 097*), hung with the paintings of the erstwhile Canon.

Müller is probably also right when he says that the supposed Shakespeare picture (*see fig. 082*) occupied a special place in the Count's collection and that the owner rejected many valuable offers to buy it.

Becker was fascinated by his find, and seems to have been constantly preoccupied by it. As the date on his "Shakespeare" miniature did not accord with the actual year of Shakespeare's death, he told the antiquaries of Mainz – according to his (Becker's) own account – that he suspected that "this picture was in all likelihood copied from an older one, or that it was possibly based on an existing death mask or statue".[130]

The key term "death mask" prompted the antiquaries to recall a "plaster head" that they had seen in the Kesselstatt collection auctioned five years earlier. Becker had the idea that this mysterious plaster cast, which without any doubt had belonged to the Mainz Canon Count Kesselstatt, was the model for his miniature death portrait and the death mask of William Shakespeare.

The Hectic Search for the Mask

Possessing a supposed picture of Shakespeare, and equipped with the information that the plaster image that accompanied it came from the same collection, Becker set off on a frantic hunt for this object. In his extensive searches he systematically combed through the Mainz antique and secondhand shops, which were very numerous at the time. We know that Mainz was already a centre for the trade in paintings by the eighteenth century, which the young Goethe liked to visit. The enterprise turned out to be more difficult than anticipated. Becker supported himself during this period as a portrait painter, and probably sold one or two items from his collection. It took about two years for his desperate search to be crowned with success. He found the death mask, last sighted in 1842 at the Kesselstatt auction, in a secondhand dealer's premises in Mainz. It was buried under rags and other worthless stuff, and it was very dirty. Becker was certain that his "Shakespeare" picture had been based on this very mask. And he sensed what an important find he had made.

In reality, however, what Becker had found was not the basis of his miniature in oils (*see fig. 082*), but the model for the funerary bust of the poet (*see fig. 021*) in the church at Stratford-upon-Avon: the authentic death mask of William Shakespeare (*see fig. 018*) - though its genuineness would not be proved until about 150 years later, after intense forensic and medical investigations (see Part III "Methods of investigation and their results").

The Circumstances and Report of the Discovery of the Mask

Regarding the circumstances under which Ludwig Becker discovered the mask, his own report of the find must suffice:

In the year 1843 Count and Canon Francis von Kesselstadt [sic] died at Mayence. In the same year his valuable Collection of Curiosities and Objects of Art was disposed of by auction. Amongst other things, there was an unorna-mented small-sized Oil Painting (the picture of a corpse) which an antiquary in the town of Mayence bought at the sale. In the year 1847 I gained possession of it by purchase. (See the Documents herewith) Professor Muller in Mayence knew the history of this Picture, and communi-cated it to me by letter. (See letter.)*[131]

It was painted in oil on parchment, and bore the date 1637. As this date does not coincide with the date of Shakespeare's death, 1616, I stated my opinion to brother antiquaries that the picture must, in all proba-bility, be copied from an older one, or possibly have been arrived at from some existing cast or statue. I then learned that in this same collection of Graf Kesselstadt [sic], there had been a plaster of Paris cast, which, on account of its melancholy appearance, had been treated with little consideration; who had bought it nobody knew. After two years' fruitless search and enquiry (in the year 1849), I discovered the lost relic in a broker's shop, amongst rags and articles of the meanest description. The back of it bears the inscription –

– A^O D$\overline{m}$ 1616

On carefully comparing the Cast with the Picture, I could no longer doubt that the pair were to be identified as the same person.

By adorning the Cast with a wreath of cypress and adding the same colour hair as in the Picture, the pale chiselled features will assuredly awaken the endless respect which his life works have gained for him.

Ludwig Becker
Edinburgh, 1850 [132]

In this report[133] Becker starts from the mistaken premise that the rediscovered death mask had served as the basis for the painter of the miniature bearing the inscription "Shakespeare" (*see fig. 082*). The report also contains a few mistakes which show that either Becker's information or his recall of details were incomplete. He tells us at the beginning of his account, for example, that Count Kesselstatt died in 1843 and that his collection was auctioned in the same year. In fact, the former Canon died in 1841, and his library and art collection were sold at separate auctions in 1842.

It is noticeable that in general this account is not very precise. It was apparently written in great haste, and – as the location "Edinburgh" indicates – written in the Scottish capital, about a year after the finding of the object. Becker describes the miniature death portrait (*see fig. 082*) as "an unornamented small-sized Oil Painting", and refrains from describing further particulars of the subject, or supplying the dimensions of the picture. He fails to mention signif-icant details, such as the laurel wreath on the forehead of the deceased, and the burning candle on his right. Neither is there any mention of the date of the picture. Both the laurel wreath and the date are noted in the auction catalogue of 1842: "A deceased man crowned with a laurel wreath 1637" (see p. 100). Becker does at least refer to it as "the picture of a corpse". While he mentions the certificate of purchase and Professor Müller's expertise,[134] he makes no reference in his report to any other names, with the exception of Shakespeare and Count Kesselstatt. So Jourdan, from whom he bought the picture; the Mainz antiquaries he spoke to; and the secondhand dealer at whose shop he found the mask, all remain anonymous. The name of the secondhand dealer was probably "Wilz". Paul Wislicenus remarks on this subject:

Herr Becker learned a year after he had bought the little picture […] that Shakespeare's death mask had likewise been in the Kesselstatt collection, and after a long search he found the former at the shop of a secondhand dealer, who was, it is thought, a certain Wilz, of whom the antiquary Jordan said that he was a very honourable man who had collected art objects with great skill.[135]

The question has been raised as to why on this occasion Becker did not ask for a receipt signed by the vendor. The most plausible answer is probably that this time it was not a knowledgeable antiquary who was involved, but a secondhand dealer who usually conducted his business without issuing receipts as the sums involved were often negligible. It should not be forgotten, though, that Becker, having finally reached the goal of his two-year long search, and being in possession of the coveted object, was in an almost intoxicated state of euphoria, and perhaps gripped by the thought of making his way as fast as possible to England in order to offer his extremely valuable purchase for sale there, so as to achieve the highest possible price for it.

It was very helpful to Becker that in 1850 his half-brother Dr Ernst Becker (*see fig. 084*) became companion and private secretary to Prince Albert. Ludwig Becker, previously constantly plagued by money worries, now believed he could achieve

Fig. 084 Portrait of the chemist Dr Ernst Becker (1826-1888). Becker, half-brother of the finder of the Shakespeare death mask, was Prince Albert's private secretary and companion.

financial independence through selling the mask. This was confirmed by a letter from a member of the extended Becker family in Darmstadt, communicating and commenting on what was then the latest family news. Writing to her son Wilhelm on 8 December 1850, Minna von Wedekind (née Schubert) discussed at length the rise of Ernst Becker, which was admired by all: he left the following day for England to take up his privileged position with Prince Albert.[136] Then she went on to talk about Ludwig Becker and his exciting find in Mainz. The writer of the letter herself seemed, for some reason, not to be particularly impressed by this discovery. She writes in a very casual and sharp-tongued way:

> That universal enthusiast Louis Becker has also found Fortuna. In Mainz he found a mask (imprint of a human face), declared the same to be the mask of Shakespeare, got a rich Englishman interested in it, travelled with him an [sic] his find to London, and got offered large sums for it; but hasn't yet clenched a deal, because he's aiming really high. Meanwhile, his person found such favour that a rich lord took him with his son on a voyage to his plantation in Van-Diems-Land [sic], while the mask is increasing in value on account of becoming so well known and L.B. will play the part of Lord Croesus when he comes back [...][137]

The Mask in the British Museum and in Stratford-upon-Avon

Once Becker had brought the mask to England, it was soon the centre of attraction. It was exhibited not only in the British Museum (*fig. 085*), where it was admired by large numbers of visitors, but also in Stratford-upon-Avon. It made a lasting impression on very many people, particularly on English artists.

In 1857 Henry Wallis painted his historical tableau, "The sculptor of the Stratford bust before his finished work, 1617-1618" (*fig. 086*), including in the scene the model used by the sculptor. It was an astonishingly good depiction of the Darmstadt Shakespeare death mask. This painting is in the Royal Shakespeare Theatre Picture Gallery in Stratford-upon-Avon. Another pictorial document that precisely reproduces the Darmstadt Shakespeare death mask is to be found in the volume *Shakespeare's Town and Times*, by H. Snowden Ward and Catharine Weed War, which appeared in *c.* 1896 (*fig. 087*). The English sculptor Lord Ronald Gower, a member of the Board of Curators of the Stratford Shakespeare Memorial Theatre at the end of the nineteenth century, based the features of his well-known Shakespeare statue in Bancroft Gardens in Stratford on the Darmstadt mask, of whose authenticity he was convinced,[138] and which he would have liked to buy for the Stratford Gallery, given an affordable price.

Fig. 085 View of the British Museum in London, where the Shakespeare death mask was kept and exhibited in the nineteenth century.

Fig. 086 Henry Wallis, "The sculptor of the Stratford bust before his finished work, 1617-1618)" (1857) –
The painter reproduces the Shakespeare death mask very accurately here. He may have seen it in the
British Museum in London or in Stratford-upon-Avon.

As already mentioned, Sir Richard Owen too wanted to buy the death mask for the British Museum, but could not make up his mind to do so because it was unclear how the mask had ended up in the Kesselstatt collection in Germany (see p. 34). The British Museum anatomist, employing the means available at the time, was already convinced that the measurements of the mask agreed with those of the funerary bust and the Droeshout engraving.

The Return of the Mask to Germany

After Ludwig Becker had perished during the disastrous Burke and Wills expedition on 29 April 1861 in Australia for which he had been selected because of his skills as an botanical illustrator, and Prince Albert too had died,[139] on 14 December 1861, Ernst Becker returned to Darmstadt with the mask. Professor Owen had previously strongly urged Becker to track down some documentary evidence of when and how Count von Kesselstatt had acquired Shakespeare's death mask. But the most intensive searches, both by Ernst Becker and by a later member of the family, failed to produce any such evidence. Even the great efforts of the German historian Paul Wislicenus in the same quest were unsuccessful.

Fig. 087 An earlier pictorial comparison of the Davenant bust and the death mask (about 1896).

By permission of the Becker family, copies were made of the original mask: the so-called Berlin copy in the State Plaster-Moulding Works in Berlin (*see fig. 065*), and the Frotscher copy, now in the possession of the Darmstadt publisher Wolfgang Frotscher.[140] The German sculptor Otto Lessing used the Darmstadt Shakespeare death mask as the model for the features of his Weimar Shakespeare monument, erected in 1904.[141]

When M. H. Spielmann in his Shakespeare article in the *Encyclopaedia Britannica* of 1911 expressed his negative verdict on the mask – a misjudgement, as the investigation results in Part III have shown – the Becker family were not prepared to accept it without further ado, especially as the English art historian had not deemed it necessary to view the death mask personally, and had made demonstrable factual errors. Marie Heidenreich, née Becker, took Spielmann particularly severely to task in her letters, as emerges from family documents which were kept in a safe together with the mask, and suffered serious fire damage during a Second World War air raid on Darmstadt.[142] She wrote on 20 March 1939 to a Mr Adamson (in English):

> It seems such a pity that the whole English speaking world should believe in the judgement of this one man [Spielmann], who is not exact at all, and so makes a dispute about the pro and contra almost impossible. [...] I wish a new authority would [a]rise and examine and critisise [sic] the history of our mask more carefully. It seems such a pity that it is hidden in our house [...]. It really ought to be in Stratford [...].

After the return of the mask to Darmstadt the Becker family received countless enquiries about the mask and numerous offers to buy it. When the prospective private American buyer Arthur Dexter of the Somerset Club in Boston, who had contacted Professor Owen at the British Museum in the first instance, approached Dr Ernst Becker on 9 October 1872 to enquire about the price of the mask, Becker turned to Owen to find out more about Dexter, and he used the opportunity to reiterate to the English expert that he (Becker) had always thought the British Museum the right home for this relic.[143]

As the later correspondence of the family shows, they occasionally considered donating the mask to the British Museum, but always refrained from doing so because they feared that shortly after being received it

would be recognised as genuine. As Magda Becker wrote on 2 December 1931 in a letter (in English) to a leading American Shakespeare scholar, B. Roland Lewis: "My father used to say: The day after I have given the mask as a present to the British Museum, the English will proclaim to possess the genuine Shakespeare Death-mask [...]."[144] By his own account, Lewis was working at the time on his *Life of Shakespeare*,[145] and had made contact with the Becker family to learn as much as he could about the death mask. It was he who suggested to the Beckers that they should offer it for sale to the then recently founded Folger Library in Washington. In his letter of 27 January 1932 he advised Magda Becker to give the suggestion serious consideration, and continued:

> Above all, keep in mind that it would be a source of deep pride to both you and to American Shakespeare scholars to have the Totenmask [sic] repose permanently in so excellent a place as The Folger Library.

But the asking price of $ 50, 000 was too high for the library, and to Lewis's great regret the sale fell through.

After the mask had survived the Second World War unscathed, having been for a time walled up in the cellar of the family property in Affolterbach in the Odenwald to keep it out of the clutches of American troops, Marie Heidenreich made contact with a friend of her youth, Lord Cherwell, one of Winston Churchill's advisers, and negotiated over exhibiting the mask at a Shakespeare festival in Stratford-upon-Avon. However, the festival never took place.[146]

The Purchase of the Mask by the City of Darmstadt at Auction

Mainly because of the negative opinions of Spielmann and Benkard (see pp. 36–7), the mask became more and more discredited, and its monetary value fell steadily, so that in 1960 the Becker/Heidenreich family, prompted and led by one of its members, the art historian Dr Magda Heidenreich (*fig. 088*),[147] decided to put the mask up for auction. The auction took place on 3 November 1960 at the Tenner auction house in Heidelberg (see Part II "The Images investigated"). The mask realised the sum of DM 52,000. Dr Hans Rasp, then Director of the Darmstadt Land and University Library, who had never doubted its authenticity - even when appearances were against it,

Fig. 088 Dr Magda Heidenreich, representative of the Becker/Heidenreich family, in her house in Affolterbach (Odenwald), approximately twelve miles north east of Heidelberg. This is where Shakespeare's death mask was bricked up after the Second World War to prevent it from falling into the hands of the American occupiers. On behalf of the family Dr Heidenreich sent the death mask for auction in Heidelberg in 1960.

through his own great personal commitment he succeeded in acquiring the Shakespeare death mask for the city of Darmstadt. He was able to beat off powerful competition, in particular that of Martin Bodmer of Zurich, the well-known collector of manuscripts and first editions. After a fierce bidding war between Bodmer and Rasp, the mask was knocked down to the latter, and he immediately sent a telegram to the then Mayor of Darmstadt, Dr Ludwig Engel: "Darmstadt Shakespeare death mask staying in Darmstadt".

Presentation of the Results of Tests of Authenticity

At a press conference held by the city of Darmstadt on 22 June 1995, in the presence of Mayor Peter Benz, head of the cultural department Roland Dotzert, and the director of the Land and University Library Dr Yorck Alexander Haase, I was given the opportunity to present the results of the tests of authenticity which had been carried out between January and May 1995 on the death mask, the Chandos portrait, and the Flower portrait.[148]

The First Known Owner: Count Franz Ludwig von Kesselstatt

The first known owner of the death mask – apart from William Shakespeare's family – was Count Franz Ludwig von Kesselstatt (*fig. 089*),[149] later canon of Mainz Cathedral and art collector, who lived from 1753 to 1841.[150] Von Kesselstatt belonged to the fourteenth generation of his aristocratic family. The von Kesselstatts originally came from Kesselstadt near Hanau (now a district of that name within Hanau), but relinquished their family seat in the twelfth century to settle initially in the eastern Rhineland, with their seat in Montabaur, where they acquired important estates. From 1349 onwards the von Kesselstatts had their residence in Kröv on the Moselle, and moved in 1438 to the old moated castle in Föhren near Trier, to become the leading aristocratic family of the Trier region. Föhren Castle, also known as Kesselstatt Castle (*fig. 090*), is still the permanent family seat.[151]

In the course of its history this highly regarded family has produced important individuals to fill prominent offices in the state or the church.[152] The distinguished ecclesiastical representatives of the family included the owner of the Shakespeare death mask, the Mainz Canon Count Franz Ludwig II von Kesselstatt, who by 1760, at only seven years of age, had already been sworn into that office in the archbishopric of Mainz.[153] Together with his brothers Philipp and Friderich he was sent off to study in Vienna in 1770. At the "k. & k. herzoglich Savoyische Ritterakademie" (Imperial, Royal and Ducal Savoyard Academy for the Nobility) he studied subjects that included German public law, international law, natural law, the history of the Reich, civics, criminal law, the theory of policing, and finance. During this time he enjoyed "the protection of the Empress and Queen Maria Theresa", who gave him and his brother an annual allowance of 1,200 Viennese florins.[154]

In 1775 the excellently educated and much travelled young Count Franz Ludwig became Capitular of the foundation for the nobility at the collegiate church of St Ferrutius in Bleidenstadt, and three years later canon at Mainz Cathedral, where he later held the important office of head of the Cathedral Chamber (*Dompräsenzkammer*) (*fig. 091*). At first he lived in the Canon's House next to the Dominican Church. It had been built by his uncle Count Franz Ludwig I, the head of the Mainz Cathedral Academy and Provost of Trier.[155] On 29 June 1793, however, during the siege of Mainz, the house went up in flames, leading to the

Fig. 089 Count Ludwig von Kesselstatt (1753-1841). The art collector and later Canon of Mainz Cathedral was the first known owner of the Shakespeare death mask (see fig. 018). He must have acquired the mask, together with the miniature death portrait of Ben Jonson (see fig. 082), in England in 1775.

loss of valuable books and costly furniture and paintings. Like many of the other art objects, however, the Shakespeare death mask - which must have been kept in this house, since the only journey to England made by the young count had taken place in 1775, eighteen years before the fire – had survived the fire unscathed.[156] The total damage was estimated at 29,924 florins.[157] Elector and Archbishop Carl Friderich of Mainz thereupon offered his distinguished canon the Bishop's Palace in Mainz,[158] which stood on the Höfchen (central square), immediately adjoining the cathedral, and was later to become known as the Kesselstatt house (*fig. 092*). It was to serve as the count's residence for the rest of his life, and he filled it with his extensive and universally admired art and antiques collection, and his large wide-ranging library.

Fig. 090 Castle Kesselstadt, seat of the Counts of Kesselstatt in Föhren near Trier.

As a result of the upheavals of the Napoleonic period, von Kesselstatt was the last canon of the old and powerful archbishopric of the Mainz Electorate, which was dissolved and redistributed by the decision of the Imperial Deputation of the German States (*Reichsdeputationshauptschluss*) in 1803. Thus he was fortunate to be able to continue enjoying a quiet life in the bishop's city (*fig. 094*) as a highly-regarded gentleman of independent means, art collector and watercolour painter, whom we have to thank for valuable views of old Mainz and its surroundings (*fig. 093*).[159] The count took a lively part in the social life of Mainz, and cultivated friendly relations with the notables of the town, its scholars and especially its artists, whom he supported to the best of his ability. His universal knowledge and refinement earned him great respect, and he was regarded as an authority on antiquities[160] and on old masters. He enjoyed the full confidence of the townspeople of Mainz, who at the time of the French Republic elected him as a

Fig. 091 Canon Franz Ludwig Kesselstatt, Head of the Cathedral Chamber (Dompräsenzkammer), in his later years.

town councillor, an honour which von Kesselstatt declined.[161] However, because of his great distinction, his expertise, and not least because of the excellent connections of his family with the Viennese court,[162] Count Kesselstatt was a member of the deputation led by Baron Mappes to represent the interests of Mainz at the Congress of Vienna which began on 18 September 1814, and ended on 9 June 1815.[163]

But the canon was not only a man of universal education with varied intellectual interests,[164] a well-regarded watercolourist, and an avid art collector and expert; he was also a great lover of the works of Shakespeare. The nineteen handwritten volumes of his *Collectanea* (Kollektaneen) in the Kesselstatt holdings of the Trier city archive bear witness to his astonishing familiarity with them. He quoted Shakespeare more than he did any other writer in world literature, including Goethe and Schiller. Von Kesselstatt was also intensely interested in any details relating to Shakespeare's life: the anecdote about the young Shakespeare being forced to make his escape because of poaching; the gloves that had been owned by David Garrick and had allegedly belonged to Shakespeare; the acquisition at auction for 1,100 talers of an autograph of Shakespeare's, the deed of purchase of his house.[165]

nach Kesselstatt 1812

Ansicht des Domes zu Mainz und der umliegenden Häuser mit Stadtgericht und Kesselstatt'schen Domstiftshaus von sogenannten Höfchen aus. Rechts im Hintergrunde die Johanniskirche.

Fig. 092 The Kesselstatt house on the Höfchen in Mainz (centre foreground), directly adjacent to the Cathedral. Count Kesselstatt lived here until the end of his life with his extensive art and antique collection, to which Shakespeare's death mask belonged for many decades.

As already noted, the miniature picture with the inscription "Shakespeare" (*fig. 082*)[166] which in fact depicts Ben Jonson on his deathbed, had a special place in the Kesselstatt collection.

The *Collectanea* notes he maintained from 1816 onwards, in which he records among other items "that the skull of the famous Descartes" had been auctioned in Stockholm for 18 talers, contain no reference to Shakespeare's death mask. Quite clearly, he did not know the identity of the person represented by the mask.

Paul Wislicenus ignored the possibility that the count did not recognise his greatest prize for what it was. He looks for other reasons why von Kesselstatt did not mention the mask, and puts forward the following rather unconvincing arguments:

> One has to consider […] how little love there is for death masks even today! To the expert, it is worth its weight in

gold – but Count Kesselstatt probably got it as an "extra" with the little Jonson picture […]. For the Count, Shakespeare's death mask was surely not a gem, but merely a venerable object – as it will have been to his contemporaries: no-one wanted to destroy it, or throw it away […].[167]

Von Kesselstatt would surely at least have mentioned this valuable treasure in his will, a document which Paul Wislicenus sought intensively but in vain at the beginning of the twentieth century.[168] For in his will he took the utmost care over the prudent and circumspect disposal of his most valuable possessions. Yet even in his last will the count fails to mention the Shakespeare death mask.[169] We can only conclude that he did not recognise his most valuable treasure, and that when he acquired it he received no hint of the person it represented – in complete contrast to the miniature death portrait.

Fig. 093 Von Kesselstatt's garden. One of the many views of old Mainz painted by Count Franz Ludwig von Kesselstatt. Shown here is Count Kesselstatt among close relatives who are visiting him.

Fig. 094 An old prospect of Mainz in the nineteenth century: by an unknown artist.

The Visit of Goethe and Sulpiz Boisserée to von Kesselstatt's Art Collection[170]

In 1815, when Johann Wolfgang Goethe (*fig. 095*)[171] was returning with his travelling companion Sulpiz Boisserée and his servant Karl Stadelmann[172] from a health cure in Wiesbaden, they made a detour on 11 August to Mainz. They set off at six in the morning, made their way first up to the heights of the Rheingau, where they enjoyed the view as far as Bingen, and by some time "after 8 o'clock they were [already] in the Drei Reichskronen [inn] in Mainz".[173] On this day – probably in the early afternoon[174] – they were accompanied by Professor Friedrich Lehné, the Mainz librarian and archaeologist, on their visit to the Kesselstatt art collection. While Sulpiz Boisserée notes with extreme brevity in his diary that "Prof Lehné took us to see Count Kesselstadt's picture gallery",[175] Goethe writes:

Fig. 095 Portrait of Johann Wolfgang von Goethe (1749-1832). After the 1828 painting by Karl Joseph Stieler in the Bavarian State Painting Collections (Bayerische Staatsgemäldesammlungen), Munich.

[...] [With Lehné to] Count [Ludwig Hyazinth] Kesselstädt [sic] [Born 1743, Canon, painter and art collector]. Collection paintings, curios. Gutenberg Square. Unfinished.
(Tgb) (diary) -[176]

The word "unfinished" suggests that Goethe was probably planning to write a longer entry, in which he would no doubt have had more to say about the collection. In his essay of 1816, "Art and Antiquity", he returns to this visit and says of the Kesselstatt collection:

> Count Kesselstädt, [sic] friend and custodian of paintings and antiquities, loses no opportunity to enrich his collection.[177]

None of those who took part in the visit, including Goethe, mentions any conversation with the owner of the collection, so that we may assume that the count was away at the time, and that the visitors were shown the collection by a servant. It is not unlikely that the count did not make his way home to Mainz immediately after the Congress of Vienna ended on 9 June 1815, but stayed on for a while in Vienna, the scene of his student days.

Goethe's visit to his house would have been the perfect opportunity for the former canon to have shown his guest – whose great admiration for Shakespeare was well known – not only his picture collection but also the plaster head and the miniature painting of 1637 with the inscription "Shakespeare".[178] But this obviously did not happen, since it is not mentioned by Goethe, Boisserée, or Count Kesselstatt. As indicated, von Kesselstatt had studied in Strasbourg (and Nancy) (see also p. 117f.) only a few years after Goethe, from September 1774 to March 1775. Strasbourg is probably the city in which the great English writer had received the most homage up to that time on the Continent. Goethe and Herder celebrated him there as the incarnation of the Ossianic original genius. For Herder Shakespeare was "*ein Sterblicher, mit Götterkraft begabt*" (a mortal endowed with divine power).[179]

The former Cathedral Curia, the residence of the erstwhile canon on the Höfchen in Mainz, looked like a museum crammed too full of pictures, other art objects, books and curios. This is shown very graphically by a small picture painted in 1830 by the French artist Victor Chailly, depicting part of the interior of the Kesselstatt house (*fig. 096*). This extremely interesting and informative painting titled "Count

Fig. 096 Victor Chailly, Interior of the Kesselstatt house on the Höfchen in Mainz. The painter has reproduced in minute detail the many paintings and art objects in this collection. The owner of the collection, Count Kesselstatt, is sitting at a table by a window, left. Land Museum (Landesmuseum), Mainz.

Kesselstadt in his collection" was previously completely unknown to Shakespeare researchers. A very slightly different version of the small picture is in the Germanic National Museum in Nuremberg (*fig. 097*). In contrast to the many imposing external views of the building, we see here the interior for the first time. The painting is among the few visual testimonies to those extensive early nineteenth-century picture collections which have been described as "part of cultural history [...] in illustrative form".[180] The Nuremberg Annual Report of 1943 contained the following description:

> [...] by one of the windows on the left, through which the sun is casting broad beams across the floor of the large living room and the bed in the alcove behind it, the white-haired Count sits at his desk, his head turned towards the observer. A flat light-grey ceiling frames the room, around whose moss-green walls Empire armchairs and small tables are set, and these walls, like those of the alcove and the corridors visible through the open door, are crowded with pictures hung closely together. Looking through to a room directly behind in the background, one can glimpse above a table with small

objects two rows of books, and above them, as far as the doorframe allows a view of it, a massive crucifix in the Gothic style. An Annunciation group near the alcove, and the Madonnas and crucifixes within it, also seem to be of Gothic origin.[181]

Goethe saw all this – obviously with great pleasure – and absorbed it.

Fig. 097 Victor Chailly, Interior of the Kesselstatt house. Another version of the painting (see fig. 096), carried out at a different time. Germanic National Museum (Germanisches Nationalmuseum), Nuremberg.

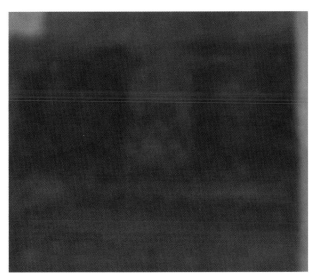

Fig. 096a Detail: the pictorial representation of the death mask (?) between two top hats on a table near the door (Mainz version).

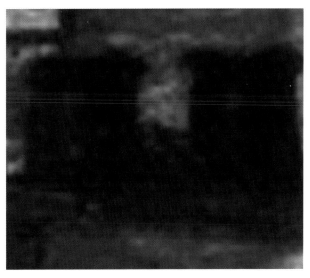

Fig. 097a Detail: pictorial representation of the death mask (?) between two top hats near the door (Nuremberg version).

The Mask in a Contemporary Painting of the Kesselstatt Collection

Before the auction of 1842 the Shakespeare death mask was in Count Kesselstatt's art collection, as is well known. Evidence of its origins in this collection has so far been provided by the statements of contemporaries,[182] and the entry in the 1842 auction catalogue: "No. 738. Male image in plaster".[183] But we now possess what is in all likelihood a further specific pointer to its presence in the Kesselstatt collection. Until now it has escaped notice that in Victor Chailly's painstakingly detailed depiction of art objects, implements, curios, and furnishings, an object can be made out which obviously represents a human face. It is to be found between two tall black top hats on a small table near the entrance on the right. The oval outline of a face is visible, a long nose, and two eye sockets filled with dark shadows. It is a face after death, very distinct from a skull. In the picture in the Mainz Landesmuseum, the face is reflected in the shiny silk material of the top hat to its right (*fig. 096 a*). In the painting in the Germanic National Museum in Nuremberg this object seems to be a little bit more outlined (*fig. 097 a*). On closer inspection the enlargement suggests that this could be Shakespeare's death mask, which had indeed been part of the collection for decades.

Guests entering the large room housing the Kesselstatt collection through the door shown on the right had to pass this small table, which stood immediately next to the doorway. It seems to have served as a hat rest. We may assume that Goethe –

who owned a cast of Torquato Tasso's death mask,[184] and so was evidently comfortable with death masks - saw this object during his visit to Kesselstatt's collection.[185] If it was indeed Shakespeare's death mask, Goethe would have had no idea of the identity of the subject. It was as concealed to him as it was to its owner. If von Kesselstatt, who loved Shakespeare and was so familiar with his works, had realised the identity of the mask's features, he would under no circumstances have kept this knowledge to himself. The writer of *Hamlet* was positively revered in Germany in the late eighteenth century. Herder's image of Shakespeare epitomises how he was seen: "If ever that tremendous image makes me think of any man: 'seated high on a rocky crag! At his feet storms, tempests, and the roaring of the sea; but his head in the beams of the heavens!' – then it is Shakespeare!"[186] Goethe himself confessed:

> The first page by him I read made me his for life, and when I had finished the first play, I stood like a man born blind given the gift of sight in an instant by a miraculous hand. I knew, I felt most vividly that my existence had been broadened to infinity [...].[187]

The Early Literature about the Mask

The information given in the early literature about the Shakespeare death mask, and repeated in print to this day, concerning the seat of the Kesselstatt family and the concentration of their total fortune – including the works of art – in the hands of the Mainz Canon Count Franz II as the last and sole surviving heir, is incorrect.

It can be traced back to the written reply of 28 February 1847 that Ludwig Becker received from the Mainz Gallery Supervisor, Müller. The conclusion drawn from Müller's erroneous information, that the Kesselstatt line had died out with the Mainz Canon, and the entire family estate had been auctioned off, was equally false. Müller's misleading information has done a good deal to underline doubts about the authenticity of the mask.

The first detailed, but incorrect, report on Franz Ludwig von Kesselstatt appeared in Friswell's monograph *Life Portraits of William Shakespeare* (1864). This report is based partly on the false information given in Müller's letter to Becker, of which the full text is reproduced in English in Friswell's book. What is more, Friswell's account contains other passages that are a complete invention:

> A German nobleman had an ancestor who was attached to one of the ambassadors accredited to the Court of King James I. This gentleman was, like many of his countrymen at a later period, a great admirer of the genius of Shakespeare, and, as a memorial of him, bought the cast, in all probability from the sculptor of the tomb, Gerard Johnson [sic], had it carefully preserved, and took it with him to his own country. There it was shown in his castle, and looked upon with much awe by his friends and neighbours.[188]

Furthermore, according to Friswill, the owner of the mask commissioned a pupil of van Dyck's to paint the miniature in oils, which had accompanied the mask ever since. Both objects, the death mask and the miniature death portrait, had remained in the family and had been passed down from generation to generation – right down to the last of his line, a church dignitary in Cologne.[189] Although it was not entirely his own fault, Friswell's totally incorrect version has done a great deal of damage, and brought the provenance of the mask into serious disrepute.

All the efforts of the Bonn anthropologist Hermann Schaaffhausen to put this right failed, although he began as early as 1874 to make crucial corrections. In his knowledgeable article, based on his own research, "*Über die Totenmaske Shakespeare's*" (On the Shakespeare death mask), where he assembled, assessed, and analysed all the facts as they were known at that time, Schaaffhausen established that: "Count von Kesselstatt, who died in Mainz in 1841, was however not the last of his line, as is often mistakenly claimed.

Neither did the family ever have their permanent seat in Cologne."[190] But Schaaffhausen's corrections failed to make an impact.

With rare exceptions, subsequent English-language research right down to the second edition of Samuel Schoenbaum's influential book *Shakespeare's Lives* (1991) relies directly or indirectly on Friswell's account, which is only partly derived from the Mainz Gallery Supervisor.

The first to refer to Friswell's account was William J. Thoms. His article "The Stratford Bust of Shakspeare" in *Notes and Queries*[191] raised two questions: "Can any reader of 'N.&Q.' […] furnish evidence of any member of the Kesselstadt family having been attached to a diplomatic mission to this country in the time of James I"; and "Can any reader of 'N.&Q.' furnish satisfactory evidence of the existence of such an admiration of Shakspeare in Germany at so early a period [i.e. the eighteenth century] as would be likely to lead a German to wish to possess a memorial of him?" While question one could not be answered at the time, it would have been easy to answer question two. It is amazing that the great, almost boundless admiration for Shakespeare in the German-speaking world in the last quarter of the eighteenth century should not have been known in nineteenth century England. Together with the celebrated Hamburg production of *Hamlet* in 1776 began the notorious so-called *Hamlet* fever, for which the way had been prepared by the circulation of the Wieland Shakespeare translation and the earlier rapturous accolades to Shakespeare from Goethe, Herder and others.

While the appeal through *Notes and Queries* failed to bear fruit, Ernst Becker, following Sir Richard Owen's advice to search specifically for the "missing link" in the history of the mask, succeeded in 1872 in tracing Josef Weismüller, the former major-domo of the Mainz Canon's household. Weismüller had looked after Count Kesselstatt's affairs in the last decade of his life, and was now manager of the estate of Calmesweiler at Buseck in the Ottweiler district. The affirmation he made in a letter of 8 July 1872 came some forty years after von Kesselstatt's death:

> With pleasure [I] hereby certify on behalf of Dr Ernst Becker of Darmstadt that Herr Franz Count von Kesselstatt, b. Trier 1753, d. Mainz 1841, travelled to England at the end of the last century, just as he travelled much in general, collecting great works of art, which were sold after his death.[192]

This declaration was received with much scepticism, and was not generally accepted – primarily, no doubt, because no precise details were provided, and the writer himself modified his statement to such an extent.

Documentary Proof of Kesselstatt's Journey to London

After roughly one hundred and fifty years, the hunt for the "missing link" in the history of the mask came to an end in early June 1995, when the author succeeded in finding the conclusive documentary evidence in the "von Kesselstatt *Depositum*" (von Kesselstatt holdings) in the Trier city archive. It was discovered in a manuscript history of the family, written by the chronicler Streitberger, in the section on the fourteenth generation, pages 218 to 220 (*fig. 098*). As this source records, the twenty-two-year-old Count Ludwig von Kesselstatt, the first known owner of the Darmstadt Shakespeare death mask, himself travelled to London in March 1775. The chronicler reports:

> After his return from Vienna, he [Count Franz Ludwig von Kesselstatt] went to Strasbourg and Nancy to improve himself, stayed there until March 1775, *and then set off on his journey to London*. [Author's emphasis][193]

During this journey Kesselstatt must have bought the death mask (*see fig. 018*) without knowing whom it represented. On the same occasion he must also have acquired the miniature oil painting with the inscription "Shakespeare" and the date "1637" (*see fig. 082*) which, as we now know, shows Ben Jonson on his deathbed.

Reading through other documents in the Kesselstatt holdings in the Trier city archives, the author was also able to establish that between the death of Shakespeare (1616) and that of Franz von Kesselstatt (1841), no member of the von Kesselstadt family was ever sent on a diplomatic or any other kind of mission to England. This is evident from annex no. 46 to the Streitberger "Family History", headed "Table of Envoys on Diplomatic and Civil Service", which lists all the ambassadors produced by the family (*fig. 099*). This precludes the possibility that the death mask might have been acquired in England much earlier by some other member of the von Kesselstatt family.

Fig. 098 Excerpt from the hand-written chronicle of the von Kesselstatt family: "von Kesselstatt holdings" ("Depositum von Kesselstatt"), Trier City Archive (Stadtarchiv Trier). This is the documentary evidence, sought for about 150 years, which proves that Count Kesselstatt, the first known owner of the Shakespeare death mask, had travelled to England at the age of 22. It was then that he must have acquired the death mask (fig. 018) and the miniature death portrait of Ben Jonson (see fig. 082). The entry reads: "After his return from Vienna, he [Franz Ludwig von Kesselstatt] went to Strasbourg and Nancy to improve himself, stayed there until March 1775, and then set off on his journey to London." The present author discovered this entry at the beginning of June 1995. If Sir Richard Owen, the famous nineteenth century anatomist at the British Museum, had been provided with a document of this kind, he would have purchased the mask for the Museum, as he has stated several times.

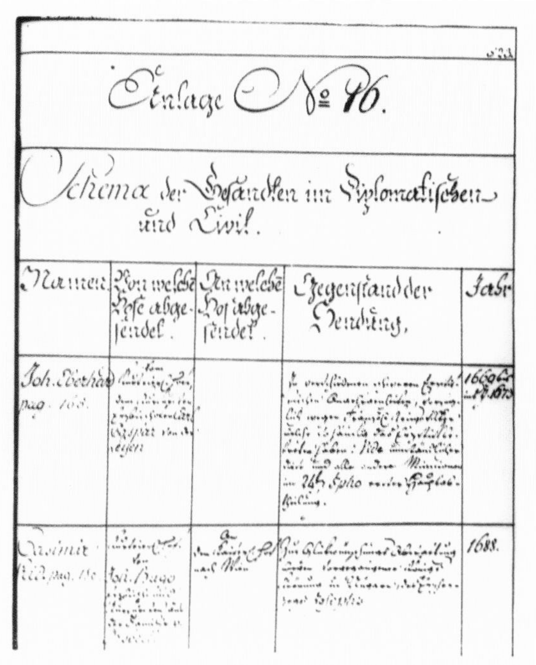

Fig 099 "Table of Envoys on Diplomatic and Civil Service". Attachment No.46 to the manuscript history of the von Kesselstatt family by the chronicler Streitberger.

The Plaster Moulder

Death masks were often taken by the sculptor himself. In the case of Shakespeare this is unlikely to have happened, because the Janssen family of sculptors were based in London. Hans Helmut Jansen and Werner Wegmann have quite reasonably conjectured that the playwright's son-in-law, the physician John Hall, may have prepared the mask.[194] If Hall treated Shakespeare in his last illness, which is highly likely, then he would also have been present after the demise of his father-in-law (with whom, moreover, he was clearly on very good terms).[195] Thus Hall is the most likely person to have moulded the plaster cast.

The Purpose of the Death Mask

The death mask had one purpose only, as was usual in the Renaissance period: it was meant to serve the sculptor Gheerart Janssen the Younger as a model for the head and face of the funerary bust of Shakespeare in the church at Stratford, which was to form the centrepiece of the monument (*see fig. 021*). The mask was never meant to be a highly prized memento, to be cherished by his relations in memory of the deceased. Thus it had no real intrinsic value, and could easily fall into oblivion.

Dating and Inscription

The results of the tests for identity and authenticity presented in Part III have shown that the death mask which was investigated was the genuine death mask of William Shakespeare. The inscription on the thick-walled back of the mask – "+ Aº D$\overline{m}$ 1616" – must therefore be regarded as correct.

Death masks had to be taken not long after the person's death, so that in Shakespeare's case too we can assume that the plaster cast from his face was prepared quite rapidly. A medical expert on death masks, Professor Hertl, having thoroughly and medically examined and also measured the mask, found on it certain specific signs that allowed him to be more precise about the timing of its preparation. In his expert report of 15 August 1997 he explained:

> The death mask was certainly not taken on the day he [the poet] died, but one or two days later. This is indicated by the presence of dried crystalline tears, about 1.5 cm in the area, which can be seen in both eyes. The

natural structure of lid and eyelashes is obscured by these sticky substances. The liquid, containing protein, is produced in the process of post-mortem decomposition and seeps for some hours from the conjunctiva, flowing slowly over the margin of the eyelid. The technique of taking a mask carefully therefore requires the corpse to be prepared. Among other things, the dried residue of tears or other traces of secretions (e.g. from the nose) must be removed before applying the plaster mixture.[196]

This medical statement leads to the conclusion that Shakespeare's death mask was taken on 24 or 25 April 1616.

THE FUNERARY BUST OF SHAKESPEARE IN THE CHURCH AT STRATFORD-UPON-AVON (1616-1617)

History

Shakespeare's funerary bust has endured many vicissitudes in its four hundred year history, the exact course of which is unclear even today. It is also unclear when, how and to what extent it was damaged and restored. Nonetheless, by drawing upon the political, religious and cultural context described in Part I, and the findings of applied methods of investigation given in Part III, an attempt will be made at a plausible reconstruction of the bust's history. Not all the vagaries that this Shakespeare image has suffered since it was erected are recorded in unambiguous written and/or visual sources. Sometimes, therefore, events and interventions will have to be taken on trust although there is no documentary evidence for them. They can be convincingly explained in terms of the background of the great political and religious conflicts of the thirties, forties and fifties of the seventeenth century, and especially of the local history of Stratford at the time of the Civil War. Further clues are provided by scattered hints among the sources, and by previously unremarked traces on the object itself and/or on copies of it.

The History of the Bust in the Seventeenth and Eighteenth Centuries

When Lieutenant Hammond went to Stratford in 1634 and visited the tomb of William Shakespeare, he was deeply impressed by the tasteful monument to the famous English poet.[197] Sir William Dugdale, who made a similar visit two years after Hammond's, was the author of the important work *The Antiquities of Warwickshire* (1656), collating and commenting on various historical sources including manuscripts, documents, tomb monuments, and coats of arms. He gives special emphasis in his book to Stratford as the town that produced the famous poet William Shakespeare, and where his bones were laid to rest.[198]

The Dugdale Engraving

When Dugdale made a drawing of Shakespeare's tomb monument in 1636, which was published in 1656 as an engraving (*fig. 100*), he created – as far as is known – the first pictorial depiction of the monument. It can give us some valuable insights into the original state of the memorial bust. At this time the sculpture must still have been undamaged. If you compare its appearance today with the Dugdale engraving, two differences can clearly be seen, the causes of which will be discussed in what follows. While the bust now has a noticeably short nose, and – correspondingly – an unusually long upper lip, the nose in the Dugdale engraving is long and prominent. Its point is slightly bent to the right. And while the bust has an unusually narrow moustache, turned upwards at the ends, the one on the Dugdale engraving is thick and luxuriant, and – extending well beyond the corners of the mouth – it turns downwards.

By 1918, the English author Charlotte Stopes in her book *Shakespeare's Environment* (2nd ed. in that year) was already pointing out the differences between the engraving and the monument.[199] Her initial conclusion about this state of affairs is right: either "Dugdale's representation was incorrect, or the tomb has been modified."[200] But the theory she goes on to elaborate, namely that the memorial bust had been radically altered in 1748/49, or had been completely replaced, fails to convince in the light of new, informed arguments. It was already being rejected as untenable by early twentieth century researchers, the leading American Shakespeare scholar B. Roland Lewis among them.[201]

It is plain from a glance at the sources on the history of the tomb bust in the seventeenth and eighteenth centuries and their contemporary historical context that there are logical explanations for the divergences between the Dugdale engraving and the bust, and – associated with them – between death mask and bust. What is known is that, threatened by decay in the first half of the eighteenth century, the whole of Shakespeare's tomb monument was thoroughly renovated in 1748/49, but that no changes were made

Fig. 100 Engraving by Sir William Dugdale (1605-1686), based on the tomb monument of William Shakespeare in the church at Stratford (sketch made in 1636). Detail: funerary bust.

to the bust, except for a new coat of paint. This was reliably confirmed by the Stratford schoolmaster and antiquary, the Reverend Joseph Greene, who as a contemporary witness plays a key role in this attempted reconstruction of historic events around Shakespeare's funerary bust.

In the context of his mammoth undertaking of recording and describing the antiquities of Warwickshire, Dugdale may only have had a relatively short time to spare for his sketch of the Shakespeare monument. In the drawing he made on the spot, he seems not to have included details he obviously regarded as unimportant. But there is no doubt that the energetic antiquary did study closely – as far as the conditions under which he was working permitted – Shakespeare's facial features and went on to reproduce them astonishingly well. Hence their explanatory usefulness within the framework of testing Shakespeare images for identity and authenticity.

Among the items that Dugdale obviously omitted in his preliminary sketch, and that were only added in - without the benefit of a model - some twenty years later when the copperplate was engraved, were the attendant figures and the cushion. The only part of the monument's important inscriptions celebrating the author that he captured were the first two words of the Latin text, "IVDICIO PYLIVM".[202] The attendant figures on the architrave differ so fundamentally from those of the original monument, that they cannot possibly have been sketched *in situ*. Furthermore, on the original monument they serve particular symbolic functions (see pp. 40–1), and fit harmoniously into the architecture as a whole, whereas in the Dugdale engraving they make more of a decorative impression. So it is plausible to suggest that the antiquary may have added them from memory, or caused them to be added. The representation of the cushion in the Dugdale engraving needs particular discussion.

The Cushion in the Dugdale Engraving

The fundamental divergence of the cushion in the Dugdale engraving (*see fig. 100*) in shape and size from that in the original monument, which shows the writer sitting in front of a writing cushion, immediately presents a very striking contradiction which demands some explanation.

The English commentator Charlotte Stopes noticed this discrepancy back at the beginning of the twentieth century. She described casually how "the hands [of the poet] are laid stiffly […] on a large cushion, suspiciously resembling a *woolsack*".[203] Stopes did great damage with this ironical remark, by giving ammunition to those who (following Delia Bacon), though lacking valid reasons, wanted to throw doubt on Shakespeare's authorship (see Part V, p. 131 and n.3) and now saw the supposed woolsack as a welcome sign of his "true" profession.

The cushion in the Dugdale engraving is indeed over-large, and looks puffed up. It shows – as the present author's comparisons of pictures have shown – clear similarities to the normal style of pillow on English beds in the 1630s. We can see such a pillow, for example, in the family scene painted in 1635 by the artist John Crouch of Chester, depicting Thomas Aston and his family gathered around the deathbed of his wife, who died in childbirth. There is no overlooking the fact that the Dugdale engraving shows a normal pillow of the day.[204]

The error can only be explained by assuming that – for whatever reason – Dugdale left the cushion out of his drawing in 1636, just as he omitted other details.

Fig. 101 Early plaster copy of the Shakespeare tomb bust in Stratford, National Portrait Gallery, London. Detail: funerary bust.

The engraver, working twenty years later from the sketch, may well never have seen Shakespeare's monument. All he may have known was that the writer's hands were resting on a cushion, which explains the above mistake.

Joseph Greene, the Stratford schoolmaster notorious for his punctiliousness, confirmed in 1749 that the Dugdale engraving is wrong about the shape of the cushion, and that what appears on the original monument is indeed a writing cushion. It was in that year that he wrote a lengthy letter to an Oxford college friend, mentioning in connection with the cushion in front of Shakespeare's tomb bust that it looked as though the writer was preparing to write on this cushion "as though at a desk" (see p. 122).

What an authentic writing or book rest on a scholar's tomb monument actually looked like in the second decade of the seventeenth century is evident from the tomb memorial, reproduced in Part I, of Bishop Giles Tomson in St George's Chapel in Windsor Castle (*see fig. 008*), which exactly matches that on the Shakespeare monument (*see fig. 021*).

An Early Plaster Copy of the Funerary Bust

Apart from the Dugdale engraving, there is another piece of evidence that can provide further information about the original appearance of the Stratford bust. The plaster copy of the tomb sculpture, dating from 1851 and housed in the National Portrait Gallery in London, was obviously made from an early copy of the original (*fig. 101*).[205] The nose and moustache of this plaster copy basically correspond to those of the authentic representations of the poet (*see figs. 014, 016, 017, and 018*). The growth of the moustache is as thick as that on the death mask, but it turns down rather less at the ends than in the Dugdale engraving, where the moustache seems to dip too acutely (*see fig. 100*). It extends far beyond the corner of the mouth on the left side, and is noticeably longer than on the right side.

The Initiative by John Ward, London Theatre Owner, to Renovate the Shakespeare Tomb Monument

It was the London theatre owner John Ward who in 1746 successfully advocated the renovation of the Shakespeare tomb monument that was urgently needed by the early eighteenth century.[206] Ward had arranged with the parish council that he would put on a Shakespeare play in Stratford, and donate the takings to the church wardens for repairs to the Shakespeare monument. *Othello* was performed on 9 September 1746. The playbill reads:

> […] as the Curious Original Monument and Bust of that incomparable Poet, erected above the Tomb that enshrines his Dust in the Church of *Stratford upon Avon Warwickshire*, Is through length of Years and other accidents become much impair'd and decay'd: An offer has been kindly made by the Judicious and much Esteem'd MR. JOHN WARD, and his Company, To Act one of SHAKESPEARE'S PLAYS, *Viz.*[207]

Discussions among the Contributors about the Restoration of the Shakespeare Monument by the Painter John Hall

A meeting was arranged for 25 November 1748 in the market hall at Stratford of "those persons who contributed for ye repairing of Shakespear's Monument" to confer and agree on "a proper method of repairing and beautifying the Monument".[208] The painter John Hall was engaged to carry out the work. He was to be paid £16 for the repair or restoration of the memorial, "provided he takes care, according to his Ability, that ye Monument shall become as like as possible to what it was when first Erected". However, according to another document with a similar text, signed by the participants, the meeting did not take place until 10 December 1748 in the Falcon in Stratford, directly opposite New Place, where Shakespeare had lived.[209] But the Reverend Kendrick, vicar of Holy Trinity, was not happy with the text prepared on 30 November 1748: in his opinion it did not define precisely what work John Hall was meant to carry out. Kendrick proceeded to draw up a version of his own. On 10 December 1748, all concerned finally signed the prepared document.[210] Unfortunately, this too fails to spell out what work on the bust and the monument had actually been contracted for with the artist:

> On Saturday Ev'ning about 9 o'clock at Lilly's at the Falcon. Mr Kenwrick having exhibited a paper signifying what Mr Hall was to do, & of what materials to repair ye monument of Shakespeare, he propos'd y^t Mr Hall & Mr Spur shou'd sign that agreement, ye Former y^t he might be oblig'd to do ye work in a compleat manner; & ye latter, that upon its being finish'd, he shou'd pay to Mr Hall ye sum of Twelve pounds ten shillings […]. [211]

Statements of the Stratford Cleric, Schoolmaster and Antiquary Joseph Greene on the Materials used in the Shakespeare Funerary Monument

The Stratford schoolmaster and antiquary, the Rev. Joseph Greene, who has frequently been mentioned here, assisted Rev. Kendrick as a clerk and was also one of the witnesses to the contract. On 27 September 1749, by request, he sent his old friend from Oxford an account of the original materials used in the Shakespeare monument. We have Greene to thank for some extremely useful information on this subject. He also reported on the replacement material used for the repairs, and the appearance and state of the tomb monument after its restoration:

> You wanted me to inform you of what *materials* ye Original Monument of Shakespeare in ye chancel of our Collegiate church was compos'd. Having had, since I saw you, a favourable opportunity (never perhaps to be repeated,) of seeing & examining the figure of the Bard, when taken down from his niche to be more commodi-

ously cleans'd from dust, &c; I can assure you that the Bust & cushion before it, (on which as on a desk this our Poet seems preparing to write,) is one entire lime-stone, naturally of a blueish or ash-colour'd casts, yet of a texture & solidity almost equal to common marble, which could be had from no quarry in our neighbourhood, except from a village call'd Wilmcote,[212] a few miles from Stratford, & which kind of stone is generally us'd for paving Halls, or ground rooms; though a finer sort, which lies deeper in the same quarry, is truly a marble, & takes a polish sufficiently beautiful for chimney pieces, even for persons of high distinction.[213]

Greene's account also contains the first useful detailed description of the Shakespeare monument:

> The two columns which support the entablatures & ornaments above the Bust, as well as the interior tables of their pedestals, are of black polished marble, if not of jet:[214] the capitals & basis of the columns, (which are of the Corinthian order, & gilded,) are of common free or sand stone; and so are the two painted naked boys, emblems of Tragedy & Comedy, which sit one on each side [on] ye upper compartment which exhibits his [Shakespeare's] coat of arms; as is also the scull, tho' not gilded, which forms the apex of the monument.[215]

The writer goes on to detail the state of the alabaster architraves ("the old architraves being much shatter'd and decay'd"), which have now been replaced with marble,[216] and states in his summary that, as far as possible, no changes had been made to the monument:

> In repairing the whole, (which was done early in ye current year by contribution of ye neighbourhood,) care was taken, as nearly as could be, not to add to or diminish what the work consisted of, and appear'd to have been when first erected: And really, except changing the substance of the architraves from alabaster to marble; nothing *has* been chang'd *nothing* alter'd, except ye supplying with ye original materials, (sav'd for that purpose,) whatsoever was by accident broken off; reviving the old colouring, and renewing the gilding that was lost.[217]

Greene's account leaves no doubt that during the restoration of 1748/49 no steps were taken that would have changed, let alone distorted the bust. Unfortunately, however, he offers no explanation for the monument's serious state of disrepair after a mere

130 years of existence. He also withholds information about exactly what parts of the monument had been broken off "by accident", as he says, and restored using the original materials. Regrettably, the artist John Hall submitted no official account of his restoration work, either.

All the same, we can assume that the meticulous account given by Greene, together with his assurance that no changes were made, are absolutely reliable.[218] The cleric and schoolmaster witnessed the proceedings in person and would certainly have reported any invasive steps - such as re-chiselling the broken-off nose or the likewise broken-off or damaged moustache - had they been taken.

In the light of this source, there is no doubt that the change in the appearance of the bust must have happened considerably earlier. This is precisely what a contemporary painting confirms.

John Hall's Pictorial Representation of the Shakespeare Monument before its Restoration in 1748/1749

John Hall, the artist commissioned to restore the monument, made a painting of the bust in 1748 – quite clearly before he began the work of restoration, and in order to document its state at that time (*fig. 102*).[219] The picture measures 48.26 x 33.02 cm, and is in the keeping of the Shakespeare Birthplace Trust in Stratford-upon-Avon. The appearance of the bust in Hall's painting basically accords with the way it looks today, i.e. in comparison with the Dugdale engraving, it already has the altered moustache and the shortened nose.

The art historian Spielmann tells us that this picture was displayed in 1910 on permanent loan from the Duke of Warwick, accompanied by the caption "showing the monument practically as it is today". On the back of the painting Spielmann found a note by the Shakespeare scholar Halliwell-Phillipps, quoted by Spielmann:

> This old painting of the monumental effigy of Shakespeare is of great curiosity, being the one painted by Hall *before he recoloured the bust* in 1748. The letters proving this are in the possession of Richard Greene, Esq., F.S.A., who presented them some years ago to *Fraser's Magazine*. I purchased the picture of Mr. Greene, who is the lineal descendant of the Rev. Joseph Greene of Stratford, the owner of the painting of about 1770. J. O. Halliwell.[220]

Fig. 102 A painting by John Hall, based on the funerary bust of William Shakespeare, apparently created before 1748.

To this, Spielmann adds simply: "I think we can leave the matter here [...]."[221]

As the present author's research has established, Hall's painting really was owned by the Reverend Greene. This is apparent from Greene's letter of 28 February 1787 to his brother and confidant Richard Greene, an apothecary in Litchfield. Joseph Greene writes:

> About 40 years ago, an ingenious limner from Bristol,[222] of the name of Hall, being at Stratford on a visit to an acquaintance, M[r] West y[e] elder,[223] if I mistake not, employ'd him to copy the Original Monument of Shakespear in y[e] Chancel of Stratford Church, with its several architectural decorations, such as its columns, entablatures, &c[224]

Greene goes on to tell his brother that the painter's client seemed not to value the outcome very highly:

> This little painting of our great Bard in his Monument, which is executed only on Pasteboard, seem'd in length of time to be disregarded by M[r] West; for after it had

been toss'd about & injured, not having any frame or guard to it, the old Gentleman, (ignorant I had one painted by M[r] Grubb of Stratford,) without asking for it, freely gave it to me, & I have for a considerable time had it in my possession.[225]

The letter also reveals that the Reverend Greene gave the painting by Hall to his brother, keeping Grubb's himself:

> I have often had thoughts of sending it to you, cou'd I have guess'd it wou'd be worth your acceptance; but having lately considered it is not so far damaged, as to prevent M[r] Stringer's easily setting it to rights, I will send it to you as a small Gift, there being nothing wanting but y[e] Apex, or top part of y[e] Monument, w[ch] was a human scull, now worn away with y[e] pasteboard.[226]

If Greene fulfilled his promise and sent the gift, as he probably did, then Hall's painting cannot - as Halliwell-Phillipps thought - have been owned by Richard Greene, the descendant of the Stratford schoolmaster. The owner must in fact have been the grandson of Joseph Greene's brother Richard, who, like Joseph Greene's son and grandson, was also called Richard.[227]

It is surprising that the Stratford schoolmaster and antiquary was prepared to part with John Hall's picture, which was older and shows the condition of the bust immediately before its restoration, but chose to keep the view of the monument painted by Grubb. Grubb was only born in 1740, so he would have been too young to have created the picture before the restoration of the monument (1748/49). It is apparent from his biography that he could not have painted it before 1774.[228]

These particulars show that Hall's painting, once presented as a gift, stayed in the possession of the apothecary Richard Greene's family, and was handed down by them. Halliwell-Phillipps must therefore have obtained it from the Richard Greene who was the grandson of the apothecary.

The Secret Cast Mould Taken by Joseph Greene from the Funerary Bust of Shakespeare

Joseph Greene's great admiration for Shakespeare led him to use means that were at some points – strictly speaking – beyond the bounds of legality. Before the Shakespeare monument was restored in 1748, the Stratford schoolmaster secretly had a plaster mould taken from it. It was not until twenty-five years later that he told his brother Richard about it, promised him the mould, and asked him for a cast in return. In his letter of 30 October 1773 he writes:

> In the year 1748 the Original Monument of Shakespeare in the Chancel of Stratford Church was repair'd & beautifi'd; as I previously consider'd that when that work should be finish'd no money or favour would procure what I wanted, namely a mould from ye carv'd face of the Poet; I therefore, with a Confederate, about a month before the intended reparation, took a good Mould in plaster of Paris from the Carving, which I now have by me, & if you will promise I shall have one plaister cast from it (for ye materials & trouble of procuring which I will most willingly pay,) the mould shall become yours, & upon your mentioning in what manner it may be safely conveyed, shall with ye first convenience be sent to you.[229]

It was not until about a year later, with a covering letter dated 15 September 1774, that Greene sent his brother the mould. He did not even mention to his family his unauthorised taking of a plaster mould of the bust.[230] On 14 November 1776 he mentions the cast (now made), and with a side-swipe at the Shakespeare monument in Westminster Abbey designed by William Kent (1685-1748) and carried out by Peter Scheemakers (1691-1782), he remarks:

> I think a bust from the Original Monument, as yours is, must be much more valuable & satisfactory, than one from his pompous Caenotaph in Westminster Abbey; which latter, [...] though in a venerable & majestic attitude, is more likely to represent Methuselah, than our Poet, who died at ye age of 53 [sic].

Greene's letter of 9 October 1777 shows that by this time he has obtained the desired cast. He praises it - "very neat and perfect" - and believes it "may pass for a Unique, as the Virtuosi term it, and consequently be of no small estimation".[231]

Around 1757, together with the Stratford sculptor Heath, Greene made for his former employer James West[232] an extremely carefully executed cast of the Shakespeare bust, as indicated by his letter to West of 16 January 1758:

> If Mr Rysbrack carves your Shakespeare from ye Mask you had of me, I am very sure it answers exactly to our

original Bust: for Heath ye Carver & I took it down from ye Chancel wall, & laid it exactly in a horizontal posture before we made ye Cast, which we executed with much care, so that no slipping of the Materials could occasion ye unnatural distance in the face with he mentions.[233]

This 'unnatural distance' in the features can only refer to that between the upper lip of the mucous membrane and the beginning of the nose (see p. 49, and *figs. 027 and 028*).

West subsequently commissioned the sculptor John Michael Rhysbrack (1694-1770) to make a bust of Shakespeare which was to be based upon this cast; the latter is now in Alscot near Preston-on-Stour. The bust, executed in marble, is in the Birmingham City Art Gallery. It is not quite clear whether Rhysbrack used Greene's cast. But he certainly made use of other sources, including the Chandos portrait.

Unfortunately the mould taken by Joseph Greene immediately *before* the restoration of 1748 has not survived or has not been identified, as far as is known. This also applies to the cast that his brother Richard made from the mould, as well as to the copies allegedly made from the head of the bust from 1737 onwards, and the one made in 1737 for the English antiquary George Vertue.[234]

Until Greene's 1748 plaster cast of the funerary bust of Shakespeare is found, and/or the other early casts come to light or are identified, we have to rely on Joseph Greene's written evidence that the renovation of the Shakespeare monument changed nothing; in other words, that *before* the restoration of 1748 the Shakespeare bust already looked as it does today.

If this is the case, the question remains as to when and under what circumstances the bust was seriously damaged, and at what point the damage was repaired.

As far as we know, there was only one repair of the Shakespeare monument before the renovation of 1748. It took place in 1649, in the year the English Civil War ended, Oliver Cromwell came to power, and King Charles I was executed.

M. H. Spielmann thought the monument had undergone little treatment at this time: "In 1649 – nearly thirty years after it was erected – the bust was as it was called 're-beautified', that is to say, repainted in its colours, for the church was damp, and the painted figure and its shrine had suffered".[235] This account seems improbable. After all, when Hammond and Dugdale visited the monument in the 1630s it was in very good condition (*see fig. 100*). It seems more likely, therefore, that Shakespeare's bust, like many other busts, statues, pictures etc, was damaged by fanatical Puritan iconoclasts, and that this damage was repaired – as far as it could be – in 1649.

On the Iconoclasm of the Puritans in the Civil War and under Cromwell's regime

Among the most important contemporary witnesses to report on the iconoclasm of the English Puritans, thus preserving valuable historical details from oblivion, was John Aubrey, frequently mentioned here. He saw these details as "fragments of a shipwreck": "These Remaines are *tanquam Tabulata Naufragy* that after the Revolution of so many Years and Governments [sic] have escaped the Teeth of Time and (which is more dangerous) the Hands of mistaken Zeale."[236] In his introduction to Aubrey's *Brief Lives*, the editor Oliver Lawson Dick says that: "It was against Idolatry [however] that the fury of the Puritans was chiefly turned […]."[237] He goes on to say that: "[…] the Puritans, having achieved power, set about their iconoclasm with such a will that Aubrey noted sadly 'that there is not a piece of glass-painting left'. […] When the glass was finished, the zealots turned their attention to the altars and statues (fig. 103),[238] the vestments, painted tombs and organs […]."[239] Apart from these objects, valuable books and manuscripts also fell prey to fanatical iconoclasm. Quite often the destruction was carried out by specially recruited demolition squads.

After Cromwell became Lord Protector of England in 1653, iconoclasm was organised and taken to extremes throughout the country. In practically every church altars, communion requisites, crucifixes, icons etc were smashed. The theatres had been closed since 1642, but they were now pulled down. Cromwell sold King Charles's valuable collection of paintings to France. Today they are in the Louvre. Furious vengeance was wreaked upon these "inanimate offenders" (statues, busts, and images), among which may well have been Shakespeare's bust, given that he was the arch-representative of the theatre that was anathema to the Puritans and given that parliamentarian as well as royalist troops were accommodated in Holy Trinity church in Stratford.

Fig. 103 "Calvinists destroying statues of the saints and communion requisites", engraving by Frans Hogenberg from the second half of the sixteenth century.

Stratford-upon-Avon at the Time of the English Civil War and the First Repair of the Bust

Shakespeare's birthplace was not spared the turmoil and ravages of the Civil War. In fact, battle raged particularly violently in and around the town, and the soldiers of both sides wrought great destruction.[240] In 1642 parliamentary troops raided the country seat of the Catholic Sir Robert Throckmorton at Coughton Court (Warwickshire), looting and destroying pictures and Catholic books. In 1643 Stratford-upon-Avon was hit particularly hard. Royalists and parliamentarians took turns with each other in the town. Destruction and plundering were the order of the day. The old market hall was badly damaged by an explosion. In May 1644 royalist soldiers forced their way into New Place, the home of Shakespeare's daughter Susanna, and in early 1645 raided the houses of the landed gentry and rampaged through Stratford, where the plague was breaking out at the same time. In May 1645 parliamentary troops occupied the area around Stratford. After their victory at Naseby they streamed into the town and its environs. In 1645 the only bridge in Stratford (Clopton Bridge) was demolished in order to deny the royalists access to the west of the country. In January 1646 many Stratford burghers reported their losses in the Civil War to the authorities in Coventry. Shakespeare's family, though equally affected, refrained from doing so. During 1646 troops under Col. Thomas Morgan were billeted in and around Stratford, and there was more looting. Soldiers on both sides used the church as a barracks; the town offered no other accommodation for troops, after all, and it was a practice followed everywhere. Mrs Charlotte Stopes made this point early in the twentieth century, and was also the first to mention the damage done in Stratford by Parliamentary forces during the Civil War.[241]

Against this background, even in the absence of written evidence it is hard to imagine that Shakespeare's monument could have remained unscathed. Shakespeare's house, New Place, was under attack before the Civil War. In connection with a legal dispute, in 1637 Alderman Baldwin Brooks and a number of under-sheriffs broke into New Place and seized from "the poet's 'Study of books' [...] Divers bookes boxes Deskes moneys bonds bills and other goods of greate value [...]".[242]

Stopes thought the bust might have been damaged even before the Civil War, pointing out that the vicar of Holy Trinity, Reverend Thomas Wilson, had misused the church for secular purposes in the 1630s. She says that he allowed his maids to dry their linen, roast chicken, and keep pigs and dogs there.[243] The church had also been desecrated by children using it as a playground.

However, the present author does not think that wanton attacks on the bust would have been very likely at this period, although it may have suffered from minor accidents. But they would not be enough to explain the considerable damage the bust must have sustained.

In reality we appear to be looking at repairs to the bust following upon damage intentionally inflicted by Puritan fanatics during the Civil War. As mentioned above, Stratford was one of the centres of the war; it saw heavy fighting, with parliamentary and royalist troops successively marching in, looting, and inflicting great damage. Thus it is quite reasonable and easy to conceive that Puritan zealots, for whom statues and busts in churches were despicable "inanimate offenders" that ought to be eradicated, carried out violent attacks on Shakespeare's bust between 1642 and 1649.

Having established that extensive repairs to the bust can no longer be dated at 1748 but should rather be placed in the year 1649, we must also assume that the damage did indeed come about during the Civil War at the hands of raging iconoclasts, who no doubt deliberately attacked in particular the monument of William Shakespeare, whose plays they regarded as reprehensible, and who in their eyes had led astray both king and country.[244]

This gives rise to the following scenario: during one or more attacks the head of the bust may have been violently struck off. J. Parker Norris pointed out as long ago as 1885 in *The Portraits of Shakespeare* that the back of the head displays an "indentation".[245] By 1911 the head was still resting loosely on the bust, as Paul Wislicenus pointed out in his essay of that year, "*Zur Untersuchung von Shakespeares Totenmaske*" (Investigating the Shakespeare death mask), referring to a remark to this effect by Canon Melville, at that time the clergyman in charge of Holy Trinity Church. It was for that reason that Wislicenus and the German sculptor who accompanied him in 1911, Robert Cauer, were warned by Canon Melville to be particularly careful in their handling of the bust.[246]

Assuming that the head did hit the stone floor of the chancel, then no doubt the nose and moustache broke off with the impact. The damage, clearly indicating a wilful attack, must have been repaired in 1649 because we know that was the only year in which work was carried out on the monument. Further, this was the year in which other Civil War damage in Stratford was reported and repaired. The restorer obviously made the best of a bad job by re-chiselling the remains of the formerly long nose and what was left of the moustache, previously large and with a downward slant.

The original appearance of the nose and moustache before the Civil War can be seen not only in the Dugdale engraving (*see fig. 100*), an early copy of the bust (*see fig. 101*), and the Droeshout engraving (*see fig. 023*), but also in the authentic Shakespeare images created at first hand: the Chandos and Flower portraits, the Davenant bust, and the death mask (*see figs. 014, 016, 017 and 018*).

The damage and makeshift repairs to the bust altered its expression, very much to the detriment of the poet: it now looked crude and unsophisticated, and not at all like that of a genius.

If the first restoration did take place in 1649 (and everything points to it), it can only have been commissioned by Shakespeare's family. The poet's son-in-law, Dr John Hall, had already fallen victim to an epidemic in 1635; the first husband of his granddaughter, Thomas Nash, had died in 1647, and his eldest daughter Susanna Hall died on 11 July 1649. It is therefore likely that Shakespeare's granddaughter, Elizabeth Nash, took the initiative to repair the Shakespeare monument. After her mother's death she was the sole heir to the Shakespeare estate. On 5 June 1649 Elizabeth had married Sir John Bernard, who had been knighted by Charles I. She only moved with him to Abington in Northamptonshire in 1653, so that she was present in Stratford to arrange her mother's funeral in June 1649, and later in the year no doubt also the repair of the damaged funerary monument to her grandfather, high above the graves of the family in the chancel.[247] Certainly she was the only person who could have had a personal interest in doing so.

We have no record of the difficulties the first, nameless restorer of the bust had to contend with. He was probably not familiar with the original appearance of the bust, and therefore an accurate historical reconstruction could not be expected, even if it had been technically possible. So the restorer must have struggled within the means available to him, and without any model of the original, to carry out the makeshift repairs to the monument described above, and especially to the face of the bust.

The Verdict of Nineteenth and Twentieth Century Scholars on Shakespeare's Funerary Bust

As discussed in Part III, in the course of the nineteenth and twentieth centuries the appearance of the bust attracted occasional criticism from Shakespeare scholars. We have just seen that there were solid grounds for this critique. But it can also be demonstrated on the basis of this book's findings that – apart from the discrepancies already explained – it authentically reproduces the poet's features.

The Fate of the Stratford Bust in the Late Twentieth Century

In October 1973 the funerary bust of Shakespeare was once again subject to attack. But what at first appeared to be an act of vandalism was later viewed by the authorities – as reflected in press statements at the time – as a deliberate but vain search for Shakespeare's manuscripts.[248] Samuel Schoenbaum, the American Shakespeare biographer, was in Stratford at the time, and reports seeing the bust standing on the floor shortly after the break-in. In a footnote to his book *William Shakespeare. A Documentary Life* (1975) he tells us: "The bust, which I examined shortly after the incident, sustained only very slight damage, and has since been put back into its place."[249] In his lecture to the International Shakespeare Congress in Berlin in 1986, Schoenbaum once again reassured Shakespeare scholars from all over the world that, apart for slight damage to its plinth, the bust had emerged unharmed from the intrusion.[250]

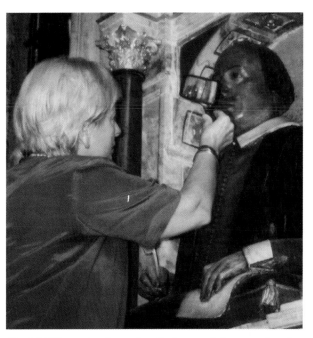

Fig. 104 The author inspecting Shakespeare's funerary bust in Stratford-upon-Avon in July 1996.

Fig. 105 Older, much darkened copy of the original funerary bust of Shakespeare in Holy Trinity Church, Stratford-upon-Avon, touched up in several places with new paint in a makeshift way.

However, when I inspected Shakespeare's funerary bust in 1996 (*fig. 104*), I noticed significant differences between the bust I saw then and the one that had occupied the wall-niche in Holy Trinity Church before 1968, which I had seen for the first time in August of 1964.[251] A documentary photograph of the bust dating from before 1968, obviously featuring the original sculpture, was reproduced in *The Life and Times of Shakespeare* and was used in all my investigations of authenticity to date (as it was for the Chandos and Flower portraits, the Davenant bust, and the Darmstadt death mask (*see fig. 021*).[252] My meticulous comparative examination of specific parts of the face, the hands, and the clothing, especially the collar, produced results which led me to the conclusion that the objects reproduced are not identical, and that the bust scrutinized in the niche of the chancel in 1996 was clearly an old, dirty and much darkened copy of the original, which in several places had been superficially repainted, but without completely covering up the old underlying grime (*fig. 105*). The most striking proof that we are dealing with two different objects is provided by the condition of the right hand. While the original bust – as written sources also attest – lacks a few fingers, which have been broken off (*fig. 106*), the fingers of the right hand on the bust photographed in 1996 are intact (*fig. 107*). The idea that there is a link with the intrusion of 1973 suggests itself. It is at that point that the original could have been replaced by a copy. When Samuel Schoenbaum stated that the bust was unharmed after the break-in, he had not carried out a comparison with reproductions of the object as it had looked before 1968. It is therefore not improbable that he was looking at a copy which – lacking opportunities for comparison – he took to be the original.

The noted English journalist and author Simon Jenkins also remarked on the dark coloration of Shakespeare's funerary bust while visiting Stratford in connection with his research for the book he published in 1999: *England's Thousand Best Churches*. Standing beneath the playwright's monument, Jenkins did not hold this detail back. With a wink to his readers, he drew attention to the "sunburnt" portrait of the poet,[253] for which, however, there may now be an explanation.

The Sculptor

The creator of the Shakespeare tomb monument was – as stated earlier (see p. 41) – the English sculptor of Dutch extraction, Gheerart Janssen the Younger.

Fig. 106 Detail of fig. 021: The Fingers on the right hand of the original funerary bust in the Holy Trinity Church at Stratford-upon-Avon. Photograph taken before 1968. While the original bust – as written sources also attest – lacks a few fingers, which have been broken off, the fingers of the right hand on the copy of the bust - photographed in 1996 - are intact (see fig. 107).

Fig. 107 Detail of fig. 105: Fingers of the right hand of the older copy of the original funerary bust of Shakespeare. Here the fingers are intact. Photographed by the author in 1996.

The Model used by the Sculptor

Gheerart Janssen must have employed the Darmstadt death mask as the model for the funerary bust of Shakespeare, as the tests of identity and authenticity have shown. This model possessed no intrinsic value, but was indispensable to the sculptor; only by using it could he achieve an exact likeness of the poet carved out of stone. The death mask may have been handed over to him when he received the commission. After serving its purpose, it probably stayed in the Janssens' workshop, where it could easily have been forgotten.[254]

The Client and the Fee

It can be taken for granted that the Shakespeare monument was commissioned by the executors of his will nominated by Shakespeare himself: his daughter Susanna Hall and his son-in-law Dr John Hall. The cost of the comparatively simple monument to John Combe was estimated in the latter's will at £60, so we can assume that Shakespeare's monument cost considerably more, being executed in an imposing Renaissance style, with additional figures and reliefs, and with valuable marble-type limestone being used for the bust, while materials for the other sections included black marble and alabaster (see pp. 120–22). The appointments and cost of the Shakespeare monument therefore corresponded to the higher social rank of the writer, also indicated by the inclusion of his family coat of arms and crest.[255]

Roughly a quarter of a century earlier, on 16 October 1591, Gheerart Janssen the Elder had been paid £200 in all for the execution and erecting of a prestigious tomb monument to the Earl of Rutland in Bottesford.[256] By this yardstick, and even allowing for inflation, the cost of the Shakespeare monument was probably not greater than £100.

By far the most expensive tomb monument in England in the first half of the seventeenth century was that of the Spencers in the church at Great Brington (near Althorp in Northamptonshire), created by the most prominent English sculptor of the day, Nicholas Stone. The cost was £600.[257] Among the family members buried there are Lord William Spencer and his wife, Lady Penelope Spencer[258].

Dating

Gheerart Janssen probably completed Shakespeare's monument in 1616 or 1617, and placed it against the left wall of the chancel in Holy Trinity Church in Stratford. It was usual in the late sixteenth and early seventeenth centuries that monuments of this kind were erected within a year. This period of time was generally agreed by contract, or laid down in the will. Thus the Stratford citizen John Combe, who died in 1614 (*see fig. 022*), ordained in his last testament that his tomb monument must be installed within a year in the church of his home town.

THE DROESHOUT ENGRAVING IN THE FIRST
FOLIO EDITION (1623)

The Various States of the Droeshout Engraving

The Droeshout engraving exists in three different states: states I, II, and III.[259] State I is the proof stage, and there are at least three copies still extant. They are in the Folger Shakespeare Library in Washington, the Bodleian Library in Oxford, and the British Museum.[260] In six or more copies of the First Folio, the engraving is reproduced in state II. All other copies of the first edition and all other editions of the Folio (see p. 44) show it in state III.[261]

Proofs were made either by the artist himself, or under his supervision. They would tell him (sometimes in consultation with his client) whether the results were satisfactory, or whether further changes were needed before the plate was handed over to a professional printer.[262]

In the case of the Droeshout engraving, corrections were carried out after the proof impressions were taken,[263] although there is no way of knowing whether at the behest of the client or on the engraver's own initiative.

One of the most noticeable divergences from state I was the addition of the shadow on the subject's collar (see p. 90). However, before Spielmann observed this in the early twentieth century, it had already been noted in the nineteenth century by William Page, among others. Page was a sculptor, and President of the New York Academy of Design: he was intensely preoccupied with the Shakespeare images, and especially with the original of the death mask in Darmstadt (see p. 35f.). Page spotted that the so-called "Halliwell Droeshout proof" differed from the well-known engraving in the printed edition of the First Folio in 1623 – chiefly because of the more natural-seeming treatment of the features. Halliwell's Droeshout, thought to be the first print impression ("Unique Proof") taken from the Droeshout plate, was named after its first known owner, the English collector and Shakespeare expert James Orchard Halliwell-Phillips (1820-1899). It passed into the hands of the American industrialist and collector of Shakespeare memorabilia, Henry Clay Folger (1857-1930), whose collection of early Shakespeare editions is among the most valuable in the world. Today the Halliwell "Proof" – together with Henry Folger's Shakespeare collection – is in the Folger Shakespeare Library in Washington DC. The American Shakespeare scholar J. Parker Norris in his book *The Portraits of Shakespeare* (1885) documented the differences between this proof print and state III, as noted by William Page.[264]

A further change noticeable in state III as against Halliwell's Droeshout was observed by the present author in connection with the medical assessments of the signs of disease visible in the Shakespeare images. It occurred in the nasal corner of the left eye. The engraver had at first – as the "Unique Proof" reveals – shown slight protuberances which correspond to those in the authentic Shakespeare images, but he omitted these in state III.

The Engraver

Since the creator of the engraving printed in 1623 in the First Folio Edition is announced at bottom left in the inscription "Martin Droeshout sculpsit London", the name of the engraver was never in doubt. It must have been Martin Droeshout the Younger, however.[265]

The Engraver's Model

From what has been said in part III (pp. 44ff.) it is clear that the young Droeshout must have used an authentic image of the dramatist for his portrait engraving of Shakespeare, as was usual at that time. This assumption is further reinforced by certain details of the Halliwell proof print. The model must have been – as set out in the sub-section above, "The sequence of Flower portrait and Droeshout engraving" (see p. 90) – the Flower portrait, painted in 1609.

The Client

In their informative address "To the great Variety of Readers" with which they prefaced the First Folio Edition in 1623, Shakespeare's close friends and fellow actors John Heminge and Henry Condell tell us that their reason for undertaking the editing of the work was that, because of his early death, it was not granted to the author William Shakespeare to edit his writings and supervise their publication:

> It had bene a thing, we confesse, worthie to haue bene wished, that the Author himselfe [William Shakespeare] had liu'd to have set forth, and ouerseen his owne writings ; But since it hath bin ordain'd otherwise, and he by death departed from that right, we pray you do not envie his Friends, the office of their care, and paine, to haue collected & publish'd them.[266]

It was surely Shakespeare himself who asked his close friends to perform this friendly service for him in the event of his early demise. This is apparent from a passage in his will. [267]

The dramatist left Heminge, Burbage, and Condell money for rings which – as it seems – were not meant to be simply mementos, but to signify their wearers'

pledge to keep faith with him. It is clear that Shakespeare must have had a very particular desire to preserve and protect his intellectual property by the careful and conscientious publication of his plays. Since this is precisely what Heminge and Condell did – on behalf of their deceased friend Shakespeare – and since they specifically stress that he himself was prevented from death by doing so, we can surely assume that they had made such a promise to Shakespeare. Richard Burbage, Shakespeare's closest friend, died an early death in 1619, too soon to have taken part in the enterprise.

Heminge and Condell carried out their editorial role under very difficult conditions, and with the greatest care and conscientiousness. In their addresss "To the great variety of readers" they themselves described their task in great detail:

> to haue collected & publish'd them; and so to haue publish'd them, as where (before) you were abus'd with diuerse stolne, and surreptitious copies, maimed, and deformed by the frauds and stealthes of iniurious imposters, that expos'd them: euen those, are now offer'd to your view cur'd, and perfect of their limbes; and all the rest, absolute in their numbers, *as he [Shakespeare] conceiued them*. [Author's emphasis] [268]

Shakespeare's friends also had to supply the engraver with a suitable model to work from enabling him to create the portrait engraving for publication in the First Folio. In keeping with the normal practice at the time, this model had to reproduce Shakespeare's features authentically, a purpose which could only be served by a portrait painted from life.

The editors may well have received the original and genuine image of the playwright – the Flower portrait, painted in 1609 – from Shakespeare's daughter and chief heir, Susanna Hall, in 1622. In this year their company went to Stratford, but were prevented from performing by the puritanical town fathers.[269] It is also conceivable that Anne Hathaway, Shakespeare's widow, who died on 6 August 1623, may have made the portrait available to them.

Under the circumstances described, no one but John Heminge and Henry Condell could have commissioned the Droeshout engraving.

V. THE RESULTS IN THEIR HISTORICAL
AND BIOGRAPHICAL CONTEXT

APPEARANCE, IDENTITY AND AUTHORSHIP

The results of the scientific tests for identity and authenticity applied to the Chandos and Flower portraits, the Davenant bust and the Darmstadt Shakespeare death mask which were presented in Part III mean that we can now be certain of the appearance of the playwright and poet William Shakespeare, born and buried in Stratford-upon-Avon, at various stages of his life. We know how he looked at about thirty to thirty-five, at forty-five, and around the age of fifty; and also how he appeared one or two days after his death.

John Aubrey, the first English biographer, in his *Brief Lives* (begun before 1667) penned an impressive verbal portrait of the physical appearance of Shakespeare, drawing upon the memories of contemporaries who had known the poet personally (see p. 81 and 86). In the past, however, this description of the dramatist was often dismissed as wishful thinking. The results we now have confirm Aubrey's verdict that Shakespeare was "a handsome, well-shap't man".[1] If we put this together with other comments by Aubrey, such as his characterisation of the playwright as "very good company" with "a very readie and pleasant smoothe Witt",[2] then a vivid and fascinating picture of Shakespeare's personality as a whole emerges.

The new findings not only supply information about Shakespeare's appearance, but also confirm – in conjunction with the background of cultural history outlined in Part I - that the images investigated show us the man who created the work of literary genius that bears the name of Shakespeare. In printed works of the early seventeenth century it was the norm, as we have seen, to document individual authorship by employing engravings exactly capturing the features of the writers portrayed. It is precisely this kind of firm announcement of "work-author-identification" that we see in the case of the First Folio Edition of Shakespeare's plays, for which Martin Droeshout the Younger, using the model of the Flower portrait, created the engraved portrait of William Shakespeare that Ben Jonson vouched for (see p. 44). Shakespeare's elaborate tomb monument with his authentic image, the symbols of his profession, and the inscriptions praising his supreme literary achievements (see pp. 41ff.), is equally a manifestation of "work-author-identification".[3] The two historical sources, the Folio edition and the tomb monument, each containing pictorial as well as textual evidence, bear witness addressed both to contemporaries and to posterity.

PAINFUL CONDITIONS, PATHOLOGICAL SYMPTOMS, AND ILLNESSES

As the medical assessment in Part III has shown, the authentic images of Shakespeare display a series of signs pointing to a long-term systemic illness from which the poet was suffering. Professor Lerche diagnosed the pathological swelling on the upper eyelids and in the area of the temples, especially visible on the left upper eyelid, as a symptom of Mikulicz syndrome, which can accompany a general illness such as lymphoma or sarcoidosis (see p. 68). He interpreted the rounded swelling in the left caruncle as a possible small caruncular tumour (see p. 68ff.). Professor Jansen took the pathological alteration to the skin on the forehead to be a benign bone tumour (see p. 71). In view of this pathological symptom and in the light of Professor Lerche's diagnosis, Professor Metz diagnosed this sign as a chronic skin sarcoidosis, a disease which - after running its course for many years - finally leads to death (see p. 71). Professor Hertl, who interpreted the protuberance in the inner corner of the left eye as a "macule on the eyelid fissure (*Lidspaltenfleck*)", and connected the yellowish spots on the lower lip of the Flower portrait with an inflammation of the oral mucous membrane indicating a general lowering of resistance, summarised by stating that William Shakespeare must have suffered from a debilitating illness that sapped his strength. This was visible in images from the Chandos portrait to the death mask, and pointed to a progressive inner disease.[4] Hertl's synopsis of these results reads:

> The images of William Shakespeare that were examined indicate that for many years the poet was a sick man, whose strength was progressively consumed by a disease that undermined it. The signs of this complaint are already in evidence by 1609, at the time of the Flower portrait.[5]

The medical findings reveal that the playwright would clearly have been suffering, and that at times he must have been in quite considerable pain. The deformation of the left eye was no doubt particularly distressing. It is known that the Mikulicz syndrome is often painful. The same applies to the noticeable swelling on the poet's forehead, as well as to the yellowish marks on his lower lip. It can also be assumed that the trilobate protuberance in the nasal corner of the left eye, causing a marked deviation of the eyelid margin (see p. 75), would have been experienced as a large and painful obstruction – whatever the diagnosis (see pp. 68–70 and 75ff.).

It will be clear from what follows that all of this corresponds to details handed down in written records from the seventeenth century. These records can be traced back to contemporary witnesses who respected and admired Shakespeare, who knew him personally, collaborated with him, or had seen him at close quarters.

In an unpublished manuscript of John Aubrey's *Brief Lives*, there are some very informative details about Shakespeare's physical state, as well as his general way of life. Once again Aubrey's source is William Beeston, who – as the biographer tells us – was best informed about Shakespeare (see p. 86f.). According to Aubrey, Beeston's knowledge came from "Master Lacy". John Lacy (d. 1681) was a player and playwright in The King's Company during the Restoration period, and had obviously gathered a great deal of information about William Shakespeare. William Beeston's father had belonged to Shakespeare's theatrical company and performed alongside the dramatist, so that in Beeston Aubrey had an informant who could draw upon two important sources and pass onto interested contemporaries what he knew about Shakespeare.

Aubrey learned from Beeston that Shakespeare had lived outside the walls of London in Shoreditch, north of Bishopsgate, "at Hoglane [Hog Lane] within 6 dores [from] – Norton – folgate [Norton Folgate]" (*figs. 108 and 109*)[6] He also found out from him something that to Aubrey's mind was quite admirable about the historical Shakespeare: "he was not a company-keeper; [...] wouldn't be debauched; and if invited to, writ he was in pain."[7] What was meant by "not a company-keeper" was primarily that he did not keep bad company. Historically, in one sense of "to keep company" or "consort" ("to cohabit [with]"), which according to the *Oxford English Dictionary* was in use in Middle English and still current until 1680, the meaning of "he was not a company-keeper" was – as it appears – that he did not live with anyone. The

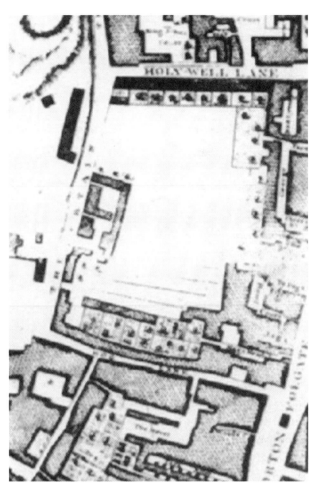

Fig. 108 John Rocque, Map of London (1737-46), excerpt: Shoreditch north of Bishopsgate. In the 1590s William Shakespeare lived in Hog Lane near Norton Folgate (below right), not far from the playhouse The Theatre.

formulations "wouldn't be debauched"[8] and "if invited to, writ he was in pain" clearly indicate that he pleaded his suffering to avoid morally offensive behaviour.

From our point of view, it is precisely this last statement that is particularly interesting, because it directly refers to the pain the writer suffered. The eminent English Shakespeare scholar Edgar Fripp picked this up: "if [Shakespeare was] 'invited' to dissipation [he] excused himself on the ground of ill-health".[9]

Thus it is evident that the results of medical assessments are in accord with one of the most important and reliable written sources of the seventeenth century. And since Aubrey's informant does not seem to be referring merely to a single occasion when Shakespeare used ill health as an excuse, but implies that he was in the habit of doing so, we can take it that with the statement "he [Shakespeare] was in pain" he (Aubrey) is not simply emphasising temporary suffering but alluding to a state of permanently impaired health, fully confirmed by the medical findings.

Fig. 109 Present-day view of Hog Lane in Shoreditch, now called Worship Street.

It is also extremely interesting that the reference to the writer's painful condition relates to the time when Shakespeare was living in Shoreditch. This is a relatively clearly defined period in Shakespeare's life. His outstandingly successful theatre company, The Chamberlain's Men, with its two leading lights Richard Burbage and William Shakespeare himself, is known to have been formed in 1594.[10] With some exceptions they performed at "The Theatre" in Shoreditch, a large theatre that was the first public playhouse to be opened in the English capital, and built in 1576 by James Burbage (father of Richard and Cuthbert). In December 1598, following a dispute with the landlord when he refused to renew the lease of the site, the building was dismantled, carted piecemeal to Southwark on the south bank of the Thames, and rebuilt there in spring 1599. The theatre was now imposingly renamed "The Globe".[11] This was when Shakespeare moved to Southwark.

We can infer from the evidence above that the dramatist was already afflicted with pain between about 1594 and 1599. The painting of the Chandos portrait coincides with the time when Shakespeare lived in Shoreditch. The Mikulicz syndrome is already well defined in this early portrait of the playwright (*see fig. 014*), so that the sufferings recorded in the sources might have been caused precisely by this disease, which is often accompanied by pain (see p. 132).

Among the noticeable traits of the Chandos and Flower portraits and the Davenant bust are Shakespeare's "plump and full" lips: the lower lip in the Flower portrait even appears swollen (see p. 76). Three contemporary authors (Joseph Hall in 1597, John Marston, 1598, and Thomas Freeman, 1614)[12] may have been alluding to this characteristic in their texts when they called a very prominent colleague by the nickname "Labeo", that is to say "the one who has large lips" or is "thick-lipped".[13] It is not difficult to identify this prominent colleague as Shakespeare, since by 1598 at the latest he was by far the most famous living author in England.[14] And, as we now know, he had noticeably full lips.

Marston is probably the most informative and interesting of the three witnesses, with his satire *Metamorphosis of Pigmalions Image and Certaine Satyres*.[15] As a playwriting colleague of Shakespeare's, he obviously had inside knowledge. When C. A. Herpich first published Marston's "Labeo" satire in *Notes and Queries*,[16] he observed that: "The chief interest of the passage, however, is in the fact that if he is girding at Shakspere, Marston has sketched for us one of the dramatist's features."[17] By this he meant Shakespeare's distinctive lips.

The playwright himself appeared on stage,[18] so Marston knew that the Elizabethan public was familiar with practically every line of his features, including every morphological and pathological characteristic, and therefore also with his lips. He was aware that Shakespeare's expressions and gestures were well known to the spectators, as was his way of speaking - with his eyes as well as his lips - and indeed the whole of his physical appearance, since he presented himself regularly as an actor. That the poet himself was uncomfortably aware of this fact is evident from Sonnet No. 110, whose autobiographical character is unmistakeable: "Alas, 'tis true I have gone here and there, / And made myself a motley to the view, / Gored mine own thoughts, sold cheap what is most dear, / [...]." The English historian and Shakespeare scholar A. L. Rowse, too, is struck by the autobiographical nature of this sonnet:

> Once more he [Shakespeare] lets us into the secret of his feelings about his profession as an actor, and in doing so, he betrays [...] what a sensitive man he was, how much he minded making himself a motley to the view, exposing his own feelings, selling cheap what was most dear to him.[19]

But Marston also introduces other subtle allusions that can be related to Shakespeare. The male character whom he calls "Labeo", as well as "Castilio" and "Castilion",[20] complains that his mistress is "stone"; obdurate (stubborn), flinty, and uniquely unyielding. "Labeo" is presented as the perfect courtier, adept at courting or wooing: he "can all poynts of courtship show." He bears a (new) coat of arms, knows how to compose elegant verses, make a pleasing face, and speak with his eyes. Marston's "Labeo" has high-flown plans and is inspired by his mistress's hanging curl[21] to "wish that he were it, to kisse her eye"[22] and is inflamed by her divine beauty. He is said to be famous for his well-turned speeches and his mastery of the sonnet. But finally Marston points out that "Labeo" "doth but champe that which another chew'd".[23]

The details of this coded character profile[24] fit Shakespeare strikingly well,[25] seen and interpreted against the background of the historical and biographical facts and events at the end of the 1590s. The poet's mistress, emotionally cold and stubbornly committed to a particular plan, has been identified in my book *Das Geheimnis um Shakespeare's 'Dark Lady'*[26](*The Secret Surrounding Shakespeare's Dark Lady*) on the basis of Marcus Gheeraerts's paintings in Hampton Court "The Persian Lady" as Shakespeare's "The Dark Lady". Between 1595 and 1598, she was caught between two men: Shakespeare and his rival. However, in the end, she left the poet out in the cold. Like "Labeo", he went away empty-handed and another man would enjoy the fruit of his love.[27]

The new sonnet in Gheeraerts's painting, ascribed to Shakespeare for the first time by the present author, describes precisely this situation. It reveals the true course of events, and as the third quatrain in particular indicates, it brings to a close the previously open-ended "Dark Lady" sequence:

> My only hope was in this goodly tree,
> which I did plant in love bring vp in care;
> but all in vaine, for now to[o] late I see
> the shales be mine, the kernels others are.[28]

To summarise: we can say that the medical findings presented in Part III, based on the authentic images of Shakespeare, are reinforced by their agreement with the allusions to the pain the poet suffered which are handed down in the historical and biographical records. The full lips noticeable in the true to life images of the poet (except the death mask and the funerary bust) were a decisive key to the decoding of the pseudonym "Labeo" in Marston's satire *Metamorphosis.*

RELIGION

Since the proofs of identity and authenticity presented in this book show that Shakespeare must have sat for the painter of the Flower portrait, the poet must also have known that the wooden board on which his image was painted was no blank panel, but displayed a religious painting from the late fifteenth or early sixteenth century,[29] a Madonna with the Christ child and St John (*see figs. 016 and 073*). This fact raised new questions, which I discussed in my book *Die verborgene Existenz des William Shakespeare (The secret life of William Shakespeare,* 2001).The results of my study on the poet's hidden life, resting in part on previously unknown sources or such ones made newly accessible, reveal that Shakespeare's parents and relations, his daughter Susanna, and also he himself were adherents of the outlawed and vigorously suppressed old Faith. This was true also of his most important teacher in Stratford, Simon Hunt. Hunt left Stratford in 1575, became a priest in Douai, a Jesuit in Rome and, in 1580, English "Penitentiary" or father confessor in the Vatican. The young Shakespeare must have studied - apparently from 1578 to 1580 - at the very popular Collegium Anglicum in Douai or Rheims, at that time the only English Catholic college on the continent. The testament of the Catholic nobleman Alexander de Hoghton in 1581 shows that subsequently Shakespeare was employed as a private tutor to the de Hoghtons, an aristocratic Catholic family in Lancashire its present head being Sir Bernard de Hoghton. This is in agreement with what John Aubrey recorded: the younger Shakespeare had served as a schoolmaster in the country.[30] In de Hoghton's testament there are (concealed) pointers to a secret (Catholic) organisation, to which the young Shakespeare obviously belonged under the name of Shakeshafte. This seems to have been a branch of the Catholic Association, founded in Rome in 1580. The role of this association of young noble and middle-class Catholics was to protect the priests of the secret Jesuit missionary movement initiated in 1580 in Rome, to accompany them and arrange for their accommodation in the houses of the English landed gentry. The dramatist stayed in Rome at least three times during the so-called "lost years" (1585-1592), using the name of his hometown, Stratford (or variants of that name), as pseudonyms. When travelling on the Continent, Shakespeare – according to a newly discovered and interpreted source – must have lodged in monasteries.[31]

Furthermore, it can be regarded as certain that he was in contact with the leading figures of the prohibited Jesuit missionary movement, Edmund Campion (1540-1581) and Robert Parsons (1546-1610), and occasionally refers to them in his plays, sometimes even by name. Near the end of his life he made a considerable contribution to the survival of the old religion.[32]

In light of this, it does not seem far-fetched to suppose that he may have inherited the Madonna image beneath the Flower portrait from his mother, who was buried on 9 September 1608.[33]

In 1609, when the Madonna picture was being painted over with Shakespeare's portrait, Shakespeare would have encountered a particularly hostile anti-Catholic mood, inflamed by the government and the established church. On 25 June 1609 Lancelot Dawes of Queen's College Oxford fulminated from the open-air pulpit of St Paul's Cathedral in London, denouncing "the abominations of Rome" and "the sins of the English Catholics", whom he called "the very scumme and excrements of this land".[34]

From his childhood, youth and early adulthood Shakespeare was familiar with the excesses of anti-Catholic legislation under Elizabeth I.[35] For his relatives, teachers and friends had all suffered from them. In 1582 the young Jesuit priest Thomas Cottom was executed.[36] He was the brother of John Cottom, who, at that time, was schoolmaster of the Stratford grammar school. Edward Arden, head of the aristocratic Arden family of Parkhall, to whom Shakespeare was related on his mother's side, was hanged for high treason in 1583 because he had been drawn into a Catholic plot, the Arden-Somerville conspiracy.[37] The execution of the Catholic priest Robert Debdale took place in 1585. Debdale was a schoolfriend of Shakespeare's and the neighbour of his later wife Anne Hathaway.[38] Shakespeare himself made a hasty escape from his home town at the beginning of 1585, and disappeared for seven years.[39] As has been mentioned above, there is new documentary evidence that the poet must have been in Rome three times during that period. In October 1613 he went to Rome once more, using the pseudonym "Ricardus Stratfordus". Richard was the name of his brother, who had died six months earlier.[40]

The significance of a Madonna picture for Catholics practising their religion in secret in the early seventeenth century is exemplified by the last moments in the life of Robert Catesby, the leader of the Gunpowder Plot conspirators. When the plan to blow up the assembled parliament along with the royal family was foiled at the last minute, Catesby fled with a few fellow-conspirators to St Legers in Northamptonshire. The group went to ground in Ashby, the Catesbys' residence. When their gunpowder exploded before the government forces had arrived, Catesby suffered severe burns. During the attack on Ashby on 8 November 1605, he and his fellow-conspirator Percy were both struck by bullets. Catesby barely managed to drag himself on his hands and knees into the house, where, clutching a picture of the Madonna, he fell to the ground and died.[41]

On his mother's side, Shakespeare was not only related to Catesby, but to all the other conspirators as well. It was probably from the Catesby household that his father John Shakespeare obtained the Borromeo Testament distributed by the Jesuits Parsons and Campion, and designed to enable English Catholics to give witness to their faith in writing. John Shakespeare may have hidden this dangerous Catholic document in the rafters of his house in Henley Street in Stratford after the discovery of the Arden-Somerville plot in 1583. It was found there by chance in 1757.[42]

When checks and house searches were carried out, it was the Madonna pictures, rosaries and Borromeo Testaments that gave their owners away. For they exposed them as followers of the forbidden Roman faith, and therefore as traitors. Many such Catholic objects came to light in August 1584 during coordinated raids ordered by the Privy Council and executed by the sheriffs and councillors of the City of London.[43]

Had the Madonna painting been in Shakespeare's or his family's possession, it would have posed a great danger to all of them. And if the image beneath the Flower portrait really had been an heirloom dear to the Shakespeares for religious reasons, then it would presumably have been out of the question for the poet to sell or destroy it. In this situation, the only possible solution seems to have been to paint the Madonna over with the poet's own portrait.

When Shakespeare died, the Flower portrait was apparently at his home, New Place. John Heminge and Henry Condell could therefore have borrowed it from Shakespeare's daughter Susanna Hall during their visit to Stratford in 1622, in order to provide a model for Martin Droeshout the Younger's First Folio engraving. It is not inconceivable that the Flower portrait was identical with the painting that was still hanging in the great hall when New Place was sold in 1758. In the list drawn up by the antiquary Wheler, the picture present there was described as "Shakespeare's head".[44] The same source tells us that in other rooms of the house Wheler discovered more Shakespeare family pictures, which may have ended up in the possession of the progeny of Shakespeare's sister Joan Hart, who were living in the poet's birthplace at the time. It seems that in 1840 the Flower portrait was still in the hands of impoverished descendants of the Harts (see p. 27).

For obvious reasons to do with the danger to life and limb, Shakespeare never openly proclaimed his Catholicism. He never made known his attitude to the religious politics of the two rulers under whom he lived (Elizabeth I and James I), or to the many faithful Catholics who died a martyr's death in the England of his day. At no point in his literary works is there any direct utterance by the poet on the subject of his country's great religious problems. But his plays, especially those too inflammatory in content to have been published in his lifetime,[45] contain many allusions to Catholic ideas as well as to Catholic rites and customs: *Romeo and Juliet* or *Hamlet* are cases in point.[46] In the reunion scene in the romance *The Winter's Tale* (V, 3) the English Shakespeare scholar Peter Milward sees a prime example of "Catholic implications".[47] For Milward, there are echoes of the Virgin Mary in the statue of Queen Hermione, mentioned in Part I (see p. 21). He draws attention to:

> [...] the statue of Hermione, 'newly performed by that rare Italian master, Julio Romano', who is significant both for his name and for his actual association with the Vatican; the kneeling of Perdita before it, as before a statue of the Virgin Mary, to 'implore her blessing'; and the apparent miracle by which 'dear life redeems' Hermione from death (V.3).[48]

The artist in question is a pupil of Raphael, Giulio Romano (?1499-1546). Highly esteemed by Rubens and Goethe, his work was clearly well known to the dramatist and admired by him. But Shakespeare could probably only have become acquainted with Romano's works on the Continent, especially in Rome or in some northern Italian cities.

We have no eye-witness accounts of Shakespeare's death. However, we do have a pictorial record of the demise of George Gilbert, founder of the Catholic Association and great patron and protector of the Jesuit mission to England, initiated in 1580. He died in Rome after a sudden fever on 6 October 1583, surrounded by priests and a few monks. The scene is preserved in an engraving.[49] The rich Catholic nobleman had gone to Rome to confer with Pope Gregory XIII on promoting the Catholic religion in England, and to help needy English Catholics in exile. The engraving shows the dying man grasping a cross in his right hand. On the wall above him hangs a picture of the Madonna and child.

We might well imagine such a scene around Shakespeare's deathbed on 23 April 1616 in New Place in Stratford, because according to a tradition handed on in the late seventeenth century, Shakespeare died a Catholic. It was the Protestant clergyman, Richard Davies, an Oxford graduate, who became rector of Sapperton in Gloucestershire, a village not too far from Stratford-upon-Avon, who made an unmistakeable remark to this effect. When his friend William Fulman, another Protestant clergyman, died in 1688, Davies acquired Fulman's personal papers. Among them were notes about Shakespeare's life. Davies added to them the sentence: "He [Shakespeare] dyed a papist."[50] The clergyman officiating at Shakespeare's deathbed was said to have been a Benedictine.[51] In researching for my book *Die verborgene Existenz des William Shakespeare* (*The hidden life of William Shakespeare*, 2001), I discovered that the clergyman in question was very probably Father Augustine (David Baker), the learned author of works on theology and ecclesiastical history, who had become a priest in Rheims a few years before Shakespeare's death, and had previously lived hidden in a Catholic nobleman's household near Stratford.[52]

In sum: financial motives probably had nothing to do with the reasons for re-using the panel with the Madonna painting on it for Shakespeare's portrait. The poet, involved in the Catholic underground, cannot have been indifferent to the picture of Mary, especially if it was a votive image that had belonged to his mother. In view of the mortal danger incurred by owning Catholic objects in the Elizabethan-Jacobean period, especially after the Gunpowder Plot of 1605, painting over the picture with a portrait of the dramatist must be seen as a brilliant solution to the problem. We can safely assume it was Shakespeare's own idea.

In the light of the findings presented in Part III, the dating of the Flower portrait, 1609, as given in the painting's inscription, could be accepted as correct (see p. 91). Now its credibility has been reinforced by the historical and biographical context sketched out above.

RETIREMENT FROM PROFESSIONAL LIFE

His contemporaries were already lamenting that Shakespeare left the stage of life far too early. Thus the commemorative lines signed I. M. [= John Marston?] in the First Folio Edition run:

VVEE [We] wondred (Shake-speare)
that thou went'st so soon
From the Worlds Stage,
To the Graues-Tyring-roome.[53]

On the basis of medical investigations presented here, we have convincing explanations for the relatively early death of the playwright, and also for his retreat from professional life when he was still only about forty-nine.

The medical findings now offer a convincing explanation of why Shakespeare gave up his activities as a professional playwright and theatre-owner in London and why he withdrew to Stratford so early. However, although he may have taken these steps mainly on medical grounds, we should not forget the part that may have been played by the drastic deterioration of the political and religious climate under James I. For precisely at this time there were further inconceivable acts of humiliation, discriminatory treatment, and persecution of the Catholic population, for example through the parliamentary bill that proposed to make Catholics wear red caps and coloured stockings, or the law that prohibited them from bearing arms.[54]

LAST ILLNESS AND POSSIBLE CAUSE OF DEATH

William Shakespeare was buried on 25 April 1616 on the left side of the chancel near the altar in Holy Trinity Church in Stratford-upon-Avon (*see fig. 020*). Like his baptismal date, the date of his funeral is recorded in the Holy Trinity parish register. The date of his death given on the marble plaque of his funerary monument is 23 April 1616. His birth in 1564 also most probably took place on 23 April, three days before his baptism on 26 April, and this happens to coincide with St George's Day, celebrating the patron saint of England. The inscription reads: "OBIIT AÑO DO^I 1616. AETATIS 53 [sic], DIE 23 AP^R."

Shakespeare scholarship has always assumed that during his last illness Shakespeare was treated by his son-in-law, Dr John Hall. He was a famous doctor with a large practice in Stratford, and was married to Shakespeare's eldest daughter Susanna. He kept casebooks in Latin about patients he treated and cured. The army surgeon Captain James Cooke[55] translated some parts of these notes into English, and published them in London in 1657 with the title *Select Observations ON ENGLISH BODIES: OR, Cures both Empericall and Historicall, performed upon very eminent Persons in desperate Diseases* (*fig. 110*).[56] The title itself names the three decisive selection criteria (presumably those of the editor) for these published notes: cures, eminent persons, and desperate diseases.[57] An interested public could therefore expect to find in this book detailed medical reports on the type of disease, the treatment and above all the *cure* of prominent and severely ill people. The standard formulation at the end of every entry states: And thus he/ or she was cured. Cooke obtained the manuscripts from Susanna Hall, who had been a widow since 1635. A former assistant of Dr Hall's had arranged for his colleague Cooke to be invited to New Place, which the Halls had inherited from the poet, and where they had lived ever since. The visit took place during the Civil War, probably in 1643, when Cooke was staying in the town.[58]

There is no record in Cooke's edition, whose entries start at 1617, of the illness that led to Shakespeare's death on 23 April 1616. In connection with her study, *John Hall and his Patients. The Medical Practice of Shakespeare's Son-in-Law* (1996), Joan Lane tried like many researchers before her to establish why Hall's notes do not include the details of the "Shakespeare case",[59] given that we can assume Hall treated Shakespeare in his last illness and would have done his utmost to save his father-in-law's life. There are good reasons to suppose that there was another casebook prior to 1617.[60] Certainly, Lane was able to show through "internal evidence" that there are accounts in Cooke's edition of a few cases dating from before 1617, or which began before that date, with one case even stretching back to 1611.[61] But this does not in any way disprove the existence of another, earlier notebook. That there was a second book was even confirmed by Cooke himself.[62] With the sole exception of Susanna Hall, Cooke, as translator and editor of the manuscripts was better placed to know this than any other contemporary witness. Therefore we may well assume that casebook I was not handed over to Cooke by Susanna Hall in 1643 because it very probably contained entries about her father's death which she wished to withhold from the public. These entries might have concerned diseases Shakespeare suffered from which Hall had cured, but also his last illness,

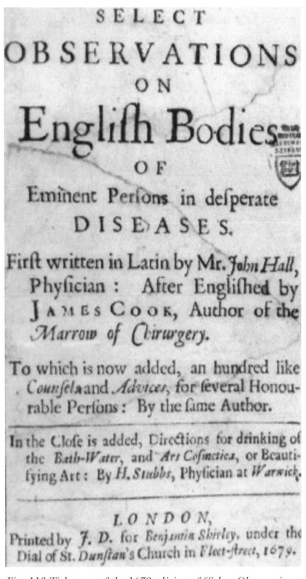

Fig. 110 Title page of the 1679 edition of "Select Observations ON ENGLISH BODIES" [...] by Dr John Hall, Shakespeare's son-in-law.

where a cure was not possible. There is every reason to think that Hall kept as precise and conscientious an account of this case as he did of all others. It cannot be ruled out that Hall's son-in-law Thomas Nash may have destroyed these notes (see p. 178 n. 69).

But if casebook 1 still existed and Susanna Hall did not give it to Cooke, but withheld it, it would have remained with the other books and manuscripts in New Place. With the death of Shakespeare's granddaughter, Lady Elizabeth Barnard, née Hall, in 1670, the direct line of his legitimate descendants was to come to an end. In 1653, however, she moved with her husband to Abington in Northamptonshire. It is debatable whether she would have taken this kind of heirloom with her. What argues against it is that in the middle of the eighteenth century there were still family portraits

of William Shakespeare (including "Shakespeare's Head") in New Place (see p. 135–6), which had not been the Barnards' property since 1674. It is quite possible that around 1750 "casebook 1" was still in New Place, too, but was later lost or destroyed.

The only reference we have to the possible cause of Shakespeare's death occurs in what was originally an orally transmitted tradition, first written down by the vicar of Holy Trinity Church, Reverend John Ward, between 1661 and 1663. However, he could not vouch for its veracity. Ward tells us that "Shakespeare, Drayton, and Ben Jhonson, had a merry meeting, and *itt seems* drank too hard, for Shakespear died of a feavour there contracted."[63] None of the participants is known to have corroborated this account. In view of the fact that Shakespeare – to judge by relevant passages from his plays – absolutely detested drunkenness,[64] and according to John Aubrey declined invitations to dissipation by pleading the pain from which he suffered (see pp. 132ff.), the tradition behind Ward's story would seem to be an invention. For the next one hundred and fifty years, nothing was to change in the situation described by John Payne Collier in 1844, when he said that "We are left in utter uncertainty as to the immediate cause of the death of Shakespeare [...]."[65] It was only with the criminological and medical investigations into the Chandos and Flower portraits, the Davenant bust, the death mask, the funerary bust and the Droeshout engraving that an entirely new perspective opened up. It has forced us to re-assess the cause of the poet's early death. Shakespeare clearly suffered from a debilitating systemic disease (see pp. 70, 73, 88 and 131), which was terminal after a long progression (see p. 70). It is therefore very likely that he died of this condition on 23 April 1616.

But a new theory about his death has also been put forward in recent English Shakespeare research. Joan Lane pointed out in her book *John Hall and his Patients* that: "By 1616, however [...], a typhus epidemic [...] appeared."[66] By this she seems to imply that Shakespeare may also have fallen victim to this epidemic. Hall does indeed say in his entry "Obser. LXXVII", concerning the twenty-eight-year-old Lady Beaufou, that the patient's burning, fierce and unremitting fever was the "New Fever" which had afflicted many townspeople.[67] But the fact that many citizens of Stratford fell ill with typhus, and some died of it,[68] in the year of Shakespeare's death and the following year is not in itself proof that the poet too died of this disease. If Shakespeare really had lost his life in the epidemic, it would surely not have gone without mention. Cook knew personally not only Hall and his assistants, but also Hall's wife Susanna. It is hard to imagine that such information would have been withheld from him. However, if Shakespeare was indeed infected, it is of course highly probable that in view of his debilitating disease and his age he would have succumbed to the contagion.

We are, however, on solid ground as far as the expert medical assessments that have been presented in Part III are concerned. By using modern methods of diagnosis available to medicine today, it is possible to recognise and classify the signs of disease which are reproduced in the images of Shakespeare with strict accuracy. It is the clearly depicted outer symptoms of illness that enable the medical experts to draw their conclusions as to the strong probability of internal illnesses whose course they can then predict.

Considering the illnesses and the untimely death of the poet within the overall historical and biographical context, there is nothing to suggest that Shakespeare succumbed to an epidemic, and therefore to a sudden and unforeseeable death.

At just fifty-one years of age, in January 1616, a few months before he died, Shakespeare drew up a very detailed and careful will. This indicates that he was aware of the critical state of his health, and was prepared for his imminent death. On 25 March 1616, about a month before he died, he altered his last testament once more.[69]

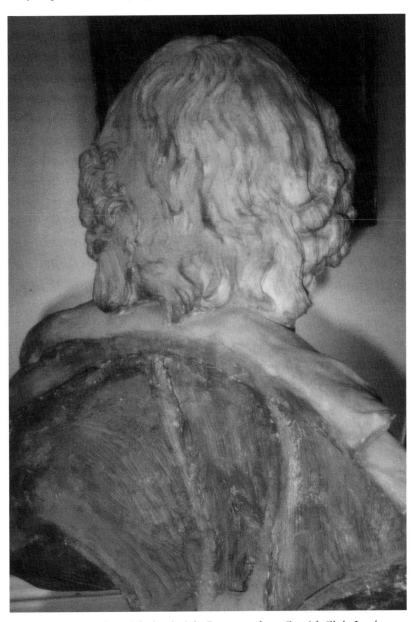

Fig. 111 Rear view of the head of the Davenant bust, Garrick Club, London.

APPENDIX I

The Prospects

The results of the investigations presented in this book have shown that we now possess a detailed conception and description of the authentic features of William Shakespeare, including all the signs of illness as they appeared in three different periods of his life and immediately after his death. Having assembled this catalogue of criteria, it should be possible in almost all cases to tell whether other images of Shakespeare with a claim to be authentic really are true-to-life representations of the poet. This can be illustrated in relation to three examples.

The Sanders Portrait

With an enormous amount of advertising activity and worldwide publicity, the so-called Sanders portrait, privately owned in Canada, was introduced to the public from 21 June to 23 September 2001 in the Art Gallery of Toronto (*fig. 112*) as a supposedly genuine portrait of Shakespeare painted in 1603. The driving force behind the campaign was the Canadian journalist Stephanie Nolen, who published a book on the picture with the ambitious title *Shakespeare's Face*, for which she recruited as co-authors the Shakespeare scholars Jonathan Bate, Marjorie Garber, Andrew Gurr, Alexander Leggatt, and Stanley Wells, as well as the historian Robert Tittler and the National Portrait Gallery curator, Tarnya Cooper.[i] But none of the contributors, including Tarnya Cooper, explicitly addressed the question of identity. This crucial question had also been left out of account in the many technical and scientific tests carried out on the Sanders portrait.[ii] The present author, however, investigated it with the help of Reinhardt Altmann, the specialist at the German Federal Bureau of Criminal Investigation. The expert compared the features of the Sanders portrait with those of the Droeshout engraving, the Chandos portrait, and the restored Flower portrait, using both criminological image comparison and trick image differentiation techniques. As documented in his image report of 8 August 2001, some striking differences emerged, some of them extreme, representing divergences in terms of the outline of the face, the area of the eyes, the eyelid cleft and parts of the eyelid plate, the mucous membrane of the lower lip, the length of the chin and the earlobes – all arguments against identifying this painting as a genuine image of Shakespeare.[iii]

The Janssen Portrait

Reinhardt Altmann also collaborated with the author in examining the so-called Janssen portrait in the Folger Shakespeare Library in Washington. James Boaden in the early eighteenth century was deeply impressed by this picture, believing it to be a true likeness of the poet; but since then, especially in the twentieth century, grave doubts have been expressed.[iv] However, being unsupported by scientific evidence, the arguments put forward for or against the authenticity of the picture have failed to convince. Drawing on the new findings in this case, certain basic agreements of the facial features immediately become apparent. The slight changes in the area of the left eye

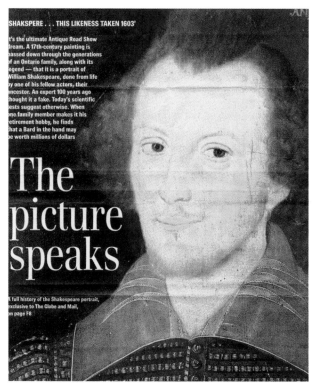

Fig. 112 The Sanders portrait, in private ownership. Picture quotation from The Globe and Mail [Toronto] (12 May 2001).

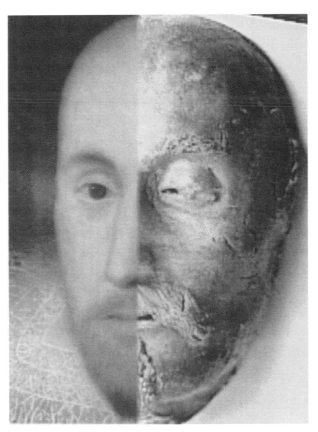

Fig. 113 Trick Image Differentiation Technique employed by BKA expert, Reinhardt Altmann: Montage of the Janssen portrait (left half) and the death mask (right half), BKA image report (1999).

(upper eyelid and inner corner of the eye) suggest an early stage of the signs of illness that became more conspicuous later. If this is the case, we could be looking at a portrait of a still youthful Shakespeare. But this theory is not in accord with the age of the portrait's subject, given on the painting as "Æ^t 46". It was Schoenbaum who had already assumed that the age could have been added in later.[v] Furthermore, it is not established that the painting really is by Cornelius Janssen, to whom it is attributed. Janssen, born in 1593, was only seventeen if the date inscribed in the portrait (1610) is correct. However, this could also be a later addition. Objections of this kind (based on inscription dates) cannot be taken as serious counterarguments.

The BKA specialist compared the Janssen portrait with the Droeshout engraving, the Chandos and Flower portraits, and the death mask. In the general comparison - as he reported in his expert assessment of 30 June 1999 - he found "approximate correspondences in the forehead area, the outline of the face, and the length of the nose including the root and bridge of the nose". He draws attention to "the peculiarity in the area of the nasal corner of the left eye", and particularly notes "the harmony of the

two halves of images 1 and 7", where he is referring to montages of the Janssen portrait and the death mask, with a section line shifted slightly away from the centre (fig. 113). But the expert also pointed out the slight divergences in the area of the left nostril and the cleft of the mouth (oral fissure), as well as the relatively narrow opening of the eyelid cleft. Another aspect he noted was that the cheekbone was more prominent in the Chandos, Flower and Droeshout portraits than in Janssen's. While these divergences in his view did not necessarily rule out identity, on the other hand the expert could neither confirm nor deny that they were in agreement with the authentic images of William Shakespeare. Discussing it with the author, he conceded that it would be worthwhile to research the history of this painting, the artist, and its ownership. For this could possibly lead to clarification.

The Grafton Portrait

Since its rediscovery in 1907, there has been speculation about whether the Grafton portrait (painted in 1588, according to its inscription) which is in the John Rylands University Library in Manchester (*fig. 114*) might be a representation of the younger William Shakespeare. The elegantly dressed young man with the slightly melancholy air has bewitched many viewers ever since. The mere thought of having the figure of the young poet before one's eyes has inspired enthusiastic adherents even among prominent Shakespeare biographers, for example John Dover Wilson, who chose the picture as the frontispiece for his book *The Essential Shakespeare*.[vi] Bernd Schmeier, reviewing the German edition of the volume (*Shakespeare. Der Mensch*[vii]), was also infected with this enthusiasm. His comment on the jacket reads: "It is difficult not to succumb to the emotional appeal of such a passionate advocate as J. Dover Wilson, and nobody will resist the temptation to accept that this is really how the young Shakespeare looked: open and cheerful, reflective and melancholy, near and distant; delicate and strong; ready for any eventuality; determined to look life in the eye, withstand its onslaught and keep his balance." Dover Wilson himself, however, was more reticent. He was gratified that the Scottish Shakespeare biographer Dr John Smart "found that it [the Grafton portrait] confirmed the way he himself imagined the young Shakespeare would have looked, and wished it were genuine".[viii] But, Dover Wilson comments, there is "no real proof"[ix] of this, and he did not expect his readers to believe it.

However, the latest Shakespeare biographer, Peter Ackroyd (whose book *Shakespeare. The Biography* was published in 2005), appearing in the BBC film about the Grafton portrait produced by John Hay and broadcast on 27 October 2005 in the programme "The Culture Show", expressed emphatically and with complete commitment his belief that this was none other than the twenty-four-year-old Shakespeare. He argued that the arms, eyes, chin and expression resembled those of the Droeshout engraving. Dr Stella Butler of the John Rylands Library, however, declared that this was extremely unlikely - without giving specific reasons.

The investigation of the picture at the National Portrait Gallery in London supervised by the curator, Dr Tarnya Cooper, promised information about the young man's identity. In her introductory remarks in Hay's film, Cooper observed: "This is the type of face you can believe wrote the love poems". She then presented the two kinds of test employed: x-ray examination and infra-red photography. But neither of these, she emphasised, could help with the question of identity.

The BKA specialist Altmann, to whom the author presented a photograph of the Grafton portrait in 1997 (*see fig. 114*), rejected firmly and without hesitation the theory that this might be an authentic image of Shakespeare, and thought no further investigation was needed. The reason he gave was that the nose of the young man in the portrait was fundamentally so different from that in the genuine Shakespeare images that the Grafton portrait could not possibly be a true to life likeness of William Shakespeare.

Looking closely at the x-ray and infra-red images that were included in John Hay's film, the present author noticed that the infra-red pictures made the significant divergence mentioned by Altmann even more obvious than it was in the original. These special images record impressively the way that the nose in the Grafton portrait becomes very thin towards the middle. There is a short section which is very narrow, and then the nose becomes very much thicker, so that towards its tip it appears fat, fleshy and bulbous. Thus

Fig. 114 The Grafton portrait. Oil on wood, John Rylands University Library, Manchester. Photographed before 1932.

this facial feature is very noticeably different from the true-to-life images of Shakespeare. At the same time the nose in the Grafton portrait appears to be shorter than in the authentic representations of the poet, while the upper lip is longer.

Beyond this there is a whole range of other aspects in which this portrait differs from the authentic features of Shakespeare in the Chandos and Flower portraits and in the Droeshout engraving. All of this is relatively easy for readers to check if, for purposes of comparison, they care to refer to the seventeen facial features (see pp. 48–9), while also bearing in mind the many signs of illness which are visible on Shakespeare's face and are named, diagnosed and discussed in detail in Part III (p. 67ff.).

In view of these circumstances, we can definitively rule out any chance that the Grafton portrait represents the youthful Shakespeare.

i 2002 in Toronto. 2003 in London. In his foreword editor Rick Archbold imaginatively describes a fantasy meeting of the experts involved: "They look at the Sanders portrait as an artifact, as a work of art, as a cultural icon and as a fascinating window into Shakespeare's world. I've met only two of these scholars in person, but like to imagine them gathered around the painting as I saw it when it went on display at the Art Gallery of Ontario, in Toronto, in the summer of 2001. [...] The conversation they might have had if they had met around the portrait is the one they now hold in the pages of this book. [...] All their skills combined [sic] in an attempt to answer the question that all of us must ask of the slightly naughty-looking fellow in the Sanders portrait: Are you Shakespeare, or aren't you? Is yours the face of genius?" (Foreword, ix–x). But the book fails to answer this question.

ii For example, the radio-carbon dating method was used to determine the age of the wood panel. But it was only a small area

of canvas, attached in later years to the back of the picture, that was investigated. With a tolerance of plus or minus roughly 50 years, it was shown to be about 340 years old.

iii This result was announced in September 2001 in a press release by the University of Mainz and published in the March 2002 issue of the journal *Anglistik. Mitteilungen des Deutschen Anglistenverbandes* (p. 231).

iv *Shakespeare's Lives*, p. 209. Schoenbaum's closing verdict is: "All in all a doubtful case."

v Op. cit., p. 208

vi (Cambridge, 1932).

vii *Betrachtungen über Leben und Werk* (Hamburg, 1953).

viii Op. cit., p. 19.

ix Ibid.

The Flower Portrait in the Royal Shakespeare Company Collection, Stratford-Upon-Avon: Original or Copy?

It has been demonstrated in this book that the Flower portrait that was radically restored by Nancy Stocker in 1979 at the Ashmolean Museum in Oxford was a true-to-life image of William Shakespeare dating from the poet's lifetime, for which he must have sat in person. The experienced restorer revealed the characteristics of Shakespeare's face in all the painting's original explicitness and attention to detail – especially including the pathological alterations. No later artist could have known about the characteristics so precisely reproduced in the Flower portrait. No painter in later years could have been aware of the various signs of disease because they progressed in the course of Shakespeare's lifetime, and could only have been presented themselves in exactly this way at that particular stage of his life. We may recall, just to give one example, the considerable increase in volume in the area of the left upper eyelid and the left caruncle that took place between the painting of the Chandos portrait and the preparation of the death mask.

I have in my possession a brilliant quality reproduction in the form of an ektachrome, a colour transparency (*see fig. 115*), officially supplied to me for publication purposes by Brian Glover in 1996,[i] then director of the Royal Shakespeare Company collection. This ektachrome shows the most minute details of the restored painting.

In spring 2005 the world media reported that the Flower portrait was "a fake". Under the supervision of Dr Tarnya Cooper at the National Portrait Gallery, the picture had been subjected to tests which had proved that the picture could not have been painted before the early nineteenth century. The experts at the National Portrait Gallery had taken pigment samples from the panel that contained chrome yellow; but chrome paints were only available "from 1814 onwards".

It has to be borne in mind that the Flower portrait was thoroughly examined by leading English scholars and specialists when it was acquired by the Stratford Memorial Theatre in the 1890s. After careful scrutiny and assessment, Sir E. J. Poynter, director of the National Gallery, later president of the Royal Academy; Lionel Cust, director of the National Portrait Gallery; and S. Colvin, curator of the print room at the British Museum, announced that the panel was old (early seventeenth century), the inscription date "1609" was correct, and the Shakespeare portrait was genuine (see p. 27 and 30) At the time technical means at their disposal were not capable of revealing that beneath the Shakespeare image there was a painting of the Madonna from the late fifteenth or early sixteenth century,[ii] proving that the wood was then already about four hundred years old. The art historian Marion H. Spielmann seems to have been the first to notice there was another painting, underlying the Shakespeare portrait, which showed through, depending on the lighting conditions. Spielmann referred to it in *The Title-Page of the First Folio of Shakespeare's Plays* (1924), but linked it with the conjecture that its subject might be Shakespeare's "Dark Lady" (see p. 30). Reporting on the condition of the panel, Spielmann said it was riddled with woodworm.

As far as the Flower portrait is concerned, the new test results from the National Portrait Gallery are most strikingly at odds with the findings of this book. In my opinion this contradiction arises out of the fact that, quite clearly, we are dealing with two different versions of the Flower portrait: the old, original painting from the playwright's own lifetime, and a copy apparently not produced until some centuries later.

It was in the autumn of 2002 that I had discovered the first specific and significant clues that the painting, exhibited in the collection of the Royal Shakespeare Company in Stratford at that time, might not be the original, but a copy. The publishers Philipp von Zabern in Mainz had requested from Stratford a transparency of the Flower portrait for reproduction in the book *William Shakespeare. Seine Zeit – Sein Leben – Sein Werk* (2003), and received a picture (*see fig. 116*) that was distinctly different from the one that – as mentioned above – Brian Glover had supplied to me in 1996 (*see fig. 115*).

It was in the late summer of 2003 that I first reported to David Howells, the new curator of the

Fig. 115 The Flower portrait, original, oil on wood, 1609, RSC collection, Stratford-upon-Avon.

Fig. 116 The Flower portrait, copy, oil on wood, RSC collection, Stratford-upon-Avon.
Created hundreds of years after the original Flower painting.

Fig. 115 a Nose and left eye (original), detail

Fig. 116 a Nose and left eye (copy), detail

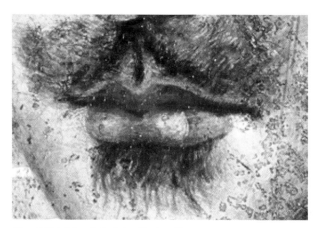

Fig. 115 b Mouth (original), detail

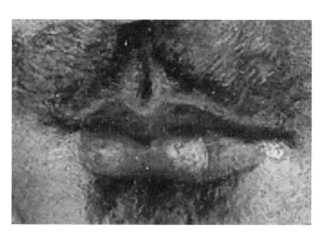

Fig. 116 b Mouth (copy), detail

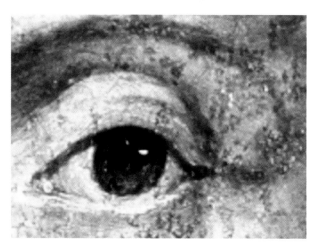

Fig. 115 c Left eye (original), detail

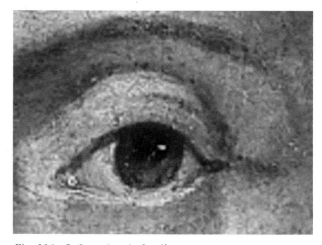

Fig. 116 c Left eye (copy), detail

Royal Shakespeare Collection in Stratford, my suspicion that the picture on display there was not the original Flower portrait.

A few weeks later I turned to the former specialist of the German Federal Bureau of Criminal Investigation (BKA), Reinhardt Altmann, requesting him to assess and report on the matter. In the written report he supplied on 21 December 2003, Altmann came to the definitive conclusion that "the new picture must be a copy of the old one".

Professor Wolfgang Speyer (University of Salzburg), an expert on Old Masters at the Dorotheum in Salzburg,[iii] whom I likewise consulted, confirmed the marked differences between the two pictures. In his assessment of 25 March 2004, he expressed the opinion that "the picture must have been restored, or, to put it more precisely, "repainted". "During this process", he continued, "everything was smoothed out on the surface but the [painting's] character had been utterly lost".

"All the blemishes in the pigment or the varnishing" had been made good, as well as "the unevenness due to the aging of the paint layers". It was obvious that "more damage had been inflicted than had been repaired". The two pictures are juxtaposed here (*figs. 115 and 116*). On close inspection the reader or observer will spot the many discrepancies between the old (original) and the new Flower portrait.

Since I had personally viewed the original picture in the presence of director Brian Glover and Prue Dunne from the Royal Shakespeare Theatre Company in July 1996 and hence can say for certain that the original was in the collection of the RSC Gallery in Stratford at that time, I therefore, at the end of 2003, asked the new curator of the Gallery, David Howells, whether the Flower portrait had undergone any changes since 1996, perhaps in the form of restoration or cleaning.

On 12 January 2004, having thoroughly examined the documentation and consulted all his colleagues, Howells officially informed me that nothing had been altered in the Flower portrait since the extensive restoration of the picture by Nancy Stocker in 1979.

When visiting the National Portrait Gallery in London in January 2004, I learned from Dr Cooper that the Gallery was planning to hold an exhibition of Shakespeare images in 2006 which would include the Flower portrait. In the meantime this image of Shakespeare was to be subjected to technical and scientific testing in the laboratories of the National Portrait Gallery. I strongly advised several times against applying comprehensive tests of authenticity to a painting suspected of being a copy; a suspicion already significantly substantiated by the above-named BKA expert opinion. On 23 June 2004 Howells informed me: "I will make sure that the scholarly team based at the National Portrait Gallery are aware of your concerns."

With the results of their tests, first presented on 21 April 2005 in John Hay's BBC film about the Flower portrait,[iv] the experts of the National Portrait Gallery have now produced proof that the portrait (*see fig. 116*) that has been displayed for some years in Stratford is not the original Flower portrait. It is now clear that we are here dealing with a copy - as Altmann has plainly stated and as the following juxtaposition of the two versions clearly demonstrates.

In view of this fact, the question arises: where is the portrait shown in figure 016 and figure 115 presently, the portrait whose authenticity I was able to prove conclusively in 1995 with the help of criminological and medical specialists, then once again in 1996, and repeatedly at many points in this book?[v]

---

i Communication from the Director, Brian Glover, to the author of 15 November 1996.

ii This was established by an x-ray examination carried out at the Courtauld Institute in London in 1966 (see p. 77 and *fig. 073*).

iii A renowned Austrian auction house that has its head office in Vienna.

iv John Hay, the producer of the film, broadcast on the BBC's "Culture Show" programme, was kind enough to send me a copy immediately after it was televised.

v See the articles mentioned in notes 17–18 (Parts I and II), 55–56, 60–61 and 82 (Part III) and 148 (Part IV) of this book. Objections raised so far have not proved tenable (see p. 182). This also applies to Marcia Pointon's arguments in "Shakespeare, Portraiture and National Identity", *Shakespeare-Jahrbuch* 133 (1997), pp. 29–53, as far as they relate to the Darmstadt Shakespeare death mask and the Chandos and Flower portraits. A revised version of Pointon's essay was published in Tarnya Cooper's catalogue *Searching for Shakespeare. With essays by Marcia Pointon, James Shapiro and Stanley Wells. National Portrait Gallery, London, 2006*, pp. 217–225: "National Identity and the Afterlife of Shakespeare's Portraits". Pointon's arguments had already been thoroughly tested and refuted by the present author in her contribution "Das Shakespeare-Bild und Bilder Shakespeares am Ende des 20. Jahrhunderts" to *Anglistik. Mitteilungen des Verbandes Deutscher Anglisten* (March 1998), pp. 117–130, p. 124 ff.

APPENDIX II

Acknowledgements

The highly commendable efforts of my British publisher, John Maxwell, and the generous understanding of my German publisher Dr W. Georg Olms, his Editorial Director Dietrich Olms, and his editors Dr Peter Guyot and Dr Doris Wendt, have enabled the English translation of this book to be published by Chaucer Press almost simultaneously with the German edition. Thanks to them, the findings of this work are now accessible to an international English-speaking readership. I owe special thanks, therefore, to John Maxwell, Managing Director of Chaucer Press, whose great personal commitment made the accelerated publication of this English edition possible. I should also like to thank Trade Director Terry Price and Marketing Director Finbarr McCabe for their energetic contributions. I am grateful too to Beth Macdougall of MGA Publishing Consultancy for her untiring efforts on behalf of the project and for her kind assistance and great help. My thanks are due, furthermore, to Victoria Huxley, who edited the text as speedily as the occasion demanded, and yet with admirable care, and whose collaboration was both pleasant and efficient. I also want to thank Rachel Burgess, who was responsible for the impressive jacket design and lay-out of the book, and the indexer, Ingrid Lock, who professionally compiled the extensive index of the work in a very short period of time.

To the translator of this book, Professor Alan Bance of the University of Southampton (kindly recommended to me by Professor Roger Paulin at Cambridge University), I owe a great debt of gratitude. I have gained enormously from working with him, and our exchanges stretching over many months have been extremely fruitful. I shall not forget his good sense and his assistance in solving difficult problems. His achievement can probably best be seen in Part III of the book, which presents the processes and results of the numerous different tests for identity and authenticity.

In view of the large numbers of people involved in the project, I hope I may be excused for listing in alphabetical order the names of those I wish to thank. The reader will be able to gauge from this list the wide range of scientific disciplines which contributed to the results achieved, or made them possible in the first place.

EMERITUS PROFESSOR RÜDIGER AHRENS, OBE, British Studies (Literature), University of Würzburg

ELIZABETH ALLEN CBIOL MIBIOL, Qvist Curator, Hunterian Museum, The Royal College of Surgeons of England, London

REINHARDT ALTMANN, EHK, Forensic Expert (Imaging Identification), German Federal Bureau of Criminal Investigation, Wiesbaden

RIMA ASTRAUSKAITE, Manchester

JÖRG BALLERSTAEDT, Director, Federal Bureau of Criminal Investigation, Wiesbaden

JOHN BASKETT, Chairman, Works of Art Committee, Garrick Club, London

ROBERT BEARMAN, Senior Archivist, Shakespeare Birthplace Trust, Stratford-upon-Avon

BERND BECKER, Chief Restorer, Hesse *Land* and University Library, Darmstadt

PETER BENZ, former Mayor of Darmstadt

TOM BISHOP, Information Services Manager, Library, The Royal College of Surgeons of England, London

ANJA BOETTCHER, Dip. Graphic Design, Wiesbaden

HEINRICH BOGE, former President of the German Federal Bureau of Criminal Investigation, Wiesbaden

H. O. BROOKS, former Sexton, Holy Trinity Church, Stratford-upon-Avon

MICHAEL BRUMBY, Archivist, Mainz City Archive

ANTHEA PELHAM BURN, Conservator, Garrick Club, London

DR GABRIELE BUSCH-SALMEN, Musicologist, Burg am Wald bei Kirchzarten

ANTHONY BUTCHER, former Chairman, Works of Art Committee, Garrick Club, London

ANDREW COHEN, Film Producer, BBC, London

DR TARNYA COOPER, Curator, 16th Century, National Portrait Gallery, London

TINA CRAIG, Deputy Head of Library and Information Services, Royal College of Surgeons of England, London

TONY DAVIS, Chief Marshal, Westminster Abbey, London

DR.-ING. ROLF-DIETER DÜPPE, Physicist, Institute for Photogrammetry and Cartography, Technical University of Darmstadt

PRUE DUNNE, Royal Shakespeare Company, Stratford-upon-Avon

ANN-MARIE EHRLICH, Director, Art Archive, London

SIR EDMUND FAIRFAX-LUCY, Charlecote Park, Warwickshire

PROFESSOR KLAUS FAISS, British Studies (Linguistics), University of Mainz

BRIAN GLOVER, former Director of the Royal Shakespeare Company Collection, Stratford-upon-Avon

THE REVD. MARTIN GORICK, Vicar, Holy Trinity Church, Stratford-upon-Avon

DR J. M. N. T. GRAY, Physicist and Mathematician, University of Manchester

DR YORCK ALEXANDER HAASE, former Chief Director of the Hesse *Land* and University Library, Darmstadt

HERTA HARTMANN, retired Senior Teacher, Wiesbaden

MECHTHILD HAWELLECK, Librarian, *Land* Library, Wiesbaden

JOHN HAY, Film Producer, BBC, London

PROFESSOR MICHAEL HERTL, Supernumerary Professor of Pediatrics, University of Heidelberg, Expert on the Physiognomy of the Sick and Death masks, former Medical Superintendent of the Children's Clinic at the Neuwerk Hospital, Mönchengladbach

DR DANIEL HESS, Curator, Germanisches Nationalmuseum, Nuremberg

WALTER HOFFMANN, Mayor of Darmstadt

THE REVD. PETER L. HOLLIDAY, former Vicar, Holy Trinity Church, Stratford-upon-Avon

GEOFFREY HOWARTH, National Trust, Tewkesbury

DAVID HOWELLS, Curator, Royal Shakespeare Company Collection, Stratford-upon-Avon

DR.-ING. CHRISTOPH HUMMEL, Dip. Physics, Wiesbaden

ANNA CORINNA HUMMEL, Student, St Andrews University, Scotland

PROFESSOR PETER HUPPERT, Institute for X-Ray Diagnostics and Nuclear Medicine, Darmstadt City Hospital

PROFESSOR HANS-HELMUT JANSEN, former Medical Superintendent of Pathology, Darmstadt City Hospital

ANDREAS KAHNERT, Photographer, Hesse Land and University Library, Darmstadt

REGINA KANIA, Librarian, Mainz City Library

CHRISTOPHER KENNEDY, former Churchwarden, Holy Trinity Church, Stratford-upon-Avon

DR ULRICH KERSTEN, former President of the Federal Bureau of Criminal Investigation, Wiesbaden

COUNT FRANZ EUGEN VON KESSELSTATT, Kesselstatt Castle, Föhren near Trier

COUNTESS LOUISETTE VON KESSELSTATT, Kesselstatt Castle, Föhren near Trier

MAVERICK KIM, Application Engineer, INUS Technology (Europe Office), Eschborn

PROFESSOR BERND KOBER, Head of the Institute for Radiology, Darmstadt City Hospital

MICHAEL LANGER, Dip. Finance, Main Customs Office, Darmstadt

KARLA LEMM, Librarian, Department of English, University of Mainz

PROFESSOR WALTER LERCHE, former Medical Superintendent of the Eye Clinic at the Wiesbaden Land Capital Hospital, Wiesbaden

RUI LINNARTZ, Restorer, Hesse Land and University Library, Darmstadt

DAVID LOWRY, Sales and Application Engineer 3D, Konica Minolta Photo Imaging Europe (UK)

CATHARINE MACCLEOD, Curator, 17th Century, National Portrait Gallery, London

MAIRIE MACDONALD, Archivist, Shakespeare Birthplace Trust, Stratford-upon-Avon

PROFESSOR JOST METZ, Medical Superintendent of the Dermatological Clinic of the Land Capital Hospital, Wiesbaden

D. MITCHELL, Royal Shakespeare Company Collection, Stratford-upon-Avon

TOM MORGAN, Head of Rights & Reproductions, National Portrait Gallery, London

CANON MICHAEL MOXON, St. George's Chapel, Windsor Castle

GRAHAM NATTRESS, former Head of West European Collections, British Library, London

DIETRICH NEUMANN, Federal Bureau of Criminal Investigation, Wiesbaden

DR GEORG NOLTE-FISCHER, Chief Director of the Hesse Land and University Library, Darmstadt

EMERITUS PROFESSOR KURT OTTEN, British Studies (Literature), University of Heidelberg, Visiting Fellow, Clare Hall, University of Cambridge

PROFESSOR RODNEY H REZNEK, Academic Department of Radiology, St Bartholomew's Hospital, London

MARGOT RINTOUL, Superintendent Radiographer, Princess Grace Hospital, London

MARCUS RISDELL, Librarian and Archivist, Garrick Club, London

EMERITUS PROFESSOR WALTER SALMEN, Musicology, University of Freiburg

CHARLES SAUMAREZ SMITH, Director of the National Gallery, London, former Director of the National Portrait Gallery, London

EDITH SCHUÉ, Head of the Central Photographic Laboratory of the University of Mainz

GEORGE E. SHIERS, former Mathematics Teacher, Grammar School, Stratford-upon-Avon

BERNHARD SIMON, Archivist, Trier City Archive

MANFRED SIMONIS, Dip. Archival Studies, Mainz City Archive

EMERITUS PROFESSOR WOLFGANG SPEYER, Classical Studies and Influence of Classical Antiquity, University of Salzburg, Expert on Old Masters at the Dorotheum, Salzburg

DR NORBERT SUHR, Curator, Land Museum (Landesmuseum), Mainz

DIPL.-ING. THORSTEN TERBOVEN, Sales and Application Engineer 3D, KONICA MINOLTA PHOTO IMAGING EUROPE (Germany), Langenhagen

HELEN TROMPETELER, Picture Librarian, National Portrait Gallery, London

CHRISTOPH VOGEL, Affolterbach (Odenwald)

ALISON WALKER, Art Archive, London

DR HORST WASSMUTH, Jurisprudence, Wiesbaden

WERNER WEGMANN, former Head Librarian, Hesse Land and University Library, Darmstadt

PROFESSOR STANLEY WELLS, Chairman of the Shakespeare Birthplace Trust, Stratford-upon-Avon, former Director of the Shakespeare Institute of the University of Birmingham at Stratford-upon-Avon

ANGELA WOODCOCK, Ashmolean Museum, Oxford

PROFESSOR JOHANN-DIETRICH WÖRNER, President of the Technical University of Darmstadt

PROFESSOR BERNHARD WROBEL, Director of the Institute for Photogrammetry and Cartography at the Technical University, Darmstadt

EMERITUS PROFESSOR DIETER WUTTKE, German Studies, University of Bamberg, Head of the Centre for Renaissance Studies.

PROFESSOR HANS-LUDWIG ZACHERT, former President of the German Federal Bureau of Criminal Investigation, Wiesbaden

MARCO ZAJAC, Manager 3D, Konica Minolta Photo Imaging Europe (Europe, Middle East, Africa), Langenhagen

JÖRG ZIERKE, President of the German Federal Bureau of Criminal Investigation, Wiesbaden

End Notes

Part I and II

1 Quoted from Pico della Mirandola, *On the Dignity of Man*, transl. by Charles Glenn Wallis, Paul J. W. Miller, and Douglas Carmichael, with an Introduction by Paul J. W. Miller (Indianapolis, 1965), p.5.

2 Pico borrowed from the classical thinker Plotinus, who in his turn drew upon Plato. Clemens Zintzen was the first to discover this. See his publication *Vom Menschenbild der Renaissance* (München/Leipzig, 2000), pp. 41–42.

3 "An apologie of Raymond Sebond", in: *Montaigne's Essays*: Renascence Editions, Book II, E-text www.uoregon.edu/~rbear/montaigne/2xii.html, provided by Ben R. Schneider, Lawrence University, Wisconsin, © 1998 The University of Oregon [101].

4 See H. Hammerschmidt-Hummel, *William Shakespeare. Seine Zeit – Sein Leben – Sein Werk* (Mainz, 2003), Part IV, p. 171 ff.

5 See Karl Christ, *Die Römer. Eine Einführung in ihre Geschichte und Zivilisation* (München, 1979), p. 125. See also Karl Schefold (in collaboration with A.-C. Bayard, H. A. Cahn, M. Guggisberg, M. T. Jenny and C. Schneider), *Die Bildnisse der antiken Dichter, Redner und Denker* (Basel, 1997).

6 Pliny the Elder, *Natural History*. A Selection. Translated with an Introduction and Notes by John F. Healy (Harmondsworth, 1991), XXXIV, XXXV and XXXVI.

7 *Skulptur* [1994] (Stuttgart/Zürich, 1995), p. 26.

8 In his publication *Nachweise zu Shakespeares Totenmaske* (p. 66) Wislicenus quotes a relevant passage from the essay *"Die Werkstätte des Bildhauers"* (The Sculptor's Workshop) by Johann Gottfried Schadow, in which the reader is given a glimpse of this art, involving the extremely meticulous use of angle gauges, plumb lines, rods, pointing, and compasses. See Schadow, *Aufsätze und Briefe*, ed. Julius Friedländer (Düsseldorf, 1864), p. 51ff.

9 *"Das Abnehmen von Totenmasken"*, in Ernst Benkard, *Das ewige Antlitz. Eine Sammlung von Totenmasken*, with a Foreword by Georg Kolbe (Berlin, 1927), XLI–XLIII, XLII. The original German text reads: "[...] *die behaarten Stellen werden mit dünn aufgelöstem Modellierton überpinselt, oder auch mit Öl, damit der aufzugießende Gips nicht festhaftet. Die Haut enthält selbst genügend Fett, braucht nicht präpariert zu werden. Die Grenze der Maske, die Teile am Hals, hinter den Ohren usw. werden mit dünnstem nassen Papier umlegt. [...] Eine große Schale Gips, suppendünn über das Antlitz gelöffelt, wenige Millimeter dick – dann ein Faden über die Stirnmitte, Nasenrücken, Mund und Kinn gelegt. Eine zweite Schale stärkeren Gips, wie ein Brei auf die erste Schicht aufgetragen (als haltende Kappe zu denken) und bevor diese bindet, wird der Faden gezogen, das Ganze in Hälften teilend. Nach dem Hartwerden der Kappe wird die zweigeteilte Form gesprengt und vorsichtig vom Kopf gelöst; das Schwierigste, denn luftdicht war der Körper mit der Form geschlossen. Die abgenommenen Hälften werden dann sofort wieder zusammengepaßt und verklammert, das Negativ gereinigt und wieder mit Gips ausgegossen. Der Mantel, die Kappe sorgfältig mit Schlägel und Meißel abgeklopft und darstellt sich das Positiv, die fertige Maske."* On the technique of taking death masks, see also Eric Maclagan, "The use of death-masks by Florentine sculptors", *The Burlington Magazine 43* (1923); Alphons Poller, *Das Pollersche Verfahren zum Abformen an Lebenden und Toten sowie an Gegenständen. Anleitung für Mediziner, Anthropologen, Kriminalisten, Museumspräparatoren, Prähistoriker, Künstler, Handfertigkeitslehrer, Amateure*, ed. by E. B. Poller und E. Fetscher, with an Introduction by C. v. Economo, 129 illustrations (Berlin/Vienna, 1931); Joseph Pohl, *Die Verwendung des Naturabgusses in der italienischen Porträtplastik in der Renaissance* (Würzburg, 1938); K.-H. Schreyl, "Geschichte und Brauchtum der Totenmaske", *Das letzte Porträt*, ed. by Fritz Eschen (Berlin, 1967); Hans Helmut Jansen, "Totenmasken", *Hessisches Ärzteblatt* 11 (Nov. 1975); H. H. Jansen und P. Leist, "The Technique of Death Masks Making. Technik der Abnahme von Totenmasken", *Beiträge zur Pathologie* 161 (1977), 385–390; Iris I. J. M. Gibson, "Death masks unlimited", *British Medical Journal* 291 (December 1985), 21–28.

10 Picture quotation from Joachim Poeschke, *Die Skulptur der Renaissance in Italien*, Vol. I: *Donatello und seine Zeit*. Photographs by Albert Hirmer und Irmgard Ernstmeier-Hirmer (München, 1990), No. 73. See also my article, *"Neuer Beweis für die Echtheit des Flower-Porträts und der Darmstädter Shakespeare-Totenmaske. Ein übereinstimmendes Krankheitssymptom im linken Stirnbereich von Gemälde und Gipsabguß"* (New evidence for the authenticity of the Flower portrait and the Darmstadt Shakespeare death mask. A corresponding symptom of illness in the area of the left forehead of painting and cast), *Anglistik. Mitteilungen des Verbandes Deutscher Anglisten* (Sept. 1996), pp. 115–136, p. 120, fig. 4.

11 *Die Verwendung des Naturabgusses in der italienischen Porträtplastik in der Renaissance* (Würzburg, 1938).

12. See the remarks in my article, *"Neuer Beweis für die Echtheit des Flower-Porträts und der Darmstädter Shakespeare-Totenmaske [...]"*, *Anglistik* (Sept. 1996), p. 123.

13 These works are reproduced in Poeschke, *Die Skulptur der Renaissance in Italien*, I, No. 63 and Nos. 192–94.

14 Dtv-*Lexikon der Kunst*, Vol. 2; see under "Grabplastik".

15 Reproduced in Poeschke, *Die Skulptur der Renaissance in Italien*, No. 187.

16 Reproduced in Poeschke, *Die Skulptur der Renaissance* in Italien, fig. 78, p. 176

17 See Hammerschmidt-Hummel, "Neuer Beweis für die Echtheit des Flower-Porträts und der Darmstädter Shakespeare-Totenmaske [...]", p. 121.

18 Hammerschmidt-Hummel, *"Neuer Beweis für die Echtheit des Flower-Porträts und der Darmstädter Shakespeare-Totenmaske* [...]", p. 118.

19 Quoted from Katherine Esdaile, *English Church Monuments,* 1510 to 1840 (London, 1946), p. 57.

20 Picture quotation from Roy Strong, *Tudor & Jacobean Portraits,* 2 Vols (London, 1969), II, No. 296.

21 *Die Verwendung des Naturabgusses in der italienischen Porträtplastik in der Renaissance,* p. 16. The original German text reads: "*Das eindrucksvollste Porträt der Zeit ist die Effigies des 1509 gestorbenen Heinrich VII. Der Charakter der Totenmaske ist unverkennbar. Das Gesicht ist eingefallen, die Haut ist welk und liegt gespannt über dem Knochengerüst.*"

22 Picture quotation from Strong, *Tudor & Jacobean Portraits,* II, No. 676.

23 Picture quotation from Strong, *Tudor & Jacobean Portraits,* II, No. 463.

24 This funerary sculpture in gilded bronze, the work of the Italian sculptor Pompeo Leoni (1533–1608), is reproduced in the volume by Mary Vincent und Robert Stradling, *Spain and Portugal* (Oxford, 1994), p. 93. As the authors point out in their caption, it resembles "the figures of the Habsburg royal family created by the same artist for the Escorial chapel".

25 See H. Hammerschmidt-Hummel, *Die verborgene Existenz des William Shakespeare. Dichter und Rebell im katholischen Untergrund* (Freiburg im Breisgau, 2001), p. 217, n. 31.

26 See *Die verborgene Existenz des William Shakespeare,* p. 25.

27 See *Die verborgene Existenz des William Shakespeare,* p. 183.

28 On this topic, Walter Salmen writes in *Musiker im Porträt 2. Das 17. Jahrhundert* (München, 1983), Introduction, p. 9: "Zur Erinnerung und Verehrung dienten auch Büsten, die zumeist in Verbindung mit Epitaphien ohne zuordnende Allegorien in Kirchen aufgestellt wurden" (There were also busts expressing admiration and respect, placed in churches and usually combined with memorial plaques without attributive allegories).

29 See letter from Professor Wells to the author of 30 November 1995.

30 Picture quotation from Paul Wislicenus, *Nachweise zu Shakespeares Totenmaske* (Jena, 1913), plate XLIX.

31 See H. Hammerschmidt, *Die Importgüter der Handelsstadt London als Sprach- und Bildbereich des elisabethanischen Dramas* (Heidelberg, 1979), p. 120.

32 Quoted from H. Hammerschmidt, *Die Importgüter der Handelsstadt London,* p. 129.

33 See Wislicenus, *Nachweise zu Shakespeares Totenmaske,* plate XLVII; M. H. Spielmann, *Shakespeare's Portraiture* (London, 1924), pp. 4–5; and Samuel Schoenbaum, *William Shakespeare. A Documentary Life* (Oxford, 1975), p. 254.

34 Photograph by H. Hammerschmidt-Hummel (1996) by kind permission of Canon Michael Moxon, St George's Chapel, Windsor Castle.

35 Photograph by H. Hammerschmidt-Hummel (1996) by kind permission of Chief Marshal Tony Davis, Westminster Abbey, London.

36 Photograph by H. Hammerschmidt-Hummel (1996), by kind permission of Chief Marshal Tony Davis, Westminster Abbey, London.

37 (New Haven/London, 1990), p. 193.

38 See Campbell, "The Functions and Uses of Portraits", in *Renaissance Portraits,* pp. 193–225. Note also Campbell's reference to further literature on the Renaissance portrait (see pp. 275–281), and the select bibliography in *Porträt [Geschichte der klassischen Bildgattungen in Quellentexten und Kommentaren,* Bd. 2], ed. by R. Preimesberger, H. Baader and N. Suthor (Berlin, 1999), pp. 478–481.

39 See Campbell, *Renaissance Portraits,* p. 225.

40 Preimesberger/Baader/Suthor, eds., *Porträt,* pp. 13–64, 15–16.

41 See for example Walter Roth, "Hautveränderungen in künstlerischen Darstellungen". I. – III. Beispiele aus dem Germanischen Nationalmuseum in Nürnberg", *Der Hautarzt* 29 (1978), pp. 86–88, 213–215 and 442–444; Albrecht Scholz, "Von kleinen und großen Tumoren in der Kunst", *Der Hautarzt* 33 (1982), p. 598–604; Walter Roth, "Keratoakanthom auf der linken Wange des Galileo Galilei", *Der Hautarzt* 37 (1986), p. 513–515; Ann G. Carmichael und Richard M. Ratzan, eds., *Medizin in Literatur und Kunst* [1991], German edition (Cologne, 1994). The author thanks Professor Jost Metz, Head of Dermatology at the Dr Horst Schmidt Clinics in Wiesbaden, for valuable information and references to the literature in this area.

42 See Heinrich Besseler, *Fünf echte Bildnisse Johann Sebastian Bachs* (Kassel/Basel, 1956), pp. 17–18.

43 See Scholz, "Von kleinen und großen Tumoren in der Kunst", p. 600, fig. 5.

44 See Carmichael/Ratzan, *Medizin in Literatur und Kunst,* p. 137, No. 41.

45 See Carmichael/Ratzan, *Medizin in Literatur und Kunst,* p. 76.

46 See Roth, "Hautveränderungen in künstlerischen Darstellungen", II, p. 214, fig. 3.

47 See Roth, "Hautveränderungen in künstlerischen Darstellungen", III, p. 443, fig. 2.

48 See the essay "Keratoakanthom auf der linken Wange des Galileo Galilei", *Der Hautarzt* 37 (1986), pp. 513–515, p. 513, fig. 1.

49 Daniel Hess, "Bildnis des Nürnberger Malers Michael Wolgemut", in *Faszination Meisterwerk. Dürer, Rembrandt, Riemenschneider.* Exhibition catalogue (Nürnberg, 2004), p. 134.

50 See Hess, "Bildnis des Nürnberger Malers Michael Wolgemut", p. 134.

51 *Die Gemälde des 16. Jahrhunderts.* Catalogue of the Germanic National Museum in Nuremberg. Compiled by Kurt Löcher in collaboration with Carola Gries. Technological findings: Anna Bartl and Magdalene Gärtner (Stuttgart, 1997), p. 211 and n. 3.

52 See *Die Gemälde des 16. Jahrhunderts,* p. 211.

53 *Die Gemälde des 16. Jahrhunderts,* p. 211.

54 See "Gabriele Paleotti: *Ähnlichkeit als Kategorie der Moral* (1582)", in *Porträt,* Commentary by Hannah Baader, pp. 297–306. At least, this applied in the Catholic countries of Europe.

55 "Gabriele Paleotti: *Ähnlichkeit als Kategorie der Moral* (1582)", in *Porträt,* Commentary by Hannah Baader, pp. 302–303. Translated by Alan Bance, who also used the original Italian text: Gabriele Paleotti, *Discorso intorno alle immagini sacre e profane* (1582; this edition Vatican City, 2002), p. 155.

56 "Paleotti: *Ähnlichkeit als Kategorie der Moral* (1582)", in *Porträt,* Commentary by H. Baader, p.302, and Paleotti, *'I ritratti di altre persone', Discorso intorno alle immagini sacre e profane* (1582) (Vatican, 2002), p. 153.

57 Here we may refer to H. Schedel's famous work *Liber chronicarum,* published in 1493 in Nuremberg.

58 On this point, see under *"Schriftsteller"* in the *Lexikon der Kunst,* VI: *"Verbreitet war im Barock das Autorenbildnis (auch als Titelkupfer)"* (Pictures of authors were widespread in the Baroque period (including copperplate frontispieces).

59 The original Latin text reads: *"Viventis Potuit Durerius Ora Philippi / Mentem non Potuit Pingere Docta / Manus".* Quoted from R. Preimesberger, "Albrecht Dürer: Das Dilemma des Porträts, epigrammatisch (1526)", in Preimesberger/Baader/ Suthor, eds., *Porträt,* Commentary, pp. 220–227, p. 220.

60 Quoted from Preimesberger, "Albrecht Dürer: *Das Dilemma des Porträts ...",* p. 222.

61 Preimesberger, "Albrecht Dürer: *Das Dilemma des Porträts ...",* p. 222.

62 Preimesberger, *"Albrecht Dürer: Das Dilemma des Porträts ...",* p. 228. The Latin original reads: "IMAGO ERASMI ROTERODA / MI AB ALBERTO DURERO AD / VIVAM EFFIGIEM DELINIATA". See also Wolfgang Speyer's astute essay, illustrated by copious examples, "Das wahrerere Porträt. Zur Rivalität von bildender Kunst und Literatur", in W. Speyer, *Frühes Christentum im antiken Strahlungsfeld* (1). Wissenschaftliche Untersuchungen zum Neuen Testament. 50 (Tübingen, 1989), pp. 395-401. Speyer demonstrates that Dürer adopted the Greek circumscription from a medallion depicting the humanist Erasmus, made by the painter Quentin Metsys in 1519. It says that the writings (of Erasmus) will show him to better advantage. The Latin part of the circumscription stresses

that the image was taken from life (*"Imago ad vivam effigiem expressa"*). Speyer comments: "In 1526 Albrecht Dürer employed this Greek inscription for his engraved portrait of Erasmus, and thereby presented the idea of 'the greater picture that the writings show' to an even larger circle of readers"(p. 400).

63 See Strong, *Tudor & Jacobean Portraits,* I, p. 282: "Collections". See also Charles Saumarez Smith, *The National Portrait Gallery* (London, 1997).

64 Malone, quoted from James Boaden, *An Inquiry into the Authenticity of Various Pictures and Prints, Which, from the Decease of the Poet to Our Own Times, Have Been Offered to the Public as Portraits of Shakspeare: Containing a Careful Examination of the Evidence on Which They Claim to Be Received; [...]* (London, 1824), p. 40.

65 Boaden records (1824) that the picture was at that time among the treasures of the Duke of Buckingham in Stowe. See *An Inquiry into the Authenticity of Various Pictures and Prints,* p. 43.

66 See Friswell, *Life-Portraits of William Shakespeare,* p. 28.

67 See Strong, *Tudor & Jacobean Portraits,* I, p. 279.

68 See "The Notebooks of George Vertue", *The Walpole Society* (Oxford, 1930–1947), I, pp. 48 and 56. In her article "The Chandos portrait: a suggested painter", *Burlington Magazine* (1982), pp. 146–149, Mary Edmond has direct recourse to the originals of Vertue's *Notebooks* in the British Library (Add. M.SS. 21, 111) and comes to the conclusion that the antiquary had only met and questioned the contemporary owner of the picture, Keck, after his first Notebook entry, and had been obliged to make some changes after this meeting. The original version of the first entry is said to read: "The Picture of Shakespear the only [replaced by "one"] Original in Possesion of / Mr. Keyck of the Tempe. he bought for forty guines / of .... who bought of Sr. W. Davenant. who had / it of Shakespeare. it was painted by one Taylor, a / Player [above "& painter"] cotemp: with Shakes & his intimate Friend." [In the left-hand margin the name "Richard Burbridge" has been written in]. According to Edmond, Vertue made three later changes: he crossed out the name "Burbridge"; above the omission mark he supplied the name "Mr. Baterton"; and he placed "it" in front of "of Sr. W. Davenant". Further, above the subordinate clause "who had / it of Shakespeare" he placed another relative clause: "to whom it was left by will. of John Taylor". The original version of the second entry – according to Edmond – reads: "Mr. Betterton told Mr.Keck several times that the Picture of Shakespear he had, was painted by John Taylor a Player, who acted for Shakespeare & this John Taylor in his will left it to Sr. Willm. Davenant. & at his death Mr. Keck bought it. in whose poses it now is [...]". Vertue, quoted from Edmond, "The Chandos portrait", p. 146.

69 See Edmond, "The Chandos portrait", pp. 146–149.

70 2 Vols. (London, 1969), I, p. 279.

71 Strong, *Tudor & Jacobean Portraits,* I, p. 279.

72 Strong, *Tudor & Jacobean Portraits,* I. p. 279.

73 *Shakespeare's Lives.* New Edition (Oxford/New York, 1991), pp. 202–206.

74 Reproduced are the painting as it was before 1979, and next to it the picture as it looked after its thorough restoration by Nancy Stocker of the Ashmolean Museum in Oxford in the year 1979.

75 The wood used was identified at the beginning of the century by G. R. M. Murray of the Botanical Department of the British Museum as "old elm-wood". Cf. the report by W. S. Brassington of 27. November 1896, quoted from J. Corbin in "Two Undescribed Portraits of Shakespeare", *Harper's New Monthly Magazine* (May 1897), p. 902. In his article "Artists' Images of Shakespeare", in *Images of Shakespeare. Proceedings of the Third Congress of the International Shakespeare Association, 1986.*, eds. Werner Habicht, D. J. Palmer and Roger Pringle (Newark/London/Toronto, 1988, pp. 19–39, p. 32), Schoenbaum declares, albeit without any substantiation, that the Flower portrait is painted on an "ancient worm-eaten panel of English oak".

76 Marion H. Spielmann refers to "Mr. H. C. Clements of Sydenham". *The Title-Page of the First Folio of Shakespeare's Plays: A Comparative Study of the Droeshout Portrait and the Stratford Monument* (Oxford/London, 1924), p. 35. Samuel Schoenbaum on the other hand has the owner residing in Peckham Rye. See *Shakespeare's Lives* (Oxford, 1975, repr. 1991), p. 334. The English Shakespeare scholar Sidney Lee characterised him as a "private gentleman with artistic tastes". *A Life of William Shakespeare* (New York, 1898), p. 288. For Schoenbaum he becomes "an artistic gentleman" (ibid, p.334).

77 The actual words used are "descendant of Shakespeare's family in whose possession it had been since the Poet sat for it". Spielmann, *The Title-Page of the First Folio of Shakespeare's Plays*, p. 35. Spielmann is very sceptical about this suggested provenance, and would even go so far as to say that it can safely be ignored.

78 Schoenbaum, *Shakespeare's Lives*, p. 334.

79 Literally, the text reads: "It was stated to have originally belonged to a descendant of Shakespeare's family." This information is based on a lecture given by Edgar Flower of the Shakespeare Memorial Theatre in Stratford-upon-Avon to the London Society of Antiquaries (p. 49).

80 An incidental scientific result presented in my book, *Das Geheimnis um Shakespeares 'Dark Lady' (The Secret of Shakespeare's Dark Lady.,* pp. 114–115) established that the poet also had an illegitimate daughter. Cf also subchapter "Autobiography in the sonnets" in my forthcoming book *The Life and Times of William Shakespeare (1564-1616)* London, 2006

81 It is alleged that one of the later, impoverished descendants of the Harts, the seventh-generation William Shakespeare Hart, who lived in Tewkesbury and died there in 1834, still possessed a walking stick of Shakespeare's. See Stanley Wells and T. J. B. Spencer, "Shakespeare in Celebration", *Shakespeare: A Celebration. 1564–1964*, ed. T. J. B. Spencer (Harmondsworth, 1964), pp. 114–132, p. 119.

82 See Hammerschmidt-Hummel, *William Shakespeare. Seine Zeit – Sein Leben – Sein Werk,* pp. 35–36, fig. 36.

83 Wells/Spencer, "Shakespeare in Celebration", pp. 119–120. Apart from this main line of descent, there were a number of subsidiary branches, bearing the name of Smith, founded by the daughters of Joan Hart. The authors point out that in the 1830s a William Shakespeare Smith went to the Stratford school; his family likeness ("the 'Shakespeare cast of countenance'") immediately struck William Howitt, an interested visitor. Howitt published his impressions in the book *Visits to Remarkable Places* (1840). Like George Shakespeare Hart, a tenth-generation descendant of Joan Hart (the playwright's sister), who emigrated to Australia in the 1860s, William Shakespeare Smith is also said to have emigrated to that antipodean country. Another member of these subsidiary branches of the family, William Smith, kept a public house in Tewkesbury in the mid-nineteenth century (p. 120).

84 Lee, *A Life of William Shakespeare*, p. 290.

85 On the origins and family relationships of the Droeshouts, see Part III p. 44.

86 Brassington, quoted from Corbin, "Two Undescribed Portaits of Shakespeare", p. 902.

87 *The Title-Page of the First Folio of Shakespeare's Plays: A Comparative Study of the Droeshout Portrait and the Stratford Monument* (Oxford/London), 1924, pp. 36–37. On the chronological order of painting and engraving, see also Spielmann's publications from 1907 onwards: "The Portraits of Shakespeare", in: *The Works of William Shakespeare. Vol. X*, ed. by A. H. Bullen (Stratford-upon-Avon, 1907), pp. 373–398; also "The Portraits of Shakespeare", *Encyclopaedia Britannica. Vol. 24*, 11th ed. (1911), pp. 787–793.

88 *Shakespeare. Man and Artist*, 2 vols. (London/Oxford, 1938), Vol. II, footnote 726.

89 Schoenbaum, *Shakespeare's Lives* (Oxford, 1970, new ed., 1991), p. 334, also Schoenbaum, *William Shakespeare: A Documentary Life* (Oxford, 1975), frontispiece, caption, and *William Shakespeare: Records and Images* (London, 1981), p. 173.

90 Schoenbaum, "Artists' Images of Shakespeare" in *Images of Shakespeare*, pp. 32–35, and *Shakespeare's Lives*, p. 334. Unfortunately, Schoenbaum's account of the circumstances of the portrait's acquisition by the Stratford Memorial Gallery in the (Berlin) lecture mentioned above contains serious factual errors. He asserts, for example, that Edgar Flower acquired the picture in 1892 from "Clements's executor", and that Mrs Flower had given the picture to the Memorial Gallery three years later (see "Artists' Images of Shakespeare", p. 34). But H. C. Clements, who loaned the Gallery the picture in 1892, died in 1895. Mrs Charles Flower bought it from his widow and donated it in the same year to the Memorial Gallery. As stated at the beginning of this chapter, Edgar Flower reported on this in December 1895 to the London Society of Antiquaries.

91 "What Shakespeare Looked Like: The Spielmann Position and the Alternatives", *Journal of the Rutgers University Libraries* 41 (June 1979), pp. 1–17, and Bertram/Cossa, "'Willm Shakespeare 1609' [...]": "Nothing about the sequence presumed in the Spielmann hypothesis (Lost Original – State I – State II – Painting)", say the authors after a thorough investigation, "is actually required by the facts of the case" (p. 87).

92 "Because of 'certain lines visible upon the picture'", according to Bertram and Cossa, drawing on Brassington, "it had long been suspected that there was an earlier painting on the elm panel beneath the painting of Shakespeare" (p. 93). Cf. the statement of Major Paul Payne, at that time "curator of the Royal Shakespeare Theatre Gallery", quoted in the article "Shakespeare Portrait X-rayed" in *The Times* of 28 May 1966.

93 "The picture is painted on gesso on a worm-eaten panel of English elm, which had previously done service for a portrait of a lady in a high ruff and a red dress (as can be traced in a good light especially when the sun is shining on it). [What if it should be 'The Dark Lady'?]", *The Title-Page of the First Folio of Shakespeare's Plays*, p. 36.

94 The fact that the picture of the Madonna and Child with St John was painted over by the Shakespeare portrait led me to undertake further scientific research; the results were published in my monograph *Die verborgene Existenz des William Shakespeare* and are briefly summarised in Part V of this book (see p. 134ff.). Since being restored in 1979 the painting has a double identity because in a few places the religious representation has been revealed and left showing. But the portrait of Shakespeare is clearly dominant.

95 They write: "Such tall elegant Madonnas set in landscapes – as this one appears to be – are fairly common in the latter part of the fifteenth century. The Christ child, twisting athletically, can be found in the work of (among others) Botticelli, Pinturicchio, and Filippino Lippi [...]. It is Leonardo da Vinci, however, who is credited with the introduction of the young Saint John into Madonna and Child scenes (as in the Madonna of the Rocks, Louvre, 1483). The Child reaching for a cross held by Saint John is a motif associated with Filippino and with Raphael (as in the Alba Madonna, National Gallery, Washington, D.C., 1509–10). If, however, the Flower Madonna is oil-on-panel (which is not certain, but which Ms Stocker says is 'probable'), this medium would greatly limit the time and the circumstances under which the painting was produced. Very few artists in Italy worked in oils in the fifteenth century. [...] The style of this Madonna in any case does not resemble that of Antonello or the Venetian painters who began using oils, but seems to be central Italian in origin. For all of the above reasons it seems likely that the work is not from the fifteenth century at all but dates from the early sixteenth century. The artist was old-fashioned in some respects but very likely was familiar with the styles of Leonardo and Raphael." "'Willm Shakespeare 1609' [...]", p. 94.

96 On this and other statements by Major Payne see Bertram/Cossa, "'Willm Shakespeare 1609' [...]", p. 93.

97 In the course of its (well-known) history the picture has been cleaned and restored several times: in 1895 by Mr Dyer on behalf of Edgar Flower; in 1942 by the firm of William Drown and Company; and in 1979, under the supervision of the Ashmolean Museum in Oxford, by Ms Nancy Stocker, who carried out probably the most radical restoration. The various earlier restorers seem to have left no records. See information provided by Bertram and Cossa (p. 93).

98 Bertram/Cossa, p.83.

99 Lee, *A Life of William Shakespeare*, pp. 289-290.

100 *A Life of William Shakespeare*, p. 289.

101 Bertram/Cossa, p. 95.

102 Photograph The Art Archive and Garrick Club, London.

103 Parker Norris, *The Portraits of Shakespeare*, p. 178.

104 Schoenbaum, *Shakespeare's Lives*, p. 337.

105 *Shakespeare's Town and Times* (London, *c.* 1896), p. 147.

106 Devonshire, quoted from *Pictures in the Garrick Club*, p. 520. There was a similar inscription on the plinth of the copy of the Davenant bust in the Royal Shakespeare Theatre Collection in Stratford-upon-Avon, where the present writer inspected and photographed it on 8 January 1998: "Workman pulling down the old Dukes Theatre in Lincoln Inn Fields London found this bust of Shakespeare which had been covered over above a doorway. (copy)" By permission of the then Director, Brian Glover, this copy was digitally measured in three dimensions by the physicist Dr J.M.N.T. Gray of the Institut für Mechanik at the Technical University of Darmstadt (now Manchester University) and his Assistant Rima Astrauskaite B.A.

107 See among others E. Beresford Chancellor, *The Romance of Lincoln's Inn Fields and its Neighbourhood* (London, 1932), p. 203: "When [...] it was necessary to enlarge the museum of the Royal College of Surgeons, in 1848, the premises were acquired for that purpose, and demolished. In the process a bust of Shakespeare was found embedded in one of the walls, and this interesting relic is now preserved in the Garrick Club."

108 Ashton, *Pictures in the Garrick Club*, p. 520: "The provenance is extremely suspect. Lincoln's Inn Fields was built in 1714 and vacated in 1732 when the manager, John Rich, moved to his new theatre in Covent Garden. There were occasional performances for 12 years, the last taking place on 11 December 1744. During the 1745 rebellion, Rich handed over the theatre to the Government to be used as a garrison. It is inconceivable that Roubiliac produced his bust before 1732, and extremely unlikely that it was made before 1744." As will be shown in Part IV (p. 94ff.), neither the reasons Ashton advances for assuming that the traditional provenance must be incorrect, nor the theory that the Davenant bust is by Roubiliac, are sustainable.

109 "The Portraits of Shakespeare", *Encyclopaedia Britannica*. Vol. 24, 11th ed. (1911): "To Roubiliac [...] must be credited the celebrated 'D'Avenant Bust' of blackened terra-cotta in the possession of the Garrick Club. This fine work of art derives its name from having been found bricked up in the old Duke's theatre in Portugal Row, Lincoln's Inn Fields, which 180 years before was d'Avenants, but which afterwards passed through various vicissitudes."

110 "The skilled sculptor who carved the Garrick Club bust", says Schoenbaum, "was probably the same L. F. Roubiliac who made the famous statue of Shakespeare for the great actor [Garrick]." *Shakespeare's Lives*, p. 337.

111 "S29*, WILLIAM SHAKESPEARE, Louis François Roubiliac, c. 1758", *A Catalogue of the Paintings, Drawings, Watercolours and Sculpture*. Compiled and written by G. Ashton, ed. by Kalman A. Burnim & Andrew Wilton (London, 1997), p. 520. The inscription on the plinth *(William Shakespeare / by / Louis François Roubiliac)* has been carried out in black letters on gilded wood; it is not clear by whom, or at what date this was done.

112 Larson, quoted from Ashton, *Pictures in the Garrick Club*, p. 521. The plaster was embedded in a "square-sectioned iron bar".

113 Ashton, *Pictures in the Garrick Club*, p. 513, p. 15.

114 With new American Supplement. Ed. Day Otis Kellogg (New York/Chicago, 1899), XXI; see under "Roubiliac". This criticism refers to Roubiliac's portraits in marble, but it also applies to his work in terracotta.

115 See the auction catalogue *Handschriften, Autographen, Wertvolle Bücher des 15. – 20. Jahrhunderts* (Heidelberg, 3 November 1960), "421 *Die Darmstädter Shakespeare-Totenmaske. Leicht gebräunter Gips, Länge* 23,5 cm. *Rückseitig eingeritzt:* 'Ao. Dm. 1616'. *Kleine Beschädigung an der Nase.* 40 000.–" (Item 421 the Darmstadt Shakespeare death mask. Plaster, turned slightly brown, length 23.5 cm, scratched into rear is, 'Ao. Dm. 1616'. Slight damage to nose. 40, 000").

116 Hermann Schaaffhausen, "Ueber die Todtenmaske Shakespeare's", *Jahrbuch der Deutschen Shakespeare-Gesellschaft* (1875), pp. 26–49, p. 41.

117 According to my research in the British Museum (between 1997 and 1999), as yet no written record of Owen's investigations has been located.

118 Schaaffhausen, "Ueber die Todtenmaske Shakespeare's", p. 42. The original German text reads: "Owen's Urtheil über die Maske war, dass dieselbe in ihren anatomischen Verhältnissen dem Bilde entspreche, welches man sich von Shakespeare machen könne. Er erkannte die ihr anklebenden Haare als wirkliche Menschenhaare und hielt es für wichtig, dass die Jahreszahl 1616 in den Ziffern jener Zeit geschrieben und, wie man an den abgerundeten Kanten derselben sehen könne, in den noch weichen Gyps eingeschrieben sei."

119 "Shakespeare's Bildnisse", *Shakespeare-Jahrbuch* (1869), pp. 308–326, p. 313. The original German text reads: "Die Kesselstadt'sche Maske [gemeint ist die Darmstädter Shakespeare-Totenmaske] ist dem Brittischen Museum zum Kauf angeboten worden, und dieses wäre, wie es heisst, darauf einzugehn geneigt, wenn nachgewiesen würde, dass irgend ein Mitglied der Familie Kesselstadt [sic], etwa im Gefolge einer Gesandtschaft, in London gewesen sei."

120 Schaaffhausen, "Ueber die Todtenmaske Shakespeare's", p. 42.

121 "Ueber die Todtenmaske Shakespeare's", p. 42.

122 Paul Wislicenus, *Dokumente zu Shakespeares Totenmaske* (Darmstadt, 1911), p. 42.

123 Wislicenus, *Dokumente zu Shakespeares Totenmaske*, p. 42.

124 A. Brandl even suggests that Wislicenus himself emphasised "old Weismüller's lack of reliability": "Zur Beurteilung der Darmstädter Shakespeare-Maske", *Shakespeare-Jahrbuch* (1928), pp. 132–140, pp. 156–171, p.158.

125 "Zur Beurteilung der Darmstädter Shakespeare-Maske", p. 157.

126 "19. *Section für Anthropologie*. 19. September – Präsident Herr Prof. Schaaffhausen", *Tageblatt der 46. Versammlung Deutscher Naturforscher und Aerzte* (1873; 19 Sept.), p. 193. The original German text reads: "Das kraniologische und physiognomische Urtheil über diese die edelsten Formen kundgebende Todtenmaske findet keinen Anhaltspunkt, um an der Aechtheit derselben zu zweifeln. Diese ist, wie die feine Zeichnung der Haut beweist, wirklich von einem Todten abgenommen worden. Die hohe volle Stirn, sowie die Schönheit der Gesichtszüge entsprechen dem Bilde, welches wir uns von dem grossen Dichter machen dürfen, und sind den bekannten bildlichen Darstellungen desselben ähnlich. [...] Es sind Gründe vorhanden, die Maske für das Original und nicht für eine Copie zu halten."

127 Since the Flower portrait had not yet been rediscovered, Page could not consider it. But for him it was clear:: "The original picture, from which this print [the Droeshout engraving] is made, I think just has been drawn or painted from the living man." William Page, "A Study of Shakespeare's Portraits", *Scribner's Monthly* (September 1875), pp. 558–574, p. 564.

128 Page, "A Study of Shakespeare's Portraits", p. 559.

129 "Dimensions of Shakespeare's Mask. Horizontal Measures. 1. Distance between hairs of eyebrows. 2. Between inner corners of eyes. 3. Between outer corners of eyes. 4. Across cheek-bones through center of eyes – (Twice the length of this measure.) 5. From center of bridge of nose between the eyes, right side, to cheek-bone. 6. From center of bridge of nose, between the eyes, left side, to cheek-bone. 7. Outer corner of right eye to center of bridge of nose. 8. Outer corner of left eye to center of bridge of nose. 9. Inner corner of both eyes to center of bridge of nose. 10. Across the fullness, above the temples. – (Twice the length of this measure.) 11. Across the nostrils. 12. Breadth from point to point of mustache. 13. Tuft on chin so wide at broadest. 14. Greatest width across lower jaws opposite the mouth. 15. Length of lower lip. 16. Opening of mouth, between mustaches. 17. Whole distance from beard on chin in front to back of cast below. 18. From throat to under part of beard. Perpendicular Measures. 19. Extreme length from peak of beard to top of head. – (Twice the length of this measure.) 20. Between eyebrows to top of mask. 21. Between eyebrows to point of nose. 22. From point of nose

to end of beard. 23. From inner corner of right eye to top of head. 24. Inner corner of right eye to bottom lobe of nostril. 25. Inner corner of right eye to mouth. 26. Opening of the mouth to turn of chin." Page, "A Study of Shakespeare's Portraits", p. 569.

130 Page, "A Study of Shakespeare's Portraits", p. 568: "Of these twenty-six measures, at least ten or twelve fit exactly corresponding points in the Stratford bust, which any one may verify if he will take the trouble to interpret the diagram here annexed, and reduce all the measurements to solid geometry."

131 Page, "A Study of Shakespeare's Portraits", p. 568.

132 One of the reasons was almost certainly of a technical nature. It would hardly have been feasible for Page, an elderly man, to undertake a risky climb on a makeshift scaffold some metres high in order to get to the bust, to carry out compass measurements and enter them into his list at the same time. While inspecting the bust in August 1996, the present writer found herself in a similar situation, but was actively assisted by Mr H. O. Brooks (Verger of Holy Trinity Church) and her husband, Dr Christoph Hummel. It is practically impossible, at that height, standing on a narrow plank, to take measurements and to write down the results oneself. Although the unnamed Stratford townsman who helped Page, and whom Wislicenus got to know personally in 1911, wrote nothing down, he did however "relate how Page expressed his astonishment from one measurement to the next on seeing how precisely the proportions fitted". Wislicenus, *Nachweise zu Shakespeares Totenmaske. Die Echtheit der Maske* (Jena, 1913), p. 72.

133 Schoenbaum failed to engage seriously with Page's 1911 measurements and results, or their clarification and confirmation by the historian Paul Wislicenus and the sculptor Robert Cauer; and neither had he ever seen the Darmstadt death mask. Nonetheless, he rejected the conclusions arrived at by the American sculptor after extensive and painstaking examination of the objects. Thus we read in *Shakespeare's Lives*: "He [Page] took many measurements and compared them with the statistics for the Stratford monument. Almost half, he asserted, corresponded; the majority that did not failed to trouble him" (p. 339).

134 Page, "A Study of Shakespeare's Portraits", p. 568.

135 Page, "A Study of Shakespeare's Portraits", p. 568.

136 Wislicenus says of Cauer that "he had grown up in his art and was very experienced in producing death masks". *Nachweise zu Shakespeares Totenmaske*, p. 74.

137 *Nachweise zu Shakespeares Totenmaske*, p. 74. The original German text reads: *"Erst prüfte Herr Cauer Page's Maße einzeln an der Totenmaske, dann übertrug er sie auf einen Abguß der Maske, "punktierte" sie nach Schadow's Darlegung [...], notierte als jeden Ansatzpunkt beider Zirkelspitzen am Abguß, machte an den Stellen – also zwei- und fünfzig – Kreuzchen, und schrieb die Nummer der Abmessungen hinzu."*

138 *Nachweise zu Shakespeares Totenmaske*, pp. 74–75. The original German text reads: *"Mit diesem Abguß und Page's Büchlein fuhren wir nach Stratford; am 4. August 1911, morgens etwa um 11 Uhr,*

trafen wir am Geburtsort des großen Dichters ein. Von Sir Sidney Lee an Mr. Wellstood, den Sekretär des "Birthhouse" empfohlen, gewannen wir bald die liebenswürdige Erlaubnis des Canon Melville, und um 3 Uhr nachmittags wurde die Büste bereits vermessen, wozu der Domherr selbst seine Hilfe lieh. Wir stellten eine Leiter neben ein Grabmal, legten über dieses eine zweite horizontal in die Sprossen der senkrechten hinein, und auf diese zweite ein Brett, das Herr Cauer erstieg. In der Rechten den Zirkel haltend, in der Linken den Abguß mit den Kreuzchen, nahm er jedes Maß erst von dem Page'schen Buche, das ich ihm emporreichte, prüfte es nochmals am Abguß und seinen Kreuzchen, und maß es dann am Büstenkopfe ab."

139 He published them on pages 77 to 80 of his book *Nachweise zu Shakespeares Totenmaske*.

140 *Nachweise zu Shakespeares Totenmaske*, pp. 81–82.

141 *Nachweise zu Shakespeares Totenmaske*, p. 81.

142 Ibidem, p. 81. It is astonishing that the differing forms of the moustache are not mentioned at this point, since – as the present writer showed in her proofs of authenticity, produced in 1995 – along with the shortness of the nose, this feature belongs to the two real "divergencies".

143 Wislicenus, Paul, *Dokumente zu Shakespeares Totenmaske*, Darmstadt, n.d..; *Shakespeares Totenmaske*, with a drawing by Hermann Pfeifer (Darmstadt, 1910, 2nd, revised edition Jena, 1911); *Nachweise zu Shakespeares Totenmaske. Die Echtheit der Maske* (Jena, 1913); "Shakespeares Totenmaske. Offener Brief an die Redaktion des Berner 'Bund'", *Der Bund* (Bern) 521 (4./5. November 1910) and "Shakespeares Totenmaske", *Jahrbuch der Deutschen Shakespeare-Gesellschaft* 48 (1912), pp. 116–124, with 2 illus.

144 "The Portraits of Shakespeare", *Encyclopaedia Britannica* (1911). The context of this quotation reads: "It [the 'Kesselstadt Death Mask'] is not in fact a death-mask at all, but a cast from one and probably not even a direct cast. [...] In searching for the link of evidence necessary to be established, through the Kesselstadt line to England and Shakespeare, a theory has been elaborated, but nothing has been proved or carried beyond the point of bare conjecture. The arguments against the authenticity of the cast are strong and cogent – the chief of which is the fact that the skull reproduced is fundamentally of a different form and type from that shown in the Droeshout print – the forehead is receding instead of upright. Other important divergencies occur." For the stunning correspondences and harmonies between these and other portraits of Shakespeare see Part III, pp. 47ff.

145 This emerges from the correspondence of the Becker family. The author received this information from Dr Magda Heidenreich, formerly the leading member of the Becker/Heidenreich community of joint heirs, when she visited the family seat in Affolterbach (Odenwald) on 17 June 1995 and consulted the family archive.

146 With a Foreword by Georg Kolbe (Berlin, 1929).

147 "Zur Beurteilung der Darmstädter Shakespeare-Maske", *Shakespeare-Jahrbuch* (1928), p. 132. The original German text

reads: "Da Benkard hier als Spezialist für Totenmasken auftritt, und eine sachgemäße Nachprüfung solcher Behauptungen oft lange auf sich warten läßt, so besteht die Gefahr, daß dieses Urteil sich als 'wissenschaftliches Ergebnis' festsetzt. Das wäre bedauerlich, denn von allen geltend gemachten Gründen ist keiner stichhaltig, und einige sind geradezu widersinnig."

148 Gundolf, "*Zur Beurteilung der Darmstädter* Shakespeare-Maske", p. 134, footnote 1.

149 Gundolf, "*Zur Beurteilung der Darmstädter* Shakespeare-Maske", p. 135. The original German text reads: "Jede sorgfältige Betrachtung [...] wird es bestätigen. Die Stirnfalten sind zweifellos organisch gewachsen [...]. An geschützten Stellen, z. B. den unteren Augenlidern, selbst noch den äußeren Augenwinkeln (Krähenfüße), dann unter dem Kinn ist die organische Hautfältelung so deutlich, daß sie jeder sehen kann [...]." See also p. 80 and *fig. 074*. Gundolf's observation is fully confirmed here.

150 "With some needle-like instrument", says Benkard, "the plaster had been pierced to create a small channel", into which the hairs had "been artificially introduced, one by one, and fixed in place with some kind of adhesive like shellack". "This idea", says Gundolf, "is so strange in itself that it is difficult to take it seriously. Just imagine: you can count a good two or three dozen extremely thin hairs; in the eyebrows, the eyelashes, both sides of the beard, all deeply and firmly stuck in the plaster, sometimes two close together. Why would anyone go to such incredible trouble to insert them in the manner described?" "Zur Beurteilung der Darmstädter Shakespeare-Maske", p. 136.

151 I was told this both in person and in telephone conversations over the summer and autumn of 1996 by Professor Jansen, who has had decades of experience in the area of death masks and produced numerous scientific publications on the subject. Professor Hertl, too, in his book *Totenmasken – was vom Leben und Sterben bleibt (Death Masks – What is Left after Living and Dying)* (Stuttgart, 2002) declared Benkard's negative verdict on the Darmstadt Shakespeare death mask to be unfounded (see pp. 121-126). He had already expressed this view in his expert report of 15.08.1997.

152 No. 12, pp. 115–125. Pohl, having demonstrated the contradictions in Spielmann's arguments right at the beginning of his essay, and having regretfully noted that "every phrase in it has been conditioning the minds of readers for half a century" (p. 115), is subjected to some unattractive disparaging remarks by Schoenbaum: "The author, [...] an enthusiast of the Vikings and Amerigo Vespucci, concluded on the basis of comparative measurements that the Mask represented the same man as the Stratford bust. Pohl puts the odds in his favour at a trillion to one; some bookmarkers, one suspects, would offer rather less"; *Shakespeare's Lives*, p. 339. The 'Kesselstadt Mask', says Schoenbaum in an ironic and derogatory comment, is in the right place, in the Darmstadt Museum (see p. 339). The Shakespeare scholar thereby demonstrates once again that he does not know the location of the Darmstadt death mask which is in the Hesse *Land* and University Library, and not in the *Landesmuseum* in Darmstadt.

Part III

1 Illustration from *The Life and Times of Shakespeare*, gen. ed.: Enzo Orlandi, text: Maria Pia Rosignoli, translator: Mary Kanani (London/New York/Sydney/Toronto, 1968), p. 74.

2 See Strong, *Tudor & Jacobean Portraits*, I, p. 284.

3 See Katherine A. Esdaile, *English Monumental Sculpture since the Renaissance*, p. 119: "the allegorical figures on the Bottesford monument are repeated by Nicholas's brother Gerard [Janssen] and elsewhere [...]."

4 In a letter of 27 September 1749 to his friend from college days, Revd. John Sympson, Greene mentions "the two naked boys" in the upper part of the monument, which he calls "emblems of Tragedy & Comedy".

5 J. C. Cooper, *An Illustrated Encyclopaedia of Traditional Symbols* (London, 1978), see under "Torch". See also G. E. Lessing, *Wie die Alten den Tod gebildet* (*How the Ancients represented Death*, Stuttgart, 1984 ; first published 1769). With reference to Lessing Katharina Braun observes that: "The youths with lowered torches stem from the Roman art of late antiquity. They belong to the iconographical type of the Eros figure, and even though they are symbolic of death and the grave, Christian art readily adopted them as decorative features". *Der Todesgenius in der frühneuzeitlichen Grabplastik.* http://www.fantom-online.de/seiten12d7.htm.

6 See William Hamper, ed., *The Life, Diary, and Correspondence of Sir William Dugdale* (London, 1827), p. 99.

7 Katharine A. Esdaile, *English Monumental Sculpture since the Renaissance* (London, 1927), pp. 117–118. See also Schoenbaum, *William Shakespeare. A Documentary Life*, p. 252.

8 The contract drawn up in 1594 with the Southamptons bears the imposing signature of the head of the family, "Garat Jhonson" (Gheerart Janssen). The original is kept in the Hampshire Record Office in Winchester under file number "Ref. 5M53/262" .

9 See Katharine A. Esdaile, *English Monumental Sculpture since the Renaissance*, pp. 117–118. It was common among neighbours to enquire about sculptors who produced particularly impressive work. So, for example, Lady Berkeley, the widow of the 17th Lord Berkeley, who died in 1613, asked Sir Robert Spencer about the artist who had carried out the work on his father's monument in Great Brington church. See Katherine Esdaile, *English Church Monuments, 1510 to 1840* (London, 1946), p. 49. In the case of John Combe it is not quite clear whether his family was directed towards the sculptor Janssen by Shakespeare, who must have known the workshop, or whether the playwright's family sought information from the Combes about the sculptor they had employed.

10 It was Mrs Charlotte C. Stopes who first drew attention to this. In "The True Story of the Stratford Bust", in: *Shakespeare's Environment* (London, 1914), p. 117, she states: "[...] I have lately found a lawsuit which proves that his [Gerard Johnsons's]

wife was acting as his widow before 1616. Therefore, if the name be correct, it [Shakespeare's bust] must have been not his, but that of his son, who succeeded him in his business."

11 On this point, see also Paul Wislicenus, *Shakespeares Totenmaske* (Jena, 1911), p. 70 ff.

12 See Nigel Llewellyn, *The Art of Death. Visual Culture in the English Death Ritual, c. 1500 – c. 1800.* Publ. in Association with the Victoria and Albert Museum (London, 1991, repr. 1992), p. 102, no. 77.

13 As Esdaile puts it: "London craftsmen like Gerard Johnson were offering 'exact portraitures' of the dead". *English Church Monuments, 1510 to 1840*, p. 48.

14 *English Monumental Sculpture since the Renaissance*, p. 119.

15 See the present writer's observations in "*Neuer Beweis für die Echtheit des Flower-Porträts und der Darmstädter Shakespeare-Totenmaske [...]*" and in "*Das Shakespeare-Bild und Bilder Shakespeares am Ende des 20. Jahrhunderts*".

16 The anonymous composer of the inscription may be using "Maronic" or "Maronem" in two different senses. Since "Maronian" is another name (no longer used in English) for the Latin poet Virgil, a connection with Virgil is suggested, as it is by the references to Nestor and Socrates. Quite rightly, as the author of many plays about the history (and pre-history) of Britain, Shakespeare is compared to the author of the *Aeneid*.

17 While T.J.B. Spencer, former Director of the Shakespeare Institute in Stratford-upon-Avon, in his article "Shakespeare as Seen by his Contemporaries", at least paraphrased part of the inscription ("The Latin epitaph on the monument [...] attributes to Shakespeare the wisdom of Nestor, the genius of Socrates, and the poetic art of Virgil", *Shakespeare: A Celebration. 1564–1964.* Ed. by T. J. B. Spencer, Harmondsworth, 1964, pp. 40–53, p. 53), Samuel Schoenbaum reproduces the Latin inscription, but without translating it, and merely remarks in passing: "the tablet under the cushion celebrates the writer". *William Shakespeare. A Documentary Life* (Oxford, 1975), p. 254.

18 On the Christian grave curse see the entry by Wolfgang Speyer in *Reallexikon für Antike und Christentum.* Vol. 7 (1969), p. 1270 f.

19 See R. B. Wheler, *History and Antiquities of Stratford-upon-Avon: Comprising A Description of the Collegiate Church, The Life of Shakspeare, and Copies of several Documents relating to him and his Family, never before printed [...]* (Stratford-upon-Avon, 1806), p. 40. Wheler was already stressing that: "[...] there is little doubt but Shakspeare held the custom of removing the bones of the dead from the grave to the charnel-house, in great horror. Of this practice he might perhaps have had ocular demonstration" (p. 76).

20 Cf. the entry under "Epitaph", in dtv. *Lexikon der Kunst*, 6 vols. (Leipzig, 1989/Munich, 1996), II.

21 See Hammerschmidt-Hummel, *William Shakespeare. Seine Zeit – Sein Leben – Sein Werk*, p. 15, fig. 18.

22 In *Mr. William Shakespeares Comedies, Histories, & Tragedies.* A facsimile edition prepared by Helge Kökeritz. With an Introduction by Charles Tyler Prouty (New Haven/London, 1954, fifth printing, 1968). The emphases in the text are the author's: she has also modernised the spelling.

23 W. Dugdale, *The Antiquities of Warwickshire Illustrated; From Records, Leiger-Books, Manuscripts, Charters, Evidences, Tombes, and Armes [...]* (London, 1656), p. 523.

24 For the complete title see footnote 64 Parts I and II p. 152.

25 Boaden, *An Inquiry*, p. 32.

26 Ibid., p. 32.

27 Such doubts, based on a misunderstanding, were first expressed by Mrs C. C. Stopes in *Shakespeare's Environment* (London, 1914), the chapter entitled "The True Story of the Stratford Bust". See also the comments in Part IV, p. 120.

28 (London, 1864), p. 6

29 *The Portraits of Shakespeare* (Philadelphia, 1885), p. 21.

30 *The Title-Page of the First Folio of Shakespeare's Plays*, p. 6.

31 B. Roland Lewis, *The Shakespeare Documents. Facsimiles, Transliterations, Translations & Commentary*, 2 vols. (Stanford/London/Oxford, 1941), II, p. 547.

32 Ibid., II, p. 547.

33 *William Shakespeare. A Documentary Life*, p. 256.

34 Picture quotation from *Mr. William Shakespeares Comedies, Histories, & Tragedies* [...].

35 Salmen, *Musiker im Porträt*, Introduction, p. 11.

36 Michiel's father, Hans Droeshout, is recorded as a painter in Antwerp in 1554. His brother Maerten (Martin Droeshout the Elder) was also born around 1570 in Brussels, and followed the profession of a painter and engraver. The latter may well have painted the Flower portrait which served his nephew as a basis for his engraving (see p. 27). Cf. The entries under 'Droeshout' in Emmanuel Bénézit, *Dictionnaire critique et documentaire des peintres, sculpteurs, dessinateurs et graveurs. Nouvelle éd., entièrement refondue, revue et corrigée sous la direction des héritiers* de E. Bénézit (Paris, 1976), Vol. 3.

37 Their names appear on the title page. In reality, however, other printers were also involved. See Charles Tyler Prouty, "Introduction", in *Mr. William Shakespeares Comedies, Histories, and Tragedies* [...], p. xxviii.

38 See Part IV: "The various states of the Droeshout engraving". In the 1663 edition, reprinted in 1664, the engraving is positioned opposite the title page. In that edition Ben Jonson's verses were placed under the picture. The Droeshout engraving and the lines of verse appear in the same arrangement in the fourth edition of the Folio. See Anon, *The Four Folios of William Shakespeare. Together with some Quartos.* Catalogue No. 138. H. P. Kraus. Old & Rare Books (New York, n. d.).

39 Here it should be borne in mind that the folio format was generally reserved at this time for the Bible and theological writings. When Ben Jonson published his works in 1616 – the year of Shakespeare's death – in a folio volume, it signified an

enormous increase in esteem for dramatic literature, a genre that had enjoyed little respect up to that point.

40 See the address "To the great Variety of Readers" in *Mr William Shakespeares Comedies, Histories, & Tragedies [...]*.

41 The entry in the Stationers' Register of sixteen of the eighteen plays that had not appeared previously was made on 8 November 1623. Cf. O. J. Campbell and E. G. Quinn, eds., *A Shakespeare Encyclopaedia* (London, 1966), see under "First Folio".

42 Charlton Hinman, "Introduction", *The Norton Facsimile. The First Folio of Shakespeare*. Based on Folios in the Folger Shakespeare Library Collection. Prepared by Ch. Hinman. Sec. Ed. with a new introd. by Peter W. M. Blayney (London, 1996).

43 A summary of the opinions of George Steevens, John Britton, James Boaden, Abraham Wivell, J. Hain Friswell, C. M. Ingleby and J. O. Halliwell-Phillipps, which we can only touch upon here, is to be found in J. Parker Norris, *The Portraits of Shakespeare* (Philadelphia, 1885), p. 47 ff. Probably the most negative personal views on the Droeshout engraving are expressed by Ingleby: "Even in its best state it is such a monstrosity, that I, for one, do not believe that it had any trustworthy exemplar" (p. 50).

44 The Cambridge graduate Steevens, together with Dr Samuel Johnson, published in 1766 twenty Shakespeare plays and edited the Shakespeare edition of 1773: he made a habit of publishing anonymous letters in the newspapers attacking his friends. See Boaden, *An Inquiry*, pp. 15–16.

45 Ibid., p. 17

46 Ibid., p. 24.

47 *Life-Portraits of William Shakespeare*, pp. 43–45.

48 *Portraits of Shakespeare*, pp. 50–51. However, the author adds that in his opinion Martin Droeshout is responsible for the mistakes and weaknesses of the engraving. He regrets that a better engraver was not appointed.

49 For the description of the conventional comparison of images using criminological investigation techniques I am indebted to Reinhardt Altmann, BKA expert in Wiesbaden, and his "Assessment of pictorial material for art-historical research, re: SHAKESPEARE", reference Federal Bureau of Criminal Investigation Wiesbaden, ZD 15 – 1170/95 (3 May 1995), text section pp. 1-101: picture file appended, pp. 1-21 ("Bildgutachten in der kunsthistorischen Forschung, hier: SHAKESPEARE", Aktenzeichen Bundeskriminalamt Wiesbaden, ZD 15 – 1170/95 (3. Mai 1995), Textteil: S. 1–10, Anlage: 1 Bildmappe, S. 1–21.)

50 Altmann, "Assessment of pictorial material [...]" (3 May 1995), text section, p. 3.

51 Ibid., text section, p. 3

52 Ibid., p. 4.

53 Ibid., text section, p. 4

54 Ibid.,p. 4.

55 The results and my evaluation of them were presented at length in my essay, "Ist die Darmstädter Shakespeare-Totenmaske echt?" [Is the Darmstadt Shakespeare Death Mask Genuine?], *Shakespeare-Jahrbuch* 132 (1996), pp. 58–74, and my article "What did Shakespeare Look Like? Authentic Portraits and the Death Mask. Methods and Results of the Tests of Authenticity", *Symbolism* 1 (2000), pp. 41–79.

56 A full account of these results is likewise to be found in "Ist die Darmstädter Shakespeare-Totenmaske echt?", *Shakespeare-Jahrbuch* (1996) and in "What did Shakespeare Look Like?, *Symbolism* (2000).

57 The description of Trick Image Differentiation Technique is also based on the text section of Reinhardt Altmann's assessment of 3 May 1995.

58 See ibid., p. 9.

59 Reinhardt Altmann, "Assessment of pictorial material in art-historical research, re: SHAKESPEARE", 6 July 1998, pp. 1-3, p. 3 [*Bildgutachten in der kunsthistorischen Forschung – hier:* SHAKESPEARE (6. Juli 1998), S. 1–3, S. 3.].

60 These findings are presented and evaluated in my publications "Ist die Darmstädter Shakespeare-Totenmaske echt?", and "What did Shakespeare Look Like?".

61 See ibid.

62 Altmann, "Photo-montage: Chandos portrait and death mask, supplement to the assessment of 3 May 1995" [Fotomontage: Chandos-Porträt/Totenmaske, Ergänzung zum Bildgutachten vom 3. Mai 1995].

63 On the first page of the assessment of 6 July 1998 there are individual descriptions of the pictorial material used; some images are shown from a variety of angles:

1. a colour image of the bust (Davenant) of a male person, image no. 1, page 1 of the attached picture file (Davenant bust) (ein Colorbild der Büste [Davenant] einer männlichen Person, Bild-Nr. 1, Seite 1, der beiliegenden Bildmappe [Davenant-Büste]).

2. a colour image of a male person, image no. 2 (Chandos portrait) (ein Colorbild einer männlichen Person, Bild-Nr. 2 [Chandos-Porträt]).

3. a colour image of a male person, image no. 3 (un-restored Flower portrait) (ein Colorbild einer männlichen Person, Bild-Nr. 3 [nicht restauriertes Flower-Porträt]).

4. a colour image of a male person, image no. 4, (restored Flower portrait) (ein Colorbild einer männlichen Person, Bild-Nr. 4 [restauriertes Flower-Porträt]).

5. a colour image of the bust (Davenant) of a male person, image no. 5 (Davenant bust) (ein Colorbild der Büste (Davenant) einer männlichen Person, Bild-Nr. 5 [Davenant-Büste]).

6. a colour image of the bust of a male person, image no. 6

(funerary bust) (ein Colorbild der Büste einer männlichen Person, Bild-Nr. 6 [Grabbüste]).

7. a black and white image (engraving) of a male person, image no. 7 (Droeshout engraving) (ein Schwarzweißbild [Stich] einer männlichen Person, Bild-Nr. 7 [Droeshout-Stich]).

8. a colour image of the bust (Davenant) of a male person, image no. 8 (Davenant bust) (ein Colorbild der Büste[Davenant] einer männlichen Person, Bild-Nr. 8 [Davenant-Büste]).

9. a black and white image of the death mask of a male person, image no. 9 (Darmstadt death mask) (ein Schwarzweißbild der Totenmaske einer männlichen Person, Bild-Nr. 9 [Darmstädter Shakespeare-Totenmaske]).

10. a colour image of the bust (Davenant) of a male person, image no. 10 (Davenant bust) (ein Colorbild der Büste [Davenant] einer männlichen Person, Bild-Nr. 10 [Davenant-Büste]).

11. a black and white image of the death mask of a male person, image no. 11 (Darmstadt Shakespeare death mask) (ein Schwarzweißbild der Totenmaske einer männlichen Person, Bild-Nr. 11 [Darmstädter Shakespeare-Totenmaske]).

64 Altmann, "Assessment [...]" (6 July 1998), p. 2.

65 Ibid., p. 2.

66 Ibid., p. 2.

67 Ibid., p. 2.

68 Ibid., p. 2.

69 Ibid., p. 2.

70 Ibid., p. 3. My italics.

71 Thus a box was constructed by Conservator Becker especially to transport the death mask in a vehicle belonging to the Hesse *Land* and University Library. The relevant police authority had also been informed.

72 The sum assured was 250,000 Euro. The premium amounted to 1,160 Euro, paid by the author.

73 Walter Lerche, "Expert opinion, 'Shakespeare portraits'" (11 April 1995) (*Gutachterliche Stellungnahme* 'Shakespeare-Portraits' (11. April 1995), p. 1.

74 Ibid., p. 1.

75 Ibid., p. 1.

76 Ibid., p. 1.

77 Ibid., p. 1.

78 Referring to the changes due to illness that are visible on the skin of subjects in early modern portraits, noted by many dermatologists, Professor Metz states in his report:

"Skin changes are also to be found in the Flower Shakespeare portrait, until now held by specialists to be a fake, and on the death mask kept in the Darmstadt Museum. These changes support Frau Professor Hammerschmidt-Hummel's recent [1995] assertion of the identity and authenticity of the two Shakespeare images, an assertion borne out by the results of her subtle researches:

In the area of the left temple in the Flower portrait, above the bump on the forehead, a roughly circular focus is visible, somewhat lighter in the middle. The rather rougher, brownish coloration around the periphery of the focus accentuates the indications of the wall-like, slightly raised character of the lesion, the middle of which appears to be sunken. On the basis of the phenomenological appearance of this change, the most obvious diagnosis would be that of a chronically inflammable granulomatose infiltration (inflammation). The change cannot be clearly demonstrated in the Chandos portrait.

However, the lesion described in the Flower portrait is immediately noticeable on the Darmstadt death mask. In the same position as in the Flower portrait there is a ring-shaped focus, measuring about 3.0 cm x 3.5, raised at the edges and somewhat sunken in the middle. The raised wall merges smoothly with the normal surface of the mask, ruling out the possibility of an artefact. The change is plainly identifiable from a dermatological point of view as a ring-shaped, inflammable (granulomatose?) infiltrate, which, given the firm base of the skull beneath, could obviously not be dispersed by pressure in the preparation of the mask" (p.1).

In the expert opinion given by Professor Jansen, he says: "At the top, two centimetres above the left eyebrow and a centimetre to the left of the centre line, there begins an almost circular, shallow protuberance (width 3.2 cm, height 3.0 cm). It is sharply delineated and raised to about 2mm. On palpation the surface is found to be fairly smooth. I could not feel a depression.

In my opinion what we are seeing is a bone tumour or an exostosis. Such tumours or exosteses occur inter alia on the skull, located particularly on the external surface of the frontal and parietal bones. The formations in question are flat or semi-spherical, with a smooth surface. Such tumours are always benign, and they grow extremely slowly.

The shallow protuberance is not only visible on the Darmstadt Shakespeare death mask, but also in the restored Flower portrait, something which – once more – Frau Hammerschmidt-Hummel was the first to notice, at almost the same time as she discovered this phenomenon on the mask. It cannot be distinguished in the unrestored Flower portrait. In the Chandos portrait, which depicts Shakespeare as a younger man, there are in my opinion indications of a protuberance on the left side of the forehead. This shows that the tumour grew extremely slowly" (p.1).

(Auch auf dem bis dato von der Fachwelt als Fälschung angesehenen Shakespeare-Portrait Flower und der im Darmstädter Museum aufbewahrten Totenmaske finden sich Hautveränderungen, welche die jüngst [1995] von Frau Prof. Hammerschmidt-Hummel vertretene, durch ihre subtilen Untersuchungsergebnisse belegte Auffassung der Identität und Echtheit der beiden Shakespeare-Abbildungen unterstützen:

Auf dem Flower-Portrait ist im Bereich der linken Stirnhälfte oberhalb des Stirnhöckers ein rundlicher, zentral etwas aufgehellter Herd zu sehen. Die etwas stärker gekörnte bräunliche Farbgebung in der Peripherie des Herdes unterstreicht einen angedeutet wallar-

tigen, etwas erhabenen Charakter der Läsion, die zentral einge-
sunken erscheint. Auf Grund des phänomenologischen
Erscheinungsbildes ist die Veränderung am ehesten als ein
chronisch-entzündliches, granulomatöses Infiltrat (Entzündung),
zu deuten. Die Veränderung ist auf dem Chandos-Portrait nicht
eindeutig nachzuweisen.

Bei der Darmstädter Totenmaske fällt jedoch die auf dem
Flower-Portrait beschriebene Läsion sofort auf. Etwa drei
Zentimeter oberhalb er linken Augenbraue findet sich in gleicher
Lokalisation wie auf dem Flower-Portrait, ein ca. 3,0 x 3,5 cm
messender, im Randbereich erhabener, zentral etwas einge-
sunkener anulärer Herd. Der erhabene Randwall geht fließend in
die weitere normale Oberflächenbeschaffenheit der Maske über,
so daß ein Artefakt auszuschließen ist. Die Veränderung ist aus
dermatologischer Sicht eindeutig als ein anuläres, entzündliches
(granulomatöses?) Infiltrat zu identifizieren, daß sich offen-
sichtlich durch die feste Unterlage des Schädelknochens auch bei
der Anfertigung der Maske nicht wegdrücken ließ" (p. 1).

In der gutachterlichen Stellungnahme von Professor Jansen wird
augeführt: "Zwei Zentimeter oberhalb der linken Augenbraue und
ein Zentimeter links der Mittellinie beginnt nach oben eine fast
kreisrunde, seichte Prominenz (Breite: 3,2 cm, Höhe: 3,0 cm). Sie
ist scharf begrenzt und etwa 2 mm erhaben. Bei Palpation ist die
Oberfläche einigermaßen glatt. Eine Delle konnte ich nicht fühlen.

Nach meiner Ansicht haben wir es mit einem Osteom bzw. einer
Exostose zu tun. Derartige Osteome bzw. Exostosen kommen u.a.
am Schädel vor. Dort sind sie besonders an der Außenfläche des
Stirn- und Scheitelbeins lokalisiert. Es handelt sich um flache oder
halbkugelige Gebilde mit glatter Oberfläche. Derartige Osteome
sind immer gutartig und wachsen außerordentlich langsam.

Die flache Stirnprominenz ist nicht nur an der Darmstädter
Shakespeare-Totenmaske sichtbar, sondern auch auf dem restaurierten
Flower-Porträt, was Frau Hammerschmidt-Hummel - nahezu
zeitgleich mit der Entdeckung des Phänomens an der Maske - auch in
diesem Fall als erste bemerkt hat. Sie ist auf dem nicht restaurierten
Flower-Porträt nicht zu erkennen. Auf dem Chandos-Porträt, das den
jüngeren Shakespeare darstellt, ist m.E. auch schon eine Prominenz
der linken Stirnseite angedeutet. Demnach wäre das Osteom im Laufe
der Jahre außerordentlich langsam gewachsen" (p. 1)).

Cf. also my article, "Neuer Beweis für die Echtheit des Flower-
Porträts und der Darmstädter Shakespeare-Totenmaske. Ein
übereinstimmendes Krankheitssymptom im linken Stirnbereich
von Gemälde und Gipsabguß" (New proof of the authenticity of
the Flower portrait and the Darmstadt death mask. A matching
symptom of disease in the left forehead area of the painting and the
plaster cast), *Anglistik* (September 1996), pp. 115–136, p. 125.

79 Jost Metz, "Expert opinion on the Chandos and Flower Shakespeare
portraits and the death mask in the Hesse *Land* and University
Library in Darmstadt (23 January 1996)" (Gutachterliche
Stellungnahme zu den Shakespeare-Portraits Chandos und Flower
und der Totenmaske in der Hessischen Landes- und
Hochschulbibliothek Darmstadt (23. Januar 1996), p. 1-2, p. 1.

80 Hans Helmut Jansen, "Expert opinion on the protuberance on
the left side of the forehead of the Darmstadt Shakespeare death
mask and in the Flower portrait (28 February 1996)"
(Gutachterliche Stellungnahme zu der Prominenz der linken
Stirnseite an der Darmstädter Shakespeare-Totenmaske und auf
dem Flower-Porträt (28. Februar 1996), p. 1-2, p. 1.

81 Cf. Metz, "Expert opinion [...]", p. 2.

82 See my observations in "Ist die Darmstädter Shakespeare-
Totenmaske echt?", p. 68: "(1) The mask was taken in a
recumbent position, whereas the portraits show the playwright
seated [Die Maske wurde in liegendem Zustand abgenommen,
die Porträts dagegen stellen den Dramatiker sitzend dar]. (2) As
a result of the suspension of blood pressure after the poet's
demise, the tissue has fallen in [Das Gewebe ist, bedingt durch
den Wegfall des Blutdrucks nach dem Ableben des Dichters, in
sich zusammengesunken]. (3) In contrast to the portraits, the
eyelid is closed, and this has the effect of smoothing out the
swelling [Das Augenlid ist im Unterschied zu den Porträts
geschlossen und vermochte auf diese Weise die Schwellung zu
glätten]. (4) The swelling was subjected to pressure from the layer
of plaster, causing the tissue to disperse, and making the left eye
of the mask altogether much more prominent than the right [Die
Schwellung war dem Druck der Gipsschicht ausgesetzt, der eine
Verteilung der Gewebsmasse bewirkt hat und auch dafür verant-
wortlich ist, daß das linke Auge der Maske insgesamt sehr viel
stärker hervortritt als das rechte]."

83 Cf. Michael Hertl, "Expert opinion on pathological symptoms
in the portraits and death mask of William Shakespeare" (15
August 1997), text section 19 pages; pictorial section 9 images
(Gutachterliche Stellungnahme: Zu Krankheitserscheinungen in
den Porträts und an der Totenmaske von William Shakespeare
(15. August 1997), *Textteil: 19 Seiten; Bildteil: 9 Abbildungen*).

84 Ibid.

85 Photograph by Andreas Kahnert, reproduced by kind permission
of the Hesse *Land* and University Library, Darmstadt.

86 Hertl, "Expert opinion [...]", (15 August 1997) p. 3.

87 Michael Hertl, "Expert opinion on the physiognomic and possibly
pathological-physiognomic features on the so-called Davenant
bust in the Garrick Club in London, in comparison with verified
painted portraits and the death mask of William Shakespeare" (11
September 1998), p. 4 (Gutachterliche Stellungnahme zu
physiognomischen und eventuellen krankenphysiognomischen
Merkmalen an der sogenannten Davenant-Büste im Londoner
Garrick-Club im Vergleich zu gesicherten malerischen Porträts
und der Totenmaske von William Shakespeare (11. September
1998), p. 4.

88 Ibid., p. 4.

89 Ibid., p. 4.

90 Ibid., p. 4.

91 Ibid., p. 3.

92 Ibid.

93 Ibid., pp. 3-4.

94 "Expert opinion" (11 September 1998), p. 4. Hertl explains that "such an intervention" is understandable "in terms of the age of the bust and the care to which it was repeatedly subjected", and explicable "as the action of those trying to restore the sculpture without having any personal relationship to the person represented, or any point of comparison with his real appearance" (daß ein "solcher Eingriff [...] beim Alter und der wiederholten Pflege der Büste leicht vorstellbar und mit der Tätigkeit restaurativ bemühter Hände, die aber ohne persönlichen Bezug und ohne Vergleichsbilder zur wahren Gestalt der dargestellten Person arbeiteten," erklärlich sei).

95 "Expert opinion [...]", (11 September 1998), p. 6. Here Hertl uses the highest degree of probability ("with utmost probability"), a term also applied by BKA expert Altmann.

96 Ibid., p. 6.

97 Ibid., p. 5. The medical specialist refers to his report of 15 August 1997, p. 12, in which he also gives the measurements of the "macule on the palpebral fissure [eyelid cleft]" or "unpigmented naevus of loose tissue and enlarged lymph vessel ducts" ["Lidspaltenfleck" bzw. "pigmentfreier Nävus aus lockerem Gewebe und erweiterten Lymphgefäßgängen] as 2.2 and 3 mm side by side, and covering 7 mm altogether ["2,2 und 3 mm nebeneinander, insgesamt für eine Strecke von 7 mm"].

98 See Hertl, "Expert opinion [...]" (15 August 1997), p. 12

99 Hertl, "Expert opinion [...] (11 September 1998), p. 5.

100 Ibid., p. 5.

101 Ibid., p. 6.

102 Ibid., p. 6.

103 See Hertl, "Expert opinion [...]" (15 August 1997), p. 13.

104 "Expert opinion [...]" (11 September 1998), p. 7.

105 Ibid., p. 7.

106 Ibid., p. 7.

107 Ibid., p. 6.

108 Ibid., p. 6.

109 See Professor Hertl's extensive report of 15 August 1997, p. 15.

110 Ibid., p. 15.

111 Ibid., p. 15.

112 The investigation results in connection with this find were published in my article "Shakespeare's Death Mask and the Shakespearian portraits 'Chandos' and 'Flower'. Additional Proofs of Authenticity on the Basis of a new Find" in *Anglistik. Mitteilungen des Verbandes Deutscher Anglisten* (March 1998), pp. 101-115. In his letter of 12 December 1996 Mr George Shiers informed me that: "Having consulted the Baronet [Sir Edmund Fairfax-Lucy] and our inventories, I have to say that no detailed record of its [the bust's] provenance now exists here. It is a marble cast and is apparently the same size as the Holy Trinity bust."

113 On this point, Parker Norris writes: "In 1793 Edmond Malone [...] advised the vicar of Holy Trinity Church to have the bust painted white. This was done, apparently by an ordinary house painter, whose coarse brush left lines in the paint. Malone's classical taste was offended by the coloring *ad vivum*, but apart from the vandalism of thus injuring so interesting and valuable a relic of the great poet, he seems to have forgotten that the Greeks frequently colored their statues." *The Portraits of Shakespeare*, p. 25.

114 In the words of Parker Norris: "This white paint was allowed to remain on the bust until 1861 [sic], when it was removed by Simon Collins, a restorer of pictures residing in London. Mr. Collins went to Stratford-upon-Avon, and on removing the white paint he found that enough of the old coloring remained to enable him to restore the bust to its original colors." *The Portraits of Shakespeare*, p. 26. The white paint was in fact removed in 1860.

115 This figure is an illustration from Schoenbaum, *Shakespeare's Lives*, between pp. 300 and 301, no. 20.

116 The Hunt portrait, also formerly known as 'The Stratford Portrait', came to light in 1860 in the house of William Oakes, Town Clerk of Stratford. The portrait had been in the family's possession for over a century, and was in a state of neglect. It too was cleaned by Simon Collins, after the latter had removed the white paint from the church bust. See Parker Norris, *The Portraits of Shakespeare*, p. 153.

117 Ibid., p. 11.

118 Ibid., p. 11.

119 Ibid., p. 13.

120 Ibid., p. 12.

Part IV

1 See *An Inquiry into the Authenticity of Various Pictures and Prints, which, from the Decease of the Poet to our own Times, have been offered to the Public as Portraits of Shakespeare [...]* (London, 1824), p. 49.

2 An Inquiry, p. 27.

3 See O. J. Campbell and E. G. Quinn, eds., *A Shakespeare Encyclopaedia* (London, 1966), under "Taylor, Joseph": "James Wright, in the *Historia Histrionica*, says that he [Taylor] played Hamlet 'incomparably well'; according to John Downes, he had been trained by 'the Author Mr. Shakespear'."

4 See Campbell/Quinn, eds., *A Shakespeare Encyclopaedia*, under "Taylor, Joseph".

5 John Downes, *Roscius Anglicanus, or an Historical Review of the Stage: After it had been Suppress'd by means of the late Unhappy Civil War, begun in 1641, till the Time of King Charles the II. Restoration in May 1660* (London, 1708), p. 21.

6 Ibid., p. 24.

7 See Parker Norris, *The Portraits of Shakespeare*, p. 69: "When

Betterton died he was a poor man, and his collection of portraits of actors and others were sold. Mrs. Barry, the actress, purchased the Chandos portrait at that sale, and she afterwards sold it to Robert Keck, of the Temple, London, for forty guineas."

8 See the summarized history of the Chandos portrait in the nineteenth century catalogue of the National Portrait Gallery, quoted by Parker Norris in *The Portraits of Shakespeare*; he had already noted that: "The John Taylor referred to here is probably a mistake for Joseph Taylor, as there was no John Taylor who was an actor." And further: "It will be noticed that the [...] history omits the ownership of the picture by Mrs. Barry [...]" (p. 70).

9 There is another seventeenth century painter of the same name: John Taylor (*ca.* 1630–1714), who can however be immediately ruled out as a possible painter of the Chandos portrait. See Ulrich Thieme und Felix Becker, *Allgemeines Lexikon der bildenden Künstler von der Antike bis zur Gegenwart*, 37 Vols. (Leipzig, 1907–1950), under "Taylor, John". This Taylor, according to Thieme/Becker, "was commissioned in 1659 by the Corporation of Oxford to paint portraits of John and Joan Nixon" (wurde 1659 von der Korporation von Oxford beauftragt, Bildnisse von John u. Joan Nixon zu malen [...]). It is obvious that it was this artist whom Edmund Malone had in mind when he reported having seen in Oxford a portrait painted by a John Taylor and dated 1655. Samuel Schoenbaum, who does not seem to know this painter, was wrong to correct Malone by stating that: "An artist by the name of John Taylor did, however, flourish in the seventeenth century: Malone reports seeing at Oxford a portrait by him dated 1655. If he is the Chandos artist, he must have had a long career. But Malone is wrong about the date: our John Taylor died in June of 1651, and was laid to rest at the parish church of St Bride in Fleet Street. He had been a leading member of the worshipful Company of Painter-Stainers, and was represented in the customary group painting [...]". *Shakespeare's Lives* (Oxford, 1970, new ed., 1991) p. 204. It is confusing that the same John Taylor is mentioned again by Schoenbaum on the same page – this time with reference to Mary Edmond's article "The Chandos portrait: a suggested painter", Burlington Magazine (1982), pp. 146–149: "A John Taylor was a leading member of the Company of Painter-Stainers, serving as Upper Warden in 1635–6, and as Master in 1643–4."

10 See "The Chandos portrait", p. 147: "25. The Master and the Wardens of 1631–32. 114.4 by 159.3 cm. (The Worshipful Company of Painter-Stainers, London)".

11 Edmond, p. 149: "John Taylor appears to be in his fifties in 1631–32, and thus would have been in his thirties during Shakespeare's last years in London, quite old enough to paint his portrait."

12 Edmond located this record in the "Court Minutes Books of the Painter-Stainers" going back to the year 1623. Cf. p.146.

13 Edmond, p. 149.

14 *An Inquiry into the Authenticity of Various Pictures and Prints*, p. 55.

15 In Scharf's own words: "It [the Chandos portrait] is painted on coarse English canvas, covered with a groundwork of greenish gray, which has been rubbed bare in several parts, where the coarse threads of the canvas happen most to project. [...] It would be folly to speculate upon the name of the artist, but any one conversant with pictures of this period would, upon careful examinations, pronounce it remarkably good if only the production of an amateur." *Notes and Queries* (April 23, 1864), S. 8

16 See Part II, n. 48.

17 See Campbell/Quinn, *A Shakespeare Encyclopaedia*, under "Taylor, Joseph".

18 Oldys, cit. J. Parker Norris, *The Portraits of Shakespeare. With numerous illustrations* (Philadelphia, 1885), p. 73.

19 See *A Literary Antiquary. Memoir of William Oldys, Esq.* by James Yeowell (London, 1862), p. xxxvii. For the London book-dealer Walker, Oldys had undertaken to produce a book on Shakespeare's life, in which – according to John Taylor in *Records of My Life* (London, 1832), I, p. 25 – he intended to write, among other things, about "ten years of the life of Shakspeare" which were unknown to biographers and commentators up to that time.

20 See Alexander Chalmers, *The General Biographical Dictionary* (London, 1815), XXIII, p. 336.

21 See J. L. Nevinson, "Shakespeare's Dress in His Portraits", *Shakespeare Quarterly* 18 (1967), pp. 101–110.

22 "*An Inquiry into the Authenticity of Various Pictures and Prints*", p. 43.

23 Entry by Benjamin E. Smith, ed., *The Century Cyclopedia of Names. A Pronouncing and Etymological Dictionary of Names in Geography, Biography, Mythology, History, Ethnology, Art, Archaeology, Fiction, etc.* [...] (London/New York, 1894, repr. 1904), under "Steevens, George".

24 Steevens, cit. Boaden, p. 45.

25 Ibid., p. 47. The verdict expressed in this skilfully chosen allusion to the familiar figure from Shakespeare directs a well-aimed blow at Steevens.

26 John Dryden, cit. Parker Norris, *The Portraits of Shakespeare*, p. 71.

27 See Boaden, *Inquiry*, p.48.

28 Under "Kneller, Sir Godfrey" in Peter and Linda Murray's *Penguin Dictionary of Art & Artists* (Harmondsworth, 1959, repr. 1982) it is pointed out that nothing is known about the painter in the years between 1678 and 1682, but that from 1683 onwards he was established in England as a much sought-after portrait painter.

29 This first copy (so far as is known) of the Chandos portrait is reproduced in Strong's *Tudor & Jacobean Portraits*, II, no. 548.

30 Boaden, p. 48. In contrast to Parker Norris, line two runs: "With awe I ask his blessing *ere* I write".

31 See Ibid., p. 48.

32 See Ibid., pp.47-48.

33 See A. H. Nethercot, *Sir William D'Avenant. Poet Laureate and Playwright-Manager* (Chicago, 1938), p. 398. In the preface to the Tempest adaptation that appeared in 1669, Dryden wrote: "I am satisfied I could never have received so much honour, in being thought the authour of any poem, how excellent soever, as I shall from the joining of my imperfections with the merit and name of Shakespeare and Sir William Davenant." *Cit.* Alfred Harbage, *Sir William Davenant. Poet. Venturer* (Philadelphia/London, 1935), p. 272.

34 In the same preface to the 1669 *Tempest* adaptation Dryden tells us that: "In the time I writ with him [Davenant], I had the opportunity to observe somewhat more nearly of him, than I had formerly done, when I had only a bare acquaintance with him [...]". Cit. Harbage, *Sir William Davenant*, p. 287.

35 He says that "Anno Domini 1660 was the happy restauration of his Majestie Charles II. Then was Sir William made, and the Tennis-Court in Little Lincolnes-Inne-fielde was turn'd into a Play-house for the Duke of Yorke's Players, where Sir William had Lodgeings, and where he dyed." *Aubrey's Lives*, entry on "Sir William Davenant".

36 Ibid.

37 "Mr William Shakespeare was wont to goe into Warwickshire once a yeare, and did commonly in his journey lye at this house in Oxon [John Davenant's Crowne Taverne in Oxford], where he was exceedingly respected. (I have heard Parson Robert say that Mr William Shakespeare haz given him a hundred kisses.) Now Sir William [Davenant] would sometimes, when he was pleasant over a glasse of wine with his most intimate friends – e.g. Sam Butler, author of Hudibras, etc, say, that it seemed to him that he writt with the very spirit that did Shakespeare, and seemed contented enough to be thought his Son." *Aubrey's Lives*, entry on "Sir William Davenant".

38 See Oscar James Campbell and Edward G. Quinn, eds., *Shakespeare Encyclopaedia* (London, 1966), under "Beeston Family".

39 Aubrey, *cit.*: Oliver Lawson Dick, "The Life and Times of John Aubrey", in: *Aubrey's Lives*, pp. 17–162, p. 79.

40 Ibid., p. 79.

41 See O. J. Campbell und E. G. Quinn, eds., *A Shakespeare Encyclopaedia* (London, 1966), under "Herbert, Sir Henry".

42 Ibid.

43 See Peter Thomson, "English Renaissance and Restauration Theatre", in *The Oxford Illustrated History of Theatre*. Ed. by John Russell Brown (Oxford/New York, 1995), pp. 173–219, p. 205.

44 Boaden, p. 47.

45 Ibid., pp. 47-48.

46 Thomson, "English Renaissance Theatre", p. 210

47 Boaden, p. 49.

48 Ibid.

49 Ibid., p. 121.

50 See my *William Shakespeare. Seine Zeit – Sein Leben – Sein Werk*, Teil IV: "Das machtpolitische Szenario am Ende der elisabethanischen Ära und Shakespeares Wende zum Tragischen" (Power politics in the late Elizabethan Age and Shakespeare's turn to tragedy), p. 171 ff.

51 Sidney Lee, *A Life of William Shakespeare*. Illustrated Library Edition (London, 1899), p. 238. This evidence is quoted by Samuel Schoenbaum both in *William Shakespeare. Records and Images* (London, 1981), p. 173, and in *Shakespeare's Lives* (Oxford, 1975, 2nd ed., 1991), p. 334. In *Shakespeare's Lives* it is stated in error that the painting had been exhibited seven (and not seventy) years (before Clements acquired it).

52 Edgar Flower of the Shakespeare Memorial Theatre in Stratford-upon-Avon had discovered it in Clements's possession in 1892.

53 Spielmann, *The Title-Page of the First Folio of Shakespeare's Plays*, pp. 35–36.

54 Ibid. See also the *Proceedings of the Society of Antiquaries of London* of 12 December 1895, where, on the basis of Edgar Flower's lecture, this phase of the history of the picture is reported: "Mr. [Edgar] Flower said that the portrait had been recently purchased and presented to the Shakespeare Memorial by Mrs. Charles Flower, and had been for a long time in the possession of a Mr. Clements, from whose widow it had been purchased. It had been exhibited in the Memorial Picture Gallery at Stratford-upon-Avon since the spring of 1892, while still the property of Mr. Clements. It had previously been exhibited at the Alexandra Palace, where it had been damaged by fire" (p. 49).

55 Brassington's report is quoted in John Corbin, "Two Undescribed Portraits of Shakespeare", *Harper's New Monthly Magazine* (May 1897), p. 902.

56 Commissioned by Edgar Flower, the cleaning was carried out in 1895 by Mr Dyer, owner of a respected picture-restoration business. Further cleaning was undertaken by the firm of William Drown and Company in 1942. As far as is known, there are no notes concerning this work and the x-rays of the picture taken at the London Courtauld Institute in 1966. See Bertram/Cossa, "'Willm Shakespeare 1609'", p. 93.

57 Lee, *A Life of William Shakespeare*, p.238

58 Lee, *William Shakespeare. Sein Leben und seine Werke* (Leipzig, 1901), p. 273.

59 The vehemence with which Spielmann sought to prove that the Flower portrait was not an authentic painting from Shakespeare's own lifetime, and also the fact that he omitted to mention aspects that pointed to the genuineness of the picture (see the comments of Paul Bertram and Frank Cossa in "'Willm Shakespeare 1609'", p. 86 ff.), suggest more factors were at play than merely concern for the facts. Sidney Lee, whose positive verdict concerning the truth to life of the Flower portrait seems to be Spielmann's primary target, enjoyed great respect as a scholar and editor. He worked from 1883 as "assistant editor" on the *Dictionary of National Biography*, and in 1891 he succeeded Sir Leslie Stephen as chief editor. He was the author of about 820 entries (the

majority concerned with the Elizabethan period). His Shakespeare biography, first published in 1898, was an immediate success at home and abroad, and was a standard work for decades. His distinguished career earned him a knighthood in 1911.

60 See the observations in the following sub-chapter ("The sequence of Flower portrait and Droeshout engraving") and later in Part IV: "The Droeshout Engraving in the First Folio Edition (1623)".

61 See the findings of my book *Die verborgene Existenz des William Shakespeare*.

62 Unfortunately, my own efforts to make contact with Mrs Stocker via the Ashmolean Museum in Oxford were unsuccessful. In response to my enquiry of 24 November 2003 Ms Angela Woodcock, the secretary of the Director of the Ashmolean Museum replied in an email : "Thank you for your fax of 24 November asking for information to contact Ms Nancy Stocker. I am sorry we are unable to help you with this. Your fax was passed around various departments at the Ashmolean, but without success."

63 Schoenbaum, *William Shakespeare. A Documentary Life*, p.258.

64 See "'Willm Shakespeare 1609': The Flower Portrait Revisited." *Shakespeare Quarterly* 37 (1986), pp. 83–96.

65 Samuel Schoenbaum, *William Shakespeare. Records and Images* (London, 1981), p. 173.

66 Schoenbaum, op. cit. p.173.

67 "From the history of the plate we know it was not a feature of the original, but introduced in the second state. So a copy of the First Folio with the engraving in a later state presumably served the anonymous artist." Schoenbaum, *William Shakespeare. Records and Images*, p. 173

68. See *Das Geheimnis um Shakespeares 'Dark Lady'*, p. 68.

69 See Bertram/Cossa, "'Willm Shakespeare 1609'", pp. 93–95.

70 See the findings of my book *Die verborgene Existenz des William Shakespeare*.

71 The Madonna painting depicts not only Mary with the Christ child, but also John the Baptist. We know that the church in Aston Cantlow was dedicated to St John the Baptist. And we know that Shakespeare's grandfather, the landed gentleman Robert Arden, and his family belonged to this parish. In his will the very devout Catholic Arden wrote that he committed his soul to Almighty God, the blessed Mary, and the blessed communion of saints in Heaven, but that he wanted his body buried in the churchyard of St John the Baptist. See my book *Die verborgene Existenz des William Shakespeare*, p. 62.

72 Schoenbaum remarked, for instance, referring to Spielmann: "As Spielmann observes, 1609 is early days for the cursive script in such inscriptions [...]". *William Shakespeare. Records and Images*, p.173

73 *Die Gemälde des 16. Jahrhunderts*. Catalogue of the Germanic National Museum in Nuremberg, compiled by Kurt Löcher with Carola Gries. Technological reports by Anna Bartl und Magdalena Gärtner (Stuttgart, 1997), p. 211.

74 During the afternoon of the day before, 11 January 1998, which was a Sunday, while I was inspecting the terrain in Lincoln's Inn Fields where in 1661 Sir William Davenant had a tennis court converted into a theatre (The Duke's Theatre), directly in front of the Royal College of Surgeons I met by chance a team from the BBC series "Tomorrow's World". The team leader was Mr Andrew Cohen, who, on behalf of BBC producer Mr Andrew Thompson, had contacted me at the end of October 1995 because of my proofs of authenticity of the Chandos and Flower portraits and the Darmstadt Shakespeare death mask. In a telephone conversation lasting more than an hour, I informed him about the methods and findings in conjunction with these tests of authenticity, before he, Andrew Thompson and S. Pakravan set to work on the production of the BBC film broadcast on 15 December 1995. In the course of this unexpected meeting in 1998 I told Mr Cohen about my interest in historical documents and writings about the architectural history of the Royal College of Surgeons, and he drew to my attention the excellent library of the College, which I visited the next day. There I found not only literature about the old theatre building as well as important images, but also the all-important source material which enabled me to clarify precisely when and under what circumstances the Davenant bust was discovered, something that was unknown until then.

75 *William Clift* (London, 1954). Dobson was at that time "Recorder of the Museum" at the Royal College of Surgeons.

76 See *Conservators of the Hunterian Museum. I. William Clift*. Repr. from Annals of the Royal College of Surgeons of England. Vol. 30 (January 1962), p. 6.

77 Dobson, *William Clift*, p.105

78 Dobson, op. cit., p.105.

79 Dobson, ibid.

80 Clift, cit. Dobson, p.105.

81 Ibid.

82 Clift talks here about having removed a *dozen* coats of paint, but elsewhere he makes it just *four*, and in the end he mentions only *three* colours. See Dobson, *William Clift*, p. 105.

83 Dobson, ibid.

84 Under "Lincoln's Inn Fields Theatre" there is the comment: "A theatre built in 1695 on the site of the former LISLE'S TENNIS COURT THEATRE [sic], in Portugal Street."

85 *Pictures in the Garrick Club. A Catalogue of the Paintings, Drawings, Watercolours and Sculpture*. Compiled and written by G. Ashton, ed. by Kalman A. Burnim & Andrew Wilton (London, 1997), p. 520. The relevant passage states: "Lincoln's Inn Fields was built in 1714 and vacated in 1732 when the manager, John Rich, moved to his new theatre in Covent Garden."

86 (London, 1983, repr. 1984); see under "Lincoln's Inn Fields Theatre".

87 Clift, cit. Dobson, p.105.

88 See Larson's report in Ashton, *Pictures in the Garrick Club*, p. 520.

89 Clift, op. cit., p.105.

90 The real owner, Mr Dennett, must have died soon after Clift found and appropriated the busts, leaving the Conservator of the Museum of the Royal College of Surgeons as the undisputed owner. Even in his earliest diary entries about the Davenant bust Clift is referring to "the late Mr. Dennett". Dobson, *Clift*, p. 105.

91 Dobson, ibid., pp. 105-106.

92 Clift, cit. Dobson, op. cit. p.106.

93 The focus on this improper conduct should not diminish William Clift's great achievements as a Conservator and a man. The Annals of the Royal College of Surgeons record in connection with Clift's death on 16 July 1849: "So ended the life of a most admirable man, one who was always ready and willing to help those anxious to learn and who was never daunted by difficulty or disappointment. He possessed those fine virtues, loyalty and courage: loyalty to John Hunter's memory; and the courage that made him fight for his master's most cherished possession." *The Conservators of the Hunterian Museum. I. William Clift.* Repr. from Annals of the Royal College of Surgeons of England. Vol. 30 -January, 1962, p. 8.

94 Given that this version of the find persisted in print until the end of the twentieth century, and that probably the demolition workers actually did find something, it is tempting to think that not only was a fictitious story of the discovery concocted, but that a real situation of discovery was attached to the earlier account after the event. In purely technical terms, this would have been possible, because the house acquired in March 1834, Lincoln's Inn Fields No. 39, was not demolished, but was fitted out as the residence of the Conservator (i.e. Clift) and was used as such. See Zacharay Cope, *The Royal College of Surgeons of England. A History* (London/Colchester, 1959), p. 248: "In March 1834 the College bought No. 39 Lincoln's Inn Fields, a smaller house on the east side of the new building, and this was used as the residence of the conservator."

95 Arthur Nethercot, *Sir William D'Avenant. Poet Laureate and Playwright-Manager* (Chicago, 1938), p. 2.

96 Nethercot, *Sir William D'Avenant*, p. 3-4: "There was, for instance, as John Sheffield asserted, an amicable letter which King James I had written to Shakespeare in his own hand, [...] which was now in D'Avenant's possession."

97 De Keyser had travelled to the English capital in 1607, with the intention of basing his plans for the stock exchange building in Amsterdam upon the London one, which in turn had been built along the lines of the one in Antwerp. There he became acquainted with the talented young stonemason Nicholas Stone, who accompanied him back to Amsterdam, and became his apprentice and eventually his son-in-law.

98 See the "Index to the Churches and Houses where Work was executed by Nicholas Stone, arranged according to Counties", in *The Seventh Volume of the Walpole Society 1918-1919*, ed. A. J. Finberg (Oxford, 1919),pp. 148-151.

99 The technique of working with terracotta, common in antiquity, was rarely used in the Middle Ages. It was revived only from the fourteenth century onwards, and had its flowering in the fifteenth century in upper Italy, and especially in Florence. See on this subject the *Lexikon der Kunst* (Leipzig, 1987; München, 1996), VI, under "Terrakotta".

100 See Leslie Stephen and Sidney Lee, eds. *The Dictionary of National Biography: From the Earliest Times to 1900.* 22 Vols. (London, 1908, repr. 1949-1950), XVIII, entry for "Stone, Nicholas (1586-1647)". The best-known works of Stone include the tomb monuments of Sir Nicholas Bacon and Lady Bacon in Redgrave Church in Suffolk, Sir Julius Caesar in St Helen's in Bishopsgate in London, and the poet and Anglican priest Dr John Donne in St Paul's Cathedral in London.

101 See Part VI of my book *William Shakespeare. Seine Zeit - Sein Leben - Sein Werk*, p. 259 ff.

102 The technique of taking a cast from a living face is described by Joseph Pohl as follows: "The first thing is to ensure that the subject can breathe during the half-hour process. You roll pieces of paper into two little tubes, fold them so that they fit the oval shape of the nostrils, and insert them into the nose. The shell of plaster must be applied in two layers, because the face of a living person is flexible, and will move under the pressure of the casing. First of all, then, a very thin layer of plaster mixed with warm water is applied, and once that has hardened off it is strengthened by a second layer. A thread separating them is not absolutely necessary". *Die Verwendung des Naturabgusses in der italienischen Porträtplastik in der Renaissance*, pp. 7-8.

103 See Pohl, op. cit., p. 8.

104 Ibid.

105 See Ashton, *Pictures in the Garrick Club*, p. 520. "It appears to relate to the life-size marble figure he produced for Garrick's Shakespeare Temple at Hampton (now in the King's Library in the British Museum). This figure dates from 1758, and although the features of the bust are less lively, the costume is exactly the same."

106 Comparing the two works, it also becomes apparent that the forehead of Roubiliac's Shakespeare statue is too low, and its chin too long. The form of the nose does not correspond to that of the Davenant bust. It follows that Roubiliac cannot have been familiar with Shakespeare's features.

107 An example is the parliamentary bill of 1613, which did not however reach the statute books, requiring English Catholics to wear red caps or yellow stockings. *See William Shakespeare. Seine Zeit - Sein Leben - Sein Werk*, p. 242.

108 Obviously this was before the fire in the theatre on St Peter's Day, 29 June 1613. The playwright may have used the

proceeds of the sale for the acquisition of the gate house in Blackfriars, or to redeem a mortgage he had taken out.

109 *Die Verwendung des Naturabgusses in der italienischen Porträtplastik in der Renaissance*, p. 9.

110 See *Das Geheimnis um Shakespeares 'Dark Lady'*, pp. 101-102.

111 In the judgement of the English art historian Roy Strong: "The most impressive likeness [of the 1st Earl of Northampton] is the kneeling tomb effigy by Nicholas Stone [...]." – "Northampton, 1st Earl of (1540-1614)", in Strong, *Tudor & Jacobean Portraits*, II, No. 548. Among the essential characteristics of the Earl of Northampton was that he was a Catholic, highly educated, and – in spite of the difficulties his religion caused him – very influential.

112 He was born in Offenbach as the first son of the later auditor of the Grand Duke's audit office in Darmstadt, Ernst Friedrich Becker, and his first wife Eleonore Charlotte Becker (née Weber), who had died by 1819. He died of emaciation and scurvy during an expedition across the then uncharted interior of the Australian continent which was to lead to the Gulf of Carpentaria. This and the following biographical information is based, unless otherwise stated, on the introduction to "The Life and Work of Ludwig Becker" in the volume *Ludwig Becker. Artist & Naturalist with the Burke & Wills Expedition*. Ed. & with an Introduction by Marjorie Tipping (Melbourne University Press, Carlton, Victoria, 1979).

113 The certificate was reproduced in English and German in Paul Wislicenus, *Dokumente zu Shakespeares Totenmaske* (Darmstadt, 1911), pp. 15-16. Original emphasis reproduced here by italics.

114 Catalogue D'Une Galerie De Tableaux. D'Une Collection De Gravures, De Croquis Antiquites Et Curiosities, Appartenant A La Succession DeFeu M. Le Comte Fr. De Kesselstatt [...] A Mayence, Le 1. Juin Prochain Et Les Jours Suivans. Mayence, 1842, No. 291. The entry contains no indication that during Count Kesselstatt's lifetime the picture was thought to depict Shakespeare on his deathbed. It would otherwise have attracted great interest, and would have sold for a very considerable sum. But the Count himself knew this, as demonstrated by the evidence from the Mainz Gallery Supervisor Müller. He received some very high offers for the supposed Shakespeare picture. See. "Professor Müller's Brief an L. Becker" [Professor Müller's letter to L. Becker] of 28 February 1847, in Wislicenus, *Dokumente*, pp. 18-19, p. 19. All emphases in this letter are italicised in the following quotations. The inscription mentioned by Müller, "Traditionen nach, Shakespeare" (According to tradition, Shakespeare, p. 19) was at that time obviously not clearly visible on the front of the picture-frame, and no doubt escaped the attention of the compiler of the catalogue, who appears not to have inspected it very closely. The fact that the inscription was not noticed can be deduced from the attribution of the miniature painting to the "German School". The same carelessness is shown in the treatment of the death mask, lot No. 738 in the catalogue. In this case the date inscribed on the rear of the mask, "+ Ã° Dm 1616", was overlooked. The allocation of the object to "sculptural works",

and in particular to "Reliefs", its description as a portrait, and especially as a "male image", as well as the precise statement of the material used, namely "Gyps" [plaster], provided sufficient detailed and unmistakeable information for an identification.

115 This information derives from the lithographer Friedrich Schönfeld, who befriended Becker in Melbourne. See Tipping, "The Life and Work of Ludwig Becker", p. 3.

116 His water colour pictures are today predominantly in family and private possession.

117 See Tipping, "The Life and Work of Ludwig Becker", p. 5. Becker (together with August Lucas) had already been employed as an illustrator for Kaup's early work *Gallerie der Amphibien* (Gallery of amphibians, 1826).

118 See the information supplied by Government Architect Becker, brother of Ludwig Becker: "Nachrichten über Ludwig Becker [...]", in Wislicenus, *Dokumente*, pp. 10-11, p.10.

119 "Nachrichten über Ludwig Becker [...]", p. 10.

120 It is hardly likely that the painter would have received financial support from his family. Becker was the eldest of five children from his father's first marriage. His mother died when he was eleven. His father remarried. There were three further children from the second marriage. When the head of the family, Ernst Friedrich Becker, died in 1826 he left a widow of thirty-nine, with eight children altogether, and with scant means of support. It therefore fell primarily to the eldest son, Ludwig, eighteen at the time, to feed the family, even if we assume that the widow's family supplied appropriate help and support. See Tipping, "The Life and Work of Ludwig Becker", p. 2-3.

121 Tipping, op. cit., p.5.

122 As quoted by Tipping, "'Not granted. 29/4/45'". "The Life and Work of Ludwig Becker", p. 5.

123 The relevant passage in the letter from the Mainz Gallery Supervisor N. Müller is confusing and misleading. "This picture" states the writer, "came into your possession after the death of Count Kesselstadt, when his effects were sold at auction, and thus you had the opportunity and the good fortune to acquire for a moderate price an artistic gem, a 'world-famous rarity'"; "Professor Müller's letter to L. Becker" of 28 February 1847, p. 19. Müller seems either not to have known, or already to have forgotten, that in reality the Mainz antiquary had bought the little painting in question at the auction. It is hard to imagine that the new owner, Becker, would not have mentioned this when he handed the picture over for the Gallery Supervisor's assessment.

124 "Professor Müller's letter to L. Becker" of 28 February 1847, pp. 18-19.

125 See Samuel Schoenbaum in *Shakespeare's Lives* (Oxford, 1970, new ed. 1991), pp. 337 ff. In the second paragraph of his letter, too, where Müller speaks of the "aristocratic Kesseltadt family in Cologne", said to have had this picture in their possession for

a hundred years, he makes some very serious mistakes which have caused considerable damage in the debate about the authenticity of the mask, and especially its provenance. See Part IV, "The first known owner: Count Franz Ludwig von Kesselstatt", pp. 108ff.

126 "Professor Müller's letter to L. Becker" of 28 February 1847, p. 19.

127 "Professor Müller's letter", ibid.

128 Müller, who held office in the Mainz Gallery for half a century, did not particularly distinguish himself in the post. On the contrary, his tenure actually harmed the collection. While the pictures were being temporarily transferred to the Franciscan monastery in Mainz, he had them rolled on to cylinders, and unfurled and rolled up again at every visit. See Rudolf Busch, "Geschichte der städtischen Gemäldegalerie in Mainz", *Mainzer Zeitschrift* 28 (1933), pp. 7-20, p. 8. Busch's overall verdict on Müller's prolonged term of office is highly critical: "In general the activities of the restorer and semi-official custodian of the Gallery Nik. Müller, who in addition had his own private gallery and dealt in pictures, were unfortunately badly lacking in public control [...]" (p. 10).

129 "Professor Müller's letter to L. Becker", Wislicenus, *Dokumente*, p. 19.

130 Ludwig Becker, "Totenmaske und Portrait von Shakespeare", in Wislicenus, *Dokumente*, pp. 23-24, p. 23

131 Becker quite clearly did not intend the following sentences, omitted in this quotation, to be printed, especially as they involve repetitions. (Their inclusion was no doubt an oversight on the part of the printer.): "It was painted etc etc" and "In the mean time I happened to see another oil painting, which being amongst his most valued pictures, was hung in his own bed-room; being considered to be a portrait of Shakespeare." This latter sentence seems to contain information that Becker apparently obtained from Müller, who claims to have known von Kesselstatt and his collection very well. If the detail in this sentence really did originate with Müller, it indicates once more that the latter could not have been a close friend of the Count. For – as Chailly's interior view reveals *(see figs 096 and 097)* - the Canon slept not in a separate bedroom, but in a bed in an alcove, clearly visible in the painting.

132 Becker, "Totenmaske und Portrait von Shakespeare", pp. 23-24.

133 There is not the slightest reason to doubt this account in principle. Presumably on the advice of interested parties in Britain, Becker wrote it and published it first in English.

134 It is noticeable that Becker talks of "documents" here. Clearly he requested and received the certificate of purchase and expert assessment some considerable time after buying the picture, on the assumption that they might be important one day.

135 *Shakespeares Totenmaske* (Jena, 2nd edn. 1911), pp. 79-80. Magda Heidenreich's positive declaration that "In 1849 Becker bought the supposed *Shakespeare death mask* from the antique dealer Wilz in Mainz [...]", is plausible but not substantiated by documentary evidence. See M. Heidenreich, *Wesentliches und Unwesentliches aus einer weltoffenen südhessischen Familie* (Darmstadt, 1980), p. 92. Factually incorrect is Heidenreich's assertion that Becker acquired the mask together with the miniature of "Ben Johnson [sic] on his death-bed" (see p. 100).

136 Letter from Minna von Wedekind (née Schubert) to Wilhelm von Wedekind on 8 December 1850, cit. Heidenreich, *Wesentliches und Unwesentliches aus einer weltoffenen südhessischen Familie*, p.68.

137 Minna von Wedekind an Wilhelm von Wedekind, 8 Dec. 1850, cit. Heidenreich, *Wesentliches und Unwesentliches aus einer weltoffenen südhessischen Familie*, p. 69.

138 This is shown by a letter from Sir Theodore Martin of 13 July 1889, which is among the Becker family papers. In this letter we read that: "Lord Ronald Gower [...] is personally fully convinced of the genuineness of the mask."

139 See Heidenreich, *Wesentliches und Unwesentliches aus einer weltoffenen südhessischen Familie*, p. 92.

140 I was informed by the present owner of this copy on 13 October 2004 that the previous owner was the Darmstadt publisher Wolfgang Schröter, who died in 1964. Before him, the object had been in the possession of a Frankfurt family (name unknown), from whose posthumous estate Schröter bought it in 1927.

141 See Balz Engler, "'Der Stein sich leise hebt': Das Shakespeare-Denkmal in Weimar", *Shakespeare-Jahrbuch* (2003), pp. 146–160.

142 These documents, from which the subsequent quotations are taken, were scanned in 1996, as far as the condition of the material would allow, by the library photographer Andreas Kahnert on the initiative of the director of the Hesse *Land* and University Library, Dr Yorck Alexander Haase. The cost was met by the city of Darmstadt. The air raid is also mentioned in a letter from Magda Heidenreich of 21 October 1975. At the time, the mask was in a safe at No. 7 Alexandraweg in Darmstadt.

143 In Becker's own words: "[...] my idea always was that eventually the proper place for this relic would be the British Museum". (27 [?] October 1872).

144 Letter of 2 December 1931.

145 See Prof. Lewis's letter of thanks of 5 January 1932.

146 See the detailed letter from Dr Magda Heidenreich of 21 October 1975 to a German academic whose name is not mentioned.

147 She was the daughter of Marie Heidenreich, née Becker (see p. 170).

148 See my lecture, "Ist die Darmstädter Shakespeare-Totenmaske echt?" (Is the Darmstadt Shakespeare death mask genuine?) which appeared in a slightly shortened version in the *Shakespeare-Jahrbuch*, Vol. 132 (1996), pp. 58–74. Professor Michael Hertl, expert on death masks and the physiognomy of the sick, checked the medical aspects of these and of my other findings, and approved them. In his expert assessment of 15

August 1997 he writes: "The efforts of Frau Professor Hildegard Hammerschmidt-Hummel meanwhile convincingly proved the identity of the Darmstadt death mask as a surviving image of William Shakespeare." In his book *Totenmasken. Was vom Leben und Sterben bleibt* (Death Masks. What remains after life and death) he states: "William Shakespeare (1564-1616), author of 38 plays, 154 sonnets, and a handful of other writings: since 1995 we can be certain that we have an authentic portrait of him. It is his original death mask (fig. 73). It belongs to the city of Darmstadt and is held in the University and *Land* Library there. The path leading to these proofs was a long one: finally, criminological methods and the criteria of medical diagnosis had to be invoked in aid, but the chain of evidence is now complete" (pp. 120-121).

149 His full name was: Franz Ludwig Hyazinth Xaver Willibald Maria II, Imperial Count von Kesselstatt. Franz Ludwig was the son of Hugo Casimir Edmund II Count von Kesselstatt and Catharina Elisabetha née Freiin (Baroness) Knebell von Catzenellenbogen, and was born in Trier.

150 The date of Canon Count Franz Ludwig II von Kesselstatt's death is incorrectly given in many English versions as 1843: this goes back to Ludwig Becker's report, "Cast and Portrait of Shakespeare", published in 1850. The text is reprinted in German and English in Wislicenus, *Dokumente*, pp. 22-24.

151 On the history of this aristocratic family, see the contribution "Reichsgrafen v. Kesselstatt" in the volume revised and edited by Hermann Friedrich Macco, *Beiträge zur Geschichte und Genealogie rheinischer Adelsfamilien*, with original drawings by Georg Macco, which appeared in Aachen in 1884; the hand-written "Family History" of the von Kesselstatts by Streitberger, held in the city archive in Trier (Depositum Kesselstatt, Kesselstatt holdings); the account "Die Reichsgrafen von Kesselstatt im Trierer Raum" in *Regierungsbezirk Trier: Monographie einer Landschaft* (no place or date of publication), pp. 209-213; and the article by Thorsten Becker "Von der Kinzig zum Kurfürsten. Ursprung in Kesselstadt: Seit über 700 Jahren besteht das Adelsgeschlecht im Trierer Land", *Hanauer Anzeiger* (6 May 1995).

152 See Streitberger, "Familiengeschichte", annex no. 46, pp. 523-526.

153 See the relevant entries under "Reichsgrafen v. Kesselstatt", in *Beiträge zur Geschichte und Genealogie rheinischer Adelsfamilien*.

154 See the entry under "Franz II. Ludwig Reichsgraf von Kesselstatt" in Streitberger, "Familiengeschichte", pp. 218-220, p. 218. This is further evidence of the good connections the Kesselstatt family had with the Imperial court in Vienna, which is also demonstrated by the many ambassadors they sent there from 1688. See "Schema der Gesandtschaften (Table of Ambassadorships) [...]", annex no. 46 to the "Familiengeschichte" by Streitberger, Depositum Kesselstatt (Kesselstatt holdings), Trier city archive. Maria Theresa must have received the young Counts personally, for among the effects of Canon Count Franz II of Mainz sold at auction in 1842,

along with a "Wedgewood tea-service for one person" which the owner of the death mask had presumably acquired in England at the same time (1775), there was also a "coffee-service, originally from the Empress Maria Theresa, with rich gilding and decoration in excellent taste." "XI. Porzellain und Möbels.", *Catalogue D'Une Galerie De Tableaux. D'Une Collection De Gravures, De Croquis Antiquites Et Curiosités, Appartenant A La Succession DeFeu M. Le Comte Fr. De Kesselstatt [...] A Mayence, Le 1. Juin Prochain Et Les Jours Suivans. Mayence, 1842, No. 928.

155 Letter from Jos. Weismüller of 8. July 1872, in Wislicenus, Dokumente, p. 11

156 Franz Ludwig I von Kesselstatt (1725-1777), the Governor and close confidant of the Elector of Trier, Archbishop Clemens Wenceslaus, was raised to the nobility as a Count of the Holy Roman Empire on 15 January 1776 by Emperor Joseph II. See the entry "Franz I Ludwig Reichsgraf von Kesselstatt" [XIII. Generation], pp. 204-205, p. 205, in the "Familiengeschichte" by Streitberger, Trier city archive, Depositum Kesselstatt (Kesselstatt holdings).

157 Many of the art treasures must have survived, for the Canon continued to own a very large and impressive collection after the fire, and he could not have assembled it on this scale only from 1793 onwards. Obviously, too, the paintings that were stolen from his collection in the Canon's absence survived more or less intact, being sighted later in various private houses in Mainz. See Jos. Weismüller's letter of reply to the Trier lawyer Zell, administrator of the Kesselstatt estate, of 19 November 1869. It states that: "During the siege of Mainz in 1792 the Kesselstatt mansion, which contained a very valuable collection of art and books, was burnt down, and since Count Franz had fled, the collection was ruined; what was not burnt was stolen; it is possible that this mask was among the latter objects." Wislicenus, *Dokumente*, p. 12. This account is incorrect on a number of essential points. *First*: the fire occurred in 1793, not 1792. *Second*: The statement here that the collection was destroyed by fire or theft and no longer existed is at odds with the statement that Weismüller made in his letter of 8.7.1872. According to this, the count's art collection was sold after his death. This is correct, and documented by the auction that took place in 1842. But it follows, therefore, that a large part of the collection must still have been in existence after the fire. *Third*: The objects rescued intact and moved to the new Kesselstatt house on the Höfchen must have included the death mask, which Weismüller, since he cannot recall it, would like to number among the items stolen. It should not be forgotten that the count's former major-domo only entered into service in the canon's house about forty years after the fire, so that he did not experience these events personally, and could only know about them from later accounts. The memories he recounted in 1869 are therefore not based on his own, unforgettable first-hand experience, but on second-hand reports which he heard about only years after the event. Furthermore, an unknown plaster death mask of no material value may well have been - especially during the confusion of wartime – less attractive to thieves than valuable

paintings. The most reliable proof of Weismüller's incorrect assumption, however, is the fact that the mask was still present when the count's collection was auctioned in 1842 – although it must be said that once again on this occasion it failed to arouse the slightest interest.

158 See the entry under "Franz II. Ludwig Reichsgraf von Kesselstatt" in Streitberger's "Familiengeschichte", history of the Kesselstatt family, which survives in a hand-written copy in the Kesselstatt holdings in the Trier city archive.

159 See Streitberger, "Franz II. Ludwig Reichsgraf von Kesselstatt", "Familiengeschichte".

160 See Streitberger, "Franz II. Ludwig Reichsgraf von Kesselstatt", where we read: "[...] his favourite pastime is practising the art of drawing and painting, at which he is particularly skilled; convincing evidence of his skills being found in his excellent extant landscape paintings [...]". The tranquillity of the retired art- and nature-loving Canon's life-style was further enhanced by the "large well-ordered garden with a very pleasant garden house" which he had laid out for him "for the sake of his health and for pleasure" on the banks of the Rhine ("below the town of Mainz") and which, tended by a gardener who lived there, served as his "summer retreat".

161 When part of a foot of a colossal Roman statue was found during excavations in the spring of 1830 in Mainz-Kastell, the knowledgeable canon was consulted. The find eventually became part of his collection. See "III. Alterthümliches von Mainz", *Quartalblätter des Vereines für Literatur und Kunst zu Mainz*, Jg. 2, H. 2 (1831), pp. 38-39, p. 38.

162 Rudolf Busch, "Graf Franz von Kesselstatt und seine Sammlungen", *Mainzer Zeitschrift* 39-40 (1944/45), pp. 55-62, p. 55.

163 See the entry under "Mappes, Johann Heinrich Ludwig Baron von. Kaufmann und Kommunalpolitiker, 1757-1845", in *Hessische Biographien*. In Verbindung mit (in association with) Karl Esselborn und Georg Lehnert. Ed. by Hermann Haupt. Unveränd. Neudr. der Ausg. V. 1918 (unrevised reprint of the first edition of 1918), Vol. 1 (Walluf bei Wiesbaden, 1973), pp. 187-188, p. 188. There it is recorded that: "When the Congress of Vienna was meeting in 1814/15, Mappes was sent there - together with Count Franz von Kesselstatt and the later president of the law court, Hadamar - in order to represent Mainz to the advantage of the city." ("Als 1814/15 der Wiener Kongreß tagte, wurde Mappes dorthin gesandt, um mit dem Grafen Franz von Kesselstadt und dem späteren Gerichtspräsidenten Hadamar die Vorteile der Stadt wahrzunehmen.")

164 His large and impressive library (like his art collection, it was auctioned off in 1842) bears witness to this.

165 This was already being pointed out by Wislicenus: see *Dokumente*, p. 37.

166 The author saw the original on 17 June 1995 in Affolterbach in the Odenwald when she was a guest of Frau Dr Magda

Heidenreich, who had the mask in her keeping on behalf of the Becker/Heidenreich family until 1960. The inscription "Shakespeare" is on the frame (front, centre, below). The inscription given in two versions by Professor Müller in his letter to Ludwig Becker of 28 February 1847, "*Traditionen nach*, Shakespeare" (according to tradition, Shakespeare) und "*Shakespeare, nach der Tradition*" (tradition has it, Shakespeare) was presumably quoted from memory and is therefore not entirely reliable. By this time Count Kesselstatt had been dead for six years. It may be assumed that Müller was quoting not the inscription, but the count's comments on the identity of the portrait's subject.

167 *Kollektaneen* (Collectanea), Vol. V, p. 15.

168 See the correspondence between Wislicenus and the administrator of the Kesselstatt estate in Trier.

169 See the count's will in the Kesselstatt holdings, Trier city archive. Von Kesselstatt gives very careful and precise instructions. He does not neglect to mention anything of importance.

170 Much of this section was published in English in my article "Goethe and Shakespeare: Goethe's Visit to the Art Collection of Franz Ludwig von Kesselstatt in Mainz", in *Symbolism. An International Annual of Critical Aesthetics*. Ed. Rüdiger Ahrens. Vol. II (New York, 2002), pp. 3-16.

171 Illustration from Eike Pies, *Goethe auf Reisen. Begegnungen mit Landschaften und Zeitgenossen* (Wuppertal, n.d.), p.41.

172 There is an erroneous reference in the volume of Johann Wolfgang von *Goethe, Goethes Leben Tag für Tag*. Vol. 6 (München, 1994), p. 246, to "*Dieter* Stadelmann". It has to be "*Diener*" (servant) Stadelmann.

173 Ibid.

174 August Gassner believes the accounts of Goethe and Boisserèe lead to this conclusion. See Gassner, *Goethe und Mainz* (Bern/Frankfurt a. M./New York/Paris, 1988), p.163, where he writes: "There can be no doubt that – contrary to the sequence in Goethe's diary – the early afternoon was devoted to visiting the two picture collections of Count Kesselstadt [sic] and the merchant, Memminger."

175 Sulpiz Boisserèe, *Tagebücher 1808-1854*. Im Auftrag der Stadt Köln (commissioned by the city of Cologne). Ed. by Hans-J. Weitz (Darmstadt, 1978), I 1808-1823, p. 245.

176 Goethe, *Goethes Leben Tag für* Tag. Vol. 6, p. 246.

177 Ibid.

178 *Goethes Werke*, Ed. Ernst Beutler. Artemisgedenkausgabe. DTV,18 vols., XII, p. 530.

179 Johann Gottfried Herder, "Shakespeare", in "Von deutscher Art und Kunst", *Deutsche Klassiker. Johann Gottfried Herder. Von deutscher Art und Kunst und andere Schriften* [1953] (Herrsching, Special Edition. n.d), pp. 109-175, p. 164.

180 Busch, "Graf Franz von Kesselstatt", p. 60.

181 Op. cit., p. 59.

182 These witnesses include above all the Mainz antique dealer S. Jourdan. In 1847 when he was selling Ludwig Becker the miniature painting (in fact depicting Ben Jonson on his death-bed) with the erroneous inscription "Shakespeare" on its frame, he had drawn Becker's attention to the "[plaster of] Paris cast", a melancholy plaster face in the Count's collection that was auctioned in 1842.

183 Catalogue D'Une Galerie De Tableaux. D'Une Collection De Gravures, De Croquis Antiquites Et Curiosités, Appartenant A La Succession DeFeu M.r Le Comte Fr. De Kesselstatt, No. 738.

184 Among Goethe's effects is a plaster cast of Torquato Tasso's death mask. The entry in his *Italian* Journey for 16 February 1787 expresses the particular focus of Goethe's interest in the physiognomy of the great Italian poet : "[...] after a long walk, [we] came to Sant' Onofrio, where Tasso lies buried in a corner [...]. His bust stands in the convent library. The face is of wax, and I can well believe that it is a death mask. It is a little blurred and damaged in places, but it still reveals better than any of his other portraits a gifted, delicate, noble and withdrawn person-ality". J. W. Goethe, *Italian Journey* 1786-1788, translation by W. H. Auden and Elizabeth Mayer (London, 1962), p. 160. (*Wir [...] kamen nach einem großen Spaziergange auf San Onofrio, wo Tasso in einem Winkel begraben liegt. Auf der Klosterbibliothek steht seine Büste. Das Gesicht ist von Wachs, und ich glaube gern, daß es über seinen Leichnam abgeformt sei. Nicht ganz scharf, und hie und da verdorben, deutet es doch im ganzen mehr als irgendein anderes seiner Bildnisse auf einen talentvollen, zarten, feinen, in sich geschlossenen Mann*). Johann Wolfgang v. Goethe, *Italienische Reise* (Munich, 1961), p. 102.

185 It must remain a matter of conjecture whether the famous guest from Weimar was shown the small death-portrait of a laurel-wreathed poet displaying the supposed designation "Shakespeare", which was evidently kept above the bed in the alcove, and so could not directly strike the visitor's eye (see the details from Victor Chailly's painting in the Mainz and Nuremberg versions, figs. 096 and 097). Certainly there is no suggestion in the written sources that he was.

186 "Wenn bei einem Mann mir jenes ungeheure Bild einfällt: 'hoch auf einem Felsengipfel sitzend! Zu seinen Füßen Sturm, Ungewitter und Brausen des Meeres; aber sein Haupt in den Strahlen des Himmels!' so ists bei Shakespeare!"

187 "Die erste Seite, die ich in ihm las, machte mich auf Zeitlebens ihm eigen, und wie ich mit dem ersten Stücke fertig war, stund ich wie ein Blindgeborner, dem eine Wunderhand das Gesicht in einem Augenblicke geschenkt. Ich erkannte, ich fühlte aufs lebhafteste meine Existenz um eine Unendlichkeit erweitert [...]". Johann Wolfgang Goethe, "Zum Shakespearestag", *Gedanken und Aufsätze. Goethes Werke.* Ed. E. Merian-Genast (Basel, 1944), Vol. XII, pp. 123-126, pp. 124-125.

188 Friswell, p. 19.

189 Ibid.

190 "Der 1841 in Mainz gestorbene Graf von Kesselstadt war indessen nicht der letzte seines Geschlechtes, wie mehrfach irrig angegeben wird. Auch hat die Familie niemals ihren ständigen Wohnsitz in Köln gehabt." *Jahrbuch der Deutschen Shakespeare-Gesellschaft* (1875), pp. 26-49, p. 44.

191 (March 19, 1864), pp. 227-228, p. 228.

192 "Mit Vergnügen bescheinige [ich] hiermit dem Herrn Dr. Ernst Becker in Darmstadt, dass Herr Franz Graf von Kesselstatt geb. zu Trier 1753, gest. zu Mainz 1841, zu Ende des vorigen Jahrhunderts England bereiste, wie er überhaupt viele Reisen gemacht und dabei grosse Kunstschätze gesammelt, welche nach seinem Tode veräussert wurden." Wislicenus, *Dokumente zu Shakespeares Totenmaske*, p. 11.

193 "Er (Franz II. Ludwig Reichsgraf von Kesselstatt) ging nach der Rückkunft von Wien nach Strasburg und Nanci zu seiner Vervollkommnung, hielt sich bis in den März 1775 dort auf, *und trat danach die Reise nach London an*." [Author's emphasis.] Streitberger, "Familiengeschichte", "Franz II. Ludwig Reichsgraf von Kesselstatt", p. 218.

194 Cf. Hans Helmut Jansen and Werner Wegmann, "Die Darmstädter Shakespeare-Totenmaske", *Jahrbuch der Deutschen Shakespeare-Gesellschaft West* (1984), pp. 270-272, p. 271.

195 Joan Lane, *John Hall and his Patients. The Medical Practice of Shakespeare's Son-in-Law.* Medical Commentary by Melvin Earles (Stratford-upon-Avon, 1996), p. xx: "There is no doubt that Hall was practising in Stratford in 1616 and that Shakespeare died there, with no suggestion that the relationship between the two men was other than amicable."

196 Die Totenmaske ist sicher nicht am Tag des Todes, sondern ein bis zwei Tage später abgenommen worden. Dafür spricht der Befund kristallin eingetrockneter Tränenflüssigkeit, die man an beiden Augen in etwa 1,5 cm Ausmaß deutlich sehen kann. Die natürliche Lid- und Wimpernstruktur wird durch diese Verklebungen verwischt. Die eiweißhaltige Flüssigkeit entsteht im Rahmen der postmortalen Zersetzung und sickert stundenlang aus dem Bindehautsack in langsamen Fluß über den Lidrand. Zu einer sorgfältigen Maskenabnahme-Technik gehört deshalb das Herrichten der Leiche. U. a. werden eingetrocknete Reste der Tränenflüssigkeit oder andere Sekretspuren (z. B. aus der Nase) vor dem Auftragen des Gipsbreis [...] beseitigt [...]." "Part II: Changes to the Face as a Whole" (Teil II: Wandel des Gesichts im ganzen). In his report, Hertl refers to Hans Helmut Jansen and P. Leist, "Technik der Abnahme von Totenmasken", *Beiträge Pathologie* 161 (1977), 385-390.

197 Literally, he speaks of the "neat Monument of that famous English Poet, Mr Wm Shakespeere". *A Relation of a short Survey of 26. Counties [...]* By a Captaine, a Lieutenant, and an Ancient. All three of the Military Company in Norwich (MS Lansdowne 213, f. 332v, EKC, ii, 243, British Library). Referring to towns and buildings, at that time the adjective "neat" according to the OED denoted primarily a beautiful and pleasing prospect. With reference to people, it meant: "Inclined to refinement or

elegance". Examples given in the OED are: "O thou Jerusalem full faire; [...] much like a Citie neat" (1549–62), and "Hampton Court the neatest pile of all the King's houses" (1675). "Neat" could also be applied to handwriting or the style of a writer: "Mr. Aubrey [...] writ a neat Hand" (1710).

198 Dugdale's actual words are "[Stratford] gave birth and sepulture to our late famous Poet Will. Shakespeare". *The Antiquities of Warwickshire Illustrated; From Records, Leiger-Books, Manuscripts, Charters, Evidences, Tombes, and Armes [...]* (London, 1656), p. 523.

199 The original text reads: "Dugdale's representation is different from what the tomb is to-day". "The True Story of the Stratford Bust", in *Shakespeare's Environment*, p.117.

200 Ibid.

201 *The Shakespeare Documents. Facsimiles, Transliterations, Translations & Commentary.* 2 Vols. (Stanford/London et al., 1941), II, "The Bust of Shakespeare set up in the Stratford Parish Church", pp. 542–547, p. 547.

202 See the complete reproductions of the Dugdale engraving und the tomb bust in Schoenbaum, *William Shakespeare. A Documentary Life*, pp. 253 and 255.

203 Stopes, *Shakespeare's Environment.* Sec. issue with additions and frontispiece (London, 1918), p. 109.

204 Reproduced in colour in my Shakespeare biography, *William Shakespeare. Seine Zeit – Sein Leben – Sein Werk*, p. 285, fig. 183.

205 Illustration also reproduced in Strong, *Tudor & Jacobean Portraits*, II, NPG 1281, fig. 554, who gives the following information: "Plaster, 31 3/4 inches, 79.7 cms, high, copy after the tomb effigy by Gerard Johnson or Janssen in Holy Trinity Church, Stratford-on-Avon, circa 1620. PLATE 554." The estimated date "1620", however, relates to the erection of the original bust. For under *"Collections"* we read: "purchased from Brucciani & Co. 1914; the firm stated that it was cast from a mould taken direct from the original in 1851; discrepancies indicate that it is a cast from a copy, but an accurate one." Strong, *Tudor & Jacobean Portraits*, I, p. 184, I, p. 284. The statement by the firm of Brucciani & Co. that the cast was made from a mould taken from the original in 1851 cannot be correct. At that time – apart from the coat of white paint that had been applied in 1793 at Malone's behest, and had not yet been removed - the bust already appeared as it does today.

206 Ward had also taken up the cause of a erecting a Shakespeare monument in Westminster Abbey and had begun to collect together funds for that purpose. The historical documents are to be found in the Halliwell-Phillipps Collection in the Folger Library in Washington, and were published as an appendix to the correspondence of the Stratford schoolmaster and antiquary Rev. John Greene. See Levi Fox, ed., *Correspondence of the Reverend Joseph Greene. Parson, Schoolmaster und Antiquary (1712–1790)* (London, 1965), pp. 164–175.

207 "Shakespearian Matters", in: *Correspondence of the Reverend Joseph Greene*, p. 164. The use of "curious" in this sense is obsolete. According to the *OED*, until 1772 the adjective meant "made with care or art", and until 1674 it was used as a synonym for "elaborate"

208 "Shakespearian Matters", in: *Correspondence of the Reverend Joseph Greene*, p. 165–166. Appended to a pre-prepared list is the declaration:: "We whose Names are under-written or annex'd, Contributors to yᵉ sum rais'd at yᵉ Townhall of Stratford upon Avon, for repairing & beautifying yᵉ Original Monument of Shakespeare yᵉ Poet; Agree that ye Direction and Execution of that Work, shall be committed to Mʳ John Hall Limner: And (provided he takes care, according to his Ability, that yᵉ Monument shall become as like as possible to what it was when first Erected,) that then the Money already rais'd for the purpose aforesaid, shall be forthwith paid him, upon finishing the Work [...]."

209 The building, demolished eleven years later by its then owner Reverend Gastrell, was still standing at this time. An old sketch of Shakespeare's property, together with views of the corner plot and the historic inn "The Falcon" are reproduced in my book *William Shakespeare. Seine Zeit – Sein Leben – Sein Werk* (see. pp. 218–219, figs. 149 and 150 a–b).

210 The names heading the document were: "Revd Mʳ Kenwrick Vicar of Stratford / Jos. Greene Clerk, Master of yᵉ Free-School [Grammar School]", followed by: "Mʳ Turbit Mercer / John Spur Black-Smith Cashier / Mʳ Benjam: Heynes Glover. / Mʳ Joseph Broome Weaver / Mʳ Samuel Morris Farmer. / Mʳ John Southam of Welcomb Farmer / Mʳ John Hall Limner. Undertaker of the Work." "Shakespearian Matters", in: *Correspondence of the Reverend Joseph Greene*, p. 169.

211 "Shakespearian Matters", in: *Correspondence of the Reverend Joseph Greene*, p. 168. Initially, the treasurer and church warden John Spur vetoed the payment, but later agreed to pay up after the completion of the work (see pp. 168–169). Eight years later, the self-confident blacksmith Spur became Chamberlain of the Corporation of Stratford, administrating in this capacity the estates of the town, as well as paying out the salary of the schoolmaster Joseph Greene. See "Schoolmaster's receipt for Salary", in *Correspondence of the Reverend Joseph Greene*, p. 154. It is not clear whether the original estimate of £16 had been reduced, or whether Hall had already received an interim payment.

212 Greene seems not to have been aware that Mary Arden, Shakespeare's mother, came from Wilmcote.

213 Letter from Joseph Greene to the Reverend John Sympson of 27 September 1749, in *Correspondence of the Reverend Joseph Greene*, pp. 170–171, p. 171.

214 "Jet" is a hard, black, highly-polished semi-precious variety of lignite (brown coal), from which jewellery for wearing in mourning used to be made.

215 Greene to Sympson, in *Correspondence of the Reverend Joseph Greene*, p. 171.

216 Ibid.

217 Ibid.

218 The assessment of B. Roland Lewis is the same: "From the Rev. Joseph Greene's letters and notes, written honestly, soberly, and clearly, it is obvious that he considers the bust (from whose face he made a mould and copy and upon which John Hall made restorations in color) to be the actual original placed in the niche by 1623. At no point does he give the least hint that any other bust was substituted [...]." *The Shakespeare Documents*, II, "The Bust of Shakespeare set up in the Stratford Parish Church", p. 546.

219 This painting is reproduced in Spielmann, *The Title-Page of the First Folio of Shakespeare's Plays*, opposite p. 24, Plate 16: "The Stratford Monument. Painted by John Hall, before 1748 – the date of its misalleged reconstruction".

220 Spielmann, op. cit. p. 24.

221 Ibid.

222 The reference is to the painter John Hall, who carried out the restoration of the Shakespeare monument in 1748.

223 The reference is to "The Honourable James West of Alscot", for whom Greene had occasionally acted as librarian.

224 *Correspondence of the Reverend Joseph Greene*, pp. 144–147, p. 145.

225 *Correspondence of the Reverend Joseph Greene*, p. 146.

226 Ibid. As the writer adds the name of the proposed mode of transport, which seems to him very secure, it may be assumed that the gift reached his brother. What is not known is whether the illustrator Edward Stringer actually did restore the picture.

227 See the information given in the Foreword to the *Correspondence of the Reverend Joseph Greene* by Levi Fox, pp. 6–7. Fox mentions the letters received in 1862 by Halliwell-Phillipps from Richard Greene, the grandson of the apothecary of the same name, who was Joseph Greene's brother and the addressee of many of his letters.

228 Grubb had indeed moved to Stratford quite early on, but worked there as a sculptor, then changing to painting and creating many portraits of Stratford townspeople, the local gentry and the clergy, including a painting of the Reverend Joseph Greene which was used as the frontispiece of the volume *Correspondence of the Reverend Joseph Greene*. Grubb lived from *c.* 1769 to *c.* 1774 in Birmingham. After marrying Anne Jeacocks he returned to Stratford.

229 Ibid., pp. 106-107.

230 Ibid., pp. 107–108, p. 108.

231 Ibid., pp. 112–114, p. 113. The full text is: "[...] I beg you will accept my sincere thanks for ye Cast of Shakespear's face, which is very neat and perfect, and seems to have been carefully taken. I question whether there is another mould or cast of the kind, since ye period mention'd, I believe ours may pass for a Unique, as the Virtuosi term it, and consequently be of no small estimation. Immediately after ye formation of

this mould, the face of Old Billy our bard was new painted; so that 'till about an hundred years to come, an attempt for another resemblance will be quashed with a *Noli me tangere*, and the taking a fresh masque from the Figure will not be allow'd upon any consideration."

232 This was the owner of Alscot near Preston-on-Stour, who also held high office in the Treasury in Whitehall.

233 *Correspondence of the Reverend Joseph Greene*, pp. 77–78, p. 77.

234 *See O Sweet Mr. Shakespeare I'll have his picture. The changing image of Shakespeare's person, 1600–1800*. National Portrait Gallery, London, Exhibition Catalogue. With an introduction by David Piper (London, 1964), p. 10: "Casts, probably of the head only, existed from at least 1737 on, when one was made for Vertue; about 1757, another for James West and in 1791 one for Malone, but no extant casts have yet been identified earlier than 1814, when George Bullock took a mould of the whole effigy from which a number of casts (3d) were made (one is still in the Soane Museum)."

235 *The Title-Page of the First Folio of Shakespeare's Plays* (London, 1924), 23.

236 "The Life and Times of John Aubrey", in: Aubrey's Lives. Ed. with the original manuscripts and with an introduction by O. L. Dick (London, 1949, Harmondsworth, repr. 1978), pp. 17–162, p. 162.

237 Op. cit., p. 42.

238 There is still evidence in English churches today of the drastic and comprehensive destruction caused by the iconoclasts. Cf. Simon Jenkins, *England's Thousand Best Churches*. With photographs by Paul Barker from the *Country Life* Archive (London/New York et al., 1999).

239 [...]. Dick, "The Life and Times of John Aubrey", p. 43.

240 Cf. with reference to this account Philip Tennant, *The Civil War in Stratford-upon-Avon* (Stratford-upon-Avon, 1996), especially the "Local Civil War Chronology 1642–7".

241 "The True Story of the Stratford Bust", in: *Shakespeare's Environment*, p. 118: "I have found in Add. MS. 28,565, a whole volume of Bills for Damages by the Parliamentary forces in Stratford 1645, from private people which are only representative of many others."

242 Oscar James Campbell and Edward G. Quinn, *Shakespeare Encyclopaedia* (1966, repr. 1974), under "Brookes, Baldwin". Cf. also F. Marcham, *William Shakespeare and his Daughter Susannah* (1931), pp. 66–71, and Schoenbaum, *William Shakespeare. A Documentary Life*, pp. 248–249.

243 On 5 June 1635, this list of charges led to the Reverend Wilson's suspension from office for three months. See Stopes, "The True Story of the Stratford Bust", in *Shakespeare's Environment*, p. 118.

244 See my article "Herrscherbildnisse Karls I. von England von Anthonis van Dyck: Herrscherkritik, Demontage und politische

Schmähung?", in Uwe Baumann, *Basileus und Tyrann. Herrscherbilder und Bilder von Herrschaft in der Englischen Renaissance* (Frankfurt am Main et al., 1999), pp. 181–210, p. 181 and p. 201.

245 (Philadelphia, 1885), p. 24.

246 *Monatshefte für Kunstwissenschaft* (1915), pp. 279–292, p. 282.

247 The plan of the Shakespeare family tombs in Stratford is reproduced in my book *William Shakespeare. Seine Zeit – Sein Leben – Sein Werk*. See fig. 187, p. 289.

248 See the reporting in the local press at the time (in, among others, the *Stratford-upon-Avon Herald*, the *Evesham Standard* and the Birmingham *Evening Mail*). The *Stratford-upon-Avon Herald* reported on 5 October 1973 with the front-page headline "Nothing there. Intruders shift church bust in vain quest for bard clues" : "IF THE objective of intruders into Stratford parish church removing the bust of William Shakespeare from its niche in the north wall of the chancel, overlooking his grave, during Tuesday night, was to find scrolls or manuscripts, they failed. Willy-nilly – but with great care not to commit damage during their nefarious and sacrilegious activity between 9 30 pm and 7 30 a m – they disposed of the claim that the niche contained anything which would either substantiate or disprove the Stratford-born genius's authorship of the works attributed to him."

249 P. 256, n. 2.

250 Samuel Schoenbaum, "Artists' Images of Shakespeare", in *Images of Shakespeare. Proceedings of the Third Congress of the International Shakespeare Association, 1986.* Eds. Werner Habicht, D. J. Palmer and Roger Pringle (Newark/London/ Toronto, 1988) pp. 19–39, p. 39.

251 As Samuel Schoenbaum writes in his preface of the 1991 edition of *Shakespeare's Lives*, the idea of writing this book entered his mind when, on 1 September 1964, he visited "(for the first time) the splendid Collegiate Church of the Holy Trinity" at Stratford-upon-Avon while attending "an international conference honouring the quartercentenary of Shakespeare's birth". Roughly a quarter of a century later he published the following colourful account of this incident: "It was late afternoon; the tourists had departed. Although outside the late summer sun still shone brilliantly, I could barely make out the monument and bust in the shadows of the north wall of the chancel.

As I stood there I thought of the pilgrims, many thousands strong, who had looked up as I now did and pondered the inconceivable mystery of creation. Keats had been there; Boswell also, and the Irelands, father and son, and Washington Irving. The scholars had come too: Malone, who dimmed his name by having the bust painted white; Halliwell-Phillipps, who had loved Stratford but in the end turned his back on the town. The mad folk had been drawn, moth-like, to the Shakesperian flame. Poor Delia Bacon had tiptoed through the portal after dusk, a candle in one hand and a lantern in the other; ignoring the gravestone malediction, she came to dig for wonderful secrets beneath the slab, but, frightened by ghosts, she fled before dawn" (p. vii).

252 Published 1968 by The Hamlyn Publishing Group, Feltham, Middlesex, © 1967 Arnoldo Mondadori Editore, gen. ed. Enzo Orlandi, text by Maria Pia Rosignoli, transl. by Mary Kanani [Portraits of Greatness], p. 74. Thus the photograph was clearly taken before the break-in of 1973.

253 (London et al., 1999), S. 713.

254 Drawing upon oral traditions, H. Snowden Ward and Catharine Weed Ward in their book *Shakespeare's Town and Times* (London, *c.* 1896) were already sketching out an amazingly realistic scenario: "It is […] traditionally recorded", they inform us, "that the bust was copied from a cast of the features, and as death-masks were not uncommonly made by doctors in those days, it is quite possible that such a cast was taken by Dr John Hall, handed to the sculptor, and, having served its purpose, left in the sculptor's hands […]" (pp. 144–145).

255 See Joseph Greene's description (p. 122). See also fig. 19 in *William Shakespeare. Seine Zeit – Sein Leben – Sein Werk*, p. 16.

256 The household accounts of Thomas Fairebarne (1590–1) record: "Paide, the xvjth of Octobre anno 1591 to Mr Garret Johnson tolme maker the somme of one hunderith poundes of laufull Englishe monye in full paiment of towe hunderithe poundes for the making of towe tolmes and settinge the same up at Bottesford for the towe Eleres, Lord Edward and Lord John, Cli." William Samuel Weatherley, "Description of the Tombs and Monuments having sculptured Effigies up to the close of the seventeenth Century: With a Digression upon the Swithland local Headstones of the seventeenth and eighteenth Centuries", in Dryden (Alice), *Memorials of Old Leicestershire* […]. (1911), p. 241.

257 See Edward Conder, *Records of the Hole Crafte and Fellowship of Masons. With a Chronicle of the history of the Worshipful Company of Masons of the City of London*. Collected from official Records in the possession of the Company, the Manuscripts in the British Museum, the Public Record Office, the Guildhall Library, etc. etc. (London/New York, 1894), Appendix: "The Company of Marblers of the City of London", p. 159. Cf. also "Index to the Churches and Houses where work was executed by Nicholas Stone, arranged according to Counties", *The Seventh Volume of the Walpole Society 1918–1919*, ed. A. J. Finberg (Oxford, 1919), pp. 148–151.

258 On the descent of Lady Penelope Spencer cf my book, *Das Geheimnis um Shakespeare 'Dark Lady'*, pp 58 ff and 84 ff, and the subchapter "Autobiography in the Sonnets" in the forthcoming English translation of my Shakespeare biography *The Life and Times of William Shakespeare (1564-1616)* (London, 2006).

259 See the exposition by the expert Charlton Hinman in *The Printing and Proof-Reading of the First Folio of Shakespeare* (Oxford, 1963).

260 As regards the fourth proof, known as the "Lilly proof", Spielmann comments that its whereabouts are unknown, if it exists at all. See *The Title-Page of the First Folio of Shakespeare's Plays*, p. 40.

261 Cf. *The Four Folios of William Shakespeare together with some Quartos.* Catalogue No. 138. H. P. Kraus. Old & Rare Books (New York, n. d.).

262 Cf. Peter and Linda Murray, *Penguin Dictionary of Art & Artists* (Harmondsworth, 1959, 4th ed., repr.1982), entry for "proof".

263 This is apparent from the engraving in the facsimile edition produced by Helge Kökeritz (see *fig. 023*), the original for which is the copy of the First Folio held by the Elizabethan Club at Yale University in New Haven; *Mr. William Shakespeares Comedies, Histories, & Tragedies.* A facsimile edition prepared by Helge Kökeritz. With an Introduction by Charles Tyler Pouty (NewHaven/London, 1954, fifth printing, 1968).

264 J. Parker Norris, *The Portraits of Shakespeare* (Philadelphia, 1885), pp. 55-58.

265 On the engraver's family, see Part III, p. 31, and n. 191.

266 *Mr. William Shakespeares Comedies, Histories, & Tragedies.*

267 See also the comments in the chapter *"Krankheit und Testament"* in my book *William Shakespeare. Seine Zeit – Sein Leben – Sein Werk*, p. 281.

268 *Mr. William Shakespeares Comedies, Histories, & Tragedies.*

269 See *William Shakespeare. Seine Zeit – Sein Leben – Sein Werk*, p. 12: "In 1622, six years after the dramatist's death, the puritanically-minded Council even went to a certain amount of expense to persuade Shakespeare's company, the famous players The King's Men, just arrived in Stratford, to leave the town again without performing. This was in spite of the fact that they had a traditional right to act in the town."

Part V

1 *Aubrey's Brief Lives.* Ed. with the original manuscripts and with an introd. by Oliver Lawson Dick (Harmondsworth/New York etc., repr. 1978); see "Sir William Davenant", p. 437.

2 Ibid.

3 The evidence on this question is so clear that Shakespeare's authorship has never been questioned by mainstream Shakespeare scholarship. But adherents of variant authorship theories, e.g. proponents of Bacon, Oxford, Marlowe, or, as has been suggested recently – Neville, have attempted to cast doubt on this middle-class son of Stratford as author of his works. Their main argument has been that Shakespeare neither enjoyed a higher education, nor went to Italy. Yet the writer of these plays, they argue, had clearly been educated at university level, and was familiar with the world of the Mediterranean. However, new research into texts and pictures has proved that William Shakespeare was a Catholic, and as such (like many other young English aristocratic and middle-class Catholics) he was educated at what was then the only Catholic college on the continent: the Collegium Anglicum in Douai or Rheims. He also travelled in Europe, especially in Italy,

and in fact stayed in Rome several times. See the relevant chapters of my book *Die verborgene Existenz des William Shakespeare*: "Identität und Verfasserschaft William Shakespeares", pp. 164-175; Part C, I. 3, "Collegausbildung auf dem Kontinent" (1578-1580)", pp. 71-90; and "Epilog", pp. 153-163.

4 In his report of 15 August 1997 he states: "During the period of the Chandos and Flower portraits, the cheek area continues to look full and rounded. But in the Flower portrait, the region of the eyes is more sharply contoured, and surely not just as a result of a different painting technique. On the one hand, the fatty tissue in which the eye sockets are embedded is reduced, making the arch of the eyes more prominent. On the other hand, the enlargement of the lachrymal glands […] becomes even more pronounced. This process of emaciation continues up to the death mask. The face now looks narrower and elongated. The cheeks have become rather sunken, the cheek bones protrude, and the eyes are surrounded by deep furrows. The red area of the lips has become narrower; the lips are thin. The effect is probably heightened by the slight slackening of the jaw with the hint of an opening mouth. There is a further contribution from the typical reduction in tissue turgor (tension), resulting from the sluggishness of circulation as dying proceeds and death ensues, when blood ebbs away into the so-called dependent parts of the body. In every corpse, the eyes sink deeper into their sockets, the temples collapse slightly, and the nose appears more pointed. There can also be a certain, albeit minor change in structure brought about by the technique of taking a death mask, through the pressure of the plaster on soft parts of the face lying directly over a hard area of bone. Hildegard Hammerschmidt-Hummel drew attention to this in her study "Neuer Beweis für die Echtheit [des Flower-Porträts] … (1996)" (New proof of the authenticity of the Flower portrait) (p.6).

5 Hertl, "Expert opinion" (15 August 1997), p. 7.

6 The relevant page of Aubrey's manuscript, which is held in the Oxford Bodleian Library, was reproduced in E. K. Chambers, *William Shakespeare. A Study of Facts and Problems.* 2 vols. (Oxford, 1930), I, p. opposite p. 252, and also in Edgar I. Fripps monograph *Shakespeare: Man and Artist* (London/New York/Toronto, 1938, sec. ed. 1964), I, opposite p. 237. Hog Lane in Shoreditch, close to where James Burbage built and ran his theatre - "The Theatre" - was not however the only place where Shakespeare lived in London. See *William Shakespeare. Seine Zeit – Sein Leben – Sein Werk*: "Ankunft, Unterkunft und Kontakte", pp. 75–89.

7 Aubrey, quoted in Fripp, *Shakespeare: Man and Artist*, p. 237.

8 The meaning of 'debauched' is practically unchanged today. *The Cambridge International Dictionary of English* (Cambridge, 1995, repr. 1999) gives the definition: "weakened or destroyed by bad sexual behaviour, drinking too much alcohol, taking drugs, etc.".

9 *Shakespeare: Man and Artist*, p. 237.

10 *William Shakespeare. Seine Zeit – Sein Leben – Sein Werk*, pp. 82-84.

11 Op. cit., p. 110 ff.

12 See *The Shakspere Allusion-Book*, I, p. 32 ff.

13 Smith's *Latin-English Dictionary*, quoted in *The Shakspere Allusion-Book*, I, p. 37, footnote.

14 See *William Shakespeare. Seine Zeit – Sein Leben – Sein Werk*, pp. 163–170.

15 Reproduced in *The Shakspere Allusion-Book*, I, p. 37, footnote.

16 9th Ser., x, p. 63.

17 Ibid.

18 Demonstrably, for example, in Jonson's *Every Man in His Humour* (1598), and clearly also in his own play *Titus Andronicus*. See Henry Peacham's stage sketch of 1594, reproduced with commentary in H. Hammerschmidt-Hummel, *Die Shakespeare-Illustration (1594-2000). Bildkünstlerische Darstellungen zu den Dramen William Shakespeares: Katalog, Geschichte, Funktion und Deutung.* (Illustrations of Shakespeare 1594-2000: artists' work on Shakespeare's plays: catalogue, history, function and interpretation.) With a lexicon of artists, classified bibliography, and indices, 3 parts and 3100 figs (Wiesbaden, 2003), I, pp. 3-5, fig. 005; see also *William Shakespeare. Seine Zeit – Sein Leben – Sein Werk*, p. 93, fig. 78 a-c.

19 *Shakespeare's Sonnets.* Ed., with Introd. and Commentary, by A. L. Rowse (New York, 1964), p. 227.

20 Robert Nares gives three meanings of "Castilian" (1) "a reproach, which probably arose after the defeat of the Armada"; (2) "a delicate courtier" and (3) "a drunken exclamation". Under (2) there is the explanation: "In this sense it was used, because the Spaniards were then thought people of the highest ceremony and polish" and "Castilian breeding was certainly most esteemed". *A Glossary of Word Phrases Names and Allusions in the Works of English Authors Particularly of Shakespeare and his Contemporaries.* New ed. (London/New York, 1905), under "Castilian". The line from Marston's text, quoted under (2) ("The absolute *Castilio*, He that can all the poynts of courtship show"), makes it clear that Marston's reference bears the sense of "delicate courtier".

21 Literally "his Mistres dangling feake". Nares could not find the word "feake" in the writings of any other author of the time. There is no other source quoted in the *OED*, either. But Nares comments: "The context seems to point to the hanging curl called a lovelock, or some part of the head-dress."

22 With this phrase Marston seems to be alluding to the famous line in *Romeo and Juliet*: "O that I were a glove upon that hand, / That I might touch that cheeke" (II, 2, 23). The playwright James Shirley was also touching in burlesque mode upon this line in Shakespeare's tragedy when in *The Schoole of Complement* (1631) he makes his character Bub[ulcus] say: "O that I were a flea vpon his lip, / There would I sucke for euer, and not skip." *The Shakspere Allusion-Book*, I, p. 357.

23 The full quotation is: "if all things were well knowne and view'd, / He doth but champe that which another chew'd".

24 The text runs:

> So *Labeo* did complaine his loue was stone,
> Obdurate, flinty, so relentlesse none:
> [...]

But Oh! the absolute *Castilio*,
He that can all the poynts of courtship show.
[...]
He, who on his glorious scutchion
Can quaintly shewe his *newe* inuention,
[...]
With some short motto of a dozen lines.
He that can purpose it in dainty rimes,
Can set his face, and with his eye can speake,
Can dally with his Mistres dangling feake,
And wish that he were it, to kisse her eye
And flare about her beauties deitie.
Tut, he is famous for his reueling,
For fine set speeches, and for sonetting;
He scornes the violl and the scraping sticke,
And yet's but Broker of anothers wit.
Certes if all things were well knowne and view'd,
He doth but champe that which another chew'd.
Come come *Castilion*, skim thy posset curd,
Show thy queere substance, worthlesse, most absurd.
Take ceremonious complement from thee,
Alas, I see *Castilios* beggary.

Marston, *Metamorphosis*, in *The Shakspere Allusion-Book*, I, pp. 35–36.

25 When C. S. Harris printed the 'Castilio' passage in *Notes and Queries*, Series, II, p. 183, he too made an effort to identify 'Castilio' as Shakespeare, noting that the line "He that can trot a Courser" referred to the days when – according to seventeenth century legend - Shakespeare looked after theatre-goers' horses.

26 See Part III of my book *Das Geheimnis um Shakespeare's 'Dark Lady'*.

27 See the sub-chapter "Autobiography in the sonnets" in my Shakespeare biography: *The Life and Times of William Shakespeare (1564-1616)* (London, 2006).

28 The full text of the new sonnet is:

> The restles swallow fits my restles minde,
> In still reuiuinge still renewinge wronges;
> her Just complaintes of cruelty vnkinde,
> are all the Musique, that my life prolonges.
> With pensiue thoughtes my weepinge Stagg I crowne
> whose Melancholy teares my cares Expresse;
> hes Teares in sylence, and my sighes vnknowne
> are all the physicke that my harmes redresse.
> My onely hope was in this goodly tree,
> which I did plant in loue bringe vp in care;
> but all in vaine, for now to[o] late I see
> the shales be mine, the kernels others are.
> My Musique may be plaintes, my physique teares
> If this be all the fruite my loue tree beares.

29 See Bertram/Cossa, "'Willm Shakespeare 1609'", p. 94.

30 See *Aubrey's Brief Lives*, p. 438. Aubrey's exact wording reads: "he understood Latin pretty well: for he had been in his younger yeares a Schoolmaster in the Countrey."

31 See William Shakespeare. *Seine Zeit - Sein Leben - Sein Werk*, p. 165.

32 These comments are based on findings presented in my book, *Die verborgene Existenz des William Shakespeare*, p. 28 ff., p. 36 ff., p. 50 ff., p. 64 ff., 91 ff., and p. 116 ff.

33 The poet's father had been dead for seven years by this time. He was buried on 8 September 1601.

34 Dawes, "Gods Mercie and Jerusalems miseries. A Sermon Preached at Pauls Crosse (1609)", cit. by Maclure, *The Paul's Cross Sermons* 1534–1643, p. 231.

35 See the chapter "Die antikatholische Gesetzgebung unter Elisabeth I. und Jakob I.", in *Die verborgene Existenz des William Shakespeare*, 16-21.

36 See *Die verborgene Existenz des William Shakespeare*, pp. 48-50.

37 See *William Shakespeare. Seine Zeit – Sein Leben – Sein Werk*, pp. 28-29.

38 See *Die verborgene Existenz des William Shakespeare*, p. 50.

39 See *William Shakespeare. Seine Zeit – Sein Leben – Sein Werk*, p. 64 ff.

40 See *Die verborgene Existenz des William Shakespeare*, Epilog, pp. 153-163.

41 *Dictionary of National Biography*. Eds. Leslie Stephen and Sidney Lee (London, 1908 ff.), III, under "Catesby, Robert".

42 See *William Shakespeare. Seine Zeit – Sein Leben – Sein Werk*, pp. 35-36.

43 See Henry Foley, *Records of the English Province of the Society of Jesus*. 7 Vols. (London, 1877–1882, repr. New York/London, 1966), VI, pp. 710–719: In his report of 27 August 1584 the deputising Alderman Banks gives an account of a search in the house of a man called Sybury: "[...] his son William [...] was committed, with two books, and a picture of our Lady put into one of the same books" (p. 710). Sheriff Spencer recorded that: "In Roger Smith's chamber certain *Papistical books*, and seven printed *suspicious pictures*" (p. 716). In the "Report of Mr. Justice Smith, Francis Mill,s and George the High Constable" concerning a search of *"Sir Thomas Tresham's house"* we read: "[...] we found and brought away [...] the things following: *A Popish painted crucifix* on a table hanging by the [...] lady's bedside; *the Jesuits' Testament in English* [meaning the so-called Borromeo testament by which English Catholics could confess their faith]; Officium Bae. Mae. Virginis ij. [this refers to the Marian Primer authorised by the Pope and printed in Paris in 1573]; A Manual of Prayers dedicated to the gentlemen of the Inns of Court; Vaux's Catechism; the first book of the Christian Exercises; a book of prayer and meditation; a painted crucifix upon orange-coloured satin; a picture of Christ upon canvas. [...] Also we found there, which we left behind, a new fashioned *picture of Christ* in a great table, and *a tabernacle of sundry painted images* ..." (p. 717). In *"Mr. Thomas Wilford's house"* Spencer found: "A *Mass Book*, very old; *a written Catechism*; *Officium Bae. Mae. V.*, very old; *an Epistle of the Persecution of Catholics in England; the same in Latin; a book against the unlawful insurrection of the Protestants*, [...]; *a Catechismus ex decreto Concil. Tridentini*" (p. 717). In the house of "Mr. Gardiner, the lawyer, in the Blackfriars", finally, Alderman Hart

also confiscated the *Officium Beatae Mariae Virginis nuper Reformatum Parisiis 1573 cum privilegio Papae et Francorum Regis*" (p. 719). The emphases are the author's.

44 "Wheler Miscellaneous Papers", ii, f. 39, quoted by Charlotte C. Stopes, *Shakespeare's Environment* (London, 1918), p. 120. The formulation "Shakespeare's head" indicates that this was a painted portrait (head and shoulders), and not a bust.

45 See *William Shakespeare. Seine Zeit – Sein Leben – Sein Werk*, p. 335.

46 See *William Shakespeare. Seine Zeit – Sein Leben – Sein Werk*, pp. 145–148 and p. 215 ff.

47 *Shakespeare's Religious Background* (London, 1973), p. 171.

48 Ibid.

49 Foley, *Records of the English Province of the Society of Jesus*, III, opposite p. 684.

50 Quoted in Campbell/Quinn, *Shakespeare Encyclopaedia*, entry for "Davies, Richard".

51 See Joseph Gillow, *Bibliographical Dictionary of English Catholics* (London, 1885–1902), under "Shakespeare".

52 On identifying this Benedictine father see *Die verborgene Existenz des William Shakespeare*, p. 121 ff.

53 "To the memorie of M. *W. Shake-speare*", in: Mr. William *Shakespeares Comedies, Histories, and Tragedies*. A facsimile edition.

54 See *William Shakespeare. Seine Zeit – Sein Leben – Sein Werk*, p. 242.

55 During the Civil War the young doctor, to whose dedication we owe the preservation of the extremely valuable medical-historical source material mentioned above, was personal surgeon to Robert Greville, Lord Brooke, who commanded the parliamentary troops in and around Stratford.

56 First, *written in Latine by Mr. John Hall Physician, living at Stratford upon Avon in Warwick-shire, where he was very famous, as also in the Counties adjacent, as appeares by these Observations drawn out of severall hundreds of his, as choysest. Now put into English for common benefit by James Cooke Practitioner in Physick and Chirurgery.*

57 The manuscript is in the British Library in London (Egerton 2065).

58 See Philip Tennant, *The Civil War in Stratford-upon-Avon. Conflict and Community in South Warwickshire, 1642–1646* (Phoenix Mill/Far Thrupp/Stroud/Stratford-upon-Avon, 1996), p. 60: "Cooke was invited to New Place by a colleague who had formerly been an assistant to Shakespeare's son-in-law, the physician John Hall. There, the poet's daughter Susanna showed Cooke her husband's medical notebooks, from which he was later to publish a selection of unique case-histories compiled by a seventeenth-century doctor going about his daily business." Regarding the date of Cooke's visit to New Place, Tennant proposes convincingly that it probably occurred during the time when Brooke and his troops were quartered in Stratford (see p. 60).

59 See Joan Lane, *John Hall and his Patients. The Medical Practice of Shakespeare's Son-in-Law*. Medical Commentary by Melvin Earles (Stratford-upon-Avon, 1996), xx.

60 Schoenbaum too observes that: "The earliest dated history in the extant case-book belongs to 1617. Conceivably a second notebook exists somewhere – Cooke refers to two Hall books – and may one day surface." S. Schoenbaum, *William Shakespeare. A Documentary Life* (Oxford, 1971), p. 241.

61 See Lane, *John Hall and his Patients*, xvi.

62 See Cooke's address "To the Friendly Reader" (1657), quoted in Schoenbaum, *William Shakespeare. A Documentary Life*, p. 238.

63 "MSS. of the Rev. John Ward, in the possession of the Medical Society of London. Printed in the 'Diary of the Rev. John Ward, A. M., Vicar of Stratford-upon-Avon, extending from 1648 to 1679," edited by C. Severn, M.D. 1839. p. 184–4," in *The Shakespeare Allusion-Book: A Collection of Allusions to Shakspere from 1591 to 1700*. Originally Compiled by C. M. Ingleby, L. Toulmin Smith, and F. J. Furnivall. Re-edited, revised, and re-arranged, with an Introduction, by John Munro (1909), re-issued with a Preface by Edmund Chambers. 2 Vols. (London/Oxford, 1932), II, 111. The emphases are the author's. Regarding the credibility of this tradition, in the eight-volume work he published in London in 1844, *The Works of William Shakespeare. The Text formed from an entirely new Collation of the old Editions: With the various Readings, Notes, a Life of the Poet, and a History of the early English Stage*, J. Payne Collier was already astutely observing: "What credit may be due to this statement, preceded as it is by the words 'it seems,' implying a doubt on the subject in the writer's mind, we must leave the reader to determine" (ccl).

64 There are numerous passages in Shakespeare's plays where drunkenness is either forcefully condemned or (with pedagogic intent) caricatured. It is impossible to list them all here. We can instead take as one representative example the scene in *Hamlet* (I, 4) where the eponymous hero criticises conditions in the England of his day by denouncing drunkenness in Denmark: "This heavy-headed revel east and west / Makes us traduc'd, and tax'd of other nations; / They clepe us drunkards, and with swinish phrase / Soil our addition; and indeed it takes / From our achievements, though perform'd at height,

/ The pith and marrow of our attribute". In *Twelfth Night*, however, where drunkenness is condemned among other vices, it is not in fact seen as the worst: "I hate ingratitude more in a man / Than lying, vainness, babbling, drunkenness, / Or any taint of vice" (II,5,81).

65 *The Works of William Shakespeare. The Text*. 8 Vols. (London, 1844), cclii.

66 Lane, *John Hall and his Patients*, xxii. She refers to the relevant investigation by J.E.D. Shrewsbury, *A History of Bubonic Plague in the British Isles* (Cambridge, 1970), pp. 276–277, which deals with the plagues of 1558, 1564, 1581, 1604 and 1608–10, and then continues: "By 1616, however, a far more severe affliction, a typhus epidemic, appeared and was noted by Hall as 'the new fever' when he attended Lady Beaufou near Warwick in July 1617."

67 "It was then called the *New Feaver*, it invaded many, I was called the third day of its Invasion." Dr. John Hall, *Select Observations*, "Observ. LXXVII", quoted in Lane, *John Hall and his Patients*, 138.

68 The unusually high number of burials in 1616 show that the epidemic must have started in that year. See the diagram published in Joan Lane's *John Hall and his Patients* (xxiv).

69 Hall's "nuncupative" (oral) last will and testament of 25 November 1635, reproduced in B. Roland Lewis (*The Shakespeare Documents. Facsimiles, Transliterations, Translations & Commentary*. 2 Vols., Stanford U. P./London/Oxford U.P., 1941, II, "Text of Nuncupative Will of John Hall, 1635", No. 260, 588) was witnessed by his son-in-law Thomas Nashe and the Stratford curate Simon Trapp. Hall's testament has attracted particular attention because in it he mentions his library ("my Study of Bookes") and his papers ("my Manuscript[es]"). This library may well also have contained many of Shakespeare's books and manuscripts. What John Hall decreed concerning his and Shakespeare's books and manuscripts is surprising. He gave his son-in-law a completely free hand with them. However, it is hard to imagine that Susanna Hall would have agreed to this. The text of the will says: "It[e]m concerning my Study of Bookes I leaue them (sayd hee) to you my son Nash to dispose of them as you see good / As for my Manu-script[es] I wold haue given them vnto M[aste]r Boles if hee had beene heere but forasmuch as hee is not heere p[re]sent you may (son Nash) burne them or else doe w[i]th them what you please."

Bibliography

Anon., *A Relation of a short Survey of 26. Counties [...]* By a Captaine, a Lieutenant, and an Ancient. All three of the Military Company in Norwich. British Library. MS Lansdowne 213, f. 332v, EKC, ii, 243.

Anon., "Die Reichsgrafen von Kesselstatt im Trierer Raum." In *Regierungsbezirk Trier: Monographie einer Landschaft.* No place or date of publication.

Anon., *The Four Folios of William Shakespeare. Together with some Quartos.* Catalogue No. 138. H. P. Kraus. Old & Rare Books. New York, n.d.

Anon., *Pictures and Sculpture from the Royal Shakespeare Theatre Picture Gallery.* Stratford-upon-Avon, n.d.

Anon., "III. Alterthümliches von Mainz", *Quartalblätter des Vereines für Literatur und Kunst zu Mainz,* 2, 2 (1831), 38-39.

Anon., *Catalogue D'Une Galerie De Tableaux, D'Une Collection De Gravures, De Croquis Antiquites Et Curiosites, Appartenant A La Succession DeFeu M Le Comte Fr. De Kesselstatt, Qui Avec Une Bibliothèque Contenant Particulièrement Des Ouvrages En Figures Anciens Et Modernes. Seront Vendus Publiquement. A Mayence, Le 1. Juin Prochain Et Les Jours Suivans,* Mayence, 1842.

Anon., "Reichsgrafen v. Kesselstatt". In *Beiträge zur Geschichte und Genealogie rheinischer Adelsfamilien* mit Originalzeichnungen von Georg Macco. Ed. Friedrich Macco, Aachen, 1884.

Anon., *Proceedings of the Society of Antiquaries of London* (12 December 1895).

Anon., *The Vestry Minute-Book of the Parish of Stratford-on-Avon from 1617 to 1699 A.D.,* London, 1899.

Anon., *Minutes and Accounts of the Corporation of Stratford-upon-Avon, 1586-1592.* Dugdale Society, 10, 1929.

Anon., *Catalogue of Pictures and Sculptures. Royal Shakespeare Theatre Picture Gallery.* 6th ed. Stratford-upon-Avon, 1970.

Anon., Bericht über das kraniologische und physiognomische Urtheil, das die Versammlung Deutscher Naturforscher und Aerzte (Anthropologische Sektion) auf ihrer Tagung im September 1873 in Wiesbaden auf Wunsch von Dr. Hermann Schaffhausen über die Totenmaske Shakespeares abgegeben hat, *Tageblatt der 46. Versammlung Deutscher Naturforscher und Aerzte* (1873), 193.

Anon., *Illustrated Catalogue of Portraits in Shakespeare's Memorial at Stratford* (1896).

Anon., "Kunst, Wissenschaft und Leben. Shakespeares Totenmaske", *Darmstädter Zeitung* (11 October 1910).

Anon., "Shakespeares Totenmaske in Darmstadt", Darmstädter Täglicher Anzeiger (11 October 1910).

Anon., "Bücherbesprechungen. Bildende Kunst. 'Shakespeares Totenmaske' von Paul Wislicenus". *Kölnische Zeitung* (11 December 1910).

Anon., "Aus Kunst, Wissenschaft und Leben. 'Shakespeares Totenmaske'". *Darmstädter Tagblatt* (12 October 1910).

Anon., "'Dokumente zu Shakespeares Totenmaske'. Von Paul Wislicenus". *Sonntagsblatt des 'Bund' (Bern)* 14 (2 April 1911).

Anon., "Shakespeare Mask Question to be Settled". *The Christian Science Monitor (Boston, Mass.)* (10 October 1912).

Anon., "Shakespeare's Likeness". *The Continental Times* (31 August 1912).

Anon., *Conservators of the Hunterian Museum. I. William Clift. Repr. from Annals of the Royal College of Surgeons of England.* Vol. 30 (January, 1962).

Anon., "Mappes, Johann Heinrich Ludwig Baron von. Kaufmann und Kommunalpolitiker, 1757-1845". In *Hessische Biographien.* In assocation with Karl Esselborn and Georg Lehnert. Ed. by Hermann Haupt. Unrevised reprint of the edition of 1918, Vol. 1, Walluf bei Wiesbaden, 1973, pp. 187-188.

Anon., *Minutes and Accounts of the Corporation of Stratford-upon-Avon,* 1593-1598. Dugdale Society, 35, 1990.

Anon., "Real life drama behind the Bard's death mask". *Herald Sun* (21 October 1995).

Anon., "German police establish what Bard looked like". *Khaleej Times* (27 October 1995).

Anon., "Totenmaske zeigt: Shakespeare war schwer erkrankt. Tumor wurde kriminalistisch aufgespürt", *Neue Presse Hannover* (1 July 1995).

Anon., "'Kein Zweifel' an Shakespeares Totenmaske. Mainzer Wissenschaftlerin erläutert in Darmstadt ihre vergleichenden Untersuchungen". *Frankfurter Allgemeine Zeitung* [Rhein-Main-Zeitung] (23 June 1995).

Anon., "Ein echter Shakespeare. Fachleute des BKA untersuchten Darmstädter Totenmaske", *Hamburger Abendblatt* (23 June 1995).

Anon., "Darmstädter Totenmaske soll die echten Gesichtszüge von Shakespeare tragen". *Frankfurter Rundschau* (23 June 1995).

Anon., "Unverwüstlicher Gips auf Reisen. Wie Shakespeares Totenmaske nach Darmstadt gelangte". *Frankfurter Allgemeine Zeitung* (23 June 1995).

Anon., "'Damit besitzen wir offenbar ein Stück von Shakespeare selbst.' Umstrittene Totenmaske ist echt". *Kölnische Rundschau* (24 June 1995).

Anon., "Shakespeare hatte einen Tumor. Totenmaske weist Veränderungen am linken Auge auf". *Mannheimer Morgen* (24 June 1995).

Anon., "Beweis für Echtheit der Totenmaske von Shakespeare". *Deutsche Tagespost* (14 May 1996).

Altmann, Reinhardt, "Bildgutachten in der kunsthistorischen Forschung, hier: SHAKESPEARE", Aktenzeichen: Bundeskriminalamt Wiesbaden, ZD 15 – 1170/95 (3 May 1995).

Altmann, Reinhardt, "Bildgutachten in der kunsthistorischen Forschung - hier: SHAKESPEARE" (6 July 1998).

Altmann, Reinhardt. "Bildgutachten in der kunsthistorischen Forschung - hier: SHAKESPEARE" (30 June 1999).

Altmann, Reinhardt. "Bildgutachten in der kunsthistorischen Forschung - hier: Sanders-Porträt" (8 August 2001).

Archbold, Rick, "Foreword". In: Stephanie Nolen (with Jonathan Bate, Tarnya Cooper, Marjorie Garber, Andrew Gurr, Alexander Leggatt, Robert Titler and Stanley Wells), *Shakespeare's Face.* Toronto, 2002, IX–XI

Ariès, Philippe, *Western Attitudes to Death.* London, 1974.

Ariès, Philippe, *The Hour of Our Death.* London, 1981.

Ariès, Philippe, *Images of Man and Death.* Cambridge, Mass., 1985.

Ashelford, Jane, *A Visual History of the Sixteenth Century.* London, 1983.

Ashelford, Jane, *Dress in the Age of Elizabeth I.* London, 1988.

Ashton, Geoffrey, *Pictures in the Garrick Club. A Catalogue of the Paintings, Drawings, Watercolours and Sculpture.* Compiled and written by G. Ashton. Eds. Kalman A. Burnim and Andrew Wilton. London, 1997.

Aubrey, John, *Aubrey's Brief Lives.* Ed. with the original manuscripts and with an introd. by Oliver Lawson Dick. Harmondsworth/New York et al., repr. 1978.

Baader, Hannah, "Gabriele Paleotti: Ähnlichkeit als Kategorie der Moral (1582)". In: *Porträt.* Geschichte der klassischen Bildgattungen in Quellentexten und Kommentaren. Eds. R. Preimesberger, H. Baader and N. Suthor. Berlin, 1999.

Backer, B. A., Hannon, N. and N. A. Russell, eds. *Death and Dying: Individuals and Institutions*. New York, 1982.

Baker, Malcolm, "Roubiliac's Models and Eighteenth-Century English Sculptors' Working Practices". *Entwurf und Ausführung in der europäischen Barockplastik*. Ed. P. Volk. Munich, 1986. 59-83.

Baker, Richard, *A Chronicle of the Kings of England. From the Time of the Romans Government unto the Raigne of our Soveraigne Lord King Charles*. London, 1643.

Baumann, Uwe, *Shakespeare und seine Zeit*. Stuttgart, 1998.

Bearman, Robert, *Shakespeare in the Stratford Records*. Phoenix Mill/Far Thrupp/Stroud, Gloucestershire/Dover NH, 1994.

Beaty, Nancy Lee, *The Craft of Dying: A Study of the Literary Tradition of The 'Ars Moriendi' in England*. New Haven, 1970.

Becker, Thorsten, "Von der Kinzig zum Kurfürsten. Ursprung in Kesselstadt: Seit über 700 Jahren besteht das Adelsgeschlecht im Trierer Land". *Hanauer Anzeiger 105* [On the origins of the Kesselstatt family] (6 May 1995).

Bénézit, Emmanuel, *Dictionnaire critique et documentaire des peintres, sculpteurs, dessinateurs et graveurs*. Nouvelle éd., entièrement refondue, revue et corrigée sous la direction des héritiers de E. Bénézit. Paris, 1976.

Benkard, Ernst, *Das ewige Antlitz. Eine Sammlung von Totenmasken*. Mit einem Geleitwort von Georg Kolbe [With a preface by Georg Kolbe]. Berlin, 1929.

Benkard, Ernst, *Undying Faces*. London, 1929.

Benndorf, Otto, *Antike Gesichtshelme und Sepulkralmasken*. Denkschriften der kaiserlichen Akademie der Wissenschaften in Wien. Vol. XXVIII. Vienna, 1878.

Bentley-Cranch, Dana, "Effigy and Portrait in Sixteenth-Century Scotland". *Rosc. Review of Scottish Culture (Dublin)* 4 (1988): 9.

Beresford Chancellor, E., *The Romance of Lincoln's Inn Fields and its Neighbourhood*. London, 1932.

Bermeitinger, Michael, "'Sein oder nicht sein' Gesicht? Wiesbadener Forscherin verifizierte mit BKA-Hilfe Shakespeares Totenmaske". *Wiesbadener Tagblatt* (22 June 1995).

Bertram, Paul, "What Shakespeare Looked Like: The Spielmann Position and the Alternatives". *Journal of the Rutgers University Libraries*, 41 (June 1979): 1–17.

Bertram, Paul and Frank Cossa, "'Willm Shakespeare 1609': The Flower Portrait Revisited". *Shakespeare Quarterly* 37 (1986): 83-96.

Besseler, Heinrich, *Fünf echte Bildnisse Johann Sebastian Bachs*. Kassel/Basel, 1956.

Bialostocki, Jan, "The Image of Death and Funerary Art in European Tradition". In: *Arte Funerario: Coloquio Internacional de Historia del Arte*. Eds. B. De La Fuente and L. Noelle. 2 Vols. Mexico City, 1987. 11-32.

Bialostocki, Jan, "The Door of Death: Survival of a Classical Motif in Sepulchral Art". *Jahrbuch der Hamburger Kunstsammlungen XVIII* (1973): 7-32.

Bland, Olivia, *The Royal Way of Death*. London, 1986.

Bloxam, Matthew Holbeche, *Warwickshire During the Civil Wars of the Seventeenth Century*. Warwick, 1880.

Boaden, James, *An Inquiry into the Authenticity of Various Pictures and Prints, Which, from the Decease of the Poet to Our Own Times, Have Been Offered to the Public as Portraits of Shakspeare: Containing a Careful Examination of the Evidence on Which They Claim to Be Received; [...]*. London, 1824.

Bode, Wilhelm von, *Italienische Portraitskulpturen des XV. Jahrhunderts in den Königlichen Museen zu Berlin*. Berlin, 1883.

Bode, Wilhelm von, *Denkmäler der Renaissance-Skulputur Toscanas*. Munich, 1892-1905.

Bode, Wilhelm von, *Florentinische Bildhauer der Renaissance*. Berlin, 1902.

Boehm, Gottfried, "Individuum und Autonomie. Zur Entwicklung der Portraitmalerei in der europäischen Neuzeit". *Reformatio. Zeitschrift für Kultur, Politik und Kirche,* 40 (1990).

Bohl, Inka, "Wie Shakespeare sein Gesicht zurückbekam". *Der Literat. Fachzeitschrift für Literatur und Kunst* 37 (July/August 1995): 15-17.

Boisserée, Sulpiz, *Tagebücher 1808-1854*. Im Auftrag der Stadt Köln [commissioned by the City of Cologne]. Ed. by Hans-J. Weitz. Darmstadt, 1978. I 1808-1823.

Bolte, O., "Über die malerische Darstellung menschlicher Haut und menschlicher Kopfbehaarung als Ausdruck stilistischer und kunstgeschichtlicher Wandlung". *Der Hautarzt* 15 (1964): 442-448.

Bolte, O., "Über die symbolische Bedeutung der gesunden und der erkrankten menschlichen Haut in der darstellenden Kunst". *Der Hautarzt* 16 (1965): 467-473.

Boltz, Ingeborg, "Shakespeare-Bildnisse". In: *Shakespeare-Handbuch*. Ed. Ina Schabert. Mit einem Geleitwort von [with a preface by] Wolfgang Clemen. Stuttgart, 3rd impression 1992, 4th impression 2000. 187-191, 179-184.

Boyes, Roger, "Computer unmasks Bard's cancer". *The Times* (24 April 1996).

Brandl, A., "Zu 'Shakespeares Totenmaske' und 'Ben Jonsons Totenbild'". *Jahrbuch der Deutschen Shakespeare-Gesellschaft* 47 (1911): 156-169.

Braun, J., *Studie zur Physiognomik nach formanalytischen Messungen an Masken*. Heidelberg, 1967.

Britton, John. *On the Monumental Bust*. London, 1816.

Burger, F., *Geschichte des florentinischen Grabmals*. Strasbourg, 1904.

Busch, Rudolf, "Graf Franz von Kesselstatt und seine Sammlungen". *Mainzer Zeitschrift* 39-40 (1944/45): 55-62.

Cambridge International Dictionary of English. Cambridge, 1995, repr. 1999.

Campbell, O. J. and E. G. Quinn, eds., *A Shakespeare Encyclopaedia*. London, 1966, repr. 1974.

Cargill, Alexander, "The Likeness of Shakespeare". *The Strand Magazine* (September, 1894): 317-324.

Carlton, Charles, *Going to the Wars: The Experience of the British Civil Wars, 1638-1651*. London. 1992.

Carmichael, Ann G, und Richard M. Ratzan, eds., *Medizin in Literatur und Kunst* [1991] German edition, Cologne, 1994.

Carpenter, Edward, ed., *A House of Kings. The Official History of Westminster Abbey*. With a Message from H.M. The Queen. Ill. London, 1966, 1972, repr. 1992.

Chalmers, Alexander, *The General Biographical Dictionary*. London, 1815.

Chambers, E. K., *William Shakespeare*. 2 Vols. Oxford 1930.

Chatwin, P. B., "The Later Monumental Effigies of the County of Warwick". *Transactions of the Birmingham Archaeological Society* 57 (1933): 122-126.

Chaunu, Pierre, *Europäische Kultur im Zeitalter des Barock*. Mit 264 Abb., 8 Farbtaf. u. 37 Karten und Plänen. [with 264 ills., 8 colour plates, and 37 maps and plans] Transl. by A. P. Zeller. [Paris, 1966]. Munich/Zürich, 1968.

Christ, Karl, *Die Römer. Eine Einführung in ihre Geschichte und Zivilisation*. Munich, 1979.

Colburn, Don, "Diagnose nach 570 Jahren: Der Kranke hatte Polio". *Welt am Sonntag* 9 (3 March 1996).

Collier, J. P., *Dissertation upon the Imputed Portraits*. London, 1851.

Conder, Edward, *Records of the Hole Crafte and Fellowship of Masons. With a Chronicle of the History of the Worshipful Company of Masons of the City of London*. Collected from official Records in the possession of the Company, the Manuscripts in the British Museum, the Public Record Office, the Guildhall Library, etc. etc. (London/New York, 1894). Including Annex: "The Company of Marblers of the City of London".

Connaughton, Colleen, "Reuters Reports" [On the Findings Regarding the Authenticity of the Darmstadt Shakespeare Death Mask and the Shakespearian Portraits 'Chandos' and 'Flower'] *Sky News* (7 March 1996) [Update: 9 May 1996].

Connell, Charles, *They Gave us Shakespeare, John Hemming & Henry Condell*. Stocksfield, 1982.

Connor, Steve, "Germans put a face to Shakespeare". *The Sunday Times* (15 March 1998).

Cope, Zacharay. *The Royal College of Surgeons of England. A History*. London/Colchester, 1959.

Cooper, J. C., *Illustriertes Lexikon der traditionellen Symbole* (1978). Transl. from English by G. und M. Middell. Leipzig, 1986.

Corbin, John, "Two Undescribed Portraits of Shakespeare". *Harper's New Monthly Magazine* (May 1897).

Craig, Edward Thomas, *Shakespeare and his Portraits, Bust, and Monument*. London, 2nd ed. 1864.

Craig, Edward Thomas, *Shakespeare's Portraits considered phrenologically*. London, 1864, Philadelphia, 1875.

Craig, Edward Thomas, *The Portraits, Bust and Monument of Shakespeare*. London, 1886.

Dawson, Aileen, *Portrait Sculpture. A Catalogue of the British Museum Collection. C. 1675-1975*. London, 1999.

Dawson, G. E., "The Arlaud-Duchange Portrait of Shakespeare". *The Library* 16, 4th ser. (1936): 290-294.

Dernburg, Friedrich, "Shakespeares Totenmaske". *Berliner Tageblatt* (6 November 1910).

Dick, Oliver Lawson, ed., "William Shakespeare". In: *Aubrey's Brief Lives*. Ed. with the original manuscripts and with an introd. by O. L. Dick [1949]. Harmondsworth, repr., 1978, 437-438.

Dobson, Jessie, *William Clift*. London, 1954.

Dtv Lexikon der Kunst. 6 Vols. Leipzig, 1989, Munich, 1996.

Dugdale, William, *The Antiquities of Warwickshire Illustrated; From Records, Leiger-Books, Manuscripts, Charters, Evidences, Tombes, and Armes* [...] London, 1656.

Durant, Will und Ariel Durant, *Gegenreformation und Elisabethisches Zeitalter*. Kulturgeschichte der Menschheit. Vol. 10. Cologne, 1985.

Dußler, Luitpold, "Unpublished Terracottas of the late Quattrocento". *The Burlington Magazine* 43 (1923).

Eddershaw, David and Eleanor Roberts, *The Civil War in Oxfordshire*. Stroud, 1995.

Edmond, Mary, "The Chandos portrait: a suggested painter". *Burlington Magazine* 124 (1982): 146-149.

Edmond, Mary, "It was for Gentle Shakespeare Cut". *Shakespeare Quarterly* 42 (1991).

Edwards, Rob, "Was Shakespeare the man behind the mask?" *New Scientist* 148.2000 (21 October 1995).

Eisenhauer, Bertram, "Bist du gebannt in diese bleiche Kruste? Eine Forscherin will die Echtheit der Totenmaske Shakespeares bewiesen haben". *Frankfurter Allgemeine Zeitung* (26 June 1995).

Encyclopaedia Britannica. A Dictionary of Arts, Sciences and General Literature. 30 Vols. With New American Supplement. Ed. Day Otis Kellogg. Orig. Ninth Ed. in 25 Vols. Ed. Spencer Baynes and W. Robertson Smith. New York/Chicago, 1899.

Engler, Balz, "'Der Stein sich leise hebt': Das Shakespeare-Denkmal in Weimar", *Shakespeare-Jahrbuch* (2003): 146–160.

Enright, D. J., ed., *The Oxford Book of Death*. Oxford, 1983.

Eschen, Fritz, *Das letzte Porträt. Totenmasken berühmter Persönlichkeiten aus Geschichte und Gegenwart*. Mit einer Einführung von [introduction by] Karl Jaspers und einem kulturhistorischen Beitrag [cultural-historical commentary] von Karl-Heinz Schreyl. Berlin, 1967.

Esdaile, Katherine Ada, *English Monumental Sculpture since the Renaissance*. With Plates. London, 1927.

Esdaile, Katherine Ada, *English Church Monuments, 1510 to 1840*. With an Introduction by S. Sitwell. With Plates. London, 1946.

Esdaile, Katherine Ada, "Some Fellow-Citizens of Shakespeare in Southwark". *Essays and Studies*. NS, 5 (1952).

Esdaile, Katherine Ada, "The Interaction of English and Low Country Sculpture in the Sixteenth Century". *Journal of The Warburg & Courtauld Institutes* VI (1943): 80-88.

Etlin, Richard A., *The Architecture of Death*. Cambridge, Mass., 1984.

Eustace, K., ed., *Michael Rysbrack, Sculptor, 1694-1770*. City of Bristol Museums & Art Gallery Exhibition Catalogue. Bristol, 1982.

Feeser, Sigrid, "Shakespeare oder nicht Shakespeare - keine Frage mehr. Eine Mainzer Anglistikprofessorin legt Beweise für die Echtheit der Totenmaske des englischen Dramatikers in Darmstädter Besitz vor". *Rheinpfalz Ludwigshafen* (1 July 1995).

Feeser, Sigrid, "Alles geklärt? - Neue Beweise für die Echtheit der Darmstädter Shakespeare-Totenmaske". *Rhein-Neckar-Zeitung Heidelberg* (5 July 1995).

Finucane, R. C., "Sacred Corpses, Profane Carrion: Social Ideals and Death Rituals in the Later Middle Ages". In: *Mirrors of Mortality: Studies in the Social History of Death*. Ed. J. Whaley. London, 1981, 40-60.

Fitzke, Franz, "Länder-Journal" [Über die Echtheitsnachweise für die die Darmstädter Shakespeare-Totenmaske und die Shakespeare-Porträts 'Chandos' und 'Flower'] *Zweites Deutsches Fernsehen* [ZDF Television] (6 December 1995).

Foley, Henry, *Records of the English Province of the Society of Jesus*. 7 Vols. London, 1877–1882, repr. New York/London, 1966. VI.

Forster, R. H., *Remarks on the Chandos Portrait*. London, 1849.

Freedman, Luba, "The Concept of Portraiture in Art Theory of the Cinquecento". *Zeitschrift für Ästhetik und Allgemeine Kunstwissenschaft* 32 (1987).

Friedel, E., *Das letzte Gesicht*. Zürich/Leipzig, 1929.

Fripp, Edgar I., *Minutes and Accounts of the Corporation of Stratford-upon-Avon and Other Records, 1553-1620*. Transcribed by R. Savage, with Introductions and Notes by E. I. Fripp. 1921-1929.

Fripp, Edgar I., *Shakespeare: Man and Artist*. 2 Vols. London, 1938, repr. 1964.

Friswell, J. Hain, *Life-Portraits of William Shakespeare*. London, 1864.

Fritz, Paul S., "From 'Public' to 'Private': The Royal Funerals in England, 1500-1830". In: *Mirrors of Mortality: Studies in the Social History of Death*. Ed. J. Whaley. London, 1981.

Fuchs, Georg, *Die Totenmaske Shakespeares*. München, 1939.

Fulton, Robert, ed., *Death and Identity*. New York, 1965.

Galbi, Douglas, "C. Epiphany, or What You Will". In: *Sense in Communication* (www.galbithink.org - 14. Januar 2004).

Galvin, Carol et al., "Pietro Torrigiano's Portrait Bust of King Henry VII". *The Burlington Magazine* 130.88 (1988).

Gans, O., "Ein Fall von Lupus erythematodes chronicus discoides disseminatus aus dem Jahre 1767". *Der Hautarzt* 15 (1964): 39-40.

Gassner, August, *Goethe und Mainz*. Bern/Frankfurt am Main/New York/Paris, 1988.

Geese, Uwe, "Skulptur der italienischen Renaissance". In: *Die Kunst der italienischen Renaissance*. Ed. Rolf Toman.Cologne, 1994. 176-237.

Gent, Lucy and Nigel Llewellyn, eds., *Renaissance Bodies: The Human Figure in English Culture, c. 1540-1660*. London, 1990.

Gerassimow, Michail Michailowitsch, *Ich suchte Gesichter*. Gütersloh, 1968.

Gibson, Iris I. J. M., "Death masks unlimited". *British Medical Journal* 291 (December 1985): 21-28.

Giesey, R. E., *The Royal Funeral Ceremony in Renaissance France*. Geneva, 1960.

Gillow, Joseph, *Bibliographical Dictionary of English Catholics*. London, 1885–1902.

Gittings, Clare, *Death, Burial and the Individual in Early Modern England*. London, 1984.

Giuliani, Luca, "Zur spätrepublikanischen Bildniskunst. Wege und Abwege der Interpretation antiker Porträts". In: *Antike und Abendland. Beiträge zum Verständnis der Griechen und Römer und ihres Nachlebens* 36 (1990): 103.

Goethe, Johann Wolfgang von, "Zum Shakespearestag". In: *Goethes Werke*. Vol 12. Ed. Ernst Merian/Genast. Basel, 1944. 123-126.

Goethe, Johann Wolfgang von, *Italienische Reise*. Munich, 1961.

Goethe, Johann Wolfgang von, *Goethes Leben Tag für Tag*. Vol. 6. Munich, 1994.

Goethe, Johann Wolfgang von, *Gedenkausgabe der Werke, Briefe und Gespräche*. Ed. Ernst Beutler. 24 Vols. and 3 Supplementary Vols. Zürich, 1948-1971 [Artemisgedenkausgabe].

Gottschalk, Heinz, *Antonio Rossellino*. Thesis, Kiel, 1930.

Gottschling, Claudia, "Das BKA fahndet nach Shakespeare. Neue Beweise sollen die Identität des berühmten Dichters endgültig entlarven". *Focus* 46 (13 November 1995): 200-204.

Gough, Richard, Sepulchral Monuments in Great Britain. 2 Vols. London, 1786-1796.

Gray, A., *Shakespeare's Son-in-Law, John Hall*. Cambridge, Mass., 1939.

Grazia, Margareta de and Stanley Wells, *The Cambridge Companion to Shakespeare*. Cambridge, 2001.

Greene, Joseph, *Correspondence of the Reverend Joseph Greene. Parson, Schoolmaster and Antiquary (1712-1790)*. Ed. Levi Fox [Historical Manuscripts Commission JP 8] London, 1965.

Greenfield, Benjamin W., "The Wriothesley Tomb in Titchfield Church: Its Effigial Statues and Heraldry". In: *Papers and Proceedings of the Hampshire Field Club*. Vol. 1. 1885-1889. Ed. by G. W. Minns. Southampton, 1890. 65-83.

Greenhill, Frank A., *Incised Effigial Slabs [...] c. 1100-c. 1700*. 2 Vols. London, 1976.

Greening Lamborn, E. A., "Great Tew and the Chandos Portrait". *Notes and Queries* 1994 (1949): 71-72.

Greenwood, Douglas, *Who's Buried Where in England*. London, 1982.

Greenwood, Granvill George, *The Straford Bust and the Droeshout Engraving*. With Plates. London, 1925.

Gresty, Hilary and Mark Lumley, eds., *Death*. Cambridge, 1988.

Grimm, Hermann, "Shakespeares Todtenmaske". *Ueber Künstler und Kunstwerke* II, 11/12. Berlin, (1876): 209ff.

Grisebach, August, *Römische Porträtbüsten der Gegenreformation*. Leipzig, 1936.

Gruhle, H., *Porträt*. Freiburg, 1948.

Gundolf, Ernst, "Zur Beurteilung der Darmstädter Shakespeare-Maske". *Shakespeare-Jahrbuch* 64, New Series, Vol. 5 (1928):132-140.

Gunnis, Rupert, *Dictionary of British Sculptors 1660-1851*. London, 1951, rev. ed. 1968.

Hale, John, *The Civilization of Europe in the Renaissance*. London, 1993.

Hale, John, *England and the Italian Renaissance. The Growth of Interest in its History and Art*. With a new introduction by Nicholas Penny. London, 1996.

Hammerschmidt, Hildegard, *Die Importgüter der Handelsstadt London als Sprach - und Bildbereich des elisabethanischen Dramas*. Heidelberg, 1979.

Hammerschmidt-Hummel, Hildegard, "Ist die Darmstädter Shakespeare-Totenmaske echt?" *Shakespeare-Jahrbuch* 132 (1996): 58-74 [Slightly abbreviated version of the address at the Darmstadt City press conference, 22 June 1995].

Hammerschmidt-Hummel, Hildegard, "William Shakespeare. Die authentischen Gesichtszüge". *JOGU* [Universität Mainz] No. 149 (February 1996).

Hammerschmidt-Hummel, Hildegard, "Neue Erkenntnisse über die Physiognomie William Shakespeares. Echtheitsnachweis der Shakespeare-Porträts 'Chandos' und 'Flower' sowie der Darmstädter Shakespeare-Toten-maske auf der Grundlage eines kriminaltechnischen Bild- und eines augenärztlichen Fachgutachtens (Zusammenfassung) [summary]". *Anglistik. Mitteilungen des verbandes Deutscher Anglisten* 7.1 (March 1996): 119-122.

Hammerschmidt-Hummel, Hildegard, "Neuer Beweis für die Echtheit des Flower-Porträts und der Darmstädter Shakespeare-Totenmaske. Ein übereinstimmendes Krankheitssymptom im linken Stirnbereich von Gemälde und Gipsabguß". *Anglistik. Mitteilungen des Verbandes Deutscher Anglisten* 7.2 (September 1996): 115-136.

Hammerschmidt-Hummel, Hildegard, "Herrscherbildnisse Karls I. von England von Anthonis van Dyck: Herrscherkritik, Demontage und politische Schmähung?" *Anglistik. Mitteilungen des Verbandes Deutscher Anglisten* 8.2 (September 1997): 117 - 131.

Hammerschmidt-Hummel, Hildegard, "Shakespeares Totenmaske und die Shakespeare-Bildnisse 'Chandos' und 'Flower'. Zusätzliche Echtheitsnachweise auf der Grundlage eines neuen Fundes". *Anglistik* 9.1 (March 1998): 101–115.

Hammerschmidt-Hummel, Hildegard, "Das Shakespeare-Bild und Bilder Shakespeares am Ende des 20. Jahrhunderts". *Anglistik* 9.1 (March 1998): 117-130.

Hammerschmidt-Hummel, Hildegard, "Herrscherbildnisse Karls I. von England von Anthonis van Dyck: Herrscherkritik, Demontage und politische Schmähung?" In: *Basileus und Tyrann. Herrscherbilder und Bilder von Herrschaft in der Englischen Renaissance*. Ed. Uwe Baumann. Frankfurt am Main et al., 1999. 181–210 [Substantially expanded version of the *Anglistik* article].

Hammerschmidt-Hummel, Hildegard, *Das Geheimnis um Shakespeare's 'Dark Lady'. Dokumentation einer Enthüllung*. Darmstadt, 1999.

Hammerschmidt-Hummel, Hildegard, "What did Shakespeare look like? Authentic Portraits and the Death Mask. Methods and results of the tests of authenticity". *Symbolism* 1 (2000): 41-79.

Hammerschmidt-Hummel, Hildegard, *Die verborgene Existenz des William Shakespeare. Dichter und Rebell im katholischen Untergrund*. Freiburg im Breisgau, 2001.

Hammerschmidt-Hummel, Hildegard. "Latest findings in the field of Shakespeare's portraiture [On the Sanders portrait]". Press release of the University of Mainz (21 September 2001). German version published in: *Anglistik. Mitteilungen des Verbandes Deutscher Anglisten* 13.1 (March 2002): 231.

Hammerschmidt-Hummel, Hildegard, "Goethe and Shakespeare: Goethe's Visit to the Art Collection of Franz Ludwig von Kesselstatt in Mainz". *Symbolism. An International Annual of Critical Aesthetics* 2. (2002): 3-16.

Hammerschmidt-Hummel, Hildegard, *Die Shakespeare-Illustration (1594–2000). Bildkünstlerische Darstellungen zu den Dramen William Shakespeares: Katalog, Geschichte, Funktion und Deutung*. Mit Künstlerlexikon, klassifizierter Bibliographie und Registern, 3 Parts, 3,100 ills. Wiesbaden, 2003.

Hammerschmidt-Hummel, Hildegard, *William Shakespeare. Seine Zeit – Sein Leben – Sein Werk*. Mainz, 2003.

Hammerschmidt-Hummel, Hildegard, "Powerful bust of Shakespeare proves to be genuine [On the Davenant bust]" Press release of the University of Mainz (14 October 2005).

Hammerschmidt-Hummel, Hildegard, *Die authentischen Gesichtszüge William Shakespeares. Die Totenmaske des Dichters und Bildnisse aus drei Lebensabschnitten*. Hildesheim, 2006.

Hamper, William, ed., *The Life, Diary, and Correspondence of Sir William Dugdale.* London, 1827.

Hanley, H. A., "Shakespeare's Family in Stratford Records". *TLS* (May 1964): 441.

Harbage, Alfred, *Sir William Davenant. Poet. Venturer.* Philadelphia/London, 1935.

Harbage, Alfred, "A Contemporary Attack Upon Shakspere?" *SAB* 16 (1941): 42-48.

Hare, Michael, "The Documentary Evidence for the Southampton Monument in Tichfield Church". *Fareham Past and Present* [Titchfield History Society, Book V, Vol. 2].

Harrison, G., *The Stratford Bust.* Brooklyn, 1865.

Hart, John S., "The Shakespear Death-mask". *Scribner's Monthly* 8 (July 1874): 304-317.

Harvey, Anthony and Richard Mortimer, eds., *The Funeral Effigies of Westminster Abbey.* Foreword by H.R.H. The Prince of Wales. Woodbridge, 1994.

Hauser, Otto, "Paul Wislicenus. 'Shakespeares Totenmaske'". *Neue freie Presse* (11 December 1910).

Hay, John, "The Flower portrait", *The Culture Show* (BBC Two) (21 April 2005).

Hay, John, "The Grafton portrait", *The Culture Show* (BBC Two) (27 October 2005).

Hazard, Mary E., "The Case for 'Case' in Reading Elizabethan Portraits". *Mosaic. A Journal for the Interdisciplinary Study of Literature* (Winnepeg) 23 (1990): 61.

Heidenreich, Magda, *Wesentliches und Unwesentliches aus einer südhessischen Familie.* Darmstadt, 1980.

Heminge, John and Henry Condell, "To the great Variety of Readers". In: *Mr. William Shakespeares Comedies, Histories, & Tragedies.* A facsimile edition prepared by Helge Kökeritz. With an Introduction by Charles Tyler Prouty. New Haven/London, 1954, fifth printing, 1968.

Hennemann, Lars, "Das Reisemitbringsel des Mainzer Domherrn. Die Darmstädter Totenmaske Shakespeares ist echt". *Wormser Zeitung* (13 April 1996), *Allgemeinen Zeitung Mainz und Wiesbadener Tagblatt* (3 April 1996).

Hertl, Michael, *Das Gesicht des kranken Kindes.* Physiognomischmimische Studie und Differentialdiagnose unter Bevorzugung des seelischen Ausdruckes. Munich, 1962.

Hertl, Michael, "Allgemeine Pathologie des Ausdrucks unter besonderer Berücksichtigung des Gesichtsausdrucks". *Handbuch für Psychologie.* Vol. 5, *Ausdruckspsychologie.* Göttingen, 1965 und 1972. 309-347.

Hertl, Michael, *Der Gesichtsausdruck des Kranken. Aussagen zur Diagnose und zum Befinden.* Stuttgart, 1993.

Hertl, Michael, "Zu Krankheitserscheinungen in den Porträts und an der Totenmaske von William Shakespeare" (15 August 1997).

Hertl, Michael, "Gutachterliche Stellungnahme zu physiognomischen und eventuellen krankenphysiognomischen Merkmalen an der sogenannten Davenant-Büste im Londoner Garrick-Club im Vergleich zu gesicherten malerischen Porträts und der Totenmaske von William Shakespeare" (11 September 1998).

Hertl, Michael, *Totenmasken. Was vom Leben und Sterben bleibt.* Stuttgart, 2002.

Hess, Daniel, "Bildnis des Nürnberger Malers Michael Wolgemut". In: *Faszination Meisterwerk. Dürer, Rembrandt, Riemenschneider. Ausstellungskatalog.* Nuremberg, 2004.

Hibbert, Christopher, *Cavaliers and Roundheads. The English at War, 1642-1649.* London, 1993.

Hinman, Charlton, *Printing and Proof-Reading of the First Folio of Shakespeare.* Oxford, 1963.

Hinman, Charlton, "Introduction". In: *The Norton Facsimile. The First Folio of Shakespeare.* Based on Folios in the Folger Shakespeare Library Collection. Prepared by Ch. Hinman. Sec. Ed. with a new introd. by Peter W. M. Blayney. London, 1996.

Hoch, Christian, "Die Sonde" [Über die Echtheitsnachweise für die Darmstädter Shakespeare-Totenmaske und die Porträts 'Chandos' und 'Flower'] *Südwest 3 (Fernsehen)*[Television] (17 March 1996).

Holländer, E., *Die Medizin in der klassischen Malerei.* Stuttgart, 1903.

Holländer, E., *Plastik und Medizin.* Stuttgart, 1912.

Hollis, George and Thomas, *The Monumental Effigies of Great Britain.* Parts 1-6. London, 1840-1842.

Hope, W. St John, "On the Funeral Effigies of the Kings and Queens of England [...]." *Archaeologia LX/2* (1907): 511-569.

Hotson, Leslie, *Shakespeare by Hilliard: A Portrait Deciphered.* London, 1977.

Hughes, Ann, *Politics, Society and Civil War in Warwickshire, 1620-1662.* Cambridge, 1987.

Hughes, Ann, "Religion and Society in Stratford-upon-Avon, 1619-1638". *Midland History* 19 (1994).

Huizinga, Johan, *Renaissance und Realismus.* Munich, 1930.

Humphreys, Sally C. and H. King, eds., *Mortality and Immortality: The Anthropology and Archaeology of Death.* London, 1981.

Huntington, R. and P. Medcalf, *Celebrations of Death: The Anthropology of Mortuary Ritual.* Cambridge, 1979.

Hutton, Ronald, *The Royalist War Effort, 1642-1646.* London, 1982.

Hyde, M. C, "Shakespeare's Head". *Shakespeare Quarterly* 16 (1965).

Ingleby, C. M., *Shakespeare: The Man and the Book.* London, 1877.

Ingleby, C. M., *Shakespeare's Bones.* London, 1883.

Ingleby, C. M., Toulmin Smith, L. and F. J. Furnivall, comps. *The Shakspere Allusion-Book: A Collection of Allusions to Shakspere from 1591 to 1700.* Re-edited, revised, and re-arranged, with an Introduction by John Munro (1909). Reissued with a Preface by Sir Edmund Chambers. 2 Vols. London/Oxford, 1932.

Jackson, David, "Verism and the Ancestral Portrait". *Greece and Rome* 34 (1987): 32.

Jahn, Ludwig und Karl Mayhoff, eds., *C. Plini Secundi Naturalis historia libri XXXVII.* Stuttgart, 1967-2002.

Janeck, A., "Metallplastik, Tonplastik, Wachsplastik". Vol. 5. *Geschichte der Kunst und der künstlerischen Techniken.* Frankfurt/Berlin, 1968.

Jansen, Hans Helmut und Werner Wegmann, "Die Darmstädter Shakespeare-Totenmaske". *Jahrbuch der Deutschen Shakespeare-Gesellschaft West* (1984): 270-272.

Jansen, H. H. und P. Leist, "The Technique of Death Masks Making [sic]. Technik der Abnahme von Totenmasken". *Beiträge zur Pathologie* 161 (1977): 385-390.

Jansen, Hans Helmut, "Gutachterliche Stellungnahme zu der Prominenz der linken Stirnseite an der Darmstädter Shakespeare-Totenmaske und auf dem Flower-Porträt". (28 February 1996).

Jenkins, Simon, *England's Thousand Best Churches.* With photographs by Paul Barker from the Country Life Archive. London/New York et al., 1999.

Jones, Barbara, *Design for Death.* New York, 1967.

Kanter, Jan, "Angst vor der Zerstörung eines Mythos. Wissenschaftler beweisen Echtheit der Totenmaske Shakespeares - und stoßen damit auf Widerstand", *DieWelt am Sonntag* (31 March 1998).

Kantner, Max, "Totenmasken". *Medizinischer Monatsspiegel Merck* 5 (1971): 99 und 106-112.

Kauffmann, H., *Donatello.* Berlin, 1935.

Kay, T., *The Story of the 'Grafton Portrait' of William Shakespeare.* London, 1914.

Kemp, Brian, *English Church Monuments.* London, 1980.

Von Kesselstatt, Franz Ludwig, *Kollektaneen.* Gebundenes Manuskript. Stadtarchiv Trier (Depositum Kesselstatt). No date or place given.

Kingman, J. und Callen J. P., "Keratoakanthom. A clinical study". *Arch. Dermatol.* 120 (1984): 736-740.

Kleine-Natrop, H. E., "Rhinophymdarstellungen auf graphischen Blättern". *Aestet. Med.* 11 (1962): 299-309.

Kleine-Natrop, H.-E., "Die historische Ikonographie des Hautarztes". *Der Hautarzt* 14 (1963): 35-37.

Knapp, A. M., *Shakespeare Catalogue* [Account of the portraits in the Barton collection, Boston Public Library]. Boston, 1880.

Kober, Bernd, "Zusatzgutachten [zur Auswertung des Vergleichs von Davenant-Büste und Totenmaske mittels Laserscanning]" (30 June 2005).

Kolbe, G., "Das Abnehmen von Totenmasken". In: H. Benkard, *Das ewige Antlitz.* Berlin, 1929. 40-42.

Kolb, Christina, "Härchen aus Shakespeares Brauen haften im Gipsabdruck. Totenmaske des Dichters im Panzerschrank der Hochschulbibliothek". *Darmstädter Echo* (23. November 1996).

Krämer-Alig, Annette, "Shakespeare im Computertomographen". *Darmstädter Echo* (23 August 2004).

Krämer-Alig, Annette, "Vom BKA zur Städtischen Klinik - Shakespeare und die moderne Technik". *Darmstädter Echo* (23 August 2004).

Kromer, Emma, "Shakespeares Totenmaske". *Neue Badische Landeszeitung (Mannheim)* (26 April 1914).

Kuenzel, Heinrich, "Die Bildnisse des Dichters". In: *William Shakespeare: Zum Gedächtnis seines dreihundertjährigen Geburtstages am 23. April 1864.* Mit einer Photographie[with a photograph]. Darmstadt, 1864. 38-43.

Lane, Joan and Melvin Earles (Medical Commentary), *John Hall and his Patients: The Medical Practice of Shakespeare's Son-in-Law* [The Shakespeare Birthplace Trust]. Stratford-upon-Avon, 1996.

Langenbach, Jürgen, "Kriminalamt identifiziert Shakespeare". *Der Standard* (Vienna) (31 October/1 November 1995).

Langer, Richard, *Totenmasken.* Leipzig, 1927.

Lange, F., *Die Sprache des menschlichen Antlitzes.* Munich/Berlin, 1940.

Laqueur, Thomas, "Bodies, Death, and Pauper Burials". *Representations* 1.1 [Univ. of California] (1983).

Lawson, S., "Cadaver Effigies: The Portrait as Prediction". *Bulletin of the Board of Celtic Studies* XXV (1974): 519-523.

Lay, D. E., "The Taylor of St. Paul's". *Times Literary Supplement* (24 May 1996).

Lee, Sir Sidney, *A Life of William Shakespeare.* London, 1898.

Lee, Sir Sidney, *William Shakespeare: Sein Leben und seine Werke.* Transl. by Richard Wülker. Leipzig, 1901.

Leftwich, Ralph W., "The Evidence of Disease in Shakespeare's Handwriting". *Proceedings of the Royal Society of Medicine, Section of the History of Medicine* 12 (1919): 28-42.

Lemaître, Alain J. und Erich Lessing, *Florenz und seine Kunst im 15. Jahrhundert.* Paris, 1992, German edition 1993.

Lerche, Walter, "Shakespeare-Portraits". Gutachterliche Stellungnahme (11 April 1995).

Lessing, G. E., *Wei de Alten den Tod Gebildet.* First Publ. 1769, Stuttgart, 1984

Lewis, B. Roland, *The Shakespeare Documents. Facsimiles, Transliterations, Translations & Commentary.* 2 Vols. Stanford /London/Oxford, 1941.

Lichtenberg, Reinhold von, *Das Porträt an Grabdenkmalen. Seine Entstehung und Entwicklung vom Altertum bis zur italienischen Renaissance.* Strasbourg, 1902.

Litten, Julian, *The English Way of Death. The Common Funeral since 1450.* London, 1991, repr. 1992.

Llewellyn, Nigel, *John Weever and English Funeral Monuments of the Sixteenth and Seventeenth Centuries.* Unpubl. Ph.D thesis, University of London, 1983.

Llewellyn, Nigel, "English Renaissance Tombs: Commemoration in Society". *Arte Funerario: Coloquio Internacional de Historia des Arte.* Eds. B. De La Fuente and L. Noelle. 2 Vols. Mexico City, 1987. 143-154.

Llewellyn, Nigel, "Claims to Status through Visual Codes: Heraldry on post-Reformation Funeral Monuments". *Chivalry in the Renaissance.* Ed. S. Anglo. Woodbridge, 1990. 145-160.

Llewellyn, Nigel, "Accident or Design? John Gildon's Funeral Monuments and Italianate Taste in Elizabethan England". *England and the Continental Renaissance: Essays in Honour of J. B. Trapp.* Eds. E. Chaney and P. Mack, Woodbridge, 1990. 143-152.

Llewellyn, Nigel, "The Royal Body: Monuments to The Dead, For The Living". *Renaissance Bodies: The Human Figure in English Culture, c. 1540-1660.* Eds. Lucy Gent and Nigel Llewellyn. London, 1990. 218-240.

Llewellyn, Nigel, *The Art of Death. Visual Culture in the English Death Ritual, c. 1500 - c. 1800.* Publ. in Association with the Victoria and Albert Museum. London, 1991, repr. 1992.

Lob, Stephanie, "To see or not to see - Shakespeare's Eye. Hildegard Hammer-schmidt-Hummel, Professor of English at Mainz University, gathers clues as to what Shakespeare really looked like ...". *Students' English Magazine [Cologne]* 6 [Shakespeare Special] (1996; June): 16-18.

Löcher, Kurt, *Die Gemälde des 16. Jahrhunderts.* Catalogue of the Germanisches Nationalmuseum Nuremberg. Compiled by K. Löcher in collaboration with Carola Gries. Technological information: Anna Bartl und Magdalene Gärtner, Stuttgart, 1997.

Loughrey, B. and G. Holderness, "Shakespearean Features". In: *The Appropriation of Shakespeare.* Ed. J. I. Marsden. New York, 1991.

Ludwig, Astrid, "Des Dichters Abbild aus Gips liegt in einer alarmgesicherten Vitrine. Die Stadt Darmstadt besitzt Shakespeares Totenmaske / Jahrhunderte während Diskurs über Echtheit oder Fälschung". *Frankfurter Rundschau* (7 November 2002).

MacLure, Millar, *The Paul's Cross Sermons.* 1534-1642. Toronto/London, 1958.

Maclagan, Eric, "The use of death-masks by Florentine sculptors". *The Burlington Magazine* 43 (1923): 303.

Mann, J. G., "Instances of Antiquarian Feeling in Medieval and Renaissance Art". *Archaeological Journal* LXXXIX (1932): 254-274.

Mann, J. G., "English Church Monuments, 1536-1625". *Walpole Society* XXI (1932-1933): 1-22.

Marcham, F., William Shakespeare and his Daughter Susannah. London, 1931.

Marchionini, A. and F. Schröpl, "Über die Darstellung von Hautkrankheiten im Bibliotheksaal des Klosters Waldsassen". *Der Hautarzt* 13 (1962): 131-134.

Marchionini, A., Schröpl, F. und K. Gagel, "Die Darstellung von Hauteffloreszenzen an der Figur des heiligen Willibald im Dom zu Eichstätt". *Der Hautarzt* 14 (1963): 368-370.

Marder, L., "The Quest for an Image". In: *His Exits and His Entrances.* London, 1963.

Mathew, F. J., *An Image of Shakespeare.* London, 1922.

McGrath, Patrick, *Papists and Puritans under Elizabeth I.* London, 1967.

Metken, Sigrid, Hg. *Die letzte Reise.* Munich, 1984.

Metz, Jost, "Gutachterliche Stellungnahme zu den Shakespeare-Portraits Chandos und Flower und der Totenmaske in der Hessischen Landes- und Hochschulbibliothek Darmstadt" (23 Januar 1996).

Meyer, A. G., *Donatello.* Bielefeld, 1908.

Meyer-Sichting, Gerhard, "Shakespeares Totenmaske". *Erlebte Vergangenheit. Darmstädter Bürger erzählen.* Darmstadt, 1986.

Meyer-Sichting, Gerhard, "Shakespeares Totenmaske". *Darmstädter Echo* (22 July 1958).

Michel, Thomas, "Kultur Südwest" [On the authenticity of the death mask and the 'Chandos' und 'Flower' portraits] *Südwest 3 (Fernsehen)* [Television] (11 April 1996).

Middleton, J. H., "Sculpture". *Encyclopaedia Britannica* XXI (1899): 556-572.

Milward, Peter, *Shakespeare's Religious Background*. London, 1973.

Montaigne, Michel de "Apologie des Raimond Sebond". In: *M. de Montaigne. Die Essais*. Ausgewählt, übertagen und eingeleitet von Arthur Franz. Leipzig, 1953, Stuttgart, 1969. 205-232.

Montaigne, Michel de "An Apologie of Raymond Sebond", in: *Montaigne's Essays*. Renascence Editions, Book II. E-text [www.uoregon.edu/~rbear/montaigne/2xii.html], provided by Ben R. Schneider, Lawrence University, Wisconsin, © 1998 The University of Oregon.

Morrill, John, ed., *Reactions to the English Civil War, 1642-1649*. London, 1982.

Morrill, John, ed., *The Impact of the English Civil War*. London, 1991.

Mosler, David, *A Social and Religious History of the English Civil War in Warwickshire*. Unpubl. Thesis. Stanford, 1975.

Murray, Peter and Linda, *Penguin Dictionary of Art & Artists*. Harmondsworth, 1959, repr. 1982.

Nares, Robert, *A Glossary of Word Phrases Names and Allusions in the Works of English Authors Particularly of Shakespeare and his Contemporaries*. New ed. London/New York, 1905.

Nethercot, H., *Sir William D'Avenant. Poet Laureate and Playwright-Manager* (Chicago, 1938).

Neumeister, Sebastian, "Renaissance und Barock – Themen am Beginn der Moderne". In: *Propyläen Geschichte der Literatur. Renaissance und Barock 1400–1700*. Berlin, 1988. III, 11–30.

Nevinson, J. L., "Shakespeare's Dress in His Portraits". *Shakespeare Quarterly* 18 (1967):

Nieder, Oliver, "Geschwollenes Auge als Beweis für Echtheit. Tränendrüse gab den Ausschlag: Shakespeare-Expertin setzte weltweiten Medienrummel in Gang". *Mainzer Rhein-Zeitung* (29 April 1998).

Nolen, Stephanie, (with Jonathan Bate, Tarnya Cooper, Marjorie Garber, Andrew Gurr, Alexander Leggatt, Robert Titler and Stanley Wells). *Shakespeare's Face*. Toronto, 2002 [On the Sanders Portrait].

Norris, J. Parker, *Bibliography of Works on the Portraits of Shakespeare*. Philadelphia, 1879.

Norris, J. Parker, *The Death Mask of Shakespeare*. London, 1884.

Norris, J. Parker, *The Portraits of Shakespeare*. With numerous illustrations. Philadelphia, 1885.

Nuding, Gertrude Prescott, "Portraits for the Nation (The National Portrait Gallery, London)." *History Today* 39 (1989): 30.

Ogden, William Sharp, "Shakespeare's Portraiture". *British Numismatic Journal* 8 (1910): 3-58.

Ogden, W. S., *Shakespeare's Portraiture: Painted, Graven, and Medallic*. London, 1912.

Oldridge, Darren, *Conflicts within the Established Church in Warwickshire, c. 1603-1642*. Unpubl. Thesis. Warwick, 1992.

Opie, Mary-Jane, *Skulptur* [1994] Stuttgart/Zürich, 1995.

Orlandi, Enzo, gen. ed., *The Life and Times of Shakespeare*. Text by Maria Pia Rosignoli. Transl. Mary Kanani [1967]. Feltham, Middlesex, 1968.

Osborn, Francis, *Traditional Memoryes of the Reign of King James*. Oxford, 1911.

Page, William, *A Study of Shakespeare's Portraits*. London, 1876, New York, 1877.

Page, William. "A Study of Shakespeare's Portraits". *Scribner's Monthly* 10 (September 1875): 558-574.

Panofsky, Erwin, *Tomb Sculpture: Its Changing Aspects From Ancient Egypt to Bernini*. London, 1964.

Pasteur Vallery-Radot, L., *Kunst und Medizin*. 3rd impression. Cologne, 1974.

Pd. "Shakespeare: Echtheitsnachweise". *Neue Zürcher Zeitung* (1/2 Juni 1996).

Peacock, John, "Inigo Jones's Catafalque for James I." *Architectural History* XXV (1982): 1-5.

Pegg, P. F. and E. Metze, *Death and Dying: A Quality of Life*. London, 1981.

Pfanner, M., "Über das Herstellen von Porträts. Ein Beitrag zu Rationalisierungsmaßnahmen und Produktionsmechanismen von Massenware im späten Hellenismus und in der römischen Kaiserzeit". *Jahrbuch des Deutschen Archäologischen Instituts* 104 (1989): 157.

Picaper, Jean-Paul, "Le vrai visage de Shakespeare. En utilisant les ordinateurs du BKA, le chercheur a trouvé les points communs des cinq portraits de référence". *Le Figaro* (8 May 1996).

Piderit, Th., *Mimik und Physiognomik*. Detmold, 1886.

Pies, Eike, *Goethe auf Reisen. Begegnungen mit Landschaften und Zeitgenossen*. Wuppertal, n.d.

Pigler, A., "Portraying the Dead". *Acta Historiae Artium* Hungarian Academy of Science, IV, i-ii (1956): 1-75.

Pigman III, G. W., *Grief and English Renaissance Elegy*. Cambridge, 1985.

Planiscig, Leo, *Venezianische Bildhauer der Renaissance*. Vienna, 1921.

Plinius der Ältere, *C. Plinius Secundus*. Pisa, 1977 ff.

Pliny the Elder, *Natural History. A Selection*. Translated with an Introduction and Notes by John F. Healy. Harmondsworth, 1991.

Poeschke, Joachim, *Die Skulptur der Renaissance in Italien*. Vol.1: *Donatello und seine Zeit*. Photographs by A. Hirmer and I. Ernstmeier-Hirmer. Munich, 1990.

Pohl, Frederick J., "The Death-Mask". *Shakespeare Quarterly* 12 (1961): 115-125.

Pohl, J., *Die Verwendung des Naturabgusses in der italienischen Porträtplastik in der Renaissance*. Würzburg, 1938.

Pointon, Marcia, "Shakespeare, Portraiture and National Identity". *Shakespeare Jahrbuch* 133 (1997): 29-53.

Poller, Alphons, *Das Pollersche Verfahren zum Abformen an Lebenden und Toten sowie an Gegenständen*. Anleitung für Mediziner, Anthropologen, Kriminalisten, Museumspräparatoren, Prähistoriker, Künstler, Handfertigkeitslehrer, Amateure. Hg. E. B. Poller und E. Fetscher. Mit einem Vorwort von C. v. Economo. Mit 129 Abb. Berlin/Vienna, 1931.

Pommer, Frank, "Das Kainsmal auf der Stirn. Neuer Beweis für die Echtheit der Darmstädter Shakespeare-Toten-maske?" *Die Rheinpfalz* (6 July 1996).

Pope-Hennessy, J., *Italian Renaissance Sculpture*. London, 1958.

Porter, S., "From death to burial in seventeenth-century England". *Local Historian* 23.4 (November 1993): 199-204.

Potterton, Homan, *Irish Church Monuments*, 1570-1880. Ulster Architectural Heritage Society. Belfast, 1975.

Preimesberger, R., "Albrecht Dürer: Das Dilemma des Porträts, epigrammatisch (1526)". In: *Porträt*. Eds. R. Preimesberger, H. Baader und N. Suthor. Berlin, 1999, pp. 220–227

Preimesberger, R. Baader, H. and N. Suthor, eds., *Porträt*. Geschichte der klassischen Bildgattungen in Quellentexten und Kommentaren. Berlin, 1999.

Pressly, W. L., "The Ashbourne Portrait of Shakespeare: Through the Looking Glass". *Shakespeare Quarterly* 44 (1993).

Price, D., "Reconsidering Shakespeare's Monument". *Review of English Studies* 48 (1997).

Puckle, B. S., *Funeral Customs: Their Origin and Development*. London, 1926.

Ratcliff, S. C. and H. C. Johnson, eds., *Warwick County Records. Quarter Sessions Order Books.* Warwick, 1935-53.

Rauch, Alexander, "Malerei der Renaissance in Venedig und Norditalien". *Die Kunst der italienischen Renaissance.* Ed. Rolf Toman. Cologne, 1994. 350-415.

Rauch, Alexander, "Malerei der Hochrenaissance und des Manierismus in Rom und Mittelitalien". *Die Kunst der italienischen Renaissance.* Ed. Rolf Toman. Cologne, 1994. 308-349.

Rayment, John L., *Monumental Inscriptions.* Federation of Family History Societies. Plymouth, 1981.

Rf., "Darmstädter Shakespeare echt". *Darmstädter Echo* (25 April 1996).

Richardson, Ruth, *Death, Dissection and the Destitute.* London, 1988.

Riehn, Angelika, "'Totenmaske ist echt'. Mainzer Shakespeare-Forscherin läßt sich nicht beirren." *Allgemeine Zeitung Mainz* (19 Januar 1996).

Rijkhoek, Guido, "'Damit besitzen wir ein Stück von ihm selber'. Die Darmstädter Totenmaske Shakespeares." *Wiesbadener Kurier* (23 Juni 1995).

Rodd, H., *The Chandos portrait of Shakespeare.* London, 1849.

Roth, Walter. "Arteriitis temporalis, dargestellt an einem Gemälde des Reichsmuseums in Amsterdam". *Der Hautarzt* 20 (1969): 330-332.

Roth, Walter, "Hautveränderungen in künstlerischen Darstellungen. I.-III Beispiele aus dem Germanischen Nationalmuseum in Nürnberg". [dermatology and art] *Der Hautarzt* 29 (1978): 86-88, 213-215, 442-444.

Roth, Walter, "Keratoakanthom auf der linken Wange des Galileo Galilei". [history of dermatology] *Der Hautarzt* 37 (1986): 513-515.

Routh, Pauline E., *Medieval Effigial Alabaster Tombs in Yorkshire.* Ipswich, 1976.

Rowse, A. L., *Shakespeare's Southampton.* London, 1965.

Rowse, A. L., "Bisham and the Hobys". *Times, Persons, Places.* London, 1965. 188-218.

Rowse, A. L., *The Elizabethan Renaissance. The Life of the Society.* London, 1971.

Rowse, A. L., *The Elizabethan Renaissance. The Cultural Achievement.* London, 1972.

Rye, W. B., *England as seen by foreigners in the Days of Elizabeth and James the First.* London, 1865.

Salmen, Walter, *Musiker im Porträt* 2. Das 17. Jahrhundert. Munich, 1983.

Savage, R. and E. I. Fripp, *Minutes and Accounts of the Corporation of Stratford-upon-Avon and Other Records 1553-1620.* 3 Vols. London, 1921, 1924, 1926.

Schaaffhausen, Hermann, "Ueber die Todtenmaske Shakespeare's". *Jahrbuch der Deutschen Shakespeare-Gesellschaft* (1875): 26-49.

Schadewaldt, H., ed., *Kunst und Medizin.* 3rd impression. Cologne, 1974.

Schadow, Johann Gottfried, "Die Werkstätte des Bildhauers". In: *Aufsätze und Briefe.* Ed. Julius Friedländer (Düsseldorf, 1864).

Schamoni, Wilhelm, *Das wahre Gesicht der Heiligen* (1937) Munich, 1967.

Schamoni, Wilhelm, *The Face of the Saints.* Transl. by Anne Fremantle. London, 1948.

Scharf, George, *On the Principal Portraits of Shakespeare.* London, 1864.

Scharf, George, "The Principal Portraits of Shakespeare". *Notes and Queries* (23 April 1864).

Scharf, George, *A few Observations connected with the Chandos Portrait of Shakespeare.* London, 1864.

Schedel, H., *Liber chronicarum.* Nuremberg, 1493.

Schefold, Karl, (in collaboration with A.-C. Bayard, H. A. Cahn, M. Guggisberg, M. T. Jenny and C. Schneider). *Die Bildnisse der antiken Dichter, Redner und Denker.* Basel, 1997.

Scheyl, K. H., "Geschichte und Brauchtum der Totenmaske". In: Karl Eschen. *Das letzte Porträt.* Berlin, 1967.

Schlosser, J. v., "Geschichte der Portraitbildnerei in Wachs". *Jahrbuch der kunsthistorischen Sammlungen des allerh. Kaiserhauses* 29 (1910): 128.

Schoenbaum, Samuel, *Shakespeare's Lives.* Oxford, 1970, new ed. 1991.

Schoenbaum, Samuel, *William Shakespeare: A Documentary Life.* Oxford, 1975.

Schoenbaum, Samuel, *William Shakespeare: Records and Images.* London, 1981.

Schoenbaum, Samuel, "Artists' Images of Shakespeare". In: *Images of Shakespeare. Proceedings of the Third Congress of the International Shakespeare Asscociation, 1986.* Eds. Werner Habicht, D. J. Palmer and Roger Pringle. Newark/London/Toronto, 1988. 19-39.

Scholz, Albrecht, "Von kleinen und großen Tumoren in der Kunst". [dermatology in art] *Der Hautarzt* 33 (1982): 598-604.

Scholz, Albrecht, "Die Altershaut im Spiegelbild der Kunst". *Medicamentum* 35 (1976): 28-32.

Schönfeld, W., "Brandmarken und Tätowierungen Europas in ihrer ärztlichen und kulturgeschichtlichen Spiegelung vom frühen Mittelalter bis zur frühen Neuzeit". *Der Hautarzt* 1 (1950): 412-418.

Schreyl, K.-H., "Geschichte und Brauchtum der Totenmaske". In: F. Eschen. *Das letzte Porträt.* Berlin, 1967.

Schubring, Paul, *Das italienische Grabmal der Frührenaissance.* Berlin, 1904.

Schwanitz, Dietrich, "Shakespeares Auge". *Die Zeit [Magazin]* 5 ["Ist das William? Auferstanden aus Indizien - Shakespeare, wie er leibt und lebt."] (26 January 1996): 10-14.

Schwerin, S., "Herstellung einer Totenmaske". In: *Anatomische Trocken-, Feucht- und Knochenpräparate.* Ed. S. Schwerin. Berlin/Göttingen/Heidelberg, 1952. 94-95.

Scott-Giles, C. W., *Shakespeare's Heraldry.* London, 1950.

Shaffer, Elinor S., "'Shakespeare between the Dramatic Muse and the Genius of Painting': From Boydell Façade to Shakespeare Shrine". *The Boydell Shakespeare Gallery.* W. Pape and F. Burwick. Bottrop, 1996. 75-87.

Shakespeare, William, *The Works of William Shakespeare. The Text formed from an entirely new Collation of the old Editions: With the various Readings, Notes, a Life of the Poet, and a History of the early English Stage.* Ed. J. Payne Collier. London, 1844.

Shakespeare, William, *Shakespeares sämtliche dramatische Werke.* Transl. by Schlegel und Tieck. With a biographical introduction by Rob. Prölss. 6 Vols. Leipzig, n.d.

Shakespeare, Willliam, *Mr. William Shakespeares Comedies, Histories, & Tragedies.* A facsimile edition prepared by Helge Kökeritz. With an Introduction by Charles Tyler Prouty. New Haven/London, 1954, fifth printing, 1968.

Shakespeare, William, *Shakespeare's Sonnets.* Ed., with Introd. and Commentary, by A. L. Rowse. New York, 1964.

Shakespeare, William, *The Complete Works.* Ed. Peter Alexander. London/Glasgow, 1951, 2. Aufl. 1978.

Sherwood, Roy, *The Civil War in the Midlands, 1642-1651.* Stroud, 1992.

Shrewsbury, J.E.D., *A History of Bubonic Plague in the British Isles.* Cambridge, 1970.

Siemens, H. W., "Der Favus auf alten Gemälden". *Der Hautarzt* 4 (1953): 431-433.

Siemens, H. W., "Die Lentigo in der Kunst". *Der Hautarzt* 15 (1964): 193-197.

Skyring, A., "Radio Interview with Hildegard Hammerschmidt-Hummel." *ORF, Österreichischer Rundfunk* [On the authenticity of the Darmstadt Shakespeare death-mask and the 'Chandos' and 'Flower'portraits] (25 October 1995).

Smith, Benjamin E., ed., *The Century Cyclopedia of Names. A Pronouncing and Etymological Dictionary of Names in Geography, Biography, Mythology, History, Ethnology, Art, Archaeology, Fiction, etc.* [...]. London/New York, 1894, repr. 1904.

Smith, Charles Saumarez, *The National Portrait Gallery*. London, 1997.

Speed, John, *The History of Great Britaine*. London, 1623.

Spencer, T. J. B., "Ben Jonson on his beloved The Author Mr William Shakespeare". *The Elizabethan Theatre* VI. London, 1974.

Speyer, Wolfgang, "Fluch". In.: *Reallexikon für Antike und Christentum*. Vol. 7 (1969): 1160-1288.

Speyer, Wolfgang, "Das wahrerere Porträt. Zur Rivalität von bildender Kunst und Literatur". In: W. Speyer, *Frühes Christentum im antiken Strahlungsfeld*.Vol. 1. Wissenschaftliche Untersuchungen zum Neuen Testament. 50. Tübingen, 1989. 395-401.

Spielmann, Marion H., "Portraits of Shakespeare". In: *The Works of William Shakespeare*. Vol. X. Ed. A. H. Bullen. Stratford-upon-Avon, 1907. 373–398

Spielmann, Marion H., "The Portraits of Shakespeare". *Encyclopaedia Britannica*. Vol. 24, 11th ed. (1911): 787–793.

Spielmann, Marion H., *The Title-Page of the First Folio of Shakespeare's Plays: A Comparative Study of the Droeshout Portrait and the Stratford Monument*. Oxford/London, 1924.

Spielmann, Marion H., *Shakespeare's Portraiture*. London, 1924.

Spielmann, Marion H. "The Janssen, or Somerset, Portrait of Shakespeare". *Connoisseur* 28, 29, 32 (1910, 1911, 1912): 51-58, 105-110, 18-24.

Spiers, W. L., "The Note book and Account Book of Nicholas Stone". *Walpole Society* VII (1918/19).

Stanley, A. P., *Historical Memorials of Westminster Abbey*. London, 1869.

Stannard, David E., *The Puritan Way of Death: A Study of Religion, Culture and Social Change*. Oxford, 1977.

Stephen, Leslie and Sidney Lee, eds., *The Dictionary of National Biography: From the Earliest Times to 1900*. 22 Vols. London, 1908 ff., repr. 1949-1950.

Stoll, Günther, "Shakespeare oder nicht Shakespeare? Mit forensischen und medizinischen Methoden versucht eine Wissenschaftlerin aus Mainz, die Echtheit einer Totenmaske zu beweisen, die Shakespeare darstellen soll". *Damals. Vereinigt mit dem Magazin 'Geschichte'* (September 1996): 48.

[Stone, Nicholas], "Index to the Churches and Houses where Work was executed by Nicholas Stone, arranged according to Counties". In: *The Seventh Volume of the Walpole Society 1918-1919*, ed. A. J. Finberg (Oxford, 1919), S. 148-151.

Stopes, Charlotte C., *The Life of Henry, third Earl of Southampton, Shakespeare's Patron*. Cambridge, 1922.

Stopes, Charlotte C., *Shakespeare's Warwickshire Contemporaries*. Strat-ford-upon-Avon, 1897.

Stopes, Charlotte C., *Shakespeare's Family, being a Record of the Ancestors and Descendants of William Shakespeare, with some account of the Ardens*. New York, 1901.

Stopes, Charlotte C., *Shakespeare's Environment*. London, 1918.

Stopes, Charlotte C., "The True Story of the Stratford Bust". In: *Shakespeare's Environment*. London, 1918.

Stothard, C. A., *The Monumental Effigies of Great Britain. Selected from our Cathedrals and Churches, [...] From the Norman Conquest to the Reign of Henry the Eighth*. With Historical Descriptions and Notes by Alfred John Kempe. A New Ed., with large Additions by John Hewitt. London, 1876.

Stow, John, *The Annales, or Generall Chronicle of England, begun by J. Stow [...] continued and augmented [...] unto the end of [...] 1631, by E. Howes*. London, 1631.

Streitberger, "Familiengeschichte" [history of the Counts of Kesselstatt]. Bound manuscript. Trier City Archive (Depositum [holdings] Kesselstatt).

Streitberger, "Schema der Gesandten [list of Kesselstatt family members in diplomatic service] im Diplomatischen und Civil", Anlage No. 46, "Familiengeschichte", pp. 523-526.

Strider, R. E. L., *Robert Greville, Lord Brooke*. Cambridge, MA, 1958.

Strong, Sir Roy, "Sir Henry Unton and his Portrait: An Elizabethan Memorial Picture and Its History". *Archaeologia* XCIX (1965): 53-76.

Strong, Sir Roy, *The English Icon: Elizabethan & Jacobean Portraiture*. Studies in British Art. The Paul Mellon Foundation for British Art 1969. London/New York, 1969.

Strong, Sir Roy, *Tudor & Jacobean Portraits*. 2 Vols. London, 1969.

Strong, Roy, "Shakespeare, William (1564-1616)". *Tudor & Jacobean Portraits*. [National Portrait Gallery] Vol.1: Text. London, 1969. 276-286.

Studing, Richard, "Survey of American Portraits of Shakespeare". *Bulletin of Bibliography* 42.4 (1985): 187-192.

Styles, Philip, "The Borough of Stratford-upon-Avon and the Parish of Alveston". *Victoria County History of Warwickshire* 3 (1946).

Suerbaum, Ulrich, *Das elisabethanische Zeitalter*. Stuttgart. 1989.

Suerbaum, Ulrich, *Der Shakespeare-Führer*. Stuttgart, 2001.

Summers, Peter, ed. *Hatchments in Britain*. Vol. VI. London, 1985.

Szita, Jane, "Age Cannot Wither Him". *Wired (San Francisco, USA)* (February 1996).

Tate, F., "Of the Antiquity, Variety and Ceremonies of Funerals in England". In: T. Tearne. *A Collection of Curious Discourses [...]*. 2 Vols. London, 2nd ed., 1771.

Taubert, Johannes, *Farbige Skulpturen. Bedeutung - Fassung - Restaurierung*. Munich, 1978.

Taylor, John, *Records of My Life*. London, 1832.

Taylor, J. H. M., ed., *Dies illa: Death in the Middle Ages*. Liverpool, 1984.

Tennant, Philip, *Edgehill and Beyond. The People's War in the South Midlands, 1642-1645*. Stroud, 1992.

Tennant, Philip, *The Civil War in Stratford-upon-Avon. Conflict and Community in South Warwickshire, 1642-1646*. Stroud, 1996.

Tenner, Helmut, "421 Die Darmstädter Shakespeare-Totenmaske. Leicht gebräunter Gips, Länge: 23,5 cm. Rückseitig eingeritzt: 'A^O. D$\overline{m}$. 1616'. Kleine Beschädigung an der Nase. 40 000.-" *Handschriften - Autographen - Wertvolle Bücher des 15. - 20. Jahrhunderts. Auction catalogue*. Auction 22, 3 November 1960. Heidelberg, 1960. 57-60.

Theaterwissenschaftliche Sammlung Universität zu Köln, Schloß Wahn, in Zusammenarbeit mit dem Bundeskriminalamt [Theatre Studies collection of the University of Cologne in Wahn Castle, in collabor*ation with the BKA: *Gefunden. Wahnbilder* [Found: Pictures from Wahn]. Cologne, 2002.

Thielemann, Andreas et al., "Bildnisstatuen stoischer Philosophen". *Mitteilungen des deutschen Archäologischen Instituts (Athenische Abteilung, Berlin)* 104 (1989): 109.

Thoma, Hans, "Brief an Paul Wislicenus vom 26.11.1908" [Auszug]. *Shakespeares Totenmaske [1910]*. P. Wislicenus Jena, 2nd impression, 1911. 39-40.

Thompson, Andrew and Shahnaz Pakravan, "Tomorrow's World" [On the Findings Regarding the Authenticity of the Darmstadt Shakespeare Death Mask and the Shakespearian Portraits 'Chandos' and 'Flower'] *BBC Television, London* (15 December 1995).

Thoms, William J., "The Kesselstadt [sic] Mask of Shakespeare". *Notes and Queries* (1864): 342.

Thoms, William J., "The Stratford Bust of Shakspeare". *Notes and Queries* (1864): 227.

Thomson, Peter, "English Renaissance and Restoration Theatre". In: *The Oxford Illustrated History of Theatre*. Ed. by John Russell Brown. Oxford/New York, 1995.

Tipping, Marjorie, *Ludwig Becker. Artist & Naturalist with the Burke & Wills Expedition.* Ed. & with an Introd. by M. Tipping. Melbourne University Press, Carlton, Victoria, 1979.

Toman, Rolf, ed., *Die Kunst der italienischen Renaissance. Architektur - Skulptur - Malerei - Zeichnung.* Cologne, 1994.

Trapesnikoff, Trifon, *Die Porträtdarstellungen der Mediceer des XV. Jahrhunderts.* Strasbourg, 1909.

Trauner, Sandra, "Mainzer Forscherin findet neues Shakespeare-Bildnis". *Dpa* (23 August 2004).

Uhlig, Robert, "Mask suggests eye cancer killed Shakespeare". *The Daily Telegraph* (19 October 1995).

Usher, Rod, (Reported by Rhea Schoenthal). "The Bard or Not the Bard: A German academic thinks she has the lowdown on Shakespeare's looks - and his premature demise". *Time. The Weekly Newsmagazine* 147.20 (13 May 1996): 55.

Vallette, Gaspard, "Le Masque de Shakespeare". *Gazette de Lausanne et Journal Suisse* 314 (13 November 1910).

Veit, Andreas Ludwig, *Mainzer Domherren vom Ende des 16. bis zum Ausgang des 18. Jahrhunderts in Leben, Haus und Habe. Ein Beitrag zur Geschichte der Kultur der Geistlichkeit. Mainz,* 1924. With 23 art plates and a frontispiece photograph of Count Franz von Kesselstatt, from a painting of 1837 situated in Kesselstatt Castle near Trier.

Vertue, George, "The Notebooks of George Vertue", *The Walpole Society* (Oxford, 1930–1947). I.

Vincent, Mary und Robert Stradling. *Spanien und Portugal.* Original English ed. Oxford, 1994, German translation Augsburg, 1997.

Volkart, Karlheinz, *Gips-Wörterbuch. Dictionnaire du Gypse et du Plâtre. Gypsum and Plaster Dictionary.* Wiesbaden/Berlin, 1971.

Wagner G. und W. Müller, *Dermatologie in der Kunst.* Biberach an der Riß, 1970.

Wainwright, Patricia, *The Parochial Church Council of The Collegiate Church of the Holy Trinity, Stratford-upon-Avon. Trinity Tales (Some lesser known Stories of Shakespeare's Church).* Illustrations by Susan Summers. Stratford-upon-Avon, 1983.

Wallace, C. W., "Shakespeare and his London Associates as Revealed in Recently Discovered Documents". *University Studies* X *(Univ. of Nebraska)* (1910).

Wall, J., *The Tombs of the Kings of England.* London, 1891.

Walter, F., "Veit Stoß als Darsteller von Hautkrankheiten". *Dermatol. Zeitschrift* 72 (1936): 17-27.

Warburg, Aby., *Bildniskunst und florentinisches Bürgertum.* Leipzig, 1901.

Ward, B. M., "The Chamberlain's Men in 1597". *Review of English Studies* IX (1933): 55.

Ward, John, "MSS. of the Rev. John Ward, in the possession of the Medical Society of London. Printed in the 'Diary of the Rev. John Ward, A. M., Vicar of Stratford-upon-Avon, extending from 1648 to 1679", edited by C. Severn, M.D. 1839.

Ward, H. Snowden and Catharine Weed Ward, *Shakespeare's Town and Times.* London, 1896.

Waser, Otto, "'Shakespeares Totenmaske'. Von Paul Wislecenus". *Sonntagsblatt des 'Bund' (Bern)* 43 (23 October 1910).

Weatherley, William Samuel, "A Description of the Tombs and Monuments having Sculptured Effigies up to the Close of the Seventeenth Century [....]". In: Dryden (Alice). *Memorials of Old Leicestershire [...].* 1911.

Weaver, Lawrence, *Memorials and Monuments.* London, 1915.

Wedgwood, C. V., *The King's War, 1641-1647.* London, 1978.

Weever, John, *Ancient funerall Monuments within the united Monarchie of Great Britaine and Ireland, and the Islands adjacent [...]* London, 1631.

Wells, Stanley and T. J. B. Spencer, "Shakespeare in Celebration". In: *Shakespeare: A Celebration. 1564–1964,* ed. T. J. B. Spencer. Harmondsworth, 1964. 114-132.

Wells, Stanley and Lena Cowen Orlin, *Shakespeare. An Oxford Guide.* Oxford, 2003.

Weinreb, Ben and Christopher Hibbert, eds., *The London Encyclopaedia.* London, 1983, repr. 1984.

Whaley, Joachim, ed., *Mirrors of Mortality: Studies in the Social History of Death.* London, 1981.

Wheler, Robert Bell, *History and Antiquities of Stratford-upon-Avon: comprising a description of the Collegiate Church, the life of Shakespeare, and copies of several documents relating to him and his family, never before printed [...].* Stratford-upon-Avon, 1806.

Whinney, Margaret D., *Sculpture in Britain, 1530-1830.* Rev. Ed. by John Physick. Harmondsworth, 1988.

White, Adam, "Classical Learning and the Early Stuart Renaissance". *Church Monuments* i/I (1985): 20-33.

White, Lesley, *Monuments and their Inscriptions.* Society of Genealogists. London, 1987.

Willoughby, Edwin Elliott, *The Printing of the First Folio of Shakespeare.* Oxford, 1932.

Wilson, Ian, *Shakespeare. The Evidence.* London, 1993.

Wilson, John Dover, *The Essential Shakespeare.* Cambridge, 1932.

Wilson, John Dover, *Shakespeare. Der Mensch. Betrachtungen über Leben und Werk.* Hamburg, 1953.

Wirbitzky, Michael, "Mittwochsforum" On the proofs of authenticity for the Darmstadt Shakespeare death mask and the portraits 'Chandos' and 'Flower'. *Südwest 3 (Fernsehen)* [Television] (17 April 1996).

Wislicenus, Paul, *Dokumente zu Shakespeares Totenmaske.* Darmstadt, n.d.

Wislicenus, Paul, *Shakespeares Totenmaske.* With a drawing by Hermann Pfeifer. Darmstadt, 1910, 2nd, revised edition. Jena, 1911.

Wislicenus, Paul, "Shakespeares Totenmaske. Offener Brief an die Redaktion des Berner 'Bund'". *Der Bund (Bern)* 521 (4/5 November 1910).

Wislicenus, Paul, "Shakespeares Totenmaske". *Jahrbuch der Deutschen Shakespeare-Gesellschaft* 48 (1912): 116-124. With 2 ills.

Wislicenus, Paul, *Nachweise zu Shakespeares Totenmaske. Die Echtheit der Maske.* Jena, 1913.

Wislicenus, Paul, "Zur Untersuchung von Shakespeares Totenmaske". *Monatshefte für Kunstwissenschaft* 8.8 (1915): 279 ff.

Wivell, Abraham, *An Inquiry into the History, Authenticity and Characteristics of the Shakespeare Portraits.* Engravings by B. and W. Holl. London, 1827.

Wivell, Abraham, *The Monumental Bust.* London, 1827.

Wright, Charles, *The Stratford Portrait of Shakespeare [...]* London, 1861.

Yeowell, James, *A Literary Antiquary. Memoir of William Oldys, Esq.* London, 1862.

Ziller, C. A., *Die Bildnerkunst. Bildhauerei und die Plastik im Kunstgewerbe. Handbuch für Kunstfreunde, Schüler und Lehrlinge.* Dresden, 1906.

Zintzen, Clemens, *Vom Menschenbild der Renaissance.* Munich/Leipzig, 2000.

List of Illustrations and Picture Credits

001 Bust of the Italian banker Niccolò da Uzzano (*c.* 1425-30), © Bargello, Florence. Picture quotation from: Joachim Poeschke, *Die Skulptur der Renaissance in Italien* Bd. 1: Donatello und seine Zeit. Photographs by Albert Hirmer and Irmgard Ernstmeier-Hirmer (Munich, 1990), no. 73 – p. 15.

002 Funeral effigy of Henry VII of England (1457-1509). Picture quotation from: Roy Strong, *Tudor & Jacobean Portraits.* 2 vols. (London, 1969), II, no. 296 – p. 16.

003 Funerary sculpture of the diplomat and cleric John Yonge (1467-1516) Picture quotation from: Roy Strong, *Tudor & Jacobean Portraits.* 2 vols. (London, 1969), II, no. 676 – p. 16.

004 Funerary monument of the Earls of Southampton in St Peter's Church, Titchfield. © H. Hammerschmidt-Hummel (1996) – p. 17.

005 Funerary sculpture of the first Earl of Northampton, Henry Howard (1540-1614). Picture quotation from: Roy Strong, *Tudor & Jacobean Portraits.* 2 vols. (London, 1969), II, no. 463 – p. 17.

006 Monument of Cornelius van Dun (d. 1577), St Margaret's Church, Westminster. © H. Hammerschmidt-Hummel (1996) – p. 18.

007 Monument of the historian John Stow (1525-1603), St Andrew Undershaft, London. Picture quotation from: Paul Wislicenus, *Nachweise zu Shakespeares Totenmaske* (Jena, 1913), plate XLIX – p. 19.

008 Monument of Bishop Giles Tomson (1553-1612), St. George's Chapel, Windsor Castle. © H. Hammerschmidt-Hummel (1996) – p. 19.

009 Monument of the English historian and antiquary William Camden (1551-1623), Westminster Abbey, London. © H. Hammerschmidt-Hummel (1996) – p. 20.

010 Monument of the Elizabethan-Jacobean poet Michael Drayton (1563-1631), Westminster Abbey, London. © H. Hammerschmidt-Hummel (1996) – p. 20.

011 Portrait of the patrician Ulrich Röhling (d. 1618) by Mathias Krodel the Younger. © Germanic National Museum, Nuremberg – p. 22.

012 Portrait of the painter Michael Wolgemut (1434/37-1519) by Albrecht Dürer. © Germanic National Museum, Nuremberg – p. 23.

013 Albrecht Dürer, portrait of Philip Melanchthon, copper engraving, 1526 – p. 24.

014 The Chandos portrait, oval, oil on canvas, National Portrait Gallery, London. © National Portrait Gallery, London – Reg. No. 1 – p. 26.

015 The Flower portrait, oil on panel, Royal Shakespeare Company Collection, Stratford-upon-Avon. [State before the 1979 restoration]. ("Copyright RSC Collection" – From the RSC Collection with the permission of the Governors of the Royal Shakespeare Company) Picture quotation from: Royal Shakespeare Theatre Picture Gallery, *Catalogue of Pictures and Sculptures* (Stratford-upon-Avon, 6th ed., 1970), opposite title – p. 28.

016 The Flower portrait, oil on panel, Royal Shakespeare Company Collection, Stratford-upon-Avon. [State after the 1979 restoration]. ("Copyright RSC Collection" – From the RSC Collection with the permission of the Governors of the Royal Shakespeare Company) – p. 29.

017 Davenant bust, terracotta, The Art Archive/Garrick Club, London – p. 31.

018 Darmstadt Shakespeare death mask, plaster of Paris, Hesse *Land* and University Library, Darmstadt. Reproduced by kind permission of the mayor of the City of Darmstadt. Andreas Kahnert (1996) – p. 33.

019 Rear view of the Darmstadt Shakespeare death mask, Hesse *Land* and University Library, Darmstadt. Reproduced by kind permission of the mayor of the City of Darmstadt. Andreas Kahnert (1996) – p. 34.

019a Detail – Inscription reading "Aº Dm 1616", Hesse *Land* and University Library, Darmstadt. Reproduced by kind permission of the mayor of the City of Darmstadt. Andreas Kahnert (1996) – p. 34.

020 The funerary monument of William Shakespeare on the left wall of the choir in Holy Trinity Church, Stratford-upon-Avon. With kind permission of the Vicar and Churchwardens of Holy Trinity Church, Stratford-upon-Avon. H. Hammerschmidt-Hummel (2002) – p. 38.

021 The funerary bust of William Shakespeare, coloured limestone, Holy Trinity Church, Stratford-upon-Avon; original photograph taken before 1968. Picture quotation from: *The Life and Times of Shakespeare*, gen. ed.: Enzo Orlandi, text: Maria Pia Rosignoli, translator: Mary Kanani (London/New York/Sydney/Toronto, 1968), p. 74. By kind permission of the Vicar and Churchwardens of Holy Trinity Church, Stratford-upon-Avon. – p. 39.

022 Recumbent funerary sculpture of John Combe. Detail of head. By kind permission of the Vicar and Churchwardens of Holy Trinity Church, Stratford-upon-Avon. H. Hammerschmidt-Hummel (2002) – p. 40.

023 Copperplate engraving of William Shakespeare by Martin Droeshout the Younger. Frontispiece of the facsimile edition of the First Folio Edition of 1623, Elizabethan Club, Yale University, New Haven (Connecticut): *Mr. William Shakespeares Comedies, Histories, & Tragedies.* A facsimile edition prepared by Helge Kökeritz. With an Introduction by Charles Tyler Prouty (New Haven/London, 1954, fifth printing, 1968) – p. 45. [Privately owned]

024 Conventional comparison of images by the German Federal Bureau of Criminal Investigation (BKA): Chandos portrait. Reinhardt Altmann, "BKA image report in arthistorical research", RE: Federal Bureau of Criminal Investigation, Wiesbaden, ZD 15 - 1170/95 (3 May 1995), images, p. 4 – p. 48.

025 Conventional comparison of images by the German Federal Bureau of Criminal Investigation (BKA): Flower portrait. Reinhardt Altmann, "BKA image report in arthistorical research: Shakespeare", RE: Federal Bureau of Criminal Investigation, Wiesbaden, ZD 15 - 1170/95 (3 May 1995), images, p. 6 – p. 48.

026 Conventional comparison of images by the German Federal Bureau of Criminal Investigation (BKA): Droeshout engraving. Reinhardt Altmann, "BKA image report in arthistorical research: Shakespeare", RE: Federal Bureau of Criminal Investigation, Wiesbaden, ZD 15 - 1170/95 (3 May 1995), images, p. 7 – p. 49.

027 Conventional comparison of images by the German Federal Bureau of Criminal Investigation (BKA): Funerary bust of Shakespeare. Reinhardt Altmann, "BKA image report in arthistorical research: Shakespeare", RE: Federal Bureau of Criminal Investigation, Wiesbaden, ZD 15 - 1170/95 (3 May 1995), images, p. 8 – p. 50

028 Conventional comparison of images by the German Federal Bureau of Criminal Investigation (BKA): Darmstadt Shakespeare death mask. Reinhardt Altmann, "BKA image report in arthistorical research: Shakespeare", RE: Federal Bureau of Criminal Investigation, Wiesbaden, ZD 15 - 1170/95 (3 May 1995), images, p. 9 – p. 50.

029 Trick Image Differentiation Technique employed by the German Federal Bureau of Criminal Investigation (BKA): Montage of the Chandos portrait (upper half) and the Flower portrait (lower half). Reinhardt Altmann, "BKA image report in arthistorical research: Shakespeare", RE: Federal Bureau of Criminal Investigation, Wiesbaden, ZD 15 - 1170/95 (3 May 1995), images, p. 11 – p. 51.

030 Trick Image Differentiation Technique employed by the German Federal Bureau of Criminal Investigation (BKA): Montage of the Chandos portrait (left half) and the Droeshout engraving (right half). Reinhardt Altmann, "BKA image report in arthistorical research: Shakespeare", RE: Federal Bureau of Criminal Investigation, Wiesbaden, ZD 15 - 1170/95 (3 May 1995), images, p. 13 – p. 51.

031 Trick Image Differentiation Technique employed by the German Federal Bureau of Criminal Investigation (BKA): Montage of the Droeshout engraving (left half) and the Flower portrait (right half). Reinhardt Altmann, "BKA image report in arthistorical research: Shakespeare", RE: Federal Bureau of Criminal Investigation, Wiesbaden, ZD 15 - 1170/95 (3 May 1995), images, p. 16 – p. 51.

032 Trick Image Differentiation Technique employed by the German Federal Bureau of Criminal Investigation (BKA): Montage of the death mask (left half) and the funerary bust (right half). Reinhardt Altmann, "BKA image report in arthistorical research: Shakespeare", RE: Federal Bureau of Criminal Investigation, Wiesbaden, ZD 15 - 1170/95 (3 May 1995), images, p. 19 – p. 52.

033 Trick Image Differentiation Technique employed by German Federal Bureau of Criminal Investigation (BKA): Montage of the Chandos portrait (left) and the death mask (right), Reinhardt Altmann, Federal Bureau of Criminal Investigation, Wiesbaden (1995) – p. 52

034 Trick Image Differentiation Technique employed by the German Federal Bureau of Criminal Investigation (BKA): Montage of the Davenant bust (left) and the Chandos portrait (right). Reinhardt Altmann, "BKA image report in arthistorical research: Shakespeare", RE: Federal Bureau of Criminal Investigation, Wiesbaden (6 July 1998), p. 12 – p. 53.

034a Trick Image Differentiation Technique employed by the German Federal Bureau of Criminal Investigation (BKA): Montage of the Davenant bust (left) and the Chandos portrait (right). Section through left eye. Reinhardt Altmann, "BKA image report in arthistorical research: Shakespeare", RE: Federal Bureau of Criminal Investigation, Wiesbaden (6 July 1998), p. 13 – p. 53.

035 Trick Image Differentiation Technique employed by the German Federal Bureau of Criminal Investigation (BKA): Montage of the Davenant bust (left half) and the Flower portrait (right half). Reinhardt Altmann, "BKA image report in arthistorical research: Shakespeare", RE: Federal Bureau of Criminal Investigation, Wiesbaden (6 July 1998), p. 13 – p. 53.

036 Trick Image Differentiation Technique employed by the German Federal Bureau of Criminal Investigation (BKA): Montage of the Davenant bust (left) and Flower portrait (right). Reinhardt Altmann, "BKA image report in arthistorical research: Shakespeare", RE: Federal Bureau of Criminal Investigation, Wiesbaden (6 July 1998), p. 14 – p. 53.

036a BKA Trick Image Differentiation Technique: detail of montage of the Davenant bust (left) and the Flower portrait (right), section through left eye. Reinhardt Altmann, "BKA image report in arthistorical research: Shakespeare", RE: Federal Bureau of Criminal Investigation, Wiesbaden (6 July 1998), p. 14 – p. 54.

037 Trick Image Differentiation Technique employed by the German Federal Bureau of Criminal Investigation (BKA): Montage of the restored Flower portrait (left half) and the Davenant bust (right half). Reinhardt Altmann, "BKA image report in arthistorical

research: Shakespeare", RE: Federal Bureau of Criminal Investigation, Wiesbaden (6 July 1998), p. 15 – p. 54.

038 Trick Image Differentiation Technique employed by the German Federal Bureau of Criminal Investigation (BKA): Montage of the funerary bust (left half) and the Davenant bust (right half). Reinhardt Altmann, "BKA image report in arthistorical research: Shakespeare", RE: Federal Bureau of Criminal Investigation, Wiesbaden (6 July 1998), p. 16 – p. 54.

039 Trick Image Differentiation Technique employed by the German Federal Bureau of Criminal Investigation (BKA): Montage of the Droeshout engraving (left half) and the Davenant bust (right half). Reinhardt Altmann, "BKA image report in arthistorical research: Shakespeare", RE: Federal Bureau of Criminal Investigation, Wiesbaden (6 July 1998), p. 17 – p. 54.

040 Trick Image Differentiation Technique employed by the German Federal Bureau of Criminal Investigation (BKA): Montage of the Droeshout engraving (left) and the Davenant bust (right), section through left eye. Reinhardt Altmann, "BKA image report in arthistorical research: Shakespeare", RE: Federal Bureau of Criminal Investigation, Wiesbaden (6 July 1998), p. 18 – p. 55.

041 Trick Image Differentiation Technique employed by the German Federal Bureau of Criminal Investigation (BKA): Montage of the death mask (left half) and Davenant bust (right half). Reinhardt Altmann, "BKA image report in arthistorical research: Shakespeare", RE: Federal Bureau of Criminal Investigation, Wiesbaden (6 July 1998), p. 19 – p. 55.

042 Trick Image Differentiation Technique employed by the German Federal Bureau of Criminal Investigation (BKA): Montage of the Davenant bust (left and right) and the death mask (centre). Reinhardt Altmann, "BKA image report in arthistorical research: Shakespeare", RE: Federal Bureau of Criminal Investigation, Wiesbaden (6 July 1998), p. 20 – p. 55.

043 Computer montage of the Davenant bust (left half) and the death mask (right half). Andreas Kahnert, Hesse *Land* and University Library, Darmstadt – p. 58.

044 Computer montage of the death mask and the Davenant bust, right profile. Andreas Kahnert, Hesse *Land* and University Library, Darmstadt – p. 58.

045 Copy of the Davenant bust in the repository of the Royal Shakespeare Company, Stratford-upon-Avon (1998) – p. 59.

046 Front view of the Davenant bust, Garrick Club, London Davenant-Büste, Dr Nico Gray (1998) – p. 60.

047 The Davenant bust seen in semi-profile (right), Garrick Club, London, Dr Nico Gray (1998) – p. 61.

048 The Davenant bust in semi-profile (left), Garrick Club, London, Dr Nico Gray (1998) – p. 62

049 Right profile of the Davenant bust, Garrick Club, London, Dr Nico Gray (1998) – p. 63.

050 Left profile of the Davenant bust, Garrick Club, London, Dr Nico Gray (1998) – p. 64.

051 The death mask under the computertomograph (centre). © Dr-Ing. Christoph Hummel (2004) – p. 65.

052 Computertomography images of the death mask. Institute of X-Ray Diagnosis and Nuclear Medicine, Darmstadt City Hospital. Prof. Peter Huppert (2004) – p. 66.

053 Laser-scan generated image of the death mask in the Hesse *Land* and University Library, Darmstadt. Dipl.-Ing. Thorsten Terboven, Konica Minolta, Germany (2004) – p. 67.

054 Archivist Marcus Risdell, Garrick Club, London, the author, David Lowry of Konica Minolta (UK), Thorsten Terboven of Konica Minolta (Germany) after the 3D measurement of the Davenant bust (2005) – p. 68.

055 Comparison of details from laser-scan generated images of the Davenant bust and the death mask. Thorsten Terboven of Konica Minolta (Germany) (2005) – p. 69.

056 Comparison of details from laser-scan generated images of the Davenant bust and the death mask. Thorsten Terboven of Konica Minolta (Germany) (2005) – p. 69.

057 Comparison of details from laser-scan generated images of the Davenant bust and the death mask. Maverick Kim of INUS Technology (Europe) (2005) – p. 71.

058 Comparison of details from laser-scan generated images of the Davenant bust and the death mask. Maverick Kim of INUS Technology (Europe) (2005) – p. 71.

059 The death mask with clearly visible protuberance on the forehead, Hesse *Land* and University Library, Darmstadt – p. 72.

060 The strikingly protruding, distorted left eye of the death mask. Andreas Kahnert, Hesse *Land* and University Library, Darmstadt (1997) – p. 73.

061 The author inspecting the (larger than life-sized) Davenant bust in the London Garrick Club. Dr Nico Gray (1998) – p. 74.

062 Swelling on the forehead of the Davenant bust, with many scratch marks. Detail of fig. 046. Dr Nico Gray (1998) – p. 75.

063 Enlargement of the right eye of the Davenant bust, Garrick Club, London. Detail of fig. 046. Dr Nico Gray (1998) – p. 76.

064 Enlargement of the left eye of the Davenant bust, Garrick Club, London. Detail of fig. 046. Dr Nico Gray (1998) – p. 76.

065 Berlin copy of the death mask, Staatliche Gipsformerei (State Plaster-moulding Works), Berlin. © H. Hammerschmidt-Hummel (1997) – p. 77.

066 Nasal corner of the left eye on the Berlin copy of the death mask, with noticeable protuberances: photogrammetric image by Dr Rolf Dieter Düppe, Institute for Photogrammetry and Cartography, Technical University Darmstadt (1997) – p. 77.

067 Nasal corner of the left eye of the death mask. Andreas Kahnert, Hesse *Land* and University Library, Darmstadt – p. 77.

068 Old marble copy of the funerary bust in Charlecote Park near Stratford-upon-Avon. George E. Shiers. With kind permission of Mr Geoffrey Howarth, Historic Buildings Representative, National Trust Severn, Tewkesbury, Gloucestershire – p. 78.

069 Nasal corner of the marble copy in Charlecote Park with noticeable trilobate protuberance. George E. Shiers. With kind permission of Mr. Geoffrey Howarth, Historic Buildings Representative, National Trust Severn, Tewkesbury, Gloucestershire – p. 78.

070 Marble copy of the funerary bust in Charlecote Park – left to right, George Shiers, the author, Rima Astrauskaite, and Dr Nico Gray. Geoffrey Howarth (1998) – p. 78.

071 Hunt portrait (from Shakespeare's funerary bust), detail. Shakespeare Birthplace Trust, Stratford-upon-Avon. Picture quotation from: Samuel Schoenbaum, *Shakespeare's Lives* (Oxford, 1970) – p. 79.

072 Infrared image [sic] of the Chandos portrait. Picture quotation from: Strong, *Tudor & Jacobean Portraits*, II, Nr. 546, NPG 1 [No longer extant at NPG] – p. 79.

072a Detail of fig. 072. Nasal corner of left eye with an incipient trilobate swelling – p. 79.

073 The Madonna beneath the Flower portrait; X-ray image, Courtauld Institute, London (1966). Picture quotation from: *Illustrated London News* (18. Juni 1966) – p. 79.

074 Nasal corner of the left eye of the death mask with the remains of a trilobate swelling. Photogrammetric measurement by Dr Rolf Dieter Düppe, Institute for Photogrammetry and Cartography, Technical University Darmstadt (1997) – p. 80.

075 Portrait engraving of Richard Burbage (c. 1567-1619) from his self-portrait in the Gallery of Dulwich. Sidney Lee, *A Life of William Shakespeare*. Illustrated Library Edition (London, 1899), between p. 32 and p. 33. [Privately owned] – p. 82.

075a First copy of the Chandos portrait painted by Sir Godfrey Kneller (1646/49-1723). Picture quotation from: Strong, *Tudor & Stuart Portraits*, II, Plates, 548 – p. 85.

076 Portrait of William Clift (1775-1849). Reproduced by kind permission of the President and Council of the Royal College of Surgeons of England – p. 92.

077 Portrait of Sir Richard Owen (1804-1892). Reproduced by kind permission of the President and Council of the Royal College of Surgeons of England – p. 92.

078 View of the Lincoln's Inn Fields Theatre or Duke's Theatre, about 1700. Reproduced by kind permission of the President and Council of the Royal College of Surgeons of England – p. 93.

079 Portrait engraving of the dramatist Sir William Davenant (1606-1668) by Io. Grenhill and William Faithorne. Detail of head. From http://www.peopleplayuk.org.uk/collections/ – p. 94.

080 Louis François Roubiliac (1702/05-1762), statue of William Shakespeare of 1758, British Museum, now British Library, London. © H. Hammerschmidt-Hummel (1999). With kind permission of the British Museum – p. 98.

081 Portrait of the Darmstadt Court Painter Ludwig Becker (1808-1861). Picture quotation from: Magda Heidenreich, *Wesentliches und Unwesentliches aus einer weltoffenen südhessischen Familie* (Darmstadt, 1980), p. 91– p. 100.

082 Miniature death portrait of Ben Jonson (1573-1637). From the estate of Dr Magda Heidenreich, Affolterbach. H. Hammerschmidt-Hummel (1996). With kind permission of Christoph Vogel, Affolterbach – p. 101.

083 Imperial Count Franz Eugen von Kesselstatt and Imperial Countess Louisette von Kesselstatt, at Kesselstatt Castle in Föhren near Trier. H. Hammerschmidt-Hummel (1996) – p. 103.

084 Portrait of Dr Ernst Becker (1826-1888). Picture quotation from: Magda Heidenreich, *Wesentliches und Unwesentliches aus einer weltoffenen südhessischen Familie* (Darmstadt, 1980), p. 94 – p. 105.

085 View of the British Museum in London. H. Hammerschmidt-Hummel (2004) – p. 105.

086 Henry Wallis, "The sculptor of the Stratford bust before his finished work, 1617-1618)" (1857). ("Copyright RSC Collection" – From the RSC Collection with the permission of the Governors of the Royal Shakespeare Company) Picture quotation from: *Pictures and Sculpture from the Royal Shakespeare Gallery* (Stratford-upon-Avon, ca. 1970), p. 43 – p. 106.

087 An earlier pictorial comparison of the Davenant bust and the death mask. Picture quotation from: H. Snowden Ward and Catharine Weed Ward, *Shakespeare's Town and Times* (London, c. 1896) – p. 106.

088 Dr Magda Heidenreich, representative of the Becker/Heidenreich family. H. Hammerschmidt-Hummel (1995) – p. 108.

089 Count Franz Ludwig von Kesselstatt (1753-1841). Stadtarchiv Mainz, BPS alph. Sammlung, 1996. Reproduced by kind permission of the City Archive of Mainz – p. 109.

090 Castle Kesselstatt, seat of the Counts of Kesselstatt in Föhren near Trier. H. Hammerschmidt-Hummel (1996) – p. 110.

091 Count Franz Ludwig von Kesselstatt, Canon of the Cathedral of Mainz. Reproduced by kind permission of the Imperial Count Franz Eugen von Kesselstatt. H. Hammerschmidt-Hummel (1996) – p. 110.

092 The Kesselstatt house on the Höfchen in Mainz. Picture quotation from: Carl Stenz, ed., *Mainz vor hundert Jahren* (Mainz, 1934) – Stadtbibliothek Mainz (City Library of Mainz): Shelfmark Mog: 20 /80 – p. 111.

093 Von Kesselstatt's garden. One of the many views of old Mainz painted by Count Franz Ludwig von Kesselstatt. Picture quotation from: Carl Stenz, ed., *Mainz vor hundert Jahren* (Mainz, 1934) – Stadtbibliothek Mainz (City Library of Mainz): Shelfmark Mog: 20 /80 – p. 112.

094 An old prospect of Mainz: artist unknown, about 1840. Picture quotation from: Carl Stenz, ed., *Mainz vor hundert Jahren* (Mainz, 1934) – Stadtbibliothek Mainz (City Library of Mainz): Shelfmark Mog: 20 /80 – p. 112.

095 Portrait of Johann Wolfgang von Goethe (1749-1832). After the 1828 painting by Karl Joseph Stieler in the Bavarian State Painting Collections (Bayerische Staatsgemäldesammlungen),

Further Information

The montages and comparisons of images, especially prepared for the present research purposes, were based on photographic reproductions of the Chandos and Flower portraits, the Davenant bust, the Darmstadt Shakespeare death mask, the funerary bust of Shakespeare, the Droeshout engraving, and the Sanders, Janssen and Grafton portraits. The photographic material either originated in older published works (with the exception of the Sanders portrait), or was commissioned by the author between 1995 and 1998, with the permission of the copyright holders or owners. The left half of the image in fig. 113 is taken from an illustration (fig. 19) in Samuel Schoenbaum's *Shakespeare's Lives* (Oxford, 1975, repr. 1991); fig. 114 is from the frontispiece of John Dover Wilson's *The Essential Shakespeare* (Cambridge, 1932). Fig. 112 reproduces text material and a photograph from the *Globe and Mail* (12 May 2001). Sir Roy Strong's work, *Tudor & Jacobean Portraits*, 2 Vols. (London, 1969), provided figs. 001-002, 005, 072, 072 a, 075 a, and 101 (see II, 296; II, 676; II, 463; II, 546; II, 548; II, 1281). Fig. 102 derives from Plate 16 of Marion H. Spielmann's *The Title-Page of the First Folio Edition of Shakespeare's Plays: A Comparative Study of the Droeshout Portrait and the Stratford Monument* (Oxford/London, 1924). Half- or part-images in Figs. 021, 024-025, 027, 029-030, 032-034, 034 a, 035-036, 036 a, and 037-038 originated in the volume *The Life and Times of Shakespeare*, gen. ed. Enzo Orlandi, text by Maria Pia Rosignoli, transl. Mary Kanani (London/New York/Sydney/Toronto, 1968), front page. Half- or part-images in Figs. 015, 025, 029, 031, 036, 036 a, and 037 are from an illustration of an earlier state of the Flower portrait, opposite the title page in the catalogue of the Royal Shakespeare Theatre Picture Gallery, *Catalogue of Pictures and Sculptures* (Stratford-upon-Avon, 6th ed., 1970) which was supplied to the author by the Stratford Gallery in the 1980s; or they are based on an ektachrome of the restored Flower portrait received by the author in 1996 from the Stratford Gallery in connection with her research projects and for publication purposes. Especially photographed for the planned scientific project, at the request of the author and with the owners' permission, were the half-, part- and full-image reproductions in figs. 034, 034 a, 035-036, 036 a, 037-044, 046-050, 055-058, 062-064. This also applies to part- and full-image reproductions in 018, 028, 032- 033, 041-044, 055-060, 067, 074, and 113. The full-face and half-image reproductions in Figs. 023, 026, 030-031, and 039-040 are taken from the facsimile edition *Mr. William Shakespeares Comedies, Histories & Tragedies.* A Facsimile edition prepared by Helge Kökeritz. With an Introduction by Charles Tyler Prouty (NewHaven/London, 1954, fifth impression, 1968), frontispiece.

Although every effort has been made to do so, it was not possible in all cases to trace the copyright owner of works or pictures reproduced.

Index